Managing the Media in the India-Burma War, 1941–1945

Managing the Media in the India-Burma War, 1941–1945

Challenging a 'Forgotten War'

Philip Woods

BLOOMSBURY ACADEMIC
LONDON • NEW YORK • OXFORD • NEW DELHI • SYDNEY

BLOOMSBURY ACADEMIC
Bloomsbury Publishing Plc
50 Bedford Square, London, WC1B 3DP, UK
1385 Broadway, New York, NY 10018, USA
29 Earlsfort Terrace, Dublin 2, Ireland

BLOOMSBURY, BLOOMSBURY ACADEMIC and the Diana logo are trademarks
of Bloomsbury Publishing Plc

First published in Great Britain 2023
This paperback edition published 2024

Copyright © Philip Woods, 2023

Philip Woods has asserted his right under the Copyright, Designs and Patents Act,
1988, to be identified as Author of this work.

For legal purposes the Acknowledgements on p. x constitute an extension of
this copyright page.

Cover image: Admiral Lord Louis Mountbatten, Supreme Allied Commander South East
Asia, sits astride a captured Japanese 75mm gun while addressing men of the Royal
Armoured Corps in Mandalay, 21 March 1945. © Imperial War Museum (SE 3484).

All rights reserved. No part of this publication may be reproduced or transmitted
in any form or by any means, electronic or mechanical, including photocopying,
recording, or any information storage or retrieval system, without prior
permission in writing from the publishers.

Bloomsbury Publishing Plc does not have any control over, or responsibility for,
any third-party websites referred to or in this book. All internet addresses given in
this book were correct at the time of going to press. The author and publisher
regret any inconvenience caused if addresses have changed or sites have ceased
to exist, but can accept no responsibility for any such changes.

A catalogue record for this book is available from the British Library.

Library of Congress Cataloging-in-Publication Data

Names: Woods, Philip, author.
Title: Managing the media in the India-Burma War : challenging a 'forgotten war' /
Philip Woods.
Description: London ; New York : Bloomsbury Academic, 2022. |
Includes bibliographical references and index.
Identifiers: LCCN 2022003691 | ISBN 9781350271647 (hardback) |
ISBN 9781350271678 (paperback) | ISBN 9781350271654 (pdf) |
ISBN 9781350271661 (epub)
Subjects: LCSH: World War, 1939–1945–Campaigns–Burma. | India. Army–History–World
War, 1939-1945. | Great Britain. Army. Army, XIV. |World War, 1939–1945–Propaganda. |
Propaganda, British–India–History–20th century.
Classification: LCC D767.6 .W66 2022 | DDC 940.54/25—dc23/eng/20220222
LC record available at https://lccn.loc.gov/2022003691

ISBN:	HB:	978-1-3502-7164-7
	PB:	978-1-3502-7167-8
	ePDF:	978-1-3502-7165-4
	eBook:	978-1-3502-7166-1

Typeset by RefineCatch Limited, Bungay, Suffolk

To find out more about our authors and books visit www.bloomsbury.com
and sign up for our newsletters.

For Judith, with love

Contents

List of Figures		viii
List of Maps		ix
Acknowledgements		x
Abbreviations		xii
Colonial-Era Names		xiv
1	Introduction	1
2	Media Covering the War in India-Burma	11
3	Managing the Media in the Burma Retreat, 1942	23
4	Managing Media Coverage of the First Arakan Campaign, 1943	37
5	Media Coverage of Operation Longcloth: Wingate's First Expedition into Burma, 1943	53
6	Mountbatten Takes Charge: Publicity and Censorship	65
7	Allies of a Kind: Public Relations Officers at War	81
8	Reporting the War, 1944	95
9	Broadcasting: BBC, All India Radio and Radio SEAC	109
10	The 'Forgotten Army'? Stepping up Publicity for the 14th Army	123
11	Film and Photography in SEAC	133
12	Race to Rangoon and Victory, 1945	149
13	Conclusion	165
Notes		175
Bibliography		213
Index		227

Figures

5.1. Left to right: Stuart Emeny (*News Chronicle*), Martin Moore (*Daily Telegraph*), Tony Beauchamp (Photographer), Captain Jack Potter (Army Conducting Officer) and Alaric Jacob (*Daily Express*), private collection. 55
5.2. Charles J. Rolo, 'Wingate's Raiders', *Milwaukee Sentinel*, 29 May 1944. 60
6.1. Air Marshal Philip Joubert de la Ferté, Deputy Chief of Staff (Information & Civil Affairs). Photo by Cecil Beaton, IB 124, IWM. 66
6.2. Supremo talks to striking war correspondents, *SEAC* newspaper, 26 April 1944. 73
7.1. Supreme Allied Commander South East Asia Mountbatten conferring with Lieutenant General J. W. Stilwell, Commander-in-Chief US Forces in China, Burma and India, March 1944, IWM, NYF 20073. 85
8.1. 'Seven Men, one a correspondent, hug the ground after a sniper's bullet pings by', adapted from *Life* magazine, Myitkyina airfield, 26 June 1944, p. 90. Note the typewriter, essential equipment wherever. Private collection. 107
9.1. Lionel Fielden (front row, second from right) surrounded by AIR station managers. Ahmed Bokhari is on Fielden's right; Zulfaqar Bokhari is on his left. GoI, *Report on the Progress of Broadcasting in India (up to the 31st March 1939)* (Simla, 1939), IOR/V/27/970/2. 110
9.2. Richard Sharp reporting for the BBC from Burma, crossing the river Irrawaddy, February 1945, courtesy of Timothy Sharp. 117
9.3. Major-General T. W. ('Pete') Rees, GOC 19 Indian Division, directing the battle for Mandalay, 9 March 1945, IWM (SE 3257). 118
10.1 The achievements of the 14th Army publicized. *Illustrated London News*, 7 October 1944, courtesy of Mary Evans Picture Library. 124
11.1. Sergeant Basil Wishart of No.9 Army Film and Photo Section films Indian troops crossing a river near Meiktila, Burma in 1945. IWM, SE5423. 142
12.1. Akyab, Burma. *c*. 3 January 1945. Lieutenant General Sir Philip Christison, Commander of the 15th Indian Corps, Group Captain W. D. David, Air Liaison Officer to the Corps, and Air Commodore the Earl of Bandon, Air Officer Commanding No. 224 Group RAF in the Arakan, landed on a village green which the local people had prepared for them. The white flag on the right of the Earl of Bandon was used by the natives to guide the aircraft down. Courtesy of Australian War Memorial Collections, SUK13681. 153

Maps

0.1.	Outline Map of Burma, courtesy of Michael D. Leigh.	xv
3.1.	Japanese Conquest of Central Burma, April–May 1942, U.S. Army Center of Military History, Wikimedia Commons.	24
4.1.	The First Arakan Campaign, December 1942–May 1943, Hilary St George Saunders, *The Royal Air Force 1939 to 1945*, Vol. III: 'The Fight Is Won', HMSO Official History of WWII, London: HMSO, 1953, p. 302.	39
8.1.	'The Fall Campaign', in Troy Sacquety, 'A Special Force Model: OSS Detachment 101 in the Myitkyina Campaign, Part 1', *Veritas*, 4, no. 1 (2008), p. 36.	96
12.1.	The Reconquest of Burma, November 1944–May 1945, Hilary St George Saunders, *The Royal Air Force 1939 to 1945*, Vol. III: 'The Fight Is Won', HMSO Official History of WWII, London: HMSO, 1953, p. 356.	150

Acknowledgements

Because of the Covid-19 pandemic and associated lockdowns, this has been a propitious time for finding the time for completing the writing of this book, but a particularly difficult time to carry out all the necessary research. Lockdowns have provided the necessary space for writing but the closure of libraries and the restrictions on travel, particularly international travel, have limited access to some of the archives that I would like to have used, particularly in the USA and, perhaps, India. This has meant a greater reliance on online sources than I would have liked ideally. I hope this has not limited the usefulness of this study too much, but it has inevitably balanced it more towards a British perspective than I originally intended.

There are a number of people who have helped me in writing the book. First and foremost is Professor Steven Casey, who has let me see preliminary drafts of his excellent studies of the role of American media in both the European and Pacific theatres. He has also provided me with access to some documents from the American archives and given excellent advice when reading my draft versions. I have found Twitter very useful in connecting with a number of military historians who have inspired me with their enthusiasm and have generously shared their knowledge. I should particularly mention Dr Robert Lyman, Dr Richard Duckett and Ian Kikuchi of the Imperial War Museum in this respect, who each provided valuable information and support. I am grateful for the help of Dr Devika Sethi in disentangling wartime censorship in India. My thanks also to the anonymous reviewers of my book proposal, who gave support, encouragement and good suggestions as to how to make improvements. I apologize if I have not managed to fulfil them all.

I am very much indebted to the excellent support given by librarians and archivists. My thanks go to those staff of the British Library (especially of the Asian & African and Newsroom reading rooms), the National Archives (Kew), the Cambridge Centre for South Asian Studies, the British Film Institute, the Imperial War Museum, the Hartley Library, University of Southampton, the School of Oriental and African Studies, University of London, the RAF Museum Archive at Hendon, and the Wisconsin Historical Society, Madison. I should particularly like to mention the help given by Els Boonen of the BBC Written Archive Centre at Caversham, who helped me navigate their wonderful archives and referencing system. I would also like to acknowledge the work of the creators and maintainers of online sources that have proved invaluable in my research: particularly the British Universities Film & Video Council 'News on Screen'; Trove, National Library of Australia, for Australian Newspapers; Steve Fogden's 'Chindit Chasing' website; and Carl Weidenburner's China-Burma-India website.

I have very much appreciated the academic environment of teaching at New York University in London over the last twenty years. I thank staff there, particularly

Professor Catherine Robson (Director) and Ruth Tucker, for granting me a Distinguished Research Fellowship over the last year so that I could complete this book.

I am grateful for those people/organizations who gave permission to use their materials in this book: Dr Mike Leigh for permission to use maps from his book; Mr Allan Girot for permission to quote from his father Eugene Girot's correspondence, held at BBC Written Archives; the BBC Written Archives itself; Messrs Timothy and Jonathan Sharp for permission to use photographs from their father Richard Sharp's collection; the Hartley Library, University of Southampton for permission to use and quote from the Mountbatten Archive.

Finally, my thanks to Abigail Lane and colleagues at Bloomsbury Academic for helping me through the publishing process.

Abbreviations

AFPFL	Anti-Fascist People's Freedom League
AFPU	Army Film and Photographic Unit
AIR	All India Radio
ALFSEA	Allied Land Forces South East Asia
AP	Associated Press [agency]
API	Associated Press India [agency]
AVG	American Volunteer Group ['Flying Tigers']
BBC	British Broadcasting Corporation
BBC WAC	BBC Written Archives Centre
BFI	British Film Institute
BIA	Burma Independence Army [later BNA]
BIS	British Information Services
BNA	Burma National Army [see also LBF, PBF]
CAS(B)	Civil Affairs Service (Burma)
CBI	China-Burma-India theatre (US)
CBS	Columbia Broadcasting System
CinC	Commander-in-Chief [Indian Army]
CSAS	Centre of South Asian Studies – University of Cambridge
DICA	Deputy Chief of Staff (Information and Civil Affairs)
(D)DPR	(Deputy) Director of Public Relations
FPI	Free Press of India [agency]
FO	Foreign Office
GOC	General Officer Commanding
GoI	Government of India
HD GoI	Home Department, Government of India
HIWR	Home Intelligence weekly reports
HQ	Headquarters
IAPR	Indian Army Public Relations
INA	Indian National Army
INS	International News Service
IO(R)	India (& Burma) Office (Records)
IWM	Imperial War Museum
JSM	Joint Staff Mission (Washington)
LBF	Local Burmese Forces
LRP	Long-Range Penetration
MoI	Ministry of Information
NCAC	Northern Combat Area Command
NRA	Newsreel Association of Great Britain and Ireland

OIOC	Oriental and Indian Office Collection, British Library
OSS	Office of Strategic Services
OWI	Office of War Information (US)
PBF	Patriot Burmese Forces [developed out of BIA, LPF, BNA]
PR(O)	Public Relations (Officer)
PWE	Political Warfare Executive
RAF	Royal Air Force
SEAC	South East Asia Command
SEAC	SEAC forces' newspaper
SACSEA	Supreme Allied Commander South East Asia [Mountbatten]
SOE	Special Operations Executive
SPRO	Service Public Relations Organisation (Burma, 1942)
SSI	Secretary of State for India/Burma [Leo Amery throughout this period]
UP	United Press [agency]
USAAF	United States Army Air Forces

Colonial-Era Names

Main place names as changed since 1941

Place names in 1941	Today
Akyab	Sittwe
Arakan	Rakhine
Bombay	Mumbai
Calcutta	Kolkata
Chungking	Chongqing (China)
Madras	Chennai
Magwe	Magway
Maymyo	Pyin Oo Lwin
Moulmein	Mawlamyine
Pegu	Bago
Prome	Pyay
Rangoon	Yangon
Toungoo	Taungoo

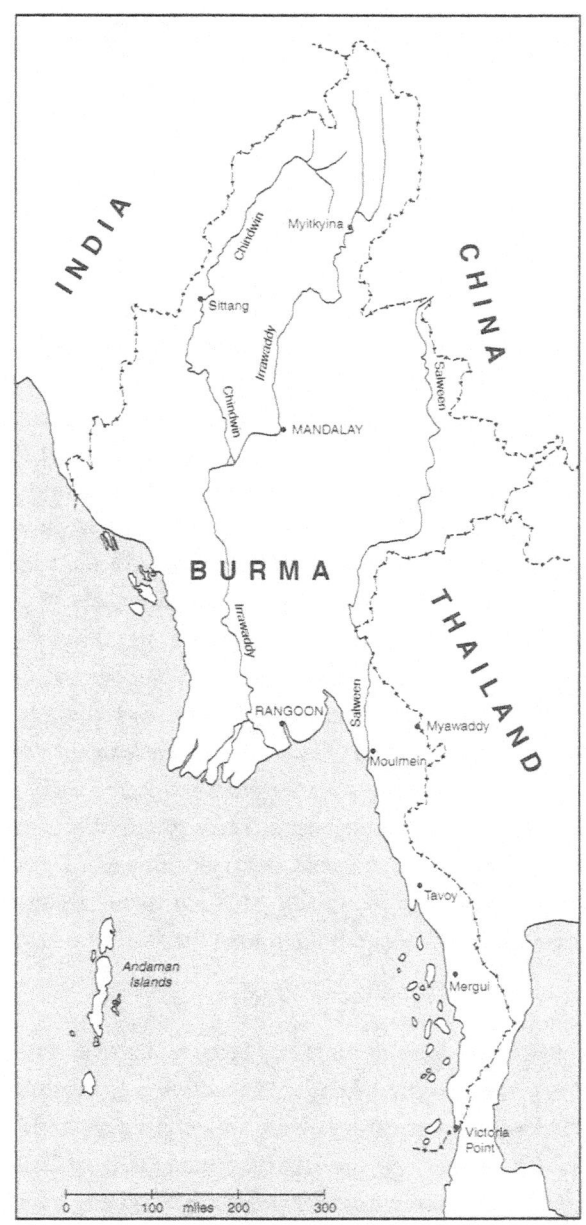

Map 0.1 Outline Map of Burma, courtesy of Michael D. Leigh.

1

Introduction

A 'Forgotten War'

In recent years, much attention has been paid by historians and others to the contribution of the Allied soldiers who fought in Burma. This reached something of a climax in the celebrations of the 75th anniversary of victory over Japan in 2020. The knighthood and publicity given to the late Sir Tom Moore, who served in Burma, and the passing of Dame Vera Lynn, who entertained troops there, brought the Burma War back to public attention. The Royal British Legion (RBL) used the 75th anniversary to explain on its website why it believed the troops fighting in Asia were given so little attention and the 14th Army became known as the 'Forgotten Army'. One of the reasons cited by the RBL was the lack of media coverage of the war against Japan: '... there were no live radio or TV broadcasts from the campaign so for most of the public they had very little knowledge beyond the odd newspaper report of what was happening'.[1] One of the purposes of this book is to question this blanket assumption that the media ignored or played down the India-Burma campaign.

Today, partly through the work of organizations like the RBL, the BBC, the Imperial War Museum (IWM), the National Army Museum, the Burma Star Association, the Kohima Educational Trust and numerous historians, I would argue that it is no longer a 'Forgotten War', and the 14th Army is no longer a 'Forgotten Army', although the clichés continue to be used in the media. These terms, which are supposed to have been coined by a British journalist in 1943, became established in the last quarter of 1944, partly because of concerns at the lack of amenities for soldiers fighting in Burma under appalling conditions.[2] This coincided with a determined public relations effort of South East Asia Command (SEAC) under Lord Louis Mountbatten to publicize the importance of the British Commonwealth contribution to the war against Japan and in particular the role of the 14th Army in India and Burma. Mountbatten had used the image early on in his command to focus the attention of his audience on his determination to bring change. He told assembled soldiers in one of his famous soapbox talks: 'I know you think of yourselves as the Forgotten Army, well, let me tell you, you're not forgotten ... nobody even knows you're here!'[3] Mountbatten and his commanders were aware that after the humiliating retreat from Burma in 1942 and the failed attempt to re-enter through Arakan in 1943 the army needed to be rebuilt, retrained and have its morale restored. The importance of troop morale during the Second World War has been increasingly recognized by historians, yet the importance of the media in supporting morale has not been properly recognized. This was partly a matter of bringing the attention of the public at home to the importance of the India-Burma War and the achievements of its soldiers, but also to the extremely difficult conditions under which it was fought. In turn, it was expected that improved media coverage would lead to soldiers receiving messages of support from home and recognition in national and local media. These efforts at publicizing the war in Burma did pay dividends, especially during the successful recapture of Mandalay and the capital Rangoon in 1945. However, it was inevitable that the media reflected the fact that the British and American public gave greater attention to the crucial events in Europe and the Pacific than to India and Burma. Public interest was, therefore, intermittent and even important events in Burma, such as the recapture of Rangoon in May 1945, could be overshadowed by events elsewhere.

This is not a traditional military history of the Burma campaign, although it depends upon the excellent work of many military historians and inevitably integrates its narrative with the way in which the Burma campaign unfolds between 1941 and 1945. Rather, it is a study of how governments and the armed forces tried to use various media to project the most positive image to domestic and international audiences of a war that often seemed neglected or, at least, misunderstood. This book focuses on Allied public relations and media, with the main emphasis on the British and, to a lesser extent, American and Indian media.[4] My previous book studied the role of war correspondents during the long retreat of Allied armies facing the Japanese invasion in the first half of 1942.[5] It was very difficult to keep journalists 'onside' during the rapid Japanese advance through Burma when it was clear that the defences were totally unprepared and under-equipped. Inevitably, censorship was the primary tool used to try to cover up the full humiliation of the defeat. Valiant attempts were made by the Army public relations organization to support correspondents with their material needs of food, transport, conducting officers, censorship and transmission of their dispatches. During the early stages of the campaign, correspondents focused their criticisms on what they saw as the failings of the civil government. It was not until the final stages of the retreat into India that correspondents felt able to make broader comments on what had gone wrong in Burma. Of the twenty-four accredited correspondents who reported from Burma at some stage in 1942, half of them published memoirs, usually within a year or two of their experiences, and almost all were critical of the way that the campaign had been run. Clearly, the army had lost control of the way that the media reported the war, and this had a damaging effect on morale in the armed forces. The contrast between the general optimism of reporting during the retreat with the stark reality of the bedraggled retreating soldiers and civilians reaching the safety of India in the summer of 1942 contributed to a heightened sense of the public having been misled, as had also happened with the fall of Singapore in February 1942. In these circumstances, a culture of blame was established in which the army tried to use the media to point the finger at Burma's civil government which had been forced into exile in India, while the governor of Burma and his staff, for their part, put up a doughty defence in the media. The US general Joseph Stilwell, who commanded Chinese troops in Burma, was much more honest in telling the press: '... We got a hell of a beating. We got run out of Burma and it is humiliating as hell. I think we ought to find out what caused it, go back and retake it.'⁶

For the next three years, there was never an agreed Allied policy of retaking all of Burma in the way that Stilwell expressed it. Because Burma was at no time a high priority for the political leaders and the Combined Chiefs of Staff, there were never the resources available for the full-scale land or amphibious operations that would be necessary to recapture the country. The Allies differed substantially over their aims in Burma, and the public relations organizations of the British and the Americans would often seem to be more at war with each other than with the enemy. What was needed was a sophisticated set of media management policies that would not make the mistake of raising public expectations too high, but which would make full use of any successes to highlight the importance of the Burma campaign. Even the phrase 'Burma campaign' is somewhat misleading, as it was really an India-Burma campaign from a British imperial perspective. The largest contingent by far in the multinational army were Indian soldiers, and the army depended on the support of Indian resources and communications. The war crossed into India in 1944 when the Japanese invaded Manipur and Assam with support from renegade soldiers of Bose's Indian National Army (INA). India presented a serious political problem for media management as the Indian nationalist civil disobedience campaign reached a height with the Quit India campaign of 1942. Correspondents were accredited to India Command until SEAC was established in the autumn of 1943. Although correspondents were approved specifically to report the war, this could be widely interpreted as allowing them to comment on the local Indian political situation, which created potential conflicts, especially in the case of American journalists, who tended to be more sympathetic to the Indian nationalist cause and hostile to British imperialism. Indian Army censorship was thought to be unnecessarily restrictive by correspondents, who claimed that political considerations were being used rather than strictly security ones. This underlines the fact that the war in this area should be seen as an India-Burma one, or in the case of the Americans, a China-Burma-India (CBI) war.

Harsh lessons in media management were learnt in the first attempt to retake territory in coastal north-west Burma, the disastrous Arakan campaign of the first half of 1943. The negative publicity of the Arakan withdrawals was somewhat fortuitously overshadowed by the great propaganda success of the publicity organized for the returning soldiers of General Wingate's first Chindit expedition in May 1943. It was ironic, however, that this publicity triumph may well have led to a distorted military investment in a second Chindit expedition in 1944, which may have taken resources and attention from the much more important defence of Indian territory at Imphal and Kohima in the same year. Lord Louis Mountbatten, appointed as Supreme Commander SEAC in August 1943, was more attuned to the need for good media management than any other commander on the British side, with the possible exception of General Montgomery. He was determined that the 14th Army, as the force fighting the Japanese was now designated, should receive as much publicity as possible to raise soldier morale and counteract the belief that this was a 'Forgotten Army'. All media were engaged in this publicity effort, from newspapers and magazines through to radio and cinema. Although it was inevitably an uphill battle to keep the attention of the

British public on Burma while the war in Europe was reaching its climax, by 1945 General Slim's successes in retaking Mandalay and Rangoon received much more professional media management and fuller press coverage than at any other stage in the campaign.

In the world wars of the twentieth century, Britain and its empire always seem to have started slowly, suffered major setbacks, but then gradually recovered, learnt from mistakes, and achieved successful momentum in the later stages leading to victory. In media management of these wars, it was a similar story. In peacetime, British politicians and civil servants tended to look down on the use of propaganda and were slow to prepare for its use in wartime. In the early phases of the Second World War, the Ministry of Information (MoI) seemed to find it hard to judge the public mood, or even to trust the public's response to the war.[7] In fact, the MoI took little part in the media management in the Burma War, devolving the initiative to the local services' public relations organizations. The same could be said further up the military and political hierarchy, too. Prime Minister Winston Churchill regarded Burma as very low in Allied priorities until Germany had been defeated. He was keen to give an impression to the Americans that Britain would play its part in a campaign to restore links in northern Burma to support China but did not want to encourage any premature public expectations of a land campaign to retake Burma.[8] Churchill seemed to pay more attention to Burma when things were going badly than he did to recognizing when they went well. Chief of Imperial General Staff Sir Alan Brooke was also very sceptical about the American focus on restoring a land bridge to China and regarded anything which took resources or attention away from his Europe-/Mediterranean-first strategy as a diversion. Even on the political side, one can detect very little in the way of a concerted pressure from Secretary of State for India and Burma Leo Amery for strengthening media coverage for the India-Burma War. He focused largely on the India side of his responsibilities and then mostly on political issues. In fact, even the Burma Office was described by one MP as 'little more than a bicycle shed at the back of the [grand India Office] building'.[9] The governor of Burma, Sir Reginald Dorman-Smith, who was forced to leave Burma for India in May 1942, did contribute ideas for propaganda on Burma but was largely taken up with planning for the eventual restoration of British civil government in Burma. As a result, military media management for India-Burma was largely left to the Indian Army and SEAC public relations organizations, which eventually established offshoots in London and Washington.

Media interest in the Burma War

The terms 'Forgotten War' and 'Forgotten Army' are widely used about the Burma campaign and do reflect a reality which was that the fighting in Burma usually held much less interest for the American and British media than the more immediate campaigns in Europe, North Africa and the Pacific. However, the war in Burma did reach the front pages at certain times of crisis, such as in February and March 1942 after Singapore and Rangoon fell to the Japanese. A number of reporters reached

Burma having been forced to leave Thailand and Singapore, which probably accounted for the increased attention.[10] 1943 was quiet for reporting in Burma, not least because the government wanted to play down any idea of a major advance there while the military hardware was not available to support it. The one exception was the short burst of publicity in May that was timed to coincide with the return of General Wingate's 1st Chindit expedition, Operation Longcloth.

Interest peaked again for the three months after March 1944 when the Japanese reached Indian soil and were repulsed. Afterwards, as the Indian journalist D. R. Mankekar noted, Burma 'resumed its proper place, third in line after Europe and the Pacific'.[11] Ever since his appointment as supreme commander, Mountbatten was determined to rebuild troop morale after the setbacks of 1943, and he saw improving media coverage of the Burma War as crucial in achieving this. He began a process of bringing in key newspaper men from Britain to set up a daily armed forces newspaper and to improve media communications with home. With the successes at Imphal and Kohima in 1944, Mountbatten pressed for SEAC to have its own personnel work within the MoI in London and for a sustained campaign to advertise the successes of the 14th Army and its generals, especially General Slim. War correspondents were given improved facilities to send their reports home, while officer observers complemented national newspaper coverage with 'personalised' press releases which were targeted at local newspapers in Britain. The BBC was brought in to provide live radio reports from the fighting, and preparations were made for an Anglo-American documentary film on the Burma War. Censorship restrictions which had irked the correspondents since the beginning of the war were eased and based only on security grounds. So, every effort was made to combat the Forgotten Army syndrome, but inevitably the British public, and therefore newspaper editors, continued to give much greater attention to events closer to home, especially the D-Day landings and the subsequent battle to defeat Germany on the Continent.

There was an increase in media interest in the Burma campaign when the 14th Army finally advanced across the Chindwin and Irrawaddy rivers, Mandalay was recaptured in March 1945 and the army raced on to recapture Rangoon. Mountbatten's campaign to have the necessary tools for the Burma campaign to be more fully publicized at home and abroad was finally achieved, but the final throes of German defeat still took precedence in the British media, as did the last stages of the Pacific war in the American media.

Changing historiography of the India-Burma War

In examining changes in the way that historians have looked at the war in Burma, I have taken a broad-brush approach and have only selected examples of the different types of historical writing in each category. I do not wish to imply any sort of hierarchy of quality or importance in the different approaches, but rather to suggest a welcome broadening of the field of study of the war, and to suggest that the study of media management is a useful addition to previous studies. For a long time, books on the Second World War in Burma tended to concentrate on the military aspects of the conflict, such as competing strategies, tactics, resources, communications and the relative qualities of the generals. Starting with the official histories, historians used the extensive range of historical material, official and unofficial, to piece together the complex manoeuvres and battles that took place. It was obviously important to record the participation of all the different units involved using campaign dispatches, regimental records and memoirs.[12] These military histories tended to pay rather less attention to other important aspects of the war, such as rivalries among the Allies,[13] the roles of indigenous peoples in the conflict, the rise of Asian nationalisms, the levels of interest in and support for the war at home, morale of the troops, and the role of intelligence gathering and ethnic rivalries in the war zones. These are all subjects which have now been much more widely researched, and some of which have been incorporated in military histories, particularly within the last two decades. It has become more important to see military operations in the context of wider social, cultural and political developments.

A real turning point in placing the Burma War in a much wider context of the challenges faced by the Japanese invasions to South East Asian empires and the crucial development of nationalist movements was Bayly and Harper's *Forgotten Armies: Britain's Asian Empire & The War with Japan*.[14] 'Forgotten Armies' was a clever title to choose because it moved away from the traditional focus on the national armies and their role in the Burma War towards a recognition that smaller armies, such as levies recruited from ethnic groups, also played a crucial role in the war.[15] The Nagas, Kachins, Chins and Karens played an important role in supporting the Allies, sometimes in conjunction with underground warriors, such as V Force, Special Operations Executive (SOE) and Office of Strategic Services (OSS). They paid a high price, both during the war and at independence; while others, such as the Burmese nationalist armed forces (up until nearly the end of the war) and the INA led by Subhas Chandra Bose, played their parts in supporting the Japanese. These different armies would have great significance for Indian and Burmese politics after the war ended. More attention has been paid to the responses of the peoples living in Burma at the time war broke out, particularly the Indian population which was so important to the economy and the effectiveness of Rangoon as a port. Journalists reported a rather different picture of the activities of Burmese 'fifth columnists' than the government of Burma, which played down the significance of organized Burmese support for the Japanese.[16] The exodus of so many Indians, Anglo-Indians, Anglo-Burmese and Europeans from Burma presented an enormous problem during the war but also had great significance for Britain's reputation and for Burma's demographic make-up after it was ended.[17] Most importantly, there has been acknowledgement of the importance of the humiliating defeats of 1942 and the growing strength of Asian nationalist movements under Japanese occupation to the process of the ending of the British Empire in South and South East Asia after the war ended. Mountbatten's adroit handling of the Burmese nationalist movement during the endgame of the war and the moves to post-war independence set precedents for the British withdrawal from India in 1947. In both Burma and India, Mountbatten saw the importance of using the media in support of his handling of nationalist movements.[18]

Military historians have increasingly emphasized the multinational nature of the Allied forces in Burma, counteracting the misleading legacy of Churchill's overemphasis on the role of British troops in Burma.¹⁹ India provided by far the largest number of soldiers in the Burma campaign, and recent works have integrated the military history with the social, political and economic histories of India in the war.²⁰ Building on the pioneering work of Ashley Jackson, there has been much greater recognition of the British imperial context of the war and the role that troops from Africa and other parts of the empire played in Burma.²¹ A very important step forward in questioning the approach to the Burma campaign which focuses on national armies is Tarak Barkawi's *Soldiers of Empire: Indian and British Armies in World War II*.²² This book has important lessons for our understanding of troop morale and, in particular, recognizing that under the stresses of war national stereotypes of soldier behaviour became less distinct and relevant as a basis for historical analysis. This also has implications for critically re-examining contemporary war reporting, which was firmly based on national stereotypes – for example, in the treatment of accounts of atrocities carried out by Japanese soldiers or of their notorious refusal to surrender. The question of morale of the British armed forces during the Second World War has now been thoroughly addressed by two studies: Alan Allport's *Browned Off and Bloody-Minded: The British Soldier Goes to War 1939–1945* and Jonathan Fennell's *Fighting the People's War: The British and Commonwealth Armies and the Second World War*.²³ These books emphasize that the brunt of the fighting (but the least of the recognition received) was taken by the infantry, and that service in India and Burma was generally unpopular with British recruits. It is clear that British soldiers, like their Indian counterparts, became increasingly politicized during the war and less sympathetic to Britain's continued imperial presence in these areas. The war correspondents also were radicalized by their experiences of reporting war, and were generally supportive of more rapid moves to the independence of India and Burma.²⁴

For all the broadening of the focus of studies of the war in Burma that has taken place, it is noticeable that the role of the media, army management of the media, and the role of war correspondents has not been given much attention to date, even in studies of soldier morale. There may be a number of reasons for this. Media historians have themselves often been sceptical about the overly patriotic role of the media in wartime and the widespread censorship and self-censorship which restricted what could be written or published at the time. The prime example of this is Phillip Knightley's classic study, *The First Casualty: The War Correspondent as Hero, Propagandist and Myth-Maker from Crimea to Iraq*.²⁵ Knightley's views were strongly supported by Connelly and Welch who accused the media of cooperating with the government and military leadership in supporting nationalistic and patriotic causes. This resulted, they argued, 'in a form of war reporting that was less concerned with accuracy than with propaganda'.²⁶ It is true that some war correspondents' dispatches and memoirs could be self-promoting and unreliable. It is also correct that, for various reasons, they held back from reporting truths which they felt would be damaging to the overall cause or to public and military morale. However, these are not arguments for ignoring the media's role in the war, but rather for treating it with the same rigour and scepticism that one treats other historical sources. It is important to keep in mind, though, the impressive range and reach of the mass media at this time. Nearly all British households read either a daily or Sunday newspaper, and local newspapers were thriving, too. Illustrated magazines like *Life* and *Picture Post* were also extremely popular, with readerships estimated to be in the millions.[27] Cinema was at the height of its popularity, with average weekly audiences in Britain increasing from 19 million at the start of the war to over 30 million at its end.[28] Forty per cent of the population were going to the cinema each week, and when there would watch newsreels, one of the main visual ways of keeping up with the war across the globe. Radio was really coming into its own, with half the adult population listening to the BBC's nightly news broadcasts. Radio had tremendous immediacy, especially as during the war the BBC developed the technical means to transmit live broadcasts from the fighting fronts. The media and official propaganda could play an important role in each of these areas. Governments could plan positive messages to be relayed through direct propaganda or through the various media. They could also try to control any negative messages, largely, but not only, through censorship, which, of course, was widely used in wartime.

Is media management in wartime just another term for propaganda?

Propaganda is a difficult word to pin down because it has acquired a set of different connotations over time and it can be used at its broadest to include almost all forms of both official and non-official forms of public persuasion. In this study, the focus is narrowed by looking at official, both military and civil organizations', attempts to use the media to project a positive view of campaigning in India-Burma during the war. In the case of the Second World War, British public memory of propaganda is a mixture of both positive and negative perceptions. On the positive side, wartime propaganda directed at the British domestic audience conjures up colourful public information campaigns such as 'Dig for Victory'. The problem is that it also brings to mind mostly negative ideas about deliberate lies, deception and the manipulation of the truth for dubious ends.[29] While these negative views of propaganda were mostly directed at enemy or dictatorial propaganda, there was a recognition that all governments had been guilty of using these methods in the First World War. In the interwar years, a perception grew in Britain that the government had used untruthful propaganda to persuade people to support the war against Germany. The example most used was the Bryce report, published by the War Propaganda Bureau in May 1915, outlining often extreme stories of German atrocities against the civilian population in Belgium. Despite the fact that later research has found that some of the evidence used was actually accurate and even sometimes understated, the resulting negative attitudes to such stories being circulated in wartime had a long-lasting impact.[30] The association of the word 'propaganda' with lies became embedded in the public consciousness, yet this failed to allow for the various types of propaganda, many of which were based on truthful information. In fact, propagandists realized that it made sense to stick to the truth wherever possible, so as not to be found out in any lie and thus lose public trust. Even so, the truth could be hidden, perhaps by censorship but also by slanting the representation of events to put a different gloss on them. Scholars have found it helpful to distinguish different forms of propaganda by colour coding, which focuses on whether the source of propaganda is revealed rather than whether it is true or not. Black propaganda hides its sources in the aim of discrediting opponents while white propaganda makes it clear what its source is. In between these two there is the tricky grey area in which the propaganda may or may not disclose its source. Black propaganda was rarely used in the Burma War, except in the practices of the Political Warfare Executive (PWE), a clandestine organization which targeted propaganda in Japanese-occupied areas.[31] Most army media management in the India-Burma theatre fitted into the white or overt category, and this included army communiqués as well as reports from correspondents in the field. This is not to deny that official communiqués or correspondents' reports often hid or glossed over military setbacks and overemphasized positive stories. However, the sources were usually indicated. Some material which was fed to the press came into a grey category because it took the form of articles prepared by official agencies, but which went out under the name of apparently independent authors. Whichever form it took, media management in wartime fits David Welch's definition of propaganda in that it was a deliberate attempt to influence public opinion favourably and to avoid creating damaging effects on morale.[32] George Orwell, who believed firmly in both the rightness of the war against fascism and the need to maintain truthfulness in his broadcasts to India for the BBC, still accepted that he was in fact a propagandist.[33]

Why is media management important?

After the largely hostile attitude adopted by the British military towards war correspondents during the First World War, there gradually evolved an acceptance that the media could play an important part in supporting the armed forces during wars. Unfortunately, this seems to have developed haphazardly and did not form part of officer training courses.[34] Ideally, commanders were supposed to keep government agencies informed, not only of what was happening in campaigns but also how they would like this information conveyed to the media. For instance, were new military operations to be given initial publicity, played down or kept strictly secret for the time being? The increased number of war correspondents would require not only facilities to carry out their work but also access to officers at various levels up to the generals. Some generals were very open to talking to war correspondents and allowed them ready access while others kept the journalists at arm's length. Generals came to realize that the media were not only important in raising the morale of their troops but also in pressing their case for support from politicians and Chiefs of Staff at home.[35] A loosening of military censorship over time is indicative of a growing recognition that it was often the best policy to trust correspondents and to work with them rather than to keep them in the dark and constantly edit what they wrote.[36]

Academic studies of military media management have tended to be weighted to the study of the post-Second World War period, particularly the Vietnam War and later conflicts. Studies of the two world wars tend to be more empirically based and focus on state propaganda and the role of war correspondents. A pioneering collection of essays focusing on military–media relations was provided by Stewart and Carruthers's *War, Culture and the Media: Representations of the Military in 20th Century Britain*.[37] From the Vietnam War onwards, studies have been stronger on theoretical approaches and emphasize changes in the nature of media management resulting from developments in communications technology and more sophisticated means of government control.[38] However, some of those changes do date back to the Second World War, and even earlier. Two examples come to mind. First, there is the system of 'pooling' correspondents' reports which involved restricting the number of journalists covering particular campaigns and requiring them to share their reports with other media outlets. This was seen at its strongest in the Falklands War of 1992, but it was certainly a requirement for newsreel cameramen in the Second World War and also applied to large military operations where numbers had to be restricted. This was much more likely in the European and North African theatres than in Burma where there was a need for more reporters rather than fewer. A second example is that of 'embedding' correspondents with particular military units so that they could be more easily controlled and also be likely to be sympathetic to the military perspective. The system was based on close monitoring of journalists and the threat of expulsion if rules which they agreed to were broken. This is seen to have been at its most obvious in the Iraq War of 2003 and came in for much criticism.[39] However, this was not that dissimilar to the system used in the two world wars when correspondents were vetted prior to approval, required to adhere to strict security rules, and operated in small groups which were accompanied by conducting officers.[40] As the journalists wore military-style uniforms, had the temporary rank of captains and messed with officers, it could be said that they were embedded, too. There were cases in Burma when military–media cooperation was very close – for instance, when two journalists rode in the tanks which were forcing an exit from Rangoon in 1942. Correspondents who were allowed to join bombing missions or fly over the Himalayas with the air force were inevitably highly sympathetic to the airmen and the operations they reported on.

British media management in the India-Burma War presents a very different picture from studies of the role of information management in the European theatre in the same period or from the role of Washington in CBI media management. This was because there was much less central control from London. Burma was very much on the periphery of concerns of bodies such as the MoI, the War Office or the Foreign Office (FO). Most of the organizations controlling the media in the Burma War were located in Army Headquarters in India and later at SEAC in Kandy, Ceylon. From the time of his appointment as Supreme Commander South East Asia, Admiral Lord Louis Mountbatten acted as the main spur to increased coordination and expansion of media activities in his command. This included newspaper, magazine correspondents, the BBC for radio, professional photographers and photographers from the services, army public relations observers, newsreel cameramen and film-makers. Mountbatten took a remarkable amount of detailed interest in all aspects of the way that the media reported the war. Critics have derided his egotism, vanity and penchant for self-publicity, but in Burma his determination to raise troop morale and to ensure that those fighting in this distant theatre were not forgotten by those at home were important elements in his successful command.[41]

2

Media Covering the War in India-Burma

In studying media management, it is important to have an overview of the various national and international media involved at the time of the Second World War. This ranges from printed media – newspapers and magazines – through to visual and audio media – newsreels, cinema, photographs and radio. It is important to be aware not only of the size of different media audiences but also to have some indication of their likely coverage of the India-Burma campaign. Different media were more or less vulnerable to pressures from their owners, from commercial considerations and, of course, from state censorship measures. In this study, the main focus will be on the British and, to a lesser extent, American and Indian media, but it is important to recognize that these were global media with interlocking links across national borders. This is clear if one looks at the strong American financial and cultural influences in cinema and newsreels, and the central role of international telegraph news agencies such as Associated Press (AP), United Press (UP) and Reuters. The war must be seen as crossing the borders between Burma and India, not just geographically, but also in terms of media management, propaganda and censorship. Most of the troops involved were recruited and trained from India, and Indian Army Public Relations (IAPR) had to be constantly attentive to the political, social and economic impact of the Burma campaign on India itself.

1. Role of the telegraph agencies

The development of telegraph communication in the mid-nineteenth century led to demand for fast transmission of stock market and other financial and commercial news from across the world. A cable connection was set up to Bombay in 1866 and Julius Reuter set up his first office there in the same year. Reuters quickly established links throughout the Far East, and when the telegraphic world was divided up between the main companies, Reuters gained the monopoly for the British Empire and the Far East.[1] It expanded to include general news as well as commercial news, as they were in any case interrelated, especially in time of war or threatened war. There was a natural symbiosis of interest between Reuters and the Government of India (GoI) based on exchange of information in return for subscription or 'subsidy' by the government. This, and the faster communications links it developed, gave Reuters an effective monopoly on telegraphic news coming into and out of India. Initially, only the Anglo-Indian (British-owned) press could afford the expensive subscription to the Reuters news service. Some progressive-minded Indian-owned papers, such as the *Bengalee* and the *Hindu*, did subscribe to Reuters, but many other Indian newspapers had to feed off the scraps by reusing material from subscribing papers. In 1899, K. C. Roy set up the Associated Press India (API) to distribute news within India. Reuters effectively took over API at the time of the First World War, but API continued to be the main distributor of news within India. Attempts to set up a nationalist alternative news agency in the interwar years failed.[2] So, the Reuters/API monopoly was maintained, with API providing the news within India and Reuters for abroad. However, there were obvious challenges, even before the war, of trying to meet the sometimes conflicting needs of the GoI for publicity and the increasingly nationalist sympathies of the Indian press and newspaper readership.[3] Before and during the Second World War, Reuters/API faced competition from the large American agencies, UP and AP. These tended to be more sympathetic to Indian nationalist aspirations, which posed problems for the Indian authorities which wanted American press coverage but resented the criticisms which resulted.[4]

Gordon Waterfield, Reuters war correspondent in Burma, pointed out in his memoir, *Morning Will Come*, that the perceived Reuters monopoly could prove a mixed blessing. On the positive side, Reuters had the advantage of fast connections from Calcutta and Delhi to Bombay for onward transmission by telegraph or wireless. On the other hand, it 'was regarded by the authorities and all the Indian Press as part of the propaganda machinery of the Government of India'.[5] Waterfield tried to go some way to counter this reputation by challenging Indian military censorship during the first Arakan campaign. Needless to say, he failed and decided to leave India.

Agency reporting differed from that of newspaper correspondents in that it was based on a reputation for obtaining stories quickly and clearly. Each agency vied to beat the others to get stories back even minutes faster than its rivals. There was not much room for the colourful adventure stories that newspaper editors valued, and there was a reputation for accuracy which needed to be maintained. The authorities did recognize the special importance of the agencies, especially in reaching local newspapers, and this could result in resentment from newspaper correspondents at what they saw as privileges being given to the agencies.[6] However, both faced problems of speedy transmission in the field. D. R. Mankekar, the Reuters/API correspondent on the India-Burma borders, pointed to the difficulties in getting a scoop there because dispatches had to be flown back to 14th Army headquarters at Comilla in East Bengal, whereas American reporters had mobile high-speed wireless transmitters at Stilwell's HQ.[7] Often stories would have to be put in a bag and sent back to the cable-point in a courier plane.[8] Correspondents would not then be in a position to try to ensure that their dispatches had priority. Where agency reporters like Mankekar could win out was by being able to stick around longer near the front than the newspaper men and thus having a chance to pick up scoops.

2. Newspapers

i. British newspapers

Before the Second World War, the British newspaper industry was definitely feeling the challenge from the growing mass media – cinema and radio. The war posed problems for the newspaper industry but also offered opportunities as against rival media. The main difficulties were obviously created by the censorship regimes implemented by the British government in the early stages of the war. Regulation 2D gave the home secretary sweeping powers to control the press, including power to ban any publication which published material 'calculated to foment opposition to the prosecution of successful issue of any war in which His Majesty is engaged'. This power was used to close two small-circulation communist papers in January 1941. Churchill and some members of the Cabinet remained ready until 1942 to widen the censorship net to include the popular but increasingly critical *Daily Mirror*, but were restrained by the likely backlash at this much larger threat to press freedom. Editors were still required to pass any items or photographs likely to be a threat to military security for approval by the Ministry of Information (MoI). This could be interpreted quite widely as it referred to obtaining, possessing or publishing materials 'in any manner likely to prejudice the efficient prosecution of the war ...'. However, as the fortunes of war improved, there were no further calls from the British government for dramatic censorship measures. Indeed, as Curran and Seaton point out, 'Coercive censorship was made, to some extent, unnecessary by self-censorship.'[9] The press were generally cooperative with the government. In any case, in the war zones, correspondents were subject to close military censorship so that unwelcome news could be hidden, downplayed or delayed.

Because of a serious shortage of newsprint, the government placed restrictions on the size of newspapers and on the proportion of advertising they could include. By 1941 the average number of pages in British newspapers was down to four, and this had the effect of actually increasing advertising revenue and making the press less reliant on chasing casual readerships.[10] Curran and Seaton argue that this, and public interest in more serious subject matter, meant that papers substantially increased the percentage of their papers devoted to such content, whether it be domestic or war news.[11] They note a marked growth of the more left-wing papers, of which the *Daily Mirror* was by far the most successful.[12] However, the reduction in pages also meant that editors had to be careful about how much space they could devote to war correspondents' dispatches from the various theatres. Stories needed to be up to date, direct in language, and preferably to combine action stories with personal ones. There was, of necessity, greater public interest in stories from nearer to home than in little-known geographical areas such as Burma. It was expensive to send correspondents to distant fields, especially if the availability of newsworthy material there was unpredictable. Newspapers had attracted large readerships in the pre-war period. More than two-thirds of the British population read a newspaper every day, with 82 per cent reading a Sunday paper.[13] The papers had made innovations in layout, typography and content to compete with rivals. The popular papers increasingly turned to 'entertainment' features rather than solid news to maintain their audiences, although inevitably they needed to, and did, alter the balance in wartime.

British newspapers had for a long time been controlled by commercial conglomerates, with the so-called 'press barons' as owners. Lord Rothermere owned the *Daily Mail* (as with other owners, additional national, evening and local papers were also in his portfolio); Lord Astor owned *The Times* and *Observer*; Lord Beaverbrook owned the *Daily Express* and *Evening Standard*; and Lords Camrose and Kemsley (Berry Brothers) owned the *Daily Telegraph*, the *Financial Times* and the *Daily Sketch*. These press lords owned about half of daily newspapers and this potentially gave them great influence. Most were Conservative in political outlook, although not formally attached to the party itself. The *News Chronicle* supported the Liberal Party, and the *Daily Herald* was set up by the trade unions in support of the Labour Party. The *Daily Mirror*, which Rothermere had sold in 1935, had become a tabloid both in format and content and was increasingly left wing in outlook. Its circulation continued to expand during the war as it took up the causes of ordinary servicemen and women along with civilians. Despite some of the owners in the interwar years using their influence to support certain political campaigns, such as Beaverbook for Empire Free Trade, and some owners showing a sympathy for fascist movements, Kevin Williams concludes for the interwar period: 'There is limited evidence to show that the press barons were successful in exerting any significant sway over British politics.'[14]

The outbreak of war in September 1939 might have thrown up the sort of crises that had allowed the press barons to have political influence in the First World War, but once Churchill was established as prime minister of a coalition government with apparently strong popular support, there was less room for such an outcome. In any case, Churchill brought Beaverbrook into the Cabinet, first as Minister for Air Production and later as Minister of Supply. Although his papers were patriotic and supportive of Churchill's leadership, Beaverbrook hired reporters and, indeed, editors whose views were much further to the left politically, such as Michael Foot, Frank Owen and Wilfred Burchett. Beaverbrook was supposed to have taken personally against Mountbatten in 1942, but it is difficult to see any sign of this antagonism reflected in his newspapers during Mountbatten's command in the Burma campaign.[15]

Some of the most popular newspapers – such as the Sundays which had the highest readerships, the *News of the World* and the *People* – focused more on popular domestic stories, sports, cartoons, music film and theatre. The papers which consistently sent correspondents to cover the Burma War were the *News Chronicle* (Jordan, Emeny, Treanor, Gelder); *Daily Mail* (Salter, Stanford, Wagg); *Daily Express* (Gallagher, Burchett, Jacob, Fitchett, Graham); *Daily Telegraph* (Gander, Moore, Legge); *Daily Herald* (Matthews, Thompson, Wills, Helliwell, McWhinnie); *Daily Sketch* and Kemsley newspapers (Hodson, Lang, Reynolds); and *The Times* (Cooper, Morrison). It was not unusual for reporters to work for more than one newspaper as long as the papers were not direct rivals, which mostly meant doubling up for foreign newspapers.

Local and regional newspapers, which had suffered circulation losses in the interwar years, benefited from the demand for news, particularly stories of local regiments and servicemen, and saw their circulation rise significantly during the war.[16] The government realized the importance of local and regional papers, especially those further away geographically from the dominance of the national press in London and the south-east, and it seems that they were treated rather more leniently by the censorship system. Officer observers, often men serving in Burma who had journalistic experience, were expected to provide stories of particular interest to the local press, and to give talks across the country when on home leave.[17]

ii. American newspapers

Burma was not the main theatre of interest to American readers and could not compete with news from Europe, North Africa and the Pacific. However, as part of the China-Burma-India (CBI) theatre, American newspapers sent correspondents to cover the activities of US General Joseph Stilwell. Stilwell only commanded Chinese troops at first, but then added America's first ground troops in the region in the form of Merrill's Marauders during the advance on Myitkyina in 1944. After Stilwell's dismissal in October, America continued to play a key role in the completion of the Ledo/Stilwell Road, linking Burma to China, and in the South East Asia Command (SEAC) under Mountbatten. American public relations started out small-scale but was very well organized under its public relations officer (PRO) Fred Eldridge. It was very supportive of Stilwell in his rivalries with British commanders. US reporters were provided with fast wireless connections in the field, something British and other national correspondents envied. Troops were provided with the first overseas forces newspaper, the very readable *CBI Roundup*, and a lively magazine *Yank*.[18]

The main US papers which provided correspondents in the theatre were the *New York Times* (Matthews, Durdin); *Chicago Daily Times* (Busvine); and *Chicago Daily News* (Stowe, Steele). The problem was that American newspapers were not national but local in circulation, and this limited their reach for British publicity in the USA. It was more important that the three American news agencies – UP, AP and the International News Service (INS) – were given every facility because they supplied foreign news to nine-tenths of the American press.[19] Photographers representing one of four organizations – AP, International News Photos, Acme Newspictures, Time Inc. – had their pictures pooled. However, *Life* magazine was allowed to have its own special photographs held for simultaneous release in its weekly edition to avoid being beaten by its daily newspaper competitors with its own photographs.[20]

American newspapers were also very interested in developments in the Indian nationalist movement, and especially the charismatic figure of Mahatma Gandhi. At key crisis points, such as the Cripps Mission and the Quit India movement of 1942, the IAPR was sensitive to the fact that American newspaper correspondents who were accredited to cover the war might turn their attention to political commentary while they waited to reach the front.[21] Some papers, like the *Chicago Tribune* and *Chicago Times,* were known to be hostile to British imperial interests, while others like the *New York Times* and *Washington Post* were thought to be more sympathetic.[22] American newspapers had a fair amount of freedom when they were publishing at home, thanks to the First Amendment to the constitution. America prided itself on establishing a system of wartime censorship based on trusting newspaper editors and journalists to use their discretion sensibly. That this worked was largely down to the man appointed to be in charge of the Office of Censorship, Byron Price. Price had been executive news editor of AP and was respected by fellow journalists. He used tactics of persuasion rather than of draconian censorship. He relied on 'missionaries' – editors and journalists who acted as liaisons to small local papers – encouraging them to understand and implement the censorship code.[23] The result was that over the course of the war no print journalist, and only one radio journalist, ever deliberately violated the censorship code after having been made aware of it and understanding its intent.[24] Even so, there were very effective and potentially wide-ranging censorship restrictions on US war reporters in the field. This censorship was obvious from the very beginning of the war as the true damage done by the Japanese attack on Pearl Harbor was covered up for a long time. At the end of the war, the news of the development of the atomic bomb and the true nature of its impact on Hiroshima and Nagasaki were also kept from the public.[25] Censorship restrictions varied over time according to what were perceived as the need to either calm or rally public opinion. A good example of this was that depictions of dead US soldiers were banned from publication until this rule was relaxed in 1943 at a time when it was felt that the American public were becoming complacent about the outcome of the war and the need for their involvement.[26]

Interestingly, no black American reporters were allowed into the CBI theatre until October 1944.[27] This reflected War Department segregationist attitudes which had restricted black reporters working for black newspapers to only be accredited to black units in Europe. In CBI there was the added concern that the Japanese were using the race issue as propaganda. So, despite the fact that the majority of the 15,000 US engineers building the Ledo Road were black, and black newspapers wanted to report on them, restrictions were tight. In SEAC, only two black reporters are recorded: Deton Brooks of the *Chicago Defender* and Frank Bolden of the Negro Press Association.

iii. Indian newspapers

Most Indian newspapers relied on agency reports rather than sending their own correspondents to cover the Burma War. English-language papers had the advantage of faster communications links, and they increased their circulations during the war as servicemen flooded into the country, and war news was given plenty of space. Newspapers in all of India were involved with the progress of the war, especially with recruitment and production, but the regions which were most immediately threatened by Japanese invasion – Calcutta in eastern India and Madras in the south-east – were most directly concerned. Two British-owned newspapers sent correspondents in both 1943 and 1944: *Times of India* (Moraes) and the *Statesman* (Pritchard, Devine, Stephens). Meanwhile a number of Indian-owned papers did so from 1944 onwards, including the *Bombay Chronicle* (Karaka), the *Hindu* (Narayan), *Blitz* (Karanjia) and *Janmabhoomi* (Yash Dev).[28]

iv. Australian newspapers

Australia had a keen interest in the Burma War, based on geographical proximity and the involvement of their troops in the theatre. There was much resentment about the Singapore debacle which had seen large numbers of Australian troops captured by the Japanese and sent to prisoner-of-war camps. Australia provided soldiers, sailors and airmen for the fight to recapture Burma. Australian war correspondents were thought to be some of the best in the business. A number of Australian journalists had worked in Fleet Street before the war and gained a favourable reputation. They were some of the most dynamic reporters during the war. They had an obvious interest in the Japanese-threatened areas in the Pacific and South East Asia. They felt that they faced some of the toughest censorship as they not only had to submit to censorship in the theatre they served in, but additional censorship was applied in Australia.[29] The main Australian papers which sent correspondents to Burma were the *Sydney Daily Telegraph* (Burchett, McKie, Wynter); *Sydney Morning Herald* (Munday, Macdonald, Standish, Gardner); *Melbourne Argus* (Johnston, Wynter); and *Melbourne Herald* (Wilkie, Jarrett). As with the American press, the size of the country meant that several correspondents provided local Australian papers with syndicated news.[30]

3. Visual media

i. Illustrated magazines

Illustrated magazines had really taken off in the 1930s with improvements in printing processes and innovative editorial policies. They were an important source of visual information about the war in the pre-television era. The most important magazines which provided coverage of the war were *Life*, *Look* and *Collier's* in the USA, and *Illustrated*, *Picture Post, Illustrated London News, The Sphere* and *The War Illustrated* in Great Britain. Photos were often syndicated between the British and American magazines. *Life* was a weekly magazine which, along with *Time*, was owned by Henry Luce, who had a strong influence over what appeared in the magazines, especially anything relating to his beloved China. *Life* alone had a circulation of over 3.25 million, but it was well known that these magazines were passed on and read by many more people, so readership may have been more than four or five times that number. *Collier's* magazine was a rather more literary-minded illustrated magazine. It had a readership of 2.5 million weekly and attracted top-class writers such as Martha Gellhorn and Ernest Hemingway. It took full-length articles from agency war correspondents, such as UP's Walter Briggs and AP's Dan De Luce.[31] *Collier's* did not pay as much attention to the CBI theatre as *Life* did and was more prepared to point to the weaknesses of the Chinese Army and the need to involve the Communist forces.[32]

It is difficult to judge the impact of the magazines. James Baughman argues that Luce's magazines were mostly read by journalists and the middle classes. He cites evidence that when Americans were asked 'which mass medium did the best job of serving the public during the war?', 67 per cent chose radio, 17 per cent newspapers, and only 3 per cent magazines. 'Many more people read newspapers than magazines. One should not exaggerate *Life*'s influence either – its determination to provide variety of entertaining materials, pin-ups, sports news, trivia, detracted from the serious stuff which in any case may not have been read rather than the pictures looked at.'[33] However, one should not underestimate the impact of even single, powerful photographs, and the cumulative effect of pages of photographs which told a story of war. Also, unlike the American newspapers, the magazines covered the whole nation and sold well overseas, and British propagandists in America thought that they were just as important in forming public opinion as any other printed sources.[34]

The magazines depended for their photos on commercial war correspondent photographers and also on official armed forces photography units.[35] Each of the armed forces had their own photographic units but there were also overarching units such as in SEAC and, in the American case, the Signals Corps. Although there were different remits for the commercial and official units, they both worked on a pooled basis so that their photographs were made widely available. The commercial photographers and newsreel cameramen worked on a rota basis to avoid unnecessary duplication of their efforts. The still photographers used a mixture of large format cameras for high-quality pictures and more portable cameras for action shots. They would often travel with newsreel cameramen who needed tripods and much heavier equipment. This and the elusive nature of the battlefront in Burma meant that it was difficult to shoot close pictures of the action, especially before the military advances of 1944–5. Additionally, there were problems of censorship, some of which were peculiar to the cameramen – for instance, the restrictions on photographing enemy prisoners of war and scenes of the dead and injured. In any case, cameramen would have known that very graphic pictures of warfare would not be published and they self-censored their work in support of the patriotic war effort and the soldiers they were embedded with.

ii. Newsreels and cinema: Britain

Studies of media management and propaganda in the British Empire, including India and Burma, have tended in the past to focus on the print media, especially newspapers.[36] British historians have tended to be less confident of using visual material, such as film and newsreel. There were always exceptions to this generalization, especially in the work of a generation of enthusiasts in the last quarter of the twentieth century who established the theory and practice of using newsreel material, for instance. However, these pioneers do not seem to have had many successors in the twenty-first century, despite the much wider accessibility of newsreels online and the excellent database of the British Universities Film and Video Council, *News on Screen*.[37] A major step forward in critical analysis of film and newsreels of empire was provided by an AHRC-funded research project (2007–10), which resulted in an online database – www.colonialfilm.org.uk – and two edited collections of essays by Grieveson and MacCabe.[38]

There were five newsreel companies in Britain at the beginning of the war: Paramount, Movietone, Gaumont-British, Pathé and Universal News. With the exception of Gaumont-British, they were owned by American parent companies or in joint ownership with British media concerns.[39] Whatever their ownership, the newsreels shown in the UK before the war were an entirely British product. Newsreels were produced by companies as a support to feature films in their cinema chains and independent cinemas. Nicholas Pronay argues that they 'were run by their parent-companies as a break-even advertising unit to keep their names before the cinema-goers and to keep off others'.[40] The implication was that they needed to cater to the demands of their public, and before the war, entertainment was often as important, if not more important, than hard news. Obviously, in wartime the news content was given greater priority and met the public's interest in visualizing how the war was going. According to Pronay, the newsreels had built up a non-provocative, consensual style, showing shared interests of government and people, which was attractive to their predominantly working-class audiences and was to stand them in good stead when a more propagandistic, patriotic approach was needed in wartime.[41]

The newsreels were popular in the early stages of the war. Over time, however, the evidence suggests that audiences tired of the news of constant military setbacks and the newsreels lost popularity. However, with cinema audiences averaging 20 million a week in 1938–9, and with films known to reach audiences who were less likely to read newspapers, the government was well aware of their importance.[42] Coverage of the war in the ten-minute reels which were produced twice a week was patriotic rather than neutral. This was reinforced by the upper-class-accented commentaries and upbeat music. As Pronay has argued, there was every reason for newsreel editors and their cameramen reporters to be supportive of the official propaganda line. Newsreels, unlike the press and broadcasting, were subject to both pre- and post-censorship. With raw film stock in short supply, it did not make sense to waste it on stories that the censors might refuse. Of all the media, the newsreels were probably the most likely to be sensitive to their public reception.[43]

iii. Newsreels and cinema: India-Burma

If the commercial newsreels reached a very large audience in Britain, they only managed a much smaller one in India. This was because their standard distribution was limited to English-speaking cinemas, of which there were only two hundred out of the estimated eleven or twelve hundred cinemas in British India.[44] These English-language cinemas catered mainly for resident Britons and for the educated elite living in the larger towns and cities of India. During wartime, the numbers would be increased in these cinemas by soldiers and war workers. The Government of India (GoI) recognized that they needed to do more to reach beyond these groups, particularly to reach vernacular speakers in areas where recruiting for the armed forces was strongest. An arrangement was made with *British Movietone News* to have a version of their newsreel dubbed into Indian languages and this reached over half the Indian-language cinemas, perhaps being seen by 2 million people each week. In addition, these newsreels were being shown in the mobile cinema vans which some provinces had set up to reach rural areas. In September 1942, this newsreel was turned into an India-based newsreel called *Indian Movietone News*, which was aimed predominantly at Indian-language cinemas. The government had thus given the American owners of Movietone, Twentieth Century Fox, a monopoly on newsreels in the vernacular cinemas. Growing American influence in Indian cinemas through the *United Newsreel* was a concern for the GoI, as was the parlous situation politically and militarily in India and Burma at the end of 1942 and into 1943.[45] The GoI decided on a much more directly interventionist policy, requiring by law every cinema in British India to show one or more films approved by the government to a minimum length of 2,000 feet. This allowed for a newsreel and a propaganda short to be shown in each cinema programme. The government took over control of the production of the *Movietone* newsreel and replaced it with a renamed version, *Indian News Parade*, starting on 15 September

1943. There was no hiding any longer that this newsreel was put out by the government. In March 1944 it was also distributed to English-speaking cinemas, though this was probably not that popular with audiences who might have to sit through this and a commercial company newsreel in the same show. The newsreel was much criticized by Indian nationalists who disliked its wartime propaganda. However, through the wide reach it attained in Indian cinemas right up until 1946, and the training of skilled Indian personnel, it helped establish the basis for official newsreel and documentary after Indian independence.

There was, however, an ongoing problem with ensuring that suitable film from the India-Burma theatre was available for the newsreels and documentaries. From the early stages of the Burma campaign, the Ministry of Information (MoI) in London was dissatisfied with the film that they were receiving from India which could be put into newsreels and documentaries and used for overseas propaganda.[46] The GoI guarded its territory jealously, arguing that the political circumstances in India were exceptional and only they knew how to address propaganda and publicity issues. Brigadier Jehu, the head of IAPR, used the few photographers and cameramen that he had available to him for use mostly in North Africa where the exploits of Indian soldiers could be shown in India. He wanted to control where cameramen were allocated, and resented pressure brought by London to make him conform to an empire-wide system of allocating cameramen to different theatres. The MoI had set up a War News Film Committee in August 1941 to coordinate both newsreel and service cameramen. It included representatives from the India Office, the Dominions, the three services and all the newsreel companies.[47] It was the Newsreel Association of Great Britain and Ireland (NRA), representing all the companies, that actually allocated newsreel cameramen to the different theatres. This was done on the basis of a rota system by which, instead of each company sending cameramen to the same theatre to compete for material, it was agreed that a limited number would be allocated but the resulting film would be shared between them. This worked quite well in wartime, although some companies chafed at the bit and pressed to have some of the material of their cameramen treated as 'exclusives'.[48]

In the 1942 retreat from Burma, there were only two newsreel cameramen filming there.[49] During 1943 and 1944 there were a very small number of British newsreel cameramen covering the war in Burma. This meant that the newsreels had to rely to a great extent on using film from the IAPR, the Army Film and Photographic Unit (AFPU) and the RAF film units. These units had a rather different remit than the commercial cameramen but one that was complementary. Towards the end of the campaign in 1945, an enlarged newsreel cameramen operation in SEAC was established.

iv. Propaganda films made in India: SEAC

Film might have been thought of as an ideal medium for reaching a largely illiterate but visually engaged Indian audience. However, there were severe practical, political and economic problems which meant that, although a number of short documentary films were made during the war, they mostly lacked the quality and, therefore, the circulation of the much more successful documentary movements in Britain and America in wartime.[50] Despite efforts to employ Indian directors, producers and technicians, the films were intended to serve imperial propaganda purposes, and this inevitably made them less attractive to Indian audiences. Although the GoI took a more interventionist role in making films after the crisis resulting from the Japanese conquest of Burma, it still proved difficult to reach target audiences in India, Britain or around the world. One of the successes was the setting up of an IAPR film unit at Tollygunge, Calcutta, where Bryan Langley pioneered the training of Indians as cameramen. This was expanded very rapidly during the summer of 1943 as the unit was reorganized with a remit to send back to Britain as much newsreel material as possible. This and the film unit responsible for making armed forces training films resulted in the building of a core of Indian cameramen and technicians who would form the basis of the post-independence Indian documentary film organization, Films Division.

Because Mountbatten was keen to build a separate SEAC film and photographic unit, he poached some of the best directors and cameramen from the Indian set-up. He focused on making a full-length documentary on the Burma campaign with the cooperation of American directors, equipment and studios. By 1945, there were, at last, plenty of newsreel and official cameramen available to capture the 14th Army's advances on Mandalay and Rangoon. The quality of film had very much improved since the retreat of 1942 and this culminated in the excellent full-length documentary film *Burma Victory*, which, unfortunately, only made it to the cinema screens after victory over Japan.

4. Broadcasting

Radio, which had really taken off in Britain and the United States, might have been thought to have been an another ideal medium through which the government could reach a large audience in India and Burma. However, for a variety of reasons, which are explained in Chapter 9, this was not a success story during the war. Once the Japanese occupied Burma, they took strong measures to ensure that the Burmese did not access enemy stations. In India, despite the efforts of the All India Radio and the BBC, there was a low take-up of wireless receivers, and the evidence suggests that people who did have radio sets were as likely to take their 'news' from Japanese or INA broadcasts.

Conclusion

As can be seen, there was a wide range of international media for the services' PROs to target in propagandizing the India-Burma War. In practice, there were constraints on reaching mass audiences in India due to the reluctance of the GoI to develop modern mass media such as radio and film. The history of this and the implications for wartime are discussed in later chapters. In the first two years of the war, there were limitations on the services' PROs in their ability to target various media for information and propaganda purposes. Largely, they had to be reactive and work with the limited number of newspapers and newsreels that were willing to send representatives to cover this distant war which had little editorial priority. It was only after Mountbatten took up his position as Supreme Commander South East Asia in October 1943 that a direct effort was made to ensure more coverage across the various media, including film and radio. Towards the end of 1944, with a growing expectation that the war with Germany would soon end, and that attention would transfer to the war against Japan, there were plans to prioritize the targeting of media outlets, especially with an American audience in mind.

3

Managing the Media in the Burma Retreat, 1942

The war in India-Burma from December 1941 to August 1945 was the longest land campaign the British, Indian and Commonwealth armies fought during the Second World War. Like the proverbial football match, this was a campaign of two halves. From the initial Japanese incursions from Thailand into southern Burma in December 1941 until the monsoon season starting May 1943, very little seemed to go right for the Allied armies in Burma. The humiliating loss of Burma to the Japanese after a five-month campaign ending in May 1942 came on top of serious setbacks to British prestige such as the loss of Hong Kong and Malaya and the sinking of two of Britain's finest warships, the *Prince of Wales* and the *Repulse*, off the coast of Malaya. Worst of all had been in February 1942 when the so-called 'impregnable' fortress of Singapore had fallen with the surrender of 130,000 Commonwealth troops to only half that number of Japanese soldiers. With the loss of Burma, Japanese forces then threatened the borders of India and could bomb cities like Calcutta or Madras almost at will. It was difficult in all these setbacks to find redeeming features or any military successes.

British forces in Burma had been caught totally unprepared for the Japanese invasion by land through Thailand and the bombing of Rangoon on 23 and 25 December 1941. It was not just that British and Burmese forces and equipment were utterly inadequate for the defence of the country but that reinforcements of Chinese, Australian, Indian or British troops were unlikely to arrive in time to save the Burmese capital. Rangoon and its port were the gateway for the crucial railway and road connecting Burma with south-west China. This was the last land-based lifeline for the Chinese Nationalist Kuomintang regime. The Burma Road, which began in Lashio in the Shan States of north-east Burma, was crucial to the American priority of providing Lend-Lease supplies to the Chiang Kai-shek regime which had been holding out against Japanese aggression since 1937. The Japanese captured the key town of Lashio before the end of April, cutting the Burma Road and forcing British and some Chinese forces to retreat across the Irrawaddy and Chindwin rivers and to make an arduous trek across deadly mountainous ranges into India. In the process, British, Indian and Burmese losses amounted to 13,463, while the Chinese may have lost three times as many, most of them during their retreat. Added to the humiliation of this retreat was the mass exodus of some half a million civilians from Burma, mostly Indians but also Anglo-Indians, Anglo-Burmese and Europeans. Many suffered appalling conditions in the retreat and tens of thousands died. Their sufferings were reported on by war correspondents and photographers, and allegations of their racially discriminatory

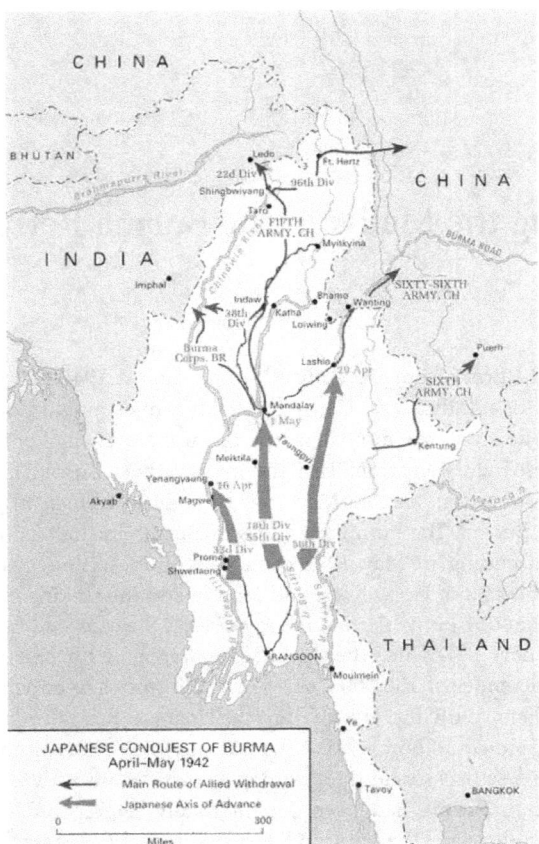

Map 3.1 Japanese Conquest of Central Burma, April–May 1942, U.S. Army Center of Military History, Wikimedia Commons.

treatment were taken up by the Indian National Congress. In truth, the army would have preferred a more rapid evacuation of the civilians to clear the routes for its forces, but the Burma government wanted to keep the port of Rangoon operating for as long as possible, and Indian labour was crucial for this.

Before looking at how army public relations managed the almost constantly bad news which it had to report during the retreat, it is important to look at the difficulties they faced, especially when meeting the demands of a corps of critical war correspondents. Their task was made more difficult by the lack of an effective propaganda machine in Burma before the campaign began. An operative Services Public Relations Organisation (SPRO) was not formally established until February 1942. Its main task was to organize and provide facilities for the large cohort of war correspondents who arrived in Rangoon from December 1941 onwards. Some of them had escaped from the fiasco in Singapore and were in no mood to be pushed around by army public relations again. Such a figure was the pugnacious O'Dowd Gallagher, who had reported for the *Daily Express* in the Spanish Civil War as well as the Abyssinian War. He had suffered the indignity of being dragged from the oily Malayan waters around the sinking battlecruiser *Repulse* in December 1941. Others, such as the veteran American reporter Leland Stowe of the *Chicago Daily News*, had come from China and were now keen to avoid the strict censorship that had been imposed by the Chungking regime. He wanted to report on the corruption that was hampering the transportation of US Lend-Lease supplies from Rangoon to China. Stowe did manage to have three articles on the subject, spread over two days, 30 and 31 December, published in the *Chicago Daily News*. T. V. Soong, the Chinese ambassador, complained to the State Department in Washington about the articles, and this was obviously relayed to the British authorities. As a result, Governor Dorman-Smith summoned Stowe and told him that, though his exposés were 'undoubtedly justified', he should not publish any more of that kind. Stowe agreed, probably recognizing that the articles had served their purpose. Undermining relations with an allied nation was an established ground for censorship but Stowe remained convinced that such censorship 'greatly delayed corrective measures and has merely served to encourage a false optimism among our home publics'.[1]

The SPRO was tasked with providing support for the war correspondents in the form of accommodation, food, transport, conducting officers, facilitating censorship and transmission of their dispatches. Journalists were provided uniforms and the temporary status of captain. As non-combatant officers, they might normally expect to receive better treatment if captured by the enemy, but no one trusted that this would count with the Japanese, and many carried guns for protection. The problem was that correspondents faced many frustrations during the retreat. In theory, they should have been able to request to move to report on the fighting front at any time. However, in Burma there was a lack of transport in the first weeks of fighting and, with a retreating army, it was often difficult to find where the front actually was, let alone to reach it. This meant that reporters were pretty much confined to Rangoon and its airfield at Mingaladon, just north of the city. The best stories were about the so-called Flying Tigers, volunteer American pilots who were in the process of being supplied to defend China. They were commanded by the charismatic Colonel Claire Chennault and, along with an RAF squadron, they put up a remarkable defence against the Japanese air force, despite being outnumbered and, in the case of the RAF, flying inferior planes. The story was covered by all the reporters, but the best coverage came from the British photographer George Rodger who supplied photos to *Life* magazine in the USA and *Illustrated* in Britain. Rodger was able to provide very personalized stories to accompany his photos while Leland Stowe kept track of the numbers of Japanese who had been shot down. Once early-warning stations south of Rangoon had been lost to the Japanese, it was no longer safe for the planes to stay at Mingaladon. Even so, the pilots continued for some time to provide one of the few positive stories of the campaign and were used to divert readers from the more negative stories elsewhere.

Back in Rangoon, if they were unable to reach the fighting fronts, correspondents tended to focus on issues such as the failure of civil defence measures in the city, the chaotic evacuation of civilians, including much-needed dockworkers, the bottleneck in the movement of goods from the docks, and the corruption involved in transporting supplies overland to China. As in Singapore, it was the local government, in this case Governor Dorman-Smith and his administration, which became the focus for media criticisms. Dorman-Smith probably compounded this problem by deciding to keep a low public profile so as to avoid hampering recovery efforts and putting up something of a 'defensive wall' against the correspondents. As in Singapore, journalists, particularly those from America and Australia, who were used to less obviously class-based societies, looked very critically on British ruling colonial societies in the East. They regarded them as living in a privileged world that was unaware of the realities of the war elsewhere. They wrote with disdain of the racial hierarchies and snobbery that they saw as pervasive in both civil and military quarters. Some criticized the so-called *burra sahibs*, or big businessmen, whom they depicted as exploiting Burma and selfishly failing to make the general war effort a priority over their own interests.[2]

General Stilwell and American reporting

American correspondents like Leland Stowe were in contact with members of the American military mission in the China-Burma-India (CBI) area – men like General John Magruder and Colonel Frank Merrill, who gave them information that was often critical of their British allies. General Joseph Stilwell arrived in Burma, at the invitation of the Chinese leader Chiang Kai-shek, shortly after the loss of Rangoon on 7 March. He was appointed as Chief of Staff to the Generalissimo and was at least nominally in command of the Chinese forces in Burma which had been belatedly and somewhat reluctantly admitted by the British to hold the vital Burma Road to China. He seemed an ideal choice because he had served in China on a number of occasions in the interwar years, culminating in a role as military attaché at the US legation in Beijing from 1935 to 1939. He had a small staff which included Fred Eldridge as his PRO. Eldridge very much reflected Stilwell's strongly Anglophobic views and they pervade his memoir, *Wrath in Burma*, published after the war ended.[3] Stilwell's new role was crucial because Chinese troops were taking up key positions defending the eastern flank of the Japanese advance, centred on Sittang valley and the town of Toungoo, and the Shan States in the north-east. The British were defending the western flank centred on the Irrawaddy river at Prome. It proved extremely difficult to coordinate these different forces along a long defensive line, not least because Chinese generals, although under Stilwell's command, largely looked to Chiang Kai-shek, over a thousand miles away, to confirm Stilwell's orders.[4] Stilwell was in the difficult position of having no American troops to work with, and control of only limited Lend-Lease supplies to use as bait for China's cooperation. In effect, Stilwell was used by President Roosevelt as a low-cost way of showing American support for keeping China in the war against Japan. He made the best of the situation, harrying both the British and the Chinese, of whose leaders he had a very poor opinion. Stilwell, 'Vinegar Joe', was an aggressive commander who loved to be in the thick of operations, which proved very attractive to American journalists like Dan De Luce (AP) and Darrell Berrigan (UP), who now had an army story in Burma to match the Flying Tigers coverage. Stilwell's belief in the offensive characterized both his military and diplomatic approaches. He found it very difficult to deal with Chiang Kai-shek's cautious and defensive approaches to China's role in the Burma War.[5]

Stilwell's attitude to the media was a mixed one. He was very open with war correspondents who found his no-nonsense style and colourful language very attractive. However, unlike some generals, he was not keen on self-publicity, preferring that reporters focused on his Chinese troops rather than himself. He was soon embarrassed by the sort of build-up that reporters were giving him. He wrote in his diary on 1 April: 'The worst has happened in the press. Before I have a chance to get my feet on the ground, a flood of crap is released, to justify which I would have to be in Rangoon within a week. What a sucker I'll look if the Japs run me out of Burma.'[6] Only a few days later he would find himself given greater media attention when he met up with Chiang Kai-shek and his wife Soon Mei-ling at the headquarters in the attractive hill station of Maymyo. Also staying there was Claire Boothe, wife of Henry Luce, the very pro-Chinese owner of the influential magazines *Time* and *Life*. As a woman reporter, Boothe could not be accredited to the military but the Luce name gave her entry to the highest circles. She arranged for a photograph session with the Chiangs and Stilwell to be presented in happy harmony, which actually matched reality, at least for these very few days. She managed to get an article out to *Time* magazine for the 24 April edition by sending it from China. The article gave fulsome praise to Stilwell and his officers. However, it would almost certainly have been stopped by the censors if she had tried to send it from Burma as her analysis was highly critical of the British military and civil government there, intimating that the Burmese people were fighting against the British and that really this should be a Chinese not a British command.[7]

The positive press coverage for Stilwell was all very well if he and the Chinese were winning in Burma, but it was pretty clear after the loss of Toungoo at the end of March that they were in a permanent retreat, trying to buy time before the monsoon set in during May. Despite the US War Department calling for the media boosting of Stilwell to be played down, over-optimistic reports continued to appear in the American press.[8] Barbara Tuchman has argued that journalists and American officials had failed for a long time to tell the American public the truth about the failings of the Chinese national leadership which so hamstrung its armies. She blamed this partly on the strong censorship they operated under in the Nationalist capital Chungking, but also to the intrinsic goodwill shown to the Chinese who had been fighting Japan on their own since 1937. In any case, she argued, journalists should not have forwarded notoriously unreliable Chinese communiqués without comment.[9] Editors sometimes made matters worse by turning these dispatches into ridiculously misleading headlines which suggested that Stilwell's forces were pushing the Japanese armies backwards while the reality was completely the opposite. A good example comes from 11 May, a week after Stilwell had actually begun his famous walk out of Burma towards India with over one hundred followers. The UP correspondent in Chungking posted a totally fantastical story about Chinese troops repelling Japanese infiltration into China along the Burma Road, and also recapturing Maymyo and closing in on Mandalay. The story was boosted in America into a front-page depiction of Stilwell, 'Another Hero for the History Books', directing these operations.[10]

How did journalists respond to this humiliating retreat?

Relations with all the correspondents worsened when they were ordered to make a rapid exit from Rangoon on 20 February and told that the government would relocate its headquarters over 450 miles north to Maymyo. As it happened, this meant that the reporters missed reporting the tragic story of the premature blowing-up of a section of the bridge across the Sittang river, which left large numbers of the 17th Indian Division soldiers on the wrong side of the river and at the mercy of the Japanese. The army scored a success in keeping the details of that story under wraps for almost two weeks. Correspondents were now forced to travel long distances from the front line at Prome and Toungoo and then return to Mandalay to have their stories censored and transmitted.

Journalists became only too aware of the Japanese dominance of the skies over Burma after the Japanese bombed Magwe airport in the middle of the country. They saw village after village burnt to the ground by incendiary bombs. On the Irrawaddy side of Burma, the British attempt In April to defend the valuable oilfields at Yenangyaung, south of Mandalay, turned into a mad scramble to destroy them and escape in the face of Japanese entrapment. Stilwell sent Chinese troops to rescue the British but the loss of the oil resources and the fact that the Japanese could reinforce men and supplies through Rangoon meant that the end was inevitable. Mandalay was almost totally devastated by Japanese bombing on Good Friday, 3 April. By this time, many correspondents were looking for ways to leave the country. The destruction of the telegraph station in Mandalay made transmission of dispatches much more difficult, as they had to be sent from the few remaining airfields in northern Burma. In any case, strict censorship meant that it was impossible to tell the full story of the Burma retreat unless reporters left the country and probably not until after it was considered completed. This would take some time as soldiers and civilians negotiated the extremely arduous mountainous routes to safety in India. In India, especially for reporters who stayed in Calcutta, there were still stories to report from aggrieved civilian refugees who saw their livelihoods and homes in Burma probably lost for good. Indian refugees had stories of hardship, suffering and racial discrimination experienced in reaching India. Nationalist politicians in India publicized the grievous failures of the civilian evacuation. It must be stressed that fuller stories of the retreat could not be published until some months after it was over, when some correspondents wrote their accounts in memoirs. Of the twenty-four correspondents who were accredited during the five months of the retreat, half wrote memoirs or sections of books, most of which were published within a year or two of the retreat. Even then, those published in Britain were subject to censorship, albeit a lighter version.[11]

What methods did the army and government use to manage the media during the retreat and its aftermath?

The army and government had a number of weapons at hand to manage the media during a very difficult retreat.

1. Accreditation of war correspondents

First, all correspondents who wanted to report from the fighting front had to be formally accredited to the India and Burma authorities, and this involved them agreeing to abide by the rules of conduct for journalists. It was possible for the authorities to refuse accreditation to correspondents or to newspapers that were thought likely to be hostile. In practice, recommendations for accreditation came from London and Washington, and local accreditation was rarely refused to established news sources, even if there were concerns expressed by Indian Army Public Relations (IAPR) about the anti-imperial attitudes expressed in some of the American papers. Accreditation could be withdrawn for contraventions of rules, but again this was unlikely to be used except in the most extreme cases because of the rumpus that it would cause at home. Some twenty-four correspondents were officially accredited during the retreat in 1942, and only one had his accreditation withdrawn.[12] However, it is worth noting that of these correspondents all were white men, representing British, American and Australian media. There were no reporters from Indian newspapers at this stage of the war, nor were there accredited women reporters.[13] Burma newspapers closed down quite early during the Japanese invasion, which meant that this perspective was also missing.

2. Practical limitations on reporting

Even when accredited, correspondents were restricted by practical concerns in what they could report, especially from the fighting front. They depended on the public relations organizations for the provision of transport without which they could not reach the battlefronts, and for the provision of accompanying conducting officers who would guide them, and check that they were safe and not undermining military security. The reliance on conducting officers often meant that correspondents operated in pairs or threes, something that they might see as inimical to their chances of scooping their rivals. So, the theoretical freedom of correspondents to cover stories wherever they liked was actually restricted, not least by concerns for their safety. This meant that some correspondents preferred to stay near headquarters rather than venturing to an unknown 'front' which might incur delays in getting their stories back home. Ideally, editors might arrange to have one reporter near the fighting and another at rear HQ to pick up army communiqués. This was a luxury that was rarely possible in the Burma campaign.[14] In any case, communiqués were usually published some days after the events described and tended to be singularly anodyne and uninformative. Reliance on these would mean that all the media would report pretty much the same material. The language that was preferred in communiqués turned retreats into 'phased withdrawals', 'regrouping' or 'straightening of lines'. However, the army often held up correspondents' dispatches until their official communiqués had been published. In addition to communiqués, the army could use press briefings from General Head Quarters (GHQ) in Delhi, or from officers in the combat zones. Some generals, such as Stilwell and later Mountbatten, were very good at dealing with the media, but in 1942, taciturn Wavell and reserved Alexander looked decidedly uncomfortable in the role. Some briefings were large-scale press conferences but otherwise they were off-record meetings with individuals or a small number of journalists. Ian Stephens, editor of the *Statesman* newspaper, reflected on the pros and cons of the private briefings. Editors might be given important information but then knew they were bound not to reveal it.[15]

3. Censorship

Having obtained their stories, correspondents needed to have them censored before dispatch. This allowed PR the greatest control over what was published. Censorship was directed primarily at stopping the publication of information which would be 'likely to assist the enemy or to be prejudicial to the national security and well-being. This control will be exercised in Burma partly by preventive measures but mainly by the voluntary and loyal cooperation of the press.'[16] The preventive measures were censorship 'stops' which were issued regularly to indicate which topics were not to be publicized. In the case of military security, these were usually temporary bans until a situation resolved itself. However, some were permanent: the strictest one being the ban on any mention of Indian soldiers who might have gone over to the Japanese after being captured in the Malaya and Singapore defeats. This became solidified over time into any mention of Subhas Chandra Bose and the Indian National Army (INA) of Indian soldiers and civilians who for various reasons had decided to fight with the Japanese for India's freedom. The withholding of military security information was generally accepted by correspondents as necessary, if sometimes overzealous in its application. However, it was the potentially wide interpretation of matters prejudicial to national security that most irked them, as it included clauses which banned the mention of 'matter calculated to impair the efficiency, morale or discipline or to prejudice recruiting for His Majesty's forces (e.g., disparagement of those in command of His Majesty's forces) or to create or encourage disaffection in any section of the population in any part of the British Empire'. Also banned was 'such information regarding subversive movements, agrarian or industrial unrest, and communal disturbances as might be calculated to raise the morale of the enemy'.[17] In the sensitive political situation in India and Burma during 1942 and the implications for the mass recruitment needed for the war effort in Britain's Asian possessions, these were restrictions that could be widely invoked.

4. Self-censorship

In addition to the censorship stops, it was expected that newspapers and their correspondents would 'self-censor', thus relieving the authorities from too many censorship clashes. Self-censorship was based on a complex of factors. First and foremost was the expectation that correspondents would see themselves as part of a just war for national survival against a ruthless enemy and therefore there was a patriotic duty not to deliberately undermine the cause. Of course, this meant the temporary suspension of the idea of a free and critical press holding authority to account, and the fact that most correspondents succumbed to this has been much criticized by media historians such as Moorcraft and Taylor.[18] Reporters were, in effect, embedded with the troops, in that they lived with them and relied on them for their safety and for information. This inevitably meant that correspondents were pretty much always supportive of ordinary soldiers and would avoid writing anything that would be seen as letting them down. There may also have been a sense of guilt involved in that reporters may well have felt that they should really have been serving in the forces themselves.[19] Self-censorship also operated within the context of the structures of the media, which were essentially moneymaking institutions. Overall, the media needed to avoid alienating their customers, whom they believed would not want to hear stories that denigrated their armed forces or which depicted graphic scenes of their dead and dying.[20] Pressure from editors for colourful stories of military derring-do meant that correspondents were rarely, if ever, able to report the realities of warfare at this stage. Even if newspapers, newsreels or broadcasters should decide to challenge the restrictions or even to transgress, they knew that the government held the whip-hand over them. Short of closing offending media, the government had control of the supply of newsprint, government advertising contracts, film stock and ministerial briefings, which could all be withheld from recalcitrant media. The power the government held in these ways can be seen most clearly when looking at the role of the BBC and also of the newsreels in wartime in later chapters. Suffice to say, by way of example, that newsreel cameramen knew not to waste precious film stock on scenes that would never pass the censors, while their editors had developed a keen sense of what their viewers would find attractive and acceptable within an entertainment programme.

During the retreat, the main issue which led to clashes between correspondents and censors was over the reporting of particular battles, which often boiled down to the naming of places or regiments which participated, or just the fact that dispatches were filed before the army had produced its own communiqués. In such cases the correspondents could appeal to higher authority and sometimes this worked, most notably when the positive publicity involved in reporting exciting stories or naming regiments was recognized. A good, but rather exceptional example, was the report of the fighting at Pegu in the army's escape from Rangoon by two Australian journalists, William Munday and Thomas Healy. The two correspondents had broken free of their conducting officer and driven by jeep to cover armoured troops which were trying to break through a strong Japanese roadblock north of Rangoon. Their story was an exciting one as they managed to travel in tanks as they broke through and they made the most of their stories by naming participating regiments: the 7th Hussars, Cameronians and West Yorkshires.[21] This information would not normally be allowed by the censors and indeed the stories were held back. Munday and Healy appealed to General Alexander who agreed that they should be allowed to go forward. In fact, the reports were very well received by the War Office which telegraphed that they 'have proved admirable stimulant home morale' and called for more reports like them. It was said that Churchill had been behind this request.[22] In view of the success of these two reporters, it might well be asked why other correspondents were not able to slip their minders and challenge censorship restrictions. Some have been criticized for avoiding the fighting and staying near headquarters where they could use the military communiqués. A minority may have done this, their reasons rarely being straightforward cowardice or laziness. There was a recognition that in Burma it was not easy to find the fighting front, which moved rapidly. Once there, it was difficult to have a broader picture of what was going on – the notorious 'fog of war'. Even then, there was the difficulty of getting reports back over long distances to censor and transmit them home. Dispatches that were out of date had little chance of being used. These considerations became even more relevant after the Japanese had destroyed the telegraph office in Mandalay at the beginning of April. Many journalists were by then thinking of leaving Burma and writing dispatches from outside the country. Correspondents did sometimes try and challenge or bypass the censorship system – for instance, by sending reports out via Chungking in China. However, they risked having their accreditation withdrawn and in most cases the censorship had the upper hand throughout the retreat.

Other issues related less to military security concerns but rather to questions of the impact of reporting on troop and civilian morale. This was obviously much more open to debate. One example was the belief that many correspondents held that parts of the Burmese population were unreliable and that some were acting as 'fifth columnists' for the Japanese. Correspondents talked of wires being spread across road at head height to decapitate jeep occupants and of fires being deliberately started to guide Japanese planes to targets. Dorman-Smith refuted these allegations and was keen to stress the overwhelming loyalty of the Burmese people to the British.[23] Burmese support for the Japanese was played down and presented as the work of a small minority of 'traitors', radical students and criminal elements. The truth was probably somewhere between the two positions. There were radical Burmese nationalists known as Thakins, some of whom had been trained by the Japanese, who fought against the retreating Allied armies, in the form of a Burma Independence Army. These probably numbered a few thousand, but it was Burmese who were not in military uniform that most drew the attention of the correspondents. There were areas of Burma where lawlessness was rife, and there were opportunists who took the chance of the chaos created by Japanese bombing to loot buildings. However, the correspondents probably exaggerated the numbers of the disaffected: most Burmese just wanted to avoid the impact of the war as best they could and adopted a wait-and-see attitude to judge which side would win.

5. Putting a positive spin on the story

It was difficult to find ways of putting a positive spin on the continuous withdrawal of British, Indian, Burmese and Chinese forces during the retreat. The only really positive story was that of the exploits of the air force resistance against the superior numbers and aircraft of the Japanese invaders. The exploits of American pilots of the American Volunteer Group (AVG) and RAF pilots in the defence of Burma made for particularly good stories. It was easy for correspondents to cover them from Rangoon and indeed their observations were an important part of the tally of 'hits', which in the case of the AVG turned into hard cash for the pilots. This only lasted a short while in 1942 because the Japanese soon gained control of the skies. Later in the Burma War, however, the British, Indian and US air forces would provide some of the most positive stories. Editors of newspapers, magazines and newsreels, perhaps following a technique used in communiqués, buried negative stories at the very end of reports of more positive ones. Sometimes, army PR turned minor successes into more important ones. An example of this was during the dangerous evacuation of the army from Burma when a small diversionary attack was made in March to recapture the town of Shwegyin on the

Sittang river from the Japanese. This was successful but, unfortunately, the correspondents were not there in time to record it. So, the army thoughtfully allowed the battle to be re-enacted for the newsreel and still cameras.[24] This form of 'faking' was frowned on by the newsreel companies but undoubtedly took place at times during the Burma campaign, when there were severe practical difficulties in getting realistic combat images. It is difficult to explain why the army allowed this re-enactment to take place during a desperate retreat. It does not seem to have been instigated by the SPRO, as its director Emile Foucar confirmed afterwards that it had happened and it was 'an incident that amused us'.[25] Throughout the campaign, journalists and the armed forces 'colluded' to make exciting stories which would make it into the press. Correspondents might, as we have seen, be allowed to ride on tanks in breaking through Japanese roadblocks. The air force was persuaded to drop its safety precautions to allow journalists to go on bombing missions. The problem was that this type of story covered up the worst realities of warfare: the inevitable atrocities, desertions, and the horrendous suffering of soldiers and civilians. Negative stories could be covered up long enough to make them stale news. The army managed to avoid press revelations about the worst setback of the retreat, the battle at the Sittang river crossing on 22–3 February, which left hundreds of soldiers of the 17th Indian Division stranded on the wrong side, having to swim to safety with the loss of most of their equipment and heavy loss of life. The battle was really significant as it left Rangoon open to the Japanese. The press secrecy was partly possible because, much to their annoyance, journalists had been told to leave Rangoon with non-essential civilians on 20 February and to relocate some 450 miles north to Maymyo. It took two journalists who were late arriving in Rangoon, J. L. Hodson and Philip Jordan, to post the first reports of the story in early March but, even then, in a sanitized form describing it as 'a kind of Dunkirk'.[26] The army had managed to delay the story for two weeks, by which time it was no longer newsworthy, but of lasting interest to military historians.[27]

6. After the retreat was over

Even before the soldiers had managed to leave Burma and reach India, the IAPR was setting up publicity guidance to explain how the defeat had come about and, more importantly, to put the best possible gloss on the defence that the army had put up. General Wavell was worried that what had happened in Burma was being depicted abroad as a 'Dunkirk and disastrous shock'. He was concerned about the impact on the morale of Indian troops and public.[28] The guidance admitted that the Japanese 'treacherous aggression' had caught the defences unprepared and that for three of the following six months '. . . Imperial forces have lacked anything in the way of adequate air support, have had no respite, relief or reinforcements and have had to fight continuous withdrawal actions in face of superior numbers and an organised 5th Column'.[29] Despite this, allied forces had 'gained many valuable weeks in aid of the defence of India . . . denied immediate exploitation of resources of Burma to the enemy [scorched earth policy] and made the conquest of Burma difficult and expensive for the Japanese, who now had to choose whether to gamble on a continued offensive through monsoon conditions or to defend over-extended lines'.[30] The argument about an organized fifth column went directly against the governor of Burma's determination to play this down so as not to damage relations with the Burmese when the army returned. Dorman-Smith believed that the army had to take responsibility for its failure in Burma. This was a form of self-defence as there is evidence that IAPR was instructed 'to use Dorman-Smith as a scapegoat and to pin all blame for the collapse of Burma in 1942 on him, so as to divert attention from the Army's failures and deflect any criticisms of the military for the defeat onto the civil administration'.[31] In any case, Dorman-Smith, who set up his exiled government in Simla, went out of his way to defend his administration against criticisms by some of the correspondents and even went as far as having subsidies paid to an American journalist, Alfred Wagg, to have his book on the retreat vetted and effectively altered to present a more favourable view of the government of Burma.[32] This must be one of the more remarkable examples of managing the media.

It is interesting that General Stilwell was able to come out of Burma with his reputation intact, and even in some respects enhanced. Finding that his original chosen land route to China was blocked, Stilwell chose to reject the option of flying, and instead led a mixed party of over a hundred people some 140 miles, over half of it on foot, over extremely difficult terrain to safety in India. It was a remarkable achievement in that Stilwell was nearly 60 years of age and not in the strongest health, but his strict discipline meant that not a single person was lost on the journey. However, Stilwell left large numbers of Chinese troops to find their own way back to India or China and did not let Chiang Kai-shek know what he was doing. Chennault regarded this as a dereliction of duty.[33] Whatever the rights or wrongs of his decision, he could not dissuade two 'publicists' to accompany him on his trek. Fred Eldridge, his PRO, took photos which appeared in *Life* magazine's 10 August edition.[34] Jack Belden also chose to follow Stilwell out of Burma but had to wait for his full story to be published in book form in 1943.[35] Stilwell's heroic image in the United States was much enhanced by this publicity.

India Command's publicity attempts to put a gloss on the defeat contrasted with the much more damning verdict of Stilwell's speech to the press in India. He was prepared to admit that they had taken 'a hell of a beating ... and it is humiliating as hell'.[36] It is not surprising that, according to Fred Eldridge, the speech proved embarrassing to the British because '[i]t refuted, officially, the carefully staged British line that the campaign had been a stubborn and brilliant delaying action to permit India to prepare for any invasion. The British didn't dare to kill it but did everything possible to delay its transmission and dissuade correspondents from filing the story at all.'[37]

Conclusion

Clearly, the wide range of media that were involved in reporting the India-Burma War indicated that this was not a 'forgotten war' in 1942. The Burma retreat featured on the front pages of British newspapers quite regularly. Indeed, it is likely that the British would have preferred less publicity for what after all was a humiliating retreat. The presence of so many journalists posed problems for the army public relations organization. During the retreat, the Burma PRO could only react to the emergency situation of international correspondents turning up in Burma and requiring facilities to report the fighting. It was not possible to pick and choose media outlets or to manage the media in any meaningful way, hence the reliance on censorship. The problem was that censorship could only be effective for a limited time. Journalists, frustrated by their inability at the time to publish their criticisms of the way that Burma had been lost to the Japanese, wrote critical reports in newspapers and in memoirs that appeared quite rapidly after the retreat had ended. These books, and stories told by aggrieved refugees fleeing Burma, were to leave a lasting negative impression of the way the British had failed in their duty to defend Burma and its people.

4

Managing Media Coverage of the First Arakan Campaign, 1943

It was a mistake to blazon the advance as an invasion of Burma. Even if the limited success aimed at were attained, it would not come up to the expectations raised, and, if we failed, the depression would be the greater. It is better to let a victory, if it comes, speak for itself; it has a voice that drowns all other sounds. If it does not come – and victory is never certain – the less preliminary drum-beating there has been the better.
Field Marshal Viscount Slim commenting on the first Arakan campaign:
Defeat into Victory[1]

Field Marshal Slim's memoirs of the long Burma campaign are widely recognized as probably the best of the Second World War generals' memoirs. From the media historian's point of view, it is interesting that he emphasized the role of media management in the first Arakan campaign, which took place between November 1942 and May 1943 and contrasted its premature publicity with the effectiveness of the delayed announcement of the first Wingate operation, which culminated soon after.[2] In fact, Slim was mistaken in thinking that the advance into the Arakan was trumpeted as the beginning of the reconquest of Burma from the Japanese. Rather the reverse was true, as every effort was made by Indian Army Public Relations (IAPR) to play down any larger significance of the attempt to recapture the strategic port of Akyab. However, it was almost inevitable that the public might misread this as indicating the beginning of the fulfilment of US General Stilwell's promise to go back and retake Burma.[3] Perhaps surprisingly, the newspapers were not responsible for building up the Arakan advance. It was only the BBC which may have overplayed news of the first successes in Arakan. Most journalists realized the difficulties of a land campaign in Burma and that even if Akyab were captured it would lead nowhere at this time. The media management of the Arakan campaign was badly handled by IAPR. When the campaign suffered severe setbacks, attempts were made to impose controls on reporting and to impose a prolonged news blackout. It was a learning curve in the art of media management which provided valuable lessons for the much more successful organization of the media coverage of the first Wingate expedition shortly afterwards.

The first Arakan campaign was covered by less than a dozen journalists, only a handful of whom were ready to cover the early stages. The Chiefs of Staff and War Cabinet had made plans for joint land and sea assaults on Burma during the 'dry season' after November 1942. An amphibious attack on the south, designed to retake Rangoon and Moulmein, was favoured by Churchill and was known as Operation Anakim. The demands from other theatres, notably in the Mediterranean, meant that the necessary naval force to implement this operation, or even to threaten the Japanese further north in the Bay of Bengal, would prove to be unavailable. There were also severe problems for any land operation in northern Burma. The slow build-up of the air force in India, the continued logistical problems in north-east India and the impact of the nationalist Quit India movement all meant that these plans had to be postponed. The Indian National Congress's civil disobedience campaign seriously disrupted communication links in northern India and meant that troops had to be diverted for internal security operations. General Stilwell, President Roosevelt and Generalissimo Chiang Kai-shek, the Chinese Nationalist leader, were all furious at British caution and delays, but General Wavell, Commander-in-Chief in India, called the shots. The alternative action which Wavell proposed, partly to keep his allies believing in British intentions to take aggressive action in Burma, and partly to restore the morale of his troops, was a limited land assault through the Arakan peninsula to the port of Akyab.[4]

The capture of Akyab in May 1942 had provided the Japanese with an airbase 100 miles from the Indian border, 160 miles from the Indian port of Chittagong and within bombing range of Calcutta, which was 300 miles away. To retake Akyab, which was seen as 'a strategical dagger pointed at the throat of India', would be an important defensive move, but also would provide an important boost to troop morale.[5] This, of course, presumed that the operation would be successful. Wavell was confident that it would be, as Japanese forces in the area would be outnumbered and he felt sure that the Japanese communication lines were overstretched after their rapid advances into northern Burma.[6] Secret intelligence units, known as V Force, had been operating in the area, and links were being made with the local Muslim population and with tribal groups in northern Burma. Unfortunately, Wavell seriously underestimated the Japanese, just as he had done in the first Burma campaign, and also overestimated the preparedness of British, Gurkha and Indian troops.[7] The terrain was the least hospitable for offensive operations, with the steep jungle-covered Mayu hills and the narrow coastal strip being intersected by *chaungs* (streams) leading down to the sea through paddy and mangrove swamp. There was only one road capable of taking mechanized transport. This crossed the Mayu range, linking Maungdaw and Buthidaung through two tunnels, and that road was inevitably highly contested. The area had very high rainfall during the monsoon and was highly malarial. An additional problem was that troops would have to transport all their food supplies as the Japanese had stripped the resources of areas around Akyab. The intrepid Australian reporter William Munday crossed into the Japanese-occupied area north of Akyab in July 1942, accompanied by A. A. Shah, the Senior District Officer for Cox's Bazaar, just across the border in India.[8] He visited the villages of Maungdaw and Buthidaung and reported on life under Japanese rule: 'On the Burma side there was desolation and burnt-out villages which I learnt later had been looted by marauding Thakins, members of Burma's pro-Japanese Nationalist party of youthful hooligans.'[9] The village headman told him of a desperate shortage of food and supplies, and the danger of civil war. Gordon Waterfield, Reuters correspondent, later said that he was not allowed to report on the civil war between

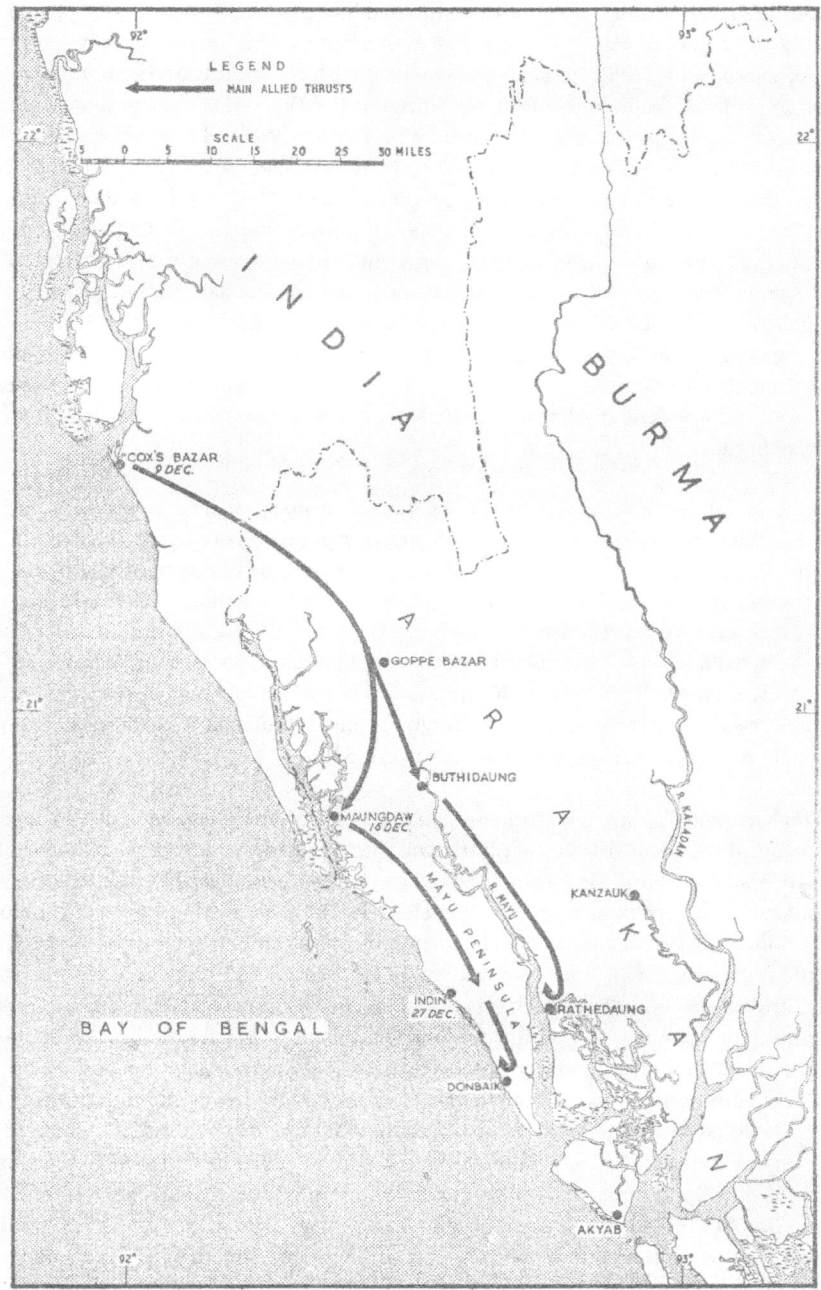

Map 4.1 The First Arakan Campaign, December 1942–May 1943, Hilary St George Saunders, *The Royal Air Force 1939 to 1945*, Vol. III: '*The Fight Is Won*', HMSO Official History of WWII, London: HMSO, 1953, p. 302.

Buddhists and Muslims which it was estimated had cost the lives of 25,000 people in spring 1942 and forced large numbers of Arakanese Muslims to flee to Bengal.[10] Muslims were still leaving Arakan even as the British troops advanced into the area in December 1942. Graham Stanford, reporting for the *Daily Mail*, told of massacres by Japanese-supporting Burmese tribesmen in the border areas and said this seemed to be 'part of a deliberate campaign to lay waste scores of villages and create a bloody No Man's land'.[11] He estimated that 20,000 people had been killed or rendered homeless in the last six months as a result.[12] Stanford reported that the British were taking countermeasures to win over villages. Quite what these measures were is not clear, but there is evidence that British and Indian troops and their ancillary staff may have acted brutally towards the local, presumably Buddhist, population.[13]

The advance on Arakan began tentatively as early as the third week of September 1942. Lieutenant General Noel Irwin, General Officer Commander of the Eastern Army in India, was not perhaps the best choice for overseeing the campaign, as Robert Lyman argues:

> His character was flawed by an aggressive temperament that brooked no questioning or argument from subordinates. Outspoken, egocentric and dictatorial, he struggled to find the wherewithal to comprehend the difficulties faced by his troops, and possessed no flexibility of mind to allow him to adjust his plans when things went wrong. His penchant for acerbity made it difficult for him to gain the respect and loyalty of his subordinates. In addition, Irwin possessed a deep-seated reverence for military rank, authority and hierarchy. He was a man of conservative and reactionary inclinations. Accordingly, he found it difficult to challenge orders and instructions when it was necessary to do so.[14]

Major-General Wilfrid Lloyd commanded the 14th Infantry Division which advanced into the Mayu peninsula from Chittagong and Cox's Bazaar in eastern India. The advance was too slow if it was intended to catch the Japanese by surprise. There were problems with torrential rain from a cyclone in October making the road-building very difficult. There was a very high incidence of malaria among the troops.[15] Reporting of the advance was withheld until just before Christmas 1942 – the only reports were of 'patrol activity', in other words small-scale reconnoitring. On 17 December, troops captured the key villages of Maungdaw and Buthidaung. They found that the Japanese had withdrawn without putting up any resistance. An advance group pushed on to Indin. A communiqué was put out by Indian Army HQ on 19 December reporting the unopposed advance, and this was broadcast on the same day by the BBC, which gave the impression that this was the prelude to a major operation designed to recapture Burma. Wavell was horrified at this publicity and immediately telegraphed General Sir Alan Brooke, the Chief of General Staff in London, asking that he 'ensure future broadcasts do not exceed scope of our communiqués and that limited nature of operations is kept constantly in foreground'.[16] Brooke, for whom Burma operations were generally a low priority, obviously felt that it would have helped if Wavell had provided clearer guidance on the line to be taken in publicity for any new military action.[17] However, far from Slim's view that the Arakan advance was oversold to the press, all the evidence shows that the army did everything it could to play down the significance of the campaign. It was probably inevitable though, in view of the build-up of troops in India and their well-known training programme, that there were expectations of some kind of military action in Burma in the dry months of 1943.[18] However, most correspondents believed that any major Allied return to Burma would not be spearheaded from the Arakan peninsula, and that the port of Akyab was, in effect, a geographical and military dead-end. It was believed that there would have to be a combined British, Chinese and American advance into northern Burma and eventually a combined naval, air force and army operation aimed at the Rangoon area in the south. The advance into Arakan could only be, as the army stressed, a limited operation with limited objectives.[19]

Initially, there were only four correspondents covering the advance into Arakan: Gordon Waterfield (Reuters), Wilfred Burchett (*Daily Express*), Graham Stanford (*Daily Mail*) and Victor Thompson (*Daily Herald*). There were two commercial newsreel cameraman: Alec Tozer (*British Movietone News*) and Maurice Ford (*British Paramount News*), although Ford left early after a dispute with the IAPR.[20] In addition there was a Ministry of Information (MoI) cameraman, Reggie Edwards, who may have filmed the occupation of Maungdaw. This low-level coverage of the start of the Arakan campaign underlines the lack of prepared publicity for it on the part of the IAPR Directorate. As the campaign developed, more correspondents were brought in, but by then it was going badly for the army and, in any case, it was often difficult for the correspondents to get near the fighting front because of the very difficult communication problems in Arakan. Correspondents relied mostly on reporting from headquarters in Maungdaw and returning to Calcutta regularly. The MoI in London was concerned at the lack of newsreel film being sent from India, and in official circles there was a suspicion that the fault lay with Brigadier Ivor Jehu, the head of IAPR. It was felt that Jehu was not taking seriously enough the need to use commercial cameramen to record operations in India-Burma, and that his relations with correspondents may have been antagonistic. Jehu defended himself from any criticisms and insisted that he had shipped over 12,000 feet of film to the MoI in the period from Christmas to the end of February 1943.[21] However, there is very little film of the first Arakan campaign now available in the newsreel company archives, less than 1,000 feet of original film, and only short sections were shown in cinemas after a two-month delay. Essentially, there are two sets of short newsreel clips from 8 April and 22 April, respectively, both probably filmed much earlier in the campaign by Alec Tozer of *British Movietone News*, possibly in February 1943, and shared with other newsreel companies through the rota system. They both reflect a positive view of the campaign, the first showing troops arriving on the Mayu peninsula by sampan and patrolling the beaches and the second showing Royal Australian Air Force crews operating over Burma.[22] The humorous pictures of a 'couple of old sweats [privates] with a fag-end between them' in the 8 April film was typical of Tozer's impish approach, but, as so often in the newsreels, the light touch masked more serious failings in the campaign.[23]

If the visual publicity for the campaign had been a failure, the coverage by the newspaper correspondents was also very troubled. One of the problems was that these were experienced war journalists who wanted a degree of freedom in their reporting.

This was bound to bring them into conflict with Jehu, who had a combative personality and wanted to keep a tight control of army publicity in India. He had been lent to the IAPR Directorate in 1940 by the *Times of India*, and been given remarkably rapid promotion to the status of colonel and later brevet brigadier. According to Ian Stephens, editor of the Calcutta-based *Statesman* newspaper, as director he developed a 'truculent woof-woof manner rather like a stage general's ... a crude person and a bully'.[24] Jehu mistrusted the independence of the war correspondents and clashed with several of them. He preferred to use his own 'observers', official reporters and cameramen, to cover the fighting fronts and provide him with the material he needed to publicize the army's role.

On 27 December, the 14th Indian Division had advanced further along the Mayu peninsula towards Rathedaung and Donbaik, which were not far from their final objective, Akyab. The information they had received that the Japanese had left Rathedaung proved to be wrong. The Japanese had set a trap and the troops ran into strong Japanese resistance, causing the first battle casualties of the campaign. There were also casualties among the war correspondents. Gordon Waterfield and Wilfred Burchett decided to try and follow the troops to Rathedaung using a large local sampan, propelled by two native oarsmen and accompanied by a conducting officer. The boat was slow, especially when the tide on the Mayu turned against it, and so, when six Japanese Zero planes appeared in the sky, it was extremely vulnerable. One of the boatmen was killed and Burchett and Waterfield were wounded in the attack. Burchett turned out to have the most serious wounds, to back and leg. They were helped back to Buthidaung, and Burchett was returned to India for hospital treatment which took him out of the campaign for the next three months. Waterfield was less seriously wounded and returned to reporting within five days.[25] The newspaper reports at the time put a gloss on the Allied lack of motorized launches on the rivers Mayu and Naf as against their Japanese opponents. Graham Stanford wrote: 'It is probably the first time that a unit has moved into action in sampans – quaint native boats rowed from the stern by a boatman known as a "Kisti Wallah".' The British Commanding Officer described his flotilla of commandeered sampans as '[l]ike Henley [regatta]'.[26] However, the correspondents did not rely on irony in their later books. Waterfield wrote angrily:

> It seemed to us extraordinary that Calcutta and Delhi should have planned an advance in Arakan without motor transport on the Mayu; as it was, it meant that the enemy could control our lines of communication ... We had not trained or equipped a force which was mobile in this type of country. We had not given them motor-launches for the rivers and made them depend for their supplies on roads which were liable to be cut at any moment by the Japs.[27]

Other correspondents who reported 'from the front' on the Arakan campaign as it developed included Martin Moore (*Daily Telegraph*), Harry Standish (*Sydney Morning Herald*), Walter Briggs (UP), Douglas Wilkie (London *Evening Standard*, Melbourne *Herald* and Sydney *Sun*) and Frank Moraes (*Times of India*). Moraes was an interesting addition – apparently, he was the first Indian correspondent to be accredited to the Indian armed forces in Burma.[28] He had been recommended by his previous newspaper boss, Ivor Jehu, and arrived in February 1943. He was in Arakan until the end of March, and he wrote regular front-page articles, in some of which he focused on the contribution of Indian and Burmese soldiers.[29] Moraes wrote later that 90 per cent of his time had been boring, being based at headquarters at Maungdaw.[30] It was a reminder that, in this campaign, it was difficult for correspondents to reach the front. Most reports they wrote, therefore, were based on army communiqués and feedback from soldiers returning from the front. Moraes said:

> I did not see a single dead Japanese in this campaign – the only action I had witnessed, apart from the desultory air bombings and duels in the skies, was the fifth battle of Donbaik, and the only live Japanese I saw at close quarters was a young prisoner who had fallen asleep at his post and had been captured by an Indian patrol.[31]

Correspondents generally wrote positively of the campaign in their dispatches even though it was clear that the advance had become bogged down in January as the Japanese reinforced their defensive positions at Rathedaung and Donbaik. At Donbaik, near to the end of the peninsula at Foul Point, they constructed thick-walled bunkers and individual foxholes which were well hidden and strategically positioned. Thoburn Wiant described the latter:

> The Japanese favorite is a foxhole six feet deep with a sodded lid, difficult to detect even by stepping on it. If necessary, the Japanese soldier can stay there a week. If troops advance past him, the Japanese lifts the lid just high enough to poke out a gun barrel, fires a couple of rounds, then drops the lid. Soldiers who look back in the direction of the shots often see nothing.[32]

The British relied on frontal assaults after preliminary artillery barrages, rather as in the First World War. As indicated in Moraes's statement above, there were a series of assaults by British and Indian troops, including the use of tanks, but all to no avail.

Correspondents had emphasized the difficulties of a campaign in Arakan from quite early on. One such journalist was Douglas Wilkie, an Australian who worked for Sir Keith Murdoch's Melbourne *Herald*, Sydney *Sun* and London *Evening Standard*. He had a reputation as being politically radical and had come to the attention of the censors in Britain and the India Office in London with four messages which he sent in October 1942 to different newspaper organizations in the USA, Britain and Australia. In these he made a number of rather scurrilous attacks on members of the Burma government in exile at Simla. In fact, his newspaper editors do not seem to have thought it appropriate to publish the controversial parts of Wilkie's messages and his published articles on the Arakan campaign were generally intelligent and informed appreciations of the military difficulties of the campaign. He showed a grasp of the broader strategic situation that was more normally the function of the professional military correspondent at home than the war correspondent reporting from the battlefront. An article of his, which was published on 6 January 1943, was one of the most realistic assessments by a journalist of the difficulties facing any Allied attempt to recapture Burma by a land operation in northern Burma launched from Assam.³³ Wilkie was trying to explain to Australian readers why such a campaign was not presently contemplated by the Allies, despite the large build-up of forces in India. Australians might have hoped this attack on the Japanese in Burma would relieve some of the pressure on their battle with the Japanese in New Guinea and the Solomon Islands. 'The answer,' he said, 'lies in the political chaos in India, the persistent lack of military lines of communication along India's eastern frontier, and special difficulties of terrain and climate in Assam.' Wilkie's article followed the line of Wavell's communiqué, stressing that the Arakan campaign was a limited operation. In this respect, the article, although very negative about the military situation in northern Burma, was probably unobjectionable. Wilkie had couched his criticisms of the Government of India (GoI) in carefully worded ways, but it was pretty clear that he felt that the failure to win the support of the Indian people was a key factor restraining potential operations in northern Burma. The military had to take account of the danger of mass civilian unrest and panic-induced evacuations from parts of eastern India. Wilkie's article coincided with a telegram from Brigadier Jehu, asking London

> to exercise careful censorship on out-going stories of correspondents who are now on Arakan front and that editors of relevant newspapers should be so informed. Detailed place names and possible attack on Akyab and detailed speculation on this latter point will have to be exercised [sic] for the present. We are informing correspondents and co-operation rather than criticism from home press and radio will therefore be of the greatest assistance to us.³⁴

This telegram was a sign that the campaign was not going to plan but it was an obvious case of trying to shut the stable door after the horse had bolted. Correspondents had reported the Arakan campaign and its obvious target, Akyab, since before Christmas 1942. Their reports had been generally optimistic, in line with the advances that the troops were making.

The whole issue of military censorship blew up when the British magazine *The Newspaper World* published an article on 20 February 1943 entitled 'War Correspondents in India Dissatisfied with Official Treatment – Australian [Wilkie] leaves as a Protest'.³⁵ Wilkie protested that 'on his return from a 2,000-mile journey covering the forward areas he found that out of twelve articles he had written at least three were completely stopped by the military press censor and that in all copy reference to climate was deleted'. He complained that his 'reference to climate, terrain and supply lines could have been gained from any guidebook or school atlas'. He felt that the unnecessary censorship had left his dispatches looking as if they had focused on trivia, and that therefore his reputation with his editors had been damaged. As a result, he decided to return to Australia. He may not have known that some of his longer dispatches, even ones mentioning the weather conditions in Burma, had actually passed through censorship and reached the Australian press.³⁶ The Wilkie affair might seem to have been a storm in a teacup, but it foreshadowed more serious discontent of the Burma correspondents with military censorship in the Burma campaign, and represented some of the mistrust of Ivor Jehu's attempts to control the press.

In fact, press coverage of the Arakan campaign remained generally positive until around the middle of March when it was clear that the empire troops were not just stalled, but in danger of being outflanked by Japanese counter-attacks and encircling movements. Earlier in the campaign, the failures to progress could be disguised with stories of British air superiority in the region and in bombing attacks on key Japanese positions, but now even this air superiority was being challenged by the Japanese. Correspondents resorted to euphemism to cover bad news. For instance, a British officer described the British position at Donbaik, where they had made at least four failed assaults on enemy positions, as 'ticklish'.[37]

Criticisms of the campaign in India led to a debate in the Indian Council of State. General Sir Alan Hartley, Deputy Commander-in-Chief, played down the importance of the Arakan campaign:

> No official statement ever implied that these operations had anything but a limited objective ... The operations have been designed to defend India's borders and occupy the enemy as fully as possible to prevent the Burmese border being used as a springboard against India and to destroy as many Japanese as possible with the aim of helping ourselves and the Chinese. We claim we succeeded in this, to a necessarily limited degree ... We have gained valuable experience and inflicted substantial casualties on the enemy.[38]

Correspondents found this defence of the campaign difficult to swallow, especially when it became clear that there was no way that the original objective of Akyab could be gained before the monsoon broke in May. It was now a matter of falling back on the Buthidaung–Maungdaw line, but even that could not be held against the reinforced Japanese troops. Waterfield wrote in his later memoir:

> According to the Public Relations Office, directed by Brigadier Jehu, the campaign was being carried out in order to kill Japs and give the troops training. Neither were very reassuring objectives to those who had seen the Inniskillings lying dead on the hill-tops round Donbaik, and knew how badly the Lancashire Fusiliers had suffered in front of Rathedaung; to suggest that warfare had no more to it than killing was to publicise failure and to depress the troops.[39]

The *Daily Mail* had used Graham Stanford's dispatches in a way that put a positive spin on the campaign even when it was clearly stalled in March 1943. However, when Stanford took a break from the fighting and returned to Calcutta in mid-March, he gave his impressions to the Australian press, and these were much more pessimistic. He said that the British advance has 'almost reached its limit' and that he could not 'foresee any important forward movement before the rains begin in April'. Although the army had shown the ability to advance against the Japanese in Burma, it had 'not, however, shown that we are strong enough to continue advancing firmly against the enemy when he has decided to stand on positions of his own choice. Rightly or wrongly, we have not taken risks, thereby denying us the advantage of surprise and speed.'[40]

It was becoming clear that, as the British forces became bogged down and then bypassed by Japanese infiltration movements in the jungle hills to the north of British positions, an effective blackout on news from Arakan was being imposed in early April 1943. The reasons were that serious setbacks that had taken place in the campaign. First, Major-General Lloyd had been replaced for going against orders by instructing the 47th Indian Infantry Brigade to retreat west of the Mayu river to avoid being entrapped by Japanese encirclement. In fact, the Japanese did manage to put a roadblock north of Indin village, thus cutting the lines of communication for the brigade, which only escaped by abandoning its heavy equipment and retreating in small parties along the beach areas. Secondly, and more seriously, the Japanese overran the 6th Brigade's headquarters on the night of 5/6 April and captured Brigadier Cavendish, his senior officers and, presumably, their battle plans.[41] The situation was extremely serious as many of the troops were suffering from malaria, were demoralized by the setbacks, and there were many desertions. One can understand, therefore, the sensitivity of the situation which led to a press blackout. The problem was that the prolonged silence only led to rumours in Calcutta and north-east India, fuelled by the stories told by soldiers returning from the front, that the Japanese counter-attack presaged a new threat to India. In these circumstances, Ian Stephens, the editor of the *Statesman* newspaper in Calcutta, wrote a short editorial note in the paper on 3 April 1943, calling for an end to the silence on land operations in Arakan.[42] This resulted in a phone-call from the IAPR Directorate in Delhi and Stephens was 'told confidentially that only operational necessity involving security of the men on the spot prevented publicity'.[43] Stephens was not convinced by this explanation and felt that the fifteen-day complete 'black-out' of news of ground operations from Arakan 'had been entirely without precedent in any war theatre'. He decided to write a long leader article on 6 April which, while admitting that the campaign had not been a total failure, amounted to a devastating critique:

> Ground (of little strategic value in itself) was won, much of it only to be relinquished later to the enemy. Good men have been killed and maimed. It requires no specialized military knowledge to deduce that there have been faults in planning or at least in synchronization, as well as tactical blunders. The lessons learnt in the 1941–42 Burma fighting seem as yet to have been dilatorily applied. Transport and equipment have proved difficulties: administrative defects may be inferred. In short, an impression is conveyed of muddle.

Stephens went on to praise the troops who 'have by all accounts fought magnificently, and their spirit is high. But reflection suggests that many of them and their junior leaders must have had but little previous acquaintance with war, or at least of hostilities in jungly tropical terrain'.[44]

Stephens's leading article caused ructions in the Indian Army establishment, and a ban was placed on the article being sent out of India or transmitted internally by the agencies, according to Stephens, 'by any means of communication, telegraphic, postal, mule, and whatnot'.[45] While Stephens tried to mollify the situation by explaining that the article, taken as a whole, was intended to be helpful, General Irwin, commanding the campaign, wrote a reply accusing Stephens of shaking public confidence in the troops and their leaders at a very sensitive time in the campaign. He said that his comments were a disservice to the troops.[46] Brigadier Jehu joined in the attack, broadening it to include other perceived editorial misdemeanours.[47] The essence of Jehu's argument was that, at a sensitive time in the campaign, it was necessary to maintain a silence which lasted, at his count, twelve days. Jehu was particularly annoyed at Stephens's second leader of 8 April that stated that 'sustained secrecy about the conduct of war, <u>whatever operational justification it may have</u>, fosters dark and ill-based popular forebodings' [author's emphasis]. He cited a dispatch by the *Times* correspondent, Robert Cooper, at General Head Quarters (GHQ) India, which took the unusual step of criticizing the *Statesman* leader for seeming to argue that no operational necessity could justify a prolonged news silence.[48]

The dispute, which caused a lot of ill-feeling all round, can only be understood within the context of Stephen's perception of the special role of the *Statesman* newspaper in India, and army public relations expectations of the role of newspapers and their war correspondents during a campaign. The *Statesman* was one of the leading British-owned papers in India. It was based in Calcutta (as well as Delhi where GHQ and IAPR Directorate were situated) and was therefore close to the fighting and indeed the bombing by Japanese airplanes. Rumours about what was happening on the battlefront were spread very easily via returning soldiers and labourers.[49] As editor, Stephens saw himself as upholding the independent reporting traditions of the newspaper, which had brought earlier editors into conflict with the authorities on more than one occasion.[50] He had a readership of some 100,000, bolstered by large numbers of British troops entering India for the war effort. He had already clashed with the government over his reporting of the large-scale evacuation of Indians from the city after the Japanese air raids in December 1942.[51] Privately, Stephens followed the developing news of the Arakan campaign with a large degree of disbelief. This was based on assessments of the very difficult geography of the peninsula and the very limited benefits of capturing Akyab, a town as he described as 'a minor port of about 40,000 inhabitants, with an airfield and some rice-mills – but virtually nothing else ... practically an island ... it led nowhere'.[52] However, his paper made no comments on the campaign until his 6 April leader, which he saw as an attempt to make some sort of assessment, while not, as he saw it, in any way undermining the army's role there. Stephens's perspective was pretty much that of an editor or military correspondent commenting on the campaign 'from a distance', aware in this case that some of what he wrote was reasonable guesswork. As it turned out, later historical assessments proved to be much harsher than anything he wrote. On the other hand, from the perspective of the army command and IAPR Directorate, Stephens was not 'playing the game'. In the India-Burma theatre it had become accepted practice that correspondents did not criticize the leadership or soldiers while a campaign was in progress. General Irwin, therefore, wrote to Stephens saying that his leader was 'unfortunately timed' and potentially undermining public confidence in the efficiency of the forces fighting the Japanese, and worse, 'shaking the confidence of the troops in themselves or their leaders'.[53] Jehu saw it as breaking an agreement with the press to restrain comment on the Arakan campaign while it was in a critical phase.

In truth, the spat between Stephens and IAPR was blown up out of proportion and owed something to the personalities of the protagonists and the pressures that they were under at the time. Stephens had chosen to clash with two very difficult men. Ivor Jehu had been on the editorial staff of the main rival British-owned newspaper in India and regarded himself as much more knowledgeable about journalism than Stephens. There is no doubt that Irwin, wrongly, took Stephens's leader as a personal criticism of his leadership in the campaign. Faced with two such powerful, authoritarian personalities, the liberal, academically minded Stephens found himself out of his depth in this dispute and tried to assure all concerned that his paper continued to be supportive of the army.[54]

The press did benefit from the row, however. The *Statesman* reported on 8 April that there had been a partial lifting of the silence on ground force operations in Arakan. General Irwin called a press conference at Barrackpore on 9 April, mainly, it seemed, to answer the criticisms in the *Statesman* leader.[55] This conference was attended by the *Statesman*'s war correspondent, Norman Devine, who took copious notes, which do not always correspond with Irwin's 'rough shorthand' notes. Irwin blamed the IAPR Directorate for the ten days' silence, which he had not approved of and had told GHQ so. According to Devine, Irwin described the *Statesman* leader of 6 April as 'misinformed, misguided and misguiding', and he obviously particularly resented the reference in it to 'muddled planning'.[56]

Irwin gave the correspondents an unprecedented amount of information on the Arakan campaign, but said that it was not to be released until a later date.[57] This was not surprising as, according to his notes, he had admitted that Buthidaung had been lost and that Maungdaw probably soon would be.[58] According to Devine, Irwin acknowledged that they were being defeated by troops numerically weaker but stronger in psychology and in training.[59] The campaign had limited objectives and he gave his analysis of the reasons for the setbacks it had suffered. Irwin said that the original aim of capturing Akyab had been thrown out of kilter by the last-minute lack of availability of the necessary ships to carry it out. As a result, the campaign had to depend on a land attack over exceedingly difficult terrain and extended lines of communication. The attack was delayed by bad weather, and this gave the Japanese time to regroup and to get into defensive positions. Japanese possession of the mouths of the Kaladan and Mayu rivers gave them a great advantage of mobility. At the beginning of February, the army concluded that capturing Akyab was not worth the effort, and by the end of the month it had determined on withdrawing to a line that could be defended when the monsoon broke. Irwin insisted that the Japanese had not put his plans out of step, with one exception, and that was their outflanking move on the Kaladan river. This was carried out by a numerically inferior but 'very effective' force from north of Rathedaung and Htizwe.[60] This was the only defeat that Irwin admitted to and, according to Devine, he plainly blamed it on his own troops who 'were driven from positions out of which we ought not to have been'. Since then, the Japanese counter-attack had been successfully resisted and heavy casualties had been inflicted on them. In answer to questions from the correspondents, Irwin insisted that the aims of the campaign had been limited and that valuable operational experience had been gained – for instance, in learning something of Japanese defensive methods. In addition, the support of the Arakanese Muslims had been won and large numbers of Japanese had been killed.[61]

Probably the most significant aspect of Irwin's analysis was his willingness to criticize the ability of British-Indian troops in jungle fighting. The Japanese soldier could execute outflanking tactics because he could live and fight on much less food than our troops could. He had the advantage of a mental attitude to war and death which made him more resilient than our troops. It would take three or four years to train our men to Japanese toughness: 'Our men are not fit like the Jap is, not trained like the Jap is, not constituted like the Jap is.'[62] Irwin's willingness to criticize his own troops in front of the press was extraordinary. He did not criticize his senior officers in this instance, but in private correspondence he was damning, and clearly felt that he had had to take the weight of decisions on his own back when local commanders should have done so.[63] In one respect, Irwin was clearly trying to shift the blame for the failure of the Arakan campaign from himself on to others. However, he was also thinking about how his superiors could learn from these mistakes for future campaigns in Burma. A few days after his press conference, he was summoned to Delhi to provide information for General Wavell to take to military planners in London. On the aeroplane, he wrote a paper on the subject which Mountbatten later claimed to have influenced his planning for SEAC.[64]

It was a grave mistake for Irwin to share his negative view of the troops with the war correspondents. They were becoming increasingly frustrated by the demands that they keep silent about the simultaneous Wingate operation in Burma, and now they were unable to report what they knew of the reasons for the failure of the Arakan campaign. Nearly a month later, at the end of the campaign, one of the correspondents, Martin Moore, tried to send a message to his paper, the *Daily Telegraph*, which repeated what Irwin had said at his earlier press briefing, criticizing both his troops and by implication those who had pressed for this premature operation. GHQ censored the message, but Irwin admitted in a handwritten note that it accurately represented his views.[65] The point was that Irwin wanted the press to follow this line as it would help take away attention from the failings of the commanders. He felt that he had run out of other excuses, such as weather conditions, for the failure to hold the Maungdaw–Buthidaung line.[66] It was not surprising that Irwin was relieved of his command by the end of the month and sent back to recuperate in Britain.

Irwin's admission of the lack of jungle training of the Indian Army was patently true, but it raised the question of whether the Arakan land campaign had been premature, and, more particularly, about General Wingate's Operation Longcloth which was taking place across the Chindwin river. This long-range penetration (LRP) expedition was hidden under a much stronger press silence but was entirely predicated on the argument that ordinary British and Indian troops could be trained quite quickly to beat the Japanese in jungle combat. The so-called Chindits showed all the qualities that Irwin had argued were missing in his Arakan troops. Although there was a strict ban on any information on Longcloth being published until the soldiers returned to base and Wingate had returned to Delhi, newspapermen knew about the operation, but no one, at any stage, asked why it was not coordinated with the Arakan campaign in order, at least, to draw off Japanese reinforcements in the area.

Despite Irwin's more honest assessment of the way the Arakan campaign was going, the correspondents continued to file relatively positive, or at least anodyne, reports from Arakan. It was not until 12 May that Graham Stanford's reports in the *Daily Mail* recognized the grim reality that the advance in Arakan had completely failed and the empire troops were back where they had started five months ago.[67] It was now only a matter of explaining how this humiliating reverse had taken place. Stanford blamed the continued vulnerability of empire forces to Japanese tactics of infiltration: 'The campaign has proved in jungle warfare the importance of small, highly mobile, attacking forces, not handicapped by a complicated supply system. Some of our troops are insufficiently trained for this type of fighting.'[68] The *Daily Express* lacked the front-line reports of its normal Burma correspondent Wilfred Burchett who was hospitalized for the first three months of 1943. While recuperating, he listened to the many soldiers returning from the front, injured or suffering from malaria. He picked up stories of low morale and poor leadership. It was not until 1946 when his book *Democracy with a Tommygun* appeared that he was able to publish his devastating critique of the Arakan campaign: 'None of the lessons of Malaya or Burma had been applied. Our troops were as ill-equipped, ill-trained and badly led as ever. The atmosphere around brigade and divisional headquarters was that of a boy-scouting expedition, except that divisions in rank were more sharply maintained.' Burchett put a great deal of the blame on the command and administration at Delhi: 'All the inefficiency, orthodoxy, stodginess, inertia, complacency and snobbishness in the British army seem to have gravitated to India, and there found a congenial resting place ... Headquarters at Delhi was far removed in both time and space from the war.'[69] Burchett had seen through the public relations excuses that the troops were just not good enough, and that the Indian troops particularly needed more time for training than British troops. Everyone knew that in North Africa, away from the stultifying atmosphere of India Command, Indian troops had performed admirably.

Another correspondent, Gordon Waterfield, also felt constrained in his contemporary dispatches, particularly so because he represented Reuters news agency which, as he recognized, had a privileged position in India and 'was regarded by the authorities and all the Indian Press as part of the machinery of the Government of India'.[70] Like other correspondents, however, he believed that the military censorship of the Indian Army was being influenced by considerations of political censorship, namely the overriding fear that negative publicity in Arakan would feed back and fuel Indian nationalist activities. Waterfield wanted to challenge the censorship system but had to recognize that as reporters were under military discipline he could not win his fight with Jehu and the censors, and he decided to leave India. He was able in 1944 to publish his criticisms of the Arakan campaign in his memoir, *Morning Will Come*. Along with the failure of tactics, he highlighted the lack of available intelligence in that very little use was made of previous V Force reconnoitring of the Mayu peninsula. He was also critical of the failure to make more use of the navy and motorboats, as these could have provided valuable cover and supplies to the troops.[71]

Whatever the journalists thought about the failure of the Arakan campaign, the impact on perceptions of the capability of the Indian Army and its generals in the eyes of British politicians and their American and Chinese allies was extremely damaging. Churchill, who was already critical of the Indian Army, of land campaigns in northern Burma and of Wavell's leadership, was furious. He minuted: 'This campaign goes from bad to worse, and we are being completely outfought and out-manoeuvred by the Japanese. Luckily, the small-scale of the operations and the attractions of other events has prevented public opinion being directed upon this lamentable scene.'[72] It is fair to say that the newspapers were not paying a great deal of attention to Burma at this time. Ironically, the Indian Army did have what it considered to be a perfect morale-boosting story on its hands, but it could not use it until 21 May 1943 because of the strict secrecy attached to General Wingate's first long-range operation, Longcloth. IAPR had learnt the necessity of managing the media, not through coercion but through cooperation. A deeply damaging Arakan campaign was almost entirely obscured by brilliant, personalized accounts of the eccentric Wingate and the colourful exploits of the newly christened 'Chindits'.

5

Media Coverage of Operation Longcloth: Wingate's First Expedition into Burma, 1943

Historians have conflicting views on the success of Operation Longcloth, as the first Wingate long-range penetration (LRP) expedition in Burma from February to May 1943 was called.[1] The most negative evaluations concentrate on the high proportion of casualties (only 2,182 out of the 3,000 men of the 77th Brigade returned to India, and only 600 of these were considered fit for further active service), the lack of wider strategic gains and the eccentric leadership of General Orde Wingate.[2] The more positive views paint Longcloth as the first time that 'ordinary' British troops showed they could fight in the jungle on equal terms with the Japanese and that the operation took 'the British Army off the roads and into the air', showing that troops could be sustained in the jungle by air.[3] However, most historians agree that the expedition was a great propaganda success and a boost for morale at a time when perceptions of the army's role in Burma was very low after the humiliating setback of the Arakan offensive.[4] As Louis Allen says: 'What the press and world opinion made of Wingate's initial exploits infused a new spirit into the affairs of Burma' and in that sense it was very positive from the perspective of British opinion.[5] Quite what the impact on the morale of the army in Burma was is more open to question. Richard Rhodes James argued that '... for a defeated and jaded army it was a wonderful shot in the arm'.[6] However, one must wonder what impression the sight of the exhausted and bedraggled Longcloth survivors must have had on the Indian soldiers, whom Wingate had disparaged and avoided using. For all soldiers, it must have been concerning to know that they could be asked to participate in an operation which allowed little or no chance of rescue and survival if you were wounded.

There has, however, been no proper analysis of the public relations operation that supported the Wingate expedition. How did Indian Army Public Relations (IAPR) recover from the many criticisms which journalists had made of their rather dictatorial and confrontational approach to the media during the Arakan campaign? How was secrecy maintained for over three months before a very full media release was made of the Wingate operation on 21 May 1943? What were the main themes which the official propaganda propounded and how effective were they in reaching target audiences? Finally, were journalists knowingly complicit in providing over-optimistic coverage of the expedition and glossing over its failures, as Phillip Knightley has argued in criticizing one journalist's account?[7]

As Churchill had argued, it was fortunate that the press and public opinion were not much focused on the setbacks of the Arakan campaign. They were much more interested in Allied successes in North Africa. Even more fortunate was that, at the same time the news of the Arakan defeat was being publicized, IAPR was presented with a perfect morale-boosting story in the form of General Wingate's first long-range operation. Wingate had been planning this operation ever since he was called to Burma in April 1942 by General Wavell as Commander-in-Chief of the Indian Army. This had not been a good time to arrive in Burma, just as the Japanese were pushing northward from having captured Rangoon in early March, and were pushing the British, Indian and Chinese armies out of the country. Wingate had time, however, to discuss his ideas with Wavell and with Major Michael Calvert, who was already training troops for clandestine operations behind enemy lines. Wingate had already had successes with his unorthodox tactics in Palestine and Abyssinia, and was now given permission to raise and train a special force, the 77th Indian Infantry Brigade, to prepare to operate in conjunction with a future Chinese attack from northern Burma and a combined naval and army assault somewhere on the Burmese coast. The brigade was very much a scratch force, and they were hardly the men Wingate would have picked himself. The British regiment, the 13th King's (Liverpool) Regiment had been taken away from coastal defence duties in Britain and was mostly made up of men in their thirties from northern England and Scotland. Wingate was given a Gurkha contingent, the 3rd/2nd Gurkha Rifles, which most commanders would have regarded as a great boon, but Wingate had an antipathy to anything associated with the Indian Army and had no understanding of the particular regimental loyalties of the Gurkhas. Lastly, there were the 2nd Burma Rifles, local soldiers officered by Britons who lived in Burma before the war, whom Wingate respected for their close knowledge of Burma and their experience in fighting during the retreat of 1942. Training took place in Saugor in the Central Provinces of India, and by all accounts was extremely arduous, as it was designed to prepare troops for extreme jungle conditions and the crossing of wide, fast-flowing rivers. The plan was for some 3,000 soldiers brought together from British, Burmese and Gurkha regiments to divide into eight columns which would cross the Chindwin river and divide into two main groups. One group would go south and act as a decoy to distract the Japanese, who were well ensconced on the Chindwin, while the northern columns would undertake long treks with the aim of destroying key Japanese lines of communication, such as the railway line running north from Mandalay to Myitkyina. It was not the intention to directly confront Japanese troops but rather to harass them in 'hit and run' operations. The key to the success of the operation was the idea that the mobile troops were no longer tied to lines of communication but would act independently and be supported by air supply, which would be called in by radio.

Operation Longcloth was nearly called off in early February 1943 because the other prongs of the attack were no longer viable. In particular, landing craft were not available for a combined operation and the Chinese were not willing to risk their troops without more substantial British intervention. General Wavell met with Wingate and the American Supply officer, Lieutenant-General Somervell, at Imphal on 6 February and Wingate argued in his usual emphatic manner that his expedition should still be allowed to go ahead. Wavell agreed and was photographed saluting the troops who would undertake this very dangerous operation. The publicity drive might be thought to have started, and, although the operation was strictly secret, Wavell had indicated to one of the correspondents, Alaric Jacob, that it might be worth his while staying around a bit longer in Imphal.[8] However, no arrangements had been made at that stage for any war correspondents to cover the expedition.

It was not until the day before the expedition left Imphal for the Chindwin river that General Geoffrey Scoones, Commander of IV Corps, invited Captain Antony Beauchamp, the official war artist, and Captain John Deane Potter, official reporter, to join the operation as official observers.[9] Beauchamp was an unusual choice in many respects. He had been a successful society portraitist and photographer before joining the army where he was taken up as an artist by Brigadier Jehu, who headed IAPR. However, his talents were better suited to photography, and he provided film of the initial stages of the expedition, some of which was used in the film *Burma Victory*. Jack Potter had formerly worked for the *Daily Express* and had volunteered for the army where he was given a public relations role as a conducting officer.[10] Anyway, Beauchamp and Potter must have realized that they could not provide full media coverage of the expedition and they managed to persuade Scoones that some professional war correspondents should also join them. So, Alaric Jacob (*Daily Express*), Stuart Emeny

Figure 5.1 Left to right: Stuart Emeny (*News Chronicle*), Martin Moore (*Daily Telegraph*), Tony Beauchamp (Photographer), Captain Jack Potter (Army Conducting Officer) and Alaric Jacob (*Daily Express*), private collection.

(*News Chronicle*) and Martin Moore (*Daily Telegraph*) were invited to make up the party.

'Without that early morning decision of Scoones,' insisted Beauchamp, 'there would have been no record of the expedition.'[11] This was not quite true as a sixth person had volunteered to accompany the operation: Captain Motilal Katju MC, an official observer with the 10th Battalion, 1st Punjab Regiment, had edited the *Pioneer* newspaper in India before the war. He wrote articles for the press in North Africa and involved himself so directly in the action that he had been awarded the Military Cross for bravery. He was a nephew of the ardent Indian nationalist, Mrs Sarojini Naidu. Katju kept a diary of the campaign and was the only 'reporter' to be allowed to accompany the whole expedition: Wingate insisted that the correspondents should only accompany him as far as the Chindwin river, and they would only carry enough rations for this. Katju was unfortunately killed towards the end of the operation on 29 April, and only a short extract of his diary, covering his arrival at the Chindwin, has survived.[12]

The last-minute arrangements for war correspondents to cover the Wingate expedition may be explained by the necessity for strict secrecy about this incursion behind Japanese lines. However, it is well known that many senior staff officers at Indian Army HQ did not like Wingate and resented the support that was being given to this potentially costly experiment.[13] Perhaps this is why so little preparation had been made for media coverage of the expedition. One might have expected commercial newsreel cameramen to be assigned to film at least the early parts of the expedition, but Jehu had shown little interest in pressing for such cameramen to be allocated to the India/Burma theatre, preferring to fill any gaps with official army cameramen and reporters.

The initial lack of coverage of the expedition was very unlikely to have reflected Wingate's wishes as he was keen on getting as much media exposure for the expedition as possible. According to Beauchamp, Wingate made sure that he obtained good photos, and even repeated his grand start to the operation, seated on a horse, because the movie camera jammed on the first take.[14] Brigadier Jehu was clearly doubtful of the capabilities of Beauchamp as a cine cameraman. He wrote:

> ... it so happened that one of my less experienced cinematographers was on the spot when the show started and did what he could in the late evening light in the depths of the jungle. The results are inevitably far from first class but, I think, are worth using in that they give some idea of the secretive way the force had to move and operate in some of the wildest country in the world.[15]

In fact, the film is very effective in showing key aspects of the Wingate expedition that the publicists wished to present. First, the operation was entirely independent of lines of communication, relying on mules and inflatable rubber boats for transport; secondly, the force was made up of ordinary soldiers – from Burma, Nepal and Britain; and lastly, they would use propaganda to win Burmese support as they advanced. The original instructions from Jehu were not to name Brigadier Wingate as the leader of the expedition but, as his past successes in Abyssinia and Palestine were mentioned in the suggested commentary, this requirement was soon dropped.[16] Jehu was wrong about the film conveying the secrecy of the expedition as all the activities portrayed in the crossing of the Chindwin were conducted in an apparently open and leisurely fashion. This included the setting up of radio communication and the demonstration of loudspeakers for local propaganda by a loyal prince of the Shan States. The material was intended to be distributed to the newsreel companies but with an embargo on its use until further notice.[17]

The correspondents retraced their steps to Imphal without a guide. They had had some small taste of what Wingate's columns would endure; long marches, often through jungle, not sure whether they were observed by the enemy, and operating on very limited rations. However, they had built up a picture of the expedition and its eccentric commander. It must have been frustrating to be forbidden from reporting it for three months. The press silence did not prove absolute. Stuart Emeny posted a story before he left base that did not name Wingate as such, but the heading 'ONIONS ARE GOOD FOR YOU – SAID A BRIGADIER IN BURMA' obviously referred to the eccentric general's dietary habits. It said that 'British and Indian troops are fit, tough and well-trained in jungle tactics. Our commanders are young, enterprising and prepared to use unorthodox methods. A brigadier who does not mind whether his men shave or not and produces onions from his pocket for you to eat because they are good for you, at least indicates a mind receptive to new ideas.'[18]

While the operation was still active on 3 April, IAPR insisted that on Wingate's return to base at the end of the operation all publicity materials should be controlled by them. General Irwin was asked to ensure that Wingate did not talk to the press and should be brought to Delhi as quickly as possible where a press conference would be arranged.[19] Wingate returned to Imphal on 3 May but there was no official communiqué on the expedition until one was released on 20 May for publication the next day. The delay may be explained by his need to recuperate, and to be debriefed on the expedition, and also the fact that some Chindits were still struggling to return to safety. On 6 May, General Irwin took Wingate from Imphal to Delhi. On 10 May, the Viceroy Lord Linlithgow met the survivors and, as Trevor Royle says, 'the Chindits got their first taste of being marketable personalities'.[20] Journalists were then allowed on 12 May to interview Chindits at Imphal, many of whom were still recovering in hospital.

According to Auchinleck's biographer, it was the Deputy Commander-in-Chief, General Sir Alan Hartley, who decided that the story could be released.[21] However, Christopher Sykes, Wingate's biographer, insists that, following pressure from the correspondents, it was General Auchinleck, as Acting Commander-in-Chief India, himself who ordered the communiqué to be released and for full publicity to be given to the expedition. The reason Sykes gives suggests that Auchinleck wanted to use the press to distract attention from the humiliating defeat in the Arakan.[22] Wingate was then paraded before more than two hundred journalists at a press conference in GHQ Delhi on 21 May. Despite the fact that he was ill, suffering from amoebic dysentery and exhaustion, he gave a very good performance, answering questions incisively and candidly. So, the journalists were able to release their stories of the Wingate expedition, which some of them had been storing up for weeks.[23] In the British newspapers it was front-page news and lead story in the *News Chronicle* (Emeny) and *Daily Mail*

(Stanford), and front-page secondary article in the *Daily Express* (Jacob) and *Daily Telegraph* (Moore), but only a single column on page four of *The Times*, which was much more circumspect in its appraisal of the expedition.[24] There was a clear correlation between the availability of stories from the correspondents who accompanied the Wingate expedition and the early prominence given to the story in their newspaper. The *News Chronicle* put a photograph of its reporter Stuart Emeny in uniform as he set off on the expedition. Otherwise, photos of Wingate kneeling and looking thoughtfully over a plan of the operation were used to accompany most front-page articles. The communiqué listed the four main achievements of the operation:

1. Serious damage was done to Japanese lines of communication, particularly to the Mandalay–Katha–Myitkyina railway line.
2. Japanese garrisons and columns were harassed and 'bamboozled' throughout a vast area, about 1,000 casualties were inflicted.
3. Enemy pressure on the Chinese Yunnan front had been relieved.
4. A large Japanese punitive expedition against the Kachin levies – allies of the British – had to be called off.

The diverse composition of the troops was stressed. Fuller details could not be divulged in case they gave the enemy information about Wingate's methods. War correspondents could fill in some of the gaps, particularly the human-interest stories, such as the requested air drop in the jungle of spare monocles for Major Bernard Fergusson, or the supply of snuff for another officer, which accidentally became mixed up with some curry powder.

What were the themes that the correspondents emphasized? It has to be said that they all used the same topics in their articles, some deriving from the official army communiqués, and many from Wingate's own interviews which he gave to journalists who accompanied him on the expedition or at the news conference in Delhi on 21 May. It was in Wingate's interests to emphasize the experimental nature of the expedition, and that many of the soldiers who participated in it were not crack troops but very ordinary English infantrymen who otherwise would have been serving on security duties in India. Wingate could also indicate the limited success of the operation in strategic terms because he was angling for a much larger, better-resourced operation in the future which formed part of a larger strategic campaign. This expedition had been experimental, but it had been successful in proving that even ordinary soldiers could operate in the distant jungle, provided they were supported by aircraft, called in by wireless radio. He had also shown that the Japanese were not invincible masters of the jungle, and that they lacked qualities of adaptability and inventiveness which the British forces could supply. Wingate had very definite views on the superior character of British troops when properly led. He had a much lower view of Indian and, to a lesser extent, Gurkha troops, unless they had British officers leading them. The journalists played up to this idea of the individualism of the British officers in their personalized accounts of their idiosyncrasies.

Wingate's own unconventional personality received a lot of coverage. Elements of his past history were mentioned, although his exploits in Abyssinia were given much more attention than his controversial support for Zionist irregular armies in Palestine before the war. Wingate's distant relationship to T. E. Lawrence was mentioned, although reference was usually given to the fact that Wingate disliked any comparison with the hero of the Arab campaign in the First World War. The term 'Chindit' was only given limited use at this time. It was an accidental mispronunciation of the Burmese half-lion, half-griffin animal that guarded Burmese temples and had been used by Wingate in an interview with Alaric Jacob at the very start of the expedition.[25] The soldiers themselves preferred, at that time, to call themselves terms like 'Wingate's Circus' or 'Wingate's Follies'.

Another important argument for the success of the expedition was the fact that it had been well received by most of the Burmese villagers whom the soldiers encountered. This, as Wilfred Burchett noted, was an important antidote to the widespread view at the end of the British retreat from Burma in 1942 that the Burmese had been hostile to them and acted as 'fifth columnists'. However, it should be remembered that many of the areas that the soldiers moved through were tribal areas, and people like the Chins and Kachins were traditionally more supportive than the Burmese Buddhists.

Overall, the immediate publicity of the Wingate expedition in the British press was prominent and very positive. The story only remained prominent in the papers, though, over that weekend of 21–4 May. Soon, the normal focus on campaigns in Europe and North Africa returned to take precedence. It was not until 7 July when a set of official photographs of the expedition was released that the story gained further widespread coverage again in the national press. *Life* photographer William Vandivert's story of the air force support given to the Wingate operation was published in *Illustrated Weekly* on 10 July 1943.[26] This was the remarkable story of a C-47 Dakota aeroplane of 31 Squadron flown by Flying Officer Michael Vlasto of the RAF, which managed to carry out a landing in a jungle clearing close to enemy lines, and to evacuate eighteen Chindit casualties. The images provided by Vandivert were some of the most iconic of the Chindit operation and made heroes of Vlasto, his cosmopolitan crew and Vandivert. Wingate acknowledged the contribution of 31 Squadron and recognized that it showed a way of not only using aeroplanes to pick up wounded soldiers from the jungle, but also to fly in large numbers of troops and supplies in a future operation. This was to form the basis for the development of Operation Thursday in 1944.[27]

Later, on 23 July, Graham Stanford, who was in Britain on leave, coined the epithet 'Wingate – Clive of Burma' in the *Daily Mail*,[28] which is supposed to have moved Churchill, on the spur of the moment, to invite Wingate to accompany him to the Quebec conference (17–24 August 1943).[29] In reality, Wingate's report on the expedition, which had been smuggled out of India, had reached Churchill via Secretary of State for India Leo Amery, and it was this which was probably most persuasive in his requiring Wingate to return home immediately, and led to his hurried inclusion at Quebec. Churchill had cleverly found a way of showing the Americans that, contrary to prevailing prejudices, the British did have plans to take the battle in Burma to the Japanese vigorously.

The Wingate mythology gained further ground with the publication of books by two journalists who recounted the stories of the Wingate expedition. The first was a triumph for British propaganda in America. British Information Services (BIS) in New

Figure 5.2 Charles J. Rolo, 'Wingate's Raiders', *Milwaukee Sentinel*, 29 May 1944.

York introduced two senior Chindit officers who happened to be in America to the American author Charles J. Rolo.[30] He first published his account in *Atlantic Monthly* magazine in October 1943, which he went on to develop into a book published in America in February 1944 called *Wingate's Raiders*.[31]

Rolo's account relied heavily on interviews with Major John B. Jefferies and Squadron Leader Robert Thompson, and also on IAPR information. Rolo's was a romanticized and uncritical account – for instance, in arguing that 'casualties for the whole campaign were fewer than anyone had dared to predict', but it gave good publicity at a time when the British role In Burma badly needed it.

The other book, *Wingate's Phantom Army*, was written by the Australian journalist Wilfred Burchett, who had been reporting the Burma campaign since early 1942 for the *Daily Express* in London.[32] Burchett had been hospitalized after the sampan he was in was strafed by Japanese fighter planes on the Mayu river at the end of December 1942. The failures of the Arakan campaign only exacerbated his inherent criticisms of British colonialism and especially of the India Army headquarters at Delhi and its public relations arm. Strict censorship meant that Burchett could not report his critical views, and this probably led him to view Wingate favourably as a fellow victim of traditional British colonialism and the Indian Army hierarchy. While he was recovering from his injuries in India, Burchett received a visit from his fellow *Express* correspondent Alaric Jacob who had returned from covering the early part of the Wingate expedition. Jacob had excited Burchett's interest in the expedition and its maverick leader but told him that the story could not be reported until official permission was given. Burchett took a chance and went to Sumprabum in northern Burma to interview some of the soldiers who were coming out of the country at the end of the campaign and, although this did not provide him with much usable material, it may have left an impression on Wingate because he had been the only journalist to take the trouble to travel there. The other correspondents presumably waited at Imphal, inside India, for the troops to return to base.[33]

Burchett's chance to interview his subject came later than the 21 May press conference, at a time when Wingate had been virtually isolated at Delhi waiting for the army command to commission a second and much larger expedition. Wingate was to be disappointed as General Auchinleck was replacing General Wavell, who had supported Wingate throughout. Auchinleck reflected the more orthodox Indian Army mistrust of Wingate and left him in isolation, writing his report on the expedition. Burchett decided to try his luck and call on Wingate at Maiden's Hotel in Delhi and

> found him stark naked on his bed, eyes buried deep in a book. He hardly glanced up as I entered, and rather gruffly asked what I wanted of him. I explained with some diffidence that I was writing a book about his Burma expedition and needed his assistance. He wasn't interested in me or my requirements, but seemed most excited about the book he was reading.[34]

This initial response to Burchett's planned book might be taken as evidence of Wingate's lack of interest in publicity, but that Burchett was able to interview his subject on a daily basis over a period of weeks suggests a rather different conclusion.[35]

In Brigadier Mike Calvert's introduction to the 1946 edition of *Wingate's Phantom Army*, he says that Burchett was chosen by Ivor Jehu to write a book on the expedition, and that he was given access to all the reports of column commanders and other Chindit officers, including Wingate's own report.[36] The idea that the Director of IAPR commissioned Burchett to write the book seems very unlikely in that Burchett would not have seemed an ideal candidate, too radical by half.[37] Burchett himself says that he did not get on with Jehu and describes him as 'pompous and incompetent' and the reluctant censor of the outline version of his book.[38]

Burchett tried for a balanced assessment of the achievements of the Wingate expedition in his concluding chapter to *Wingate's Phantom Army*:

> From a strictly operational point of view, the results were not spectacular. They put the main railway out of commission for several weeks by cutting the line and blowing the great Bonchaung Gorge. They killed a number of Japs directly, and many more through information given to the R.A.F. And that was about all. But they *did* tie down a force between four and five times as great as their own, and forced Jap headquarters to call off operations which they had already started ... For four vital months from February to June, a proportion of Jap forces in Burma were engaged in running this ghost army to earth ... Meanwhile, in Northern Burma they had lost the use of the dry season ... The Japs lost the last chance for seizing the initiative. They never again had such opportunities as they missed during the dry season of 1943.[39]

Despite the attempt at a balanced verdict, Burchett's account overstated the impact on Japanese plans and was overwhelmingly supportive of Wingate and very much captivated by his personality and achievements. Phillip Knightley argues that Burchett's multiple interviews with Wingate 'clouded his journalistic judgement'.[40] He goes on to say:

> The blame for over-glamorizing a comparatively minor and very costly operation in the Burma campaign must lie with all the correspondents and especially with Burchett who allowed his admiration for Wingate (another outsider), his distaste for British Army blimps, and his attraction to guerrilla warfare to distort his assessment of the expedition.[41]

If the expedition was well covered in Britain, there were complaints that the Indian newspapers showed little interest. *The Times* complained:

> For sheer physical adventure, with a Wellsian blend of modern science, there can never have been anything quite like the Wingate jungle expedition; yet oddly enough it is almost completely ignored by the Indian newspapers which, for political reasons, have been loudest in their criticism of the Arakan campaign and their exploitation of the Japanese peril. Such are the depths of men's ingratitude.[42]

Marsland Gander, writing in the *Daily Telegraph*, also criticized the nationalist newspapers saying that the Indian National Congress party's paper *Hindustan Times* only published the official communiqué, while Mr Jinnah's Moslem League paper *Dawn* had nothing except a reference to Captain Katju who had accompanied the expedition as official observer.[43] Indian opinion, said Gander, 'seems unimpressed, once again demonstrating extraordinary preoccupation with internal politics'. Gander exempted British-owned Indian papers, such as the *Statesman*, from this criticism. Indeed, the *Statesman*, whose editor Ian Stephens may have been compensating for past 'transgressions' on the subject of the Arakan campaign, gave very full coverage to the Wingate expedition, including a special multipage supplement.[44] Even though the media coverage of the Wingate expedition was not really very prolonged and was far greater in Britain than in India, it did mark an important turning point in the popular view in both countries of the war in Burma.[45]

Conclusion

The campaigns up until that date had been marked by a retreat which could not be redeemed in any kind of Dunkirk-style propaganda, and a humiliating setback in the first Arakan campaign. The Wingate expedition provided the first real signs that British, Burmese, Indian and Gurkha troops could take on and get the better of Japanese troops in jungle warfare. The story had provided a media boon at a time when the war was also going much better for the Allies elsewhere in the world. In terms of media management, it might be thought to be a well-planned triumph. However, as we have seen, the achievement owed as much to luck as good judgment and planning. There had been no planning for any extensive newspaper or visual coverage of the Wingate expedition. This may have been because of jealousies of Wingate within GHQ or because of the experimental nature of the operation. Most likely, it was because the expedition depended on total secrecy and thus it was considered safer to rely on official observers and cameramen. It may also have been considered an unattractive expedition to cover for professional newsmen as it would take them away for several weeks on an extremely arduous and dangerous operation. Whatever the reasons, the fact that three professional correspondents did go with the initial part of the expedition, and maintained a silence about it for three months, made for colourful stories ready for publication when the expedition returned. Of course, Wingate was the perfect general for the newsmen to focus their colourful stories and pictures on. He was an excellent communicator and appeared to be a man with new military ideas who could turn the war against the Japanese around. His eccentricities, and those of some of his company commanders, provided interesting stories. Like Lawrence of Arabia, to whom Wingate was often compared, Wingate was lucky to have his story quickly immortalized by a skilful biographer, in fact two biographers in his case.

Wingate needed the publicity in order to make the case for his next, much larger LRP operation. He was fortunate that through the press coverage he came to the attention of Churchill at just the moment when the prime minister needed a means of convincing the Americans at the Quebec Conference that Britain had the men and the means to take the fight to the Japanese, even though he actually intended very limited operations in Burma until Germany had been defeated. It is ironic, though, that the very success of the Chindit propaganda may have led the Allies to support an inappropriately large expansion of LRP in 1944 – Operation Thursday. Jon Latimer suggests: 'Perhaps the publicity went to his [Wingate's] head' and led him to argue for a much more grandiose second operation.[46] The Quebec Conference was notable also for setting up a unified South East Asia Command (SEAC) with Lord Louis Mountbatten as Supreme Commander. Mountbatten would drive forward an integrated media campaign to restore the morale of the troops In Burma and ensure that the publicity that Wingate had received was continued and expanded.

6

Mountbatten Takes Charge: Publicity and Censorship

Lord Louis Mountbatten's arrival in India in October 1943 to take up his post as Supreme Commander of South East Asia Command (SEAC) marked important changes, not just in military arrangements but also in media management of the war. Winston Churchill had asked Mountbatten to coordinate public relations across the whole Command. He had arranged for Charles Eade, managing editor of the *Sunday Dispatch* (Rothermere Press), to go out to manage setting this up as his public relations adviser. Eade's role was rather vague. Churchill told him that his job would be to mind Mountbatten's back, and that he was not keen on any great publicity for the SEAC theatre over the coming months. He wrote to General Ismay, his chief military adviser: 'I cannot too strongly emphasise the importance of damping down all publicity about this theatre for at least 3 months.'[1] Eade's job turned out to be not so much advising as actually setting up a working public relations organization for SEAC within the six months that he had allotted himself to be away from his paper. Eade reckoned that he would need to find some sixty new officers who would be based across SEAC from Delhi through to Calcutta, Imphal and Ceylon.[2] This new set-up would have important implications for the existing publicity and censorship regimes, which were based on India Command, not least in the demands that would be made for the transfer of staff to SEAC.

SEAC had been set up at the Quebec Conference in August 1943 in order to establish an overall control of military operations over a very widespread theatre. It would bring together not only the various Allied nations but also the different services: army, navy and air force. India Command was now restricted to looking after internal security, the North-West Frontier and those troops serving overseas, plus supply and training functions for the war against Japan. For General Auchinleck, having been relieved of his command in the Middle East and left to languish in India before being appointed Commander-in-Chief in June 1943, it must have been difficult to take this diminution of responsibility for operations in Burma. A further awkwardness was created by Mountbatten's creation of a new post of Deputy Chief of Staff (Information and Civil Affairs), DICA for short, which would bring together not only responsibility for public relations and censorship in SEAC but also psychological warfare and military administration of reconquered Burma, or civil affairs as it was now called. Each of these areas impinged on pre-existing India Command activities and would inevitably lay claim to some of their established staff. The man appointed to the daunting task of overseeing this new empire was Air Marshal Philip Joubert de la Ferté, who was flown

Figure 6.1 Air Marshal Philip Joubert de la Ferté, Deputy Chief of Staff (Information & Civil Affairs). Photo by Cecil Beaton, IB 124, IWM.

out from Britain at the end of October 1943. Ian Stephens, editor of the influential *Statesman* newspaper, welcomed Joubert: 'An excellent choice: publicity-minded; already a successful BBC broadcaster in his own right; with previous Indian experience too as A.O.C. [Air Officer Commanding] in '37–'39; and having amply enough rank to offset Jehu [Indian Army Public Relations Director] when needed.'[3] Joubert would need all his administrative and diplomatic skills to steer him through his new job, especially with Mountbatten as his very demanding superior.[4]

SEAC forces' newspaper

The full impact of these changes was not felt immediately because SEAC, being based in Delhi, had to operate alongside the Indian Army organization, and it would take time to introduce new policies and, most importantly, new staff. The new Supreme Commander was seen as a breath of fresh air by many, including Ian Stephens, who met him soon after his arrival. His enthusiasm for Mountbatten was somewhat checked, however, when he realized that the 'Supremo' had radical ideas for improving the morale of troops in India and Burma, which was known to have reached a low point. One of these ideas was to set up a new daily newspaper for troops serving east of the Brahmaputra river, in other words the main areas in Burma and eastern India where combat troops were likely to be placed.[5] It was to be called simply, but not very originally, *SEAC*. Stephens saw the planned paper as both an opportunity and a threat to the *Statesman*'s business.[6] The *Statesman* presses in Delhi were already printing three different army publications, though these were journals not daily newspapers covering up-to-date events, and did not in any way compete with the *Statesman*.[7] The new proposals for a daily paper provided a direct challenge as the suggested price was 1 anna, which would undercut the *Statesman*, which charged 2 annas.[8] It would be flown daily by air to eastern areas, including places like Shillong and Chittagong in eastern India, where the *Statesman* had established sales already.

For Stephens, this was a particularly discomforting turn of events as it meant that all the time that had been spent preparing for an airmail edition of the *Statesman* to be sent to the troops was now wasted and there seemed to be no recognition of how stretched he and his staff were in wartime. He argued that the paper should be priced at 2 annas or, if not, should be provided free. He probably thought that he had a strong negotiating hand because *SEAC* would have to be printed in Calcutta on the *Statesman*'s presses if it were to appear within the next few months. No other presses were suitable, and it would take too long to import new presses under wartime conditions. Stephens made headway in negotiations with the paper's newly arrived editor Frank Owen. Stephens admired Owen for his liberal political views and his experience as a former editor of the *Evening Standard* in London. However, it was Mountbatten who saw the new paper as very much his child and was determined that it should not be provided free but should be sold at a price that was affordable to the troops. He also wanted that the paper would be seen to be both widely read and self-supporting. To Mountbatten, the 1-anna cover price was essential and he provided his own aircraft to fly Stephens to Delhi to persuade him. Stephens admitted that Mountbatten was charming but also that, in effect, he was ruthlessly bullied into accepting the 1-anna price. The best that he could do in the face of *force majeure* was to submit gracefully and offer staff accommodation and the use of *Statesman* presses in Calcutta, even though his paper would lose money as a result. He felt that the *Statesman* could afford the losses in view of its additional wartime profits, but he asked that each edition of the new paper should at least acknowledge the contribution that the *Statesman* was making.

The first edition of the new paper appeared on 10 January 1944. It was a four-page daily, with a larger Sunday paper soon added. Stephens later reflected that 'from now on things went very well, the *SEAC–Statesman* link-up developing into one of the war's more surprising minor success-stories, journalists and the Calcutta climate being what they are'.[9] The front cover showed a photograph of Mountbatten, beaming at the birth of his 'new baby'. His welcoming address emphasized the purpose of the paper:

> In one sense it should be regarded as a supplement to letters from home and in another as a means of keeping those fighting in remote places in touch with the wider issues of the War. *SEAC* is designed to ensure that the men of this Command, whatever their nationality, rank or branch of service will not forget nor be forgotten.

To this practical aim of maintaining and raising morale, Mountbatten promised freedom to the editors and stressed that in the war against fascism a free press was crucial. Chief of Staff Pownall wondered whether Mountbatten had gone too far in extolling press freedom. In his view correspondents sometimes abused this freedom.[10] The commitment would be an important test of Mountbatten's resolve when he had to deal with criticisms of *SEAC*'s editorial policies, especially when these were considered to be too left-wing politically, too outspoken about those in authority, or allowing too much space to soldiers' grievances.

Frank Owen came from editing the *Evening Standard* in London and was therefore connected to the influential Beaverbrook empire. Assisting him as editor were Ian Coster, also of the *Evening Standard*, Len Jackson of the *Daily Mirror*, Tom Wilcox, who was formerly foreign news subeditor of the *Daily Express*, and H. S. T. Tillotson, formerly staff reporter of the *Lancashire Daily Post*. This was a powerful editorial team, which ensured that the paper was a quality product with a popular appeal.[11] The newspaper started with circulation figures of 10,000 and by June 1944 had reached 20,000, and eventually 100,000, according to Mountbatten.[12] Distribution to troops who were stationed over widespread and often inhospitable terrain was a remarkable achievement in itself. Four Avro Anson planes were dedicated to delivering newspapers, which had only started leaving the Calcutta presses very early in the morning at 01.30 but were delivered by 10.00 each day.[13] Eade used his contacts in Fleet Street to receive copies of the British newspapers and permission to use some of their articles and correspondents. The *SEAC* editorial staff and advisers, having been drawn from the popular press in Britain, knew how to reach their audience.

There were various methods used by the *SEAC* newspaper to raise troop morale. First, an important justification for providing a separate forces newspaper was to provide news from home, which could not be found in Indian papers. This included a range of topics from politics through to crime reports and, of course, sports news and results. Sometimes this took on a romantic or nostalgic tone as regular pictures were provided of scenic places and landscapes in Britain – for example, of the Lake District and Stratford-upon-Avon to remind combatants perhaps of the land they were fighting for.

Secondly, the paper provided information about progress in the SEAC theatre. This amounted, as Mountbatten had indicated when arguing the case for a top-flight Fleet Street editor, to a form of hidden propaganda. In only the second issue of *SEAC*, the Australian journalist Wilfred Burchett addressed the difficult issue of the previous military setbacks in Burma. The poor reputation that some soldiers still fighting in Burma received as a result of the retreat in 1942 and the failure of the Arakan campaign in early 1943 needed to be challenged. Burchett (mistakenly named Peter Burchett under his *Daily Express* by-line) managed this superbly well by telling of his personal involvement in both campaigns. He described the retreat not as a humiliation but as another Dunkirk and Battle of Britain rolled into one. It was an heroic rearguard action, fought with inadequate numbers and weapons, which 'saved the world and the Army'.[14]

Thirdly, it provided personal stories and pictures about named members of the armed forces. *SEAC* was much more restrained than the American press, which gave full home details of those who appeared in publications, but the paper attempted to ensure that all the services were covered, and also all of the regions and nationalities participating. A good example was when *SEAC* ran an article based on visiting society photographer Cecil Beaton's photos, which was headed 'Personalities Down Arakan Way'. One photograph was of soldier Albert Millard of Tonypandy, South Wales, who told Beaton that it was the first time ever that he had had his photo taken and, if he had known it would happen now, he would have shaved.[15]

Fourthly, it gave an opportunity for combatants to voice their opinions via the letters page – for example, about pay, conditions, repatriation arrangements and other matters that concerned them. Owen was keen to be seen to be on the side of the ordinary serviceman, but this could sometimes get him into trouble with his bosses. An example in his editorial in *SEAC* on 17 June 1944 attacking the Bristol North member of parliament, Captain Bernays, who thought that an unmarried soldier's pay was quite adequate. Owen took Bernays to task and asked what right his nine months in the army (none of it on overseas service) and his MP's salary gave him to speak for the ordinary soldier. Philip Joubert was disturbed by this criticism of a Westminster politician, and told Mountbatten: 'I do feel very strongly that Mr Owen has got to be disciplined. As you know, I have ridden him with a very light rein but there have been quite a number of instances where, in spite of my instructions to him, he has allowed undesirable matter to be published.'[16] Mountbatten agreed that there should be no attacks on MPs in his papers but generally stood by Owen on such occasions. When General Christison reported complaints he had heard about the left-wing tendencies of *SEAC*, Mountbatten disagreed, and emphasized that the paper was not to be 'muzzled'. He argued that its readers were a large citizen army, not a small professional one, and their paper must reflect what the majority thought and felt. 'Its whole value, he was sure, lay in the fact that the troops believed in it as their own paper, which fearlessly published their own views.'[17] However, Owen was thought to have gone too far in allowing a letter from a soldier to be published which made 'derogatory references' about the Secretary of State for War, Sir James Grigg, Mountbatten's immediate boss.[18]

Last, but definitely not least, the paper provided entertainment – for example, in the form of strip cartoons, the most popular one being Jane, which was provided courtesy of the *Daily Mirror*, and also glamour photos or pin-ups. Perhaps these were the most important boost to morale?

Phoenix magazine

Official reports on troop morale confirmed that *SEAC* did contribute to raising it. It was said that the soldiers appreciated the rapid delivery of the paper to frontline areas, and that some posted copies home to show what they were doing.[19] Setting up *SEAC* newspaper proved to be relatively plain sailing compared with Mountbatten's next project which was to establish a weekly pictorial magazine for the troops. The magazine was first proposed in May 1944, but the first edition of *Phoenix* was not actually ready until January 1945. Even then, the first three editions, 75,000 copies, had to be pulped because they did not meet Mountbatten's strict requirements that it be a joint Anglo-American publication.[20] It took two months of deliberations in the War Office to approve the magazine, largely because its proposed staffing was considered larger than other comparable forces' magazines. In fact, the magazine was designed to be self-supporting, partly because offices could be shared with the *Statesman* in Calcutta. The American staffing for the magazine was ready long before the British equivalent was established with the result that the Americans lost patience and withdrew their staff and support for the magazine at the beginning of October 1944.[21] It was strange that Mountbatten was not informed of this until the very end of 1944 and as a result had to plead with the Americans to return their staff and support.[22] Joubert pressed Mountbatten to allow the production and distribution of the magazine to continue while awaiting the American involvement. The editor, Ian Coster, also threatened to resign, but Mountbatten stuck to his guns and had the first three draft editions pulped. The first edition of the magazine was produced on 24 February 1945.[23]

Mountbatten took a close interest in both the magazine and the newspaper and would intervene to ask for changes to captions or to ensure that a balance was kept in the articles between British and American content. Ralph Arnold who worked at the SEAC HQ said:

> Supremo's intense interest in everything to do with PR could be a bit awkward. As a start he took a keen interest in his own personal publicity, and made no bones about it. Either, it seemed, he got too much, or else he got too little. Too much, or the wrong kind of publicity, embarrassed and annoyed him. Too little upset him. It was difficult to achieve the happy mean.[24]

Despite the views of Stilwell and his entourage that Mountbatten was publicity-mad, it does seem that he genuinely did not want publicity to focus on him, although, strangely, it often did.[25] The reason he allowed it to was not personal vanity, as might have been expected from an obviously vain person, but that he believed it was essential to contributing to improving the image and standing of the South East Asia Command (SEAC). He did, however, work incredibly hard on publicity issues. Arnold commented on Mountbatten's remarkable practice of reading press cuttings and all the signals about public relations, both incoming and outgoing. 'If a signal could be re-drafted, he would re-draft it. It nearly drove us mad.'[26]

Censorship

The other major change instituted by SEAC was in the censorship system, the crucial alter ego of the propaganda machine. If censorship was too strict, editors would refuse to send reporters on such distant and expensive assignments. Again, the new SEAC control of censorship took time to achieve, and, in effect, operational censorship was shared with Indian Army GHQ until mid-April 1944, when SEAC HQ moved to Kandy and SEAC took over these censorship functions in its area. Although this worked reasonably well, the censorship attitudes and policies of the two commands differed substantially, and this would blow up into a full-scale row just as SEAC was taking over control. Ever since the war in Burma began, Indian Army censorship had always borne the brunt of complaints from correspondents. This continued to be the case in 1944. Douglas Gardner of the *Sydney Morning Herald* wrote in October on his return to Australia: 'Censorship in India, both civil and military is the most severe in the Empire. There has been some relaxation recently, but previously correspondents of the world's Press were unable to send out despatches giving anything like a complete picture of events.' He complained that a 'blind' system was used for outgoing messages so correspondents did not know what changes had been made to their dispatches. A double check was made at Bombay of messages going out, even though they had been passed elsewhere. Censorship of incoming messages was equally severe, despite the fact that they had been censored elsewhere.[27]

Whereas Mountbatten wanted censorship restricted to matters strictly relating to military security, this had never been considered possible by the Indian authorities who were acutely aware of the implications of military information and scares for domestic politics and civilian and soldier morale. It is necessary to distinguish between India's censorship of correspondents' dispatches sent overseas and the problem of what could be allowed for publication within India itself. Because of the very sensitive political situation in India during the war, domestic censorship was different from that followed in the United Kingdom. It was designed to maintain a balance between military and political considerations. Properly speaking, the military were in charge of censorship in India with the Commander-in-Chief and his Chief Censor taking responsibility. However, they were expected to work with the civilian authorities represented by a civilian Chief Press Censor, later Chief Press Advisor. As Devika Sethi has pointed out, it became standard practice to use journalists, such as Desmond Young and Bernard Kirchner, to carry out these 'advisory' roles at both central and local levels. In her view this gave 'the perfect alibi for state censorship masquerading as self-regulation'.[28] However, it could also be seen as a sensible way of winning the cooperation of Indian newspapers, which was in fact achieved by agreements in 1940 and 1942 with the newspaper editors' organization. This system of advisory consultation between editors and censors worked well but broke down under the strains of the Quit India crisis of August 1942 and censorship of the Bengal Famine of 1943.[29] The Government of India (GoI) was acutely aware of the potential for civilian panic in the case of rumours of Japanese bombing of cities or invasion of Indian territory. In these circumstances, political considerations could not be separated from military security issues, and this caused conflicts with war correspondents and also with the government in London.

Correspondents' dispatches that were to be sent abroad were supposedly censored on grounds of military security alone. However, the GoI realized that reports published in London or New York could find their way back into Indian newspapers, sometimes via Japanese propaganda. This provided the GoI with another ground for internal censorship. Journalists called the wider form of censorship used in India 'political' or 'policy' censorship to contrast it with that based strictly on military security only. This was the basis for Indian censorship of stories which circulated in April 1944 following an article by Hanson Baldwin, military correspondent of the *New York Times*, which revealed a fundamental rift over strategy in Burma between Stilwell and Mountbatten.[30]

Problems rarely arise singly, and in this case the *New York Times* controversy coincided with two more military censorship issues in April. Both resulted from a very serious military situation when the Japanese advanced towards India and threatened crucial British positions at Imphal, Kohima and Dimapur. This endangered crucial lines of communication supporting Stilwell's advance from Ledo. This was obviously a very dangerous moment for India and there were concerns that the public should not be panicked, which might lead to mass evacuations from key strategic areas. An additional problem was that Subhas Chandra Bose's Indian National Army (INA) was involved in significant numbers in what the INA called the 'March on Delhi', and this provided obvious propaganda opportunities for the Japanese.

The problem started when a message on 13 April filed by Martin Moore, the *Daily Telegraph* correspondent, was censored because it suggested that that the first Japanese attack on Kohima 'was repulsed by scratch lot of semi-invalids from [the] convalescent camp'.[31] The overall tone of the dispatch was considered positive and 'good publicity' and the defence of Kohima section of the story was probably intended to highlight the heroism involved. However, it was obviously open to censorship in that it revealed to the Japanese the very limited manpower and resources there. The story was also filed by four other correspondents: Ian Fitchett (Sydney *Daily Telegraph* and London *Daily Express*), Graham Stanford (*Daily Mail*), Ian Laing (*Daily Sketch* and *Sunday Times*) and Philip Wynter (Australian Consolidated Newspapers). It was duly stopped by 11th Army censors. The censorship was only supposed to apply to the offending section of the articles but, apparently by mistake, was applied to the whole. By 20 April, the articles had been approved, with the offending section taken out. The journalists were not satisfied, however. There had been an additional operational ban on speculation that the Japanese advance might threaten Assam communications in the Brahmaputra valley which was in operation from 7 to 22 April. This had been imposed by SEAC on the advice of India Command which was concerned at the impact of ill-informed speculation on Indian public opinion. The journalists' frustration at these two bans reflected their belief that the army was withholding the truth about the Japanese assault on Assam and the danger that Kohima, Imphal and the railhead at Dimapur faced of being overrun. In fact, they were correct: the situation at Kohima was desperate, but news of the situation was kept not only from the public but even from the British government, parliament and the Indian Assembly. Misleadingly optimistic statements were put out.[32]

The journalists contacted their newspapers and complained that this dispute was the culmination of long-standing complaints about censorship by GHQ India. They determined to go on strike and stop providing copy until the censorship regime was changed. The censorship was undertaken in Delhi only a day or two before the headquarters of SEAC moved from Delhi to Kandy in Ceylon, and a clearer direction now needed to be made about SEAC's censorship policy. On 22 April, SEAC HQ put out a statement explaining the censorship but countered by listing the improvements made to facilities for war correspondents since SEAC took over six months previously.[33] It was obviously intended to show that the majority of correspondents were satisfied with arrangements and had not joined the five striking correspondents. It pointed out that now that SEAC was based at Kandy it had taken over responsibility for censorship which was now based both there and at 14th Army headquarters at Comilla. It concluded: 'The only censorship imposed is that dictated by the needs of military security.' The statement only seemed to annoy the correspondents more, and they wrote messages which they requested be sent home through Reuters outlining their complaints against the Indian censorship and PR organization. They argued that they had a right to make their protest public. The PR adviser for SEAC, Charles Eade, agreed that their protests should not be censored. In London, the correspondents' editors asked that a representative of the journalists should be allowed to fly home and explain their case. Martin Moore was chosen but, first of all, he was invited to meet with Mountbatten at Kandy. The two men met on 28 April and Moore reported back a summary of the meeting to his editor A. E. Watson.[34] Mountbatten assured him that

> future censorship will in only two matters step beyond grounds of purely security considerations. Firstly, a story may be stopped or cut if its publication is thought likely to have a damaging effect on the morale of the men actually fighting – i.e., if it discloses temporary adverse developments which may not be fully known to the troops. Secondly, censorship may intervene if publication of a story is considered to affect the security of India as SEAC's supply base.[35]

Moore commented: 'Everything depends on how these two points are interpreted. The wide interpretation of the second, in particular, has been the basic cause of most of our censorship difficulties in the past.' However, he recognized the intention to treat censorship more reasonably and that censors had now been given more freedom to use their judgment on individual messages, rather than working to a rigid list of 'stops'. Only one absolute stop remained in place and that was on what he described as the actions in Burma of 'renegade Indians recruited from among prisoners of war in Malaya and elsewhere'. This was the INA and its charismatic leader Subhas Chandra

THE SUPREMO talks to war correspondents during his recent visit to the front. Left to right: Geoffrey Tebbutt, Melbourne Herald and London Evening Standard, Martin Moore, Daily Telegraph and Statesman, Graham Stanford, Daily Mail.

Figure 6.2 Supremo talks to striking war correspondents, *SEAC* newspaper, 26 April 1944.

Bose. The INA had been established initially from Indian soldiers who were captured by the Japanese in Malaya and Singapore in 1942, some of whom decided to fight for Indian freedom alongside the Japanese. Correspondents did ask to report on the INA in the overseas press but, for the most part, the media adhered to the embargo throughout the war.[36]

Moore took up the issue of why correspondents were not tipped off either about the recent Sabang naval air operation off Sumatra or Wingate's glider-borne operation. Neither, he said, was properly explained. He should have known, however, that correspondents were invited to cover Wingate's second expedition, Operation Thursday, but only a few agreed to take up the offer.[37] Moore concluded by telling his editor that the journalists' strike, and the publicity it had received, had 'achieved their result in jolting the censorship and public relations organisation and bringing matters to the attention of the Supreme Command. I think conditions will now be easier, and I am personally satisfied that I can continue to work without friction. After this showdown it will be possible to take any future grievances to the highest quarter.'[38]

Mountbatten met with correspondents in Kandy on 4 May.[39] He had been able to instil a much better relationship between SEAC and the war correspondents. He had set down the aim of reducing censorship as much as possible in line with security needs. He also insisted on a centralized system of censorship and press releases for the SEAC area, though Stilwell was able to maintain the right to send communiqués from his command to Chungking.[40] A policy was established to clarify the arrangement for censorship 'stops' and to try to encourage commanders to limit the time these stops remained in force, and to keep correspondents informed about them and when they were to be lifted. The censorship maintained by the GoI and India Command was limited to material intended directly for India and the Indian press, apart from matters of strictly military security where they could ask for stops on material sent overseas.

The irony was that the correspondents had achieved their victory by aiming their protest at the wrong target in this instance. They had seen the banning of their Kohima message as the culmination of long-standing grievances with the India Command's censorship and public relations set-up. SEAC had taken control of the response to the correspondents' strike and gone along with the idea that it resulted from fundamental problems with India Command's mixing of Indian domestic concerns with the overriding need for military security to drive censorship. There was some general basis to this view, but not in relation to this particular censorship. Eventually, the Deputy Director IAPR was able to address correspondents in Delhi on 4 May to explain the situation off the record. The essence of this was that the Kohima message had been censored by both GHQ *and* SEAC, which was the system of joint censorship in operation. The Indian Army did not deal with operational censorship relating to the 14th Army (SEAC) area but its censors were consulted on matters which had wider implications for India's security. The correspondents' wider complaint about 'policy censorship' did not refer to political censorship but rather to the ban on speculation about future military plans which might threaten India, which the Indian Army censors were responsible for.[41] Although correspondents continued to be suspicious of India Command's role in censorship of their dispatches, it had not apparently been guilty in April 1944. The two-week period of press silence at a crucial point in the Japanese invasion of India had caused much consternation in India and in Britain. Home Intelligence reports indicated that people knew of the strike and feared that 'bad news is being kept back'.[42] Reports of the public being confused about the situation in Burma and believing that news was being censored continued to be reported up to the middle of May.

An amusing postscript to the story is that, shortly after his meeting with Mountbatten, Martin Moore decided to test the new liberal censorship policy by writing a long descriptive article on the luxurious set-up at SEAC HQ in Kandy.[43] The article, which was published in the *Daily Telegraph* on 6 May, could have graced any luxury property magazine and was an acute embarrassment to Mountbatten, who already faced criticism for the move to Kandy and the very large number of staff at his headquarters:

> Admiral Mountbatten has chosen for his new headquarters one of the loveliest places in the garden island of Ceylon ... The amenities of the several camps are astonishing ... Three cinemas, each with seating capacity for four hundred, are being built ... and more amenities are being added. There are to be three swimming pools, one for officers, one for men, and a third for the Wrens and W.A.A.C.s. Coolies are now busy laying tennis courts, and squash courts will soon be added.

Not surprisingly, Mountbatten gave immediate orders for the cancellation of new tennis courts and squash courts. He wanted to know why the article had not been censored.[44] Mountbatten had been hoist with his own petard. Colonel Crook, the Chief Press Censor, pointed out that he was only carrying out Mountbatten's newly stated censorship policy and there were no military security or troop morale grounds for censoring it.[45] Obviously, there were limits to Mountbatten's use of charm and control.

Stuart Gelder and the challenge to the 'Gentleman's Agreement' with China

It was probably no coincidence that, following the 'victory' on censorship by the SEAC correspondents, there was another challenge to India's system of censorship. This time it related to relations with the Nationalist Chinese regime, and it was the *News Chronicle*'s Chungking correspondent, Stuart Gelder, who was responsible for confronting the authorities, something pretty much in character for this combative reporter. He had left China where censorship was strong and sent a couple of dispatches from Calcutta which were highly critical of the Chinese regime. The first was sent and published by his paper on 2nd May. The second, which was considered even more critical, was held up by the Indian censors and was referred to Delhi. Gelder obviously felt strongly that the article should not be censored and threatened his immediate return to London if it were. He felt that the British public should know about the serious political, social and military flaws in their Chinese allies.[46] He sparked a serious confrontation between Secretary of State Leo Amery and Viceroy Wavell. The position in London was clearly stated: 'Such "political censorship" as was exercised here since 1942 on grounds of promoting disharmony among Allied or Empire Governments has recently been in practice abandoned and save where negotiations are prejudiced or in wholly exceptional cases censors here would never go beyond discussion.'[47] The External Affairs Department in Delhi replied that there was a 'Gentleman's Agreement' in place with the Chinese that sensitive messages about India which were filed in Chungking were referred to the British Embassy before passing censorship and vice versa for messages filed in India.[48] They were worried about breaking this agreement. The matter was referred to Wavell who agreed that the dispatch should be censored and that they should not give in to Gelder.[49] Amery countered that Gelder's dispatch should be released subject possibly to deletion of some points in one paragraph. He added that Foreign Office (FO) staff had spoken to the editorial staff of the *News Chronicle* pointing out that some of the criticism of China in the message did seem to be 'biased and exaggerated' and hoped that the article would be carefully scrutinized before publication. He added that the editorial staff seemed 'receptive'.[50] Amery pointed out that similar criticisms of Chiang Kai-shek's regime had been published in America and these had reached British newspapers already. So, the message was released on 17 May.[51]

This was not, however, the end of the affair as Gelder wanted a third, even more critical article, sent home. It was held up in censorship and referred to the British Embassy in Chungking under the 'Gentleman's Agreement'. The Embassy favoured suppressing the message if possible and was apparently supported by General Stilwell's headquarters on the rather dubious grounds that Gelder was accredited to it. It was agreed, once again, that the message should be released subject to minor cuts. Unfortunately, this did not satisfy Gelder, who insisted on sending a message to his editor which protested the censorship which he contrasted with Amery's recent statement in the House of Commons that there was no political censorship imposed on messages from India.[52] Once again, the FO had a word in the ear of the editor of the *News Chronicle* and Gelder's dispatch was not published.[53] Amery realized that the 'Gentleman's Agreement' with China had to be dropped as it could breach his House of Commons promise and pressed Wavell to do this.[54] Wavell was obviously reluctant to comply and a highly unusual issue arose which allowed him to argue that these matters had to be dealt with on a case-by-case basis. This derived from rumours that Chiang Kai-shek was being unfaithful to his wife and had a child with a mistress. Chiang held a tea party in July, which included members of the foreign press, to strongly deny these rumours which he clearly saw as an attack on China.[55] Would the press agree to suppress this news? Not Stuart Gelder, apparently. He picked up the story in September and sent a dispatch on it home. Once again, the FO had to be called into action to use its powers of persuasion on the *Chronicle*. It worked, and the story was not published.[56] These examples were indicative of the 'behind the scenes' contacts with editors in London that government preferred to avoid public confrontations over censorship issues.

The Gelder censorship affair indicated how much the GoI's position on censorship had become distanced from the policies of SEAC and the government in London. Delhi had always felt that its needs were special because of the threat of Indian nationalism and the sensitivities of the Indian Army and the civilian war effort. By the middle of 1944 it was made clear that it was expected to limit censorship essentially to military security issues. It had been forced to recognize that its powers of censorship were limited as correspondents could direct their dispatches through SEAC in Ceylon if they wanted a 'softer' censorship. The affair had also shown the newly found strength of correspondents if they wished to challenge censorship decisions in SEAC or India. The threat of raising the issue in Britain seemed to be enough to make governments think again about anything that could be deemed political censorship. The answer in this case at least was for the authorities in Britain to use their power of persuasion on newspaper editors rather than coercion. Appeals on the basis of the patriotic needs of wartime could be effective. It is a reminder that forms of self-censorship almost certainly outnumbered formal censorship, although they tend not, by their nature, to be as well documented.

Geoffrey Tebbutt convinces Mountbatten

Another example of Mountbatten's personal intervention in censorship issues came in July 1944 and underlined his determination to avoid any charge of SEAC using political rather than security censorship. The issue concerned Geoffrey Tebbutt, the distinguished Australian correspondent of the Melbourne *Herald* and London *Evening Standard*, who was preparing to leave SEAC after covering the fighting at Arakan, Imphal, Myitkyina and Mogaung. He was a very thoughtful journalist who liked to go beyond conventional war reporting to analyse longer-term trends in the progress of the Burma campaign. This approach was always likely to create security issues if the critical analysis could be deemed by the censors to give encouragement to the enemy by pointing out weaknesses in the Allied side. In a number of articles, he had already shown that he was not at all impressed with the way that the Arakan campaign was going, commenting: 'We are now holding less territory than we held in December 1942.'[57] He also commented on the length of time it was taking to displace the Japanese from Myitkyina, despite their overwhelming inferiority in numbers. However, he regarded Stilwell's advance as the one major territorial advance of that season's campaigning.[58] He praised the Imphal campaign but as in other theatres he predicted that any advance would be seriously slowed by the monsoon. This was very much against the advice that the Director of Public Relations (DPR) was putting out which was that the monsoon should not be treated as a reason for any delay or stop in fighting.[59] Tebbutt also argued that the multinational, polyglot nature of SEAC troops had disadvantages in terms of communication and cohesion. It was pretty clear that he thought that volunteer troops from India and Africa could never be fully engaged in a battle to liberate Burma, although he recognized that British troops also disliked being there.[60] However, he contrasted this inherent disunity with the palpable willingness of the soldiers to fight and die on behalf of their cause.

Tebbutt had already attracted the attention of censors before he wrote his final dispatch on 14 July to his newspapers and protested that this was being censored as some of his previous articles had been. The article reflected on the reasons for slow progress or 'holding' situation in SEAC, in which various armies seemed to be fighting their own private wars. It ascribed these problems to the enormous size of the command

and the difficulties of centralizing it. Most importantly, SEAC still relied on India to supply the troops and materials, and this slowed everything down in a tangle of eastern bureaucracy. The IAPR wanted to censor the article on several security grounds. Joubert backed the censorship request.[61] Tebbutt protested and cited the agreement that Mountbatten had made with the striking correspondents that there was to be no political censorship in SEAC.[62] Mountbatten decided to take up the issue personally and met more than once with Tebbutt, finally agreeing a compromise version of the dispatch on 16 July. Mountbatten acknowledged that the article was trying to be helpful in emphasizing the difficulties SEAC faced in fighting a war on such an enormous geographical scale. He described Tebbutt as 'most reasonable' and realized that there was no point in censoring just parts of the article as it would no longer make any sense. He also knew that Tebbutt could always publish the article when he reached home.[63] So, he agreed to pass the article with some alterations made particularly to appease the Indian Army command and sent a pacifying message to Auchinleck.[64]

Joubert believed these changes were so small as to not make much difference but had to concur with the Supreme Commander. The article was published in Australia on 19 July under the rather provocative headline, '"Old Order" Clogs East Asia'.[65] Mountbatten obviously learnt a few things about the practice of journalism in the process of his talks with Tebbutt. He learnt, first, that war correspondents rather resented the role that officer observers had come to play and felt that they were so close to the formations they were attached to that they could distort the way the war was reported, and their reports were received as having had official imprimatur. Mountbatten also, somewhat surprisingly, learnt that correspondents worked to word limits for their dispatches and that if official communiqués were too long they could find their reports reduced in the published articles.[66] He gave instructions to shorten communiqués for lesser engagements.

Another means by which the GoI could try and control foreign reporting of India was by means of vetting the correspondents who were given permission to report there. This was something that Indian Army HQ in the person of Brigadier Jehu, DPR, had been used to doing for war correspondent applications to theatres in India and Burma. What concerned the GoI, however, were journalists, particularly from the United States, who did not apply for military accreditation but could come to India on a visa and send dispatches home on sensitive issues such as the Quit India movement or the famine in Bengal.[67] In addition, it was inevitable that accredited war correspondents would arrive in India and base themselves there while travelling intermittently to the Assam or Burma fronts. They, too, could comment on sensitive issues, such as the famine in Bengal in 1943, which in the view of the government could undermine morale both at home and among serving soldiers. The establishment of SEAC in charge of operations in India and Burma threatened to undermine any control which India might have over foreign journalists. They expressed these concerns when the question of the formalization of allocation of quotas for SEAC war correspondent accreditations was raised early in 1944. An agreement was reached in February 1944 that eighty correspondents could be accredited in total and that they would be divided between the UK, USA and India and the Dominions at a ratio of 2:2:1. The India and Dominion correspondents would be recommended by recognized bodies such as the

Empire Press Union, something which the GoI had to accept, albeit reluctantly. The Air Ministry in London would coordinate accreditations for the UK, and the War Department would do so in Washington. The GoI tried to insist that it should be able to comment on American applications but again it had to accept that it could have no veto over such applications and, only as a courtesy, the names of applicants would be passed to the Indian Agency General in Washington. It was made very clear that it would be SEAC that gave final approval to applications, though it was very unlikely that they would turn down those approved by their home authorities. The whole issue, which ran on in official correspondence until August 1944, was coloured by the perception in London that India was out of line in its censorship policies, going further than requirements of military security to include wider political concerns, namely the sensibilities of Indian public opinion. It was recognized that India had powers to control or influence its domestic press, through the office of a press adviser for instance, and also it could censor incoming newspaper articles. London argued, however, that it should not try and control correspondents' dispatches going outside of India on any other than grounds of military security. Otherwise, it would be construed as a restriction of the freedom of the press which was much valued in the USA. Alec Joyce at the India Office underlined the point by writing 'and let us scotch, once and for all, the foolish notion that a war correspondent can't open his mouth on any other than operational matters'.[68]

Conclusion

The Government of India (GoI) and the Indian Army HQ, which had fought throughout to have their own distinctive approach to censorship issues, had finally been brought into line with wider British policies. Mountbatten had been instrumental in ensuring more open and less restrictive policies were applied to journalists both within the forces' journals, *SEAC* and *Phoenix*, and also to war correspondents. *SEAC* newspaper was produced and distributed very professionally. It made an important contribution to boosting morale by keeping the troops in touch with home news and giving them an outlet for their frustrations about pay, conditions and delays to demobilization. The limitations on censorship, and improvements in the speed of transmitting dispatches, encouraged editors to send correspondents to what was, after all, a very distant assignment. The next chapters look at some of the issues involved in managing the reporting of the crucial campaigns of 1944, starting with the very different priorities of the British and American public relations organizations.

7

Allies of a Kind: Public Relations Officers at War

The three major Allies in the war against Japan in South East Asia and the Far East were divided on everything except the overriding need to defeat the enemy. They were at odds both on their overall war aims and the strategies for achieving them. This inevitably impacted on the media management of the different allies. The British and American public relations organizations seemed to be in perpetual rivalry, which often seemed to involve the difficult relations between General Stilwell and Admiral Mountbatten. The awkward command structure exacerbated the tensions because Mountbatten, despite being Supreme Commander, did not have direct operational control over Stilwell's Chinese and American forces. Stilwell was supposed to keep Mountbatten informed of his plans and progress, but at times he operated virtually independently. This tension would reach a height in February 1944 when the American press brought the conflicting Allied strategies out into the public domain. Relations only eased after Stilwell was recalled in October 1944.

China's war aims

The Chinese had the strictest censorship regime and were sensitive to any slurs on their leaders and war effort in the Western media. This sensitivity derived from the precarious position the Chinese were in. Nationalist China under Chiang Kai-shek and the Kuomintang had been fighting the Japanese continuously since 1937, long before either the British or Americans became involved. The Chinese regime had been thrown back by 1941 to the centre and south-west of the vast country, with its capital at Chungking. It was not just the Japanese that Chiang had to contend with: the Chinese Communists under Mao Tse-Tung were a growing force in the area around Yenan to the north and there were a number of warlords who threatened the regime as well. China's armies were poorly trained and even more poorly armed, and in these circumstances Chiang's main aim was, not surprisingly, survival. This involved keeping the Communists at bay while attracting as much American and Allied aid as possible in order to play a long, defensive strategy. Most American war correspondents, much influenced by General Stilwell, criticized this strategy at the time and were followed later by historians such as Barbara Tuchman. Since then, historians of Chinese military history have looked at Chiang's defensive strategy with rather more understanding, if not always approval.[1]

American war aims

The main route by which American Lend-Lease aid could reach China up until 1942 was along the Burma Road which reached from Kunming in south-west China through to Lashio in Burma, and thence by rail to the port of Rangoon. However, the Japanese had cut off this route by May 1942 as a result of their successful invasion of Burma from Thailand. For the Americans the priority was to reopen this supply route as soon as possible, and thereby keep the Chinese in the war against Japan. The building of a new road was sanctioned. This was the Ledo Road, later renamed the Stilwell Road, which was being driven painfully by American engineers and local labourers across the most difficult terrain and weather conditions from Assam through northern Burma to link with the old Burma Road. In the meantime, it would be necessary to provide supplies by a highly dangerous airlift over the Himalayas, known as the Hump.

American policy towards China was influenced by long-standing historical connections. American missionaries had been present in China for several decades previously. Interestingly, this legacy resulted in several influential American soldiers, politicians, publishers and journalists being the children of China missionaries and being actively involved in the China-Burma-India (CBI) campaign of World War Two. Most notable of these were General Stilwell; his political adviser John Paton Davies; John S. Service of the State Department in China; Henry Luce, the publisher of *Time* and *Life* magazines; and John Hersey, *Time* correspondent.[2] America hoped to develop its economic and political interests in East Asia as an outcome of the war, and it was prepared to sacrifice its long-standing extra-territorial concessions as a sweetener to improve America's relations with China. There was, additionally, a sense of guilt that so little had been done to defend China during the 1930s and a desire to try to compensate now. President Roosevelt envisaged China playing an important role as a friendly power in Asia when Japan was defeated. By inviting the Chinese leader Chiang Kai-shek to participate on equal terms in the Cairo Conference in November 1943, he gave China an important diplomatic boost.

American support was based on the calculation that China was tying down some 1 million Japanese troops on the mainland and it was crucial that it be kept in the war so that American forces could concentrate their efforts on conquering Japan in the Pacific. Chiang Kai-shek and the Kuomintang were seen as the best hope of holding China together when there were rival warlords and Mao Tse-tung's Communists threatening Chinese unity. However, there were those like General Stilwell who believed that the Chinese regime was unreliable, incompetent and corrupt. Worst of all, it was taking American money and supplies while avoiding fully committing troops in Burma so that the regime could be bolstered at home against its Communist rivals. A number of journalists who reported from China and Burma supported Stilwell's assessment, as was shown in an outpouring of criticism of Chiang when Stilwell was recalled in October 1944. A number of correspondents took the opportunity to visit Mao at the Communist headquarters in Yenan. They reported favourably on the integrity of the Communists and the support they had among the people and contrasted this with the ineffectiveness and disdain for the ordinary Chinese people shown by the Kuomintang. Roosevelt, however, had strong domestic reasons to remain committed to Chiang. The impact of these conflicting American approaches to China would play out with long-lasting consequences in the post-war world.

British war aims

Britain actually had more long-standing and better established trade links with China than the United States. It also had extra-territorial treaties imposed on China, most important of which was its ninety-nine-year lease on the New Territories of Hong Kong, signed in 1898. This colonial history, and China's borders with Burma and India, instilled mistrust between the two powers, which was not helped when Britain closed the Burma Road temporarily in July 1940 under pressure from Japan. Britain was pressured by US pre-emptive action to give up some of these treaty rights in 1943, but not those relating to Hong Kong. For Britain, the main aim in South East Asia and the Far East was to restore those parts of its empire that had been lost to the Japanese: Hong Kong, Malaya, Singapore and Burma, to defend the borders of India, and to restore the prestige it had lost as a result of Japanese conquests. For Winston Churchill, the restoration of the British Empire was imperative, and this inevitably brought him into conflict with President Roosevelt, who was determined that America should not be seen to be sending its soldiers to support the return of European empires in Asia.[3] Churchill's preferred strategy was to use combined operations with marine forces attacking the Japanese from the south, either via Sumatra and Java or more directly to Rangoon. He did not like the idea of a long land campaign from northern Burma because the lines of communication through very difficult territory were extremely difficult, whereas the Japanese could defend behind interior lines. Above all else, Churchill prioritized his Mediterranean and Middle East strategy, which meant that military supplies were always given precedence to that area rather than Burma and the Far East. This had the effect of frustrating not only Mountbatten's ambitions for combined operations to recover Burma but also the American desire to give aid to China by an aggressive land campaign in northern Burma. The Americans interpreted this British reluctance to press on with a land campaign in Burma in support of Stilwell as resulting from their focus on regaining their lost imperial territories. These different perceptions plagued Allied relations throughout much of the war.

The British also had a more negative, not to say more realistic, view of the value of Chiang Kai-shek's China in playing a major role in the defeat of Japan. They doubted that Stilwell's drive, using predominantly Chinese troops, to capture Myitkyina, the key town and airfield in north-east Burma, could be achieved before the onset of the monsoon in May 1944. They believed that even if the land route to China could be reopened it would not be in time to play a decisive role in the war. They proved to be correct, but this would not win much favour with the Americans who saw the final opening of the Ledo Road in January 1945 as one of their greatest achievements.

Problems of command structure exacerbate differences

These differences between the Allies over war aims and strategies were exacerbated by the complicated overlapping command structures in the South East Asia area. US general Joseph Stilwell was deputy to Mountbatten as Supreme Allied Commander while he retained his other roles as commander of American troops in the CBI theatre and as Chief of Staff to Chiang Kai-shek. This peculiar arrangement made him responsible through three different lines of command. In addition, he was in operational command of the Chinese forces that had been trained at Ramgarh in India and which were called the Northern Combat Area Command (NCAC). In the 1944 campaign, NCAC was bolstered for the first time by American troops, three battalions of a long-range penetration (LRP) force, 5307 Composite Unit (Provisional), known by the press as Merrill's Marauders, after its commander Brigadier General Frank Merrill. This confused command situation was bound to cause friction between Stilwell and British commanders in the field.

If this was a difficult chain of command for Stilwell to deal with, it also presented major problems for Mountbatten as Supreme Commander. Each of the three service chiefs in SEAC had the right of direct communication with their headquarters in London. Furthermore, some of the commanders, such as Admiral Sir James Somerville, had every reason to regard Mountbatten as having leapfrogged over their previous seniority. It required great tact and forbearance for this command to work in practice. There was also the problem that India, the main source of troops, training and supplies for SEAC, was not included in its area. General Auchinleck, Commander-in-Chief, India, as an experienced commander, could well have resented Mountbatten's appointment and the negative view of the India Command that underlay it. However, despite difficulties, particularly over censorship and publicity issues, he proved supportive. Mountbatten had not been given the sort of unquestioned supreme command that US General MacArthur enjoyed in the Pacific theatre, so his diplomatic skills would be crucial in making a success of his command. He was keen to assert overall control over SEAC publicity, but Stilwell was able to resist him and ultimately keep control of communiqués and press notes going to the United States and Britain by using his prerogative of sending them through his Chinese 'bosses' in Chungking.

Mountbatten and Stilwell – their use of the press

Both Stilwell and Mountbatten used the media to support their aims in this theatre. However, they each had different audiences to consider. Stilwell faced the major problem that the United States government, while it was committed to keeping China in the war and winning the war in the Pacific, had to be convinced that his plan of a land offensive into China through Burma would actually bring a significant improvement in supplies to China in the time available. Stilwell argued that the existing supply route to China by air over the Himalayas, the so-called Hump, was dangerous both from high altitude weather conditions and also from Japanese fighter attacks from Myitkyina airfield. Capturing Myitkyina would allow for a shorter and safer air route

Allies of a Kind

Figure 7.1 Supreme Allied Commander South East Asia Mountbatten conferring with Lieutenant General J. W. Stilwell, Commander-in-Chief US Forces in China, Burma and India, March 1944, IWM, NYF 20073.

to China and result eventually in a road and oil pipeline connecting to the Burma Road and thence to China. Stilwell's American-trained Chinese troops could use the new route for a land campaign in China itself. This looked very ambitious and there was always the lure of the US Air Commander in China Brigadier General Claire Chennault's alternative plan based on an airborne assault on the Japanese mainland from aircraft based in China. Stilwell had to counter Chennault's plan, which would divert material resources and aircraft from the land-war option. Additionally, Stilwell needed to bring pressure on Chiang Kai-shek to engage Chinese troops in Burma rather than holding them in reserve in China to ward off future Japanese attacks or moves by his Communist rivals. This would mean persuading President Roosevelt to use American Lend-Lease supplies to China as a means of sustaining a Chinese offensive. Finally, Stilwell needed Roosevelt to use the major allied conferences to push for a land offensive from India into North Burma and to deny British strategies of relying on naval operations against Rangoon or Java/Sumatra which would focus on the restoration of British colonial rule in the territories they had lost to the Japanese in 1942. Stilwell could usually rely on his patron, US Chief of Staff General George Marshall, for support, but Roosevelt was preparing to contest a presidential election in 1944 and was much more focused on prioritizing a successful European military campaign than refereeing command conflicts in South East Asia. The opportunity was there for Stilwell to use the press to support his aims, just as General MacArthur in the Pacific or General Montgomery in Europe did with some panache.[4] However, it was not Stilwell's style to play politics, unless he felt really compelled to. Fred Eldridge, Stilwell's PRO, commented: 'Stilwell was a strange contradiction of astute and inept politician.... He played a masterful game with the British, but he neglected to develop a strong coterie of powerful American backers to counteract his natural enemies when he had opportunities right in his lap.'[5]

Stilwell was popular with the press corps: he was always prepared to talk to journalists and his straight-talking manner was refreshing.[6] Barbara Tuchman describes this very well:

> Vinegar Joe was becoming a public personality. He made good copy, and the press made the most of it, developing a picturesque stereotype, the crusty cracker-barrel soldier's soldier, tough, leathery, wiry, down-to-earth, wise-cracking, Chinese-speaking, a disciplinarian loved by his troops, with lack of swank and a warm smile, an American 'Chinese Gordon', an 'Uncle Joe'.[7]

Mountbatten was a much more sophisticated communicator than Stilwell. He was very aware of the power of the media, especially film and visual media. He had good contacts in the London newspaper industry as well as in the film industry. The question was not, therefore, whether he would use the media, but to what ends. Clearly, it was important to focus on the British domestic audience, whether it be politicians like Churchill, the Chiefs of Staff or the general British public. The problem was that the needs of these audiences might be contradictory. Churchill made it clear at the outset of Mountbatten's command that he wanted the Burma campaign to be downplayed in the early months of SEAC. He did not want false expectations raised of an early advance.[8] Europe and North Africa were the priorities and resources would not be available in large enough numbers to support a combined operation until the dry season starting in October 1944. Mountbatten, on the other hand, prioritized restoring the morale of the British and Indian armies in Burma, and countering their perception that they were the 'forgotten armies'. The only way that this could be done effectively was through achieving military victories over the Japanese. This would take time and, in the meantime, action was urgently needed to restore troop morale. Practical steps could be taken, for instance, to reduce the incidence of malaria and to ensure rapid treatment of those who were wounded. Mountbatten thought it important for soldiers to see their commanders in person and he travelled to various fronts where he conducted 'impromptu' soapbox talks to troops in which he promised that they would no longer be forgotten. He believed that the regular supply of the soldiers' newspaper *SEAC* was crucial in restoring and maintaining morale. It would include stories from families at home which would help convince the troops that they really were not overlooked. At the same time, *SEAC* could be used to project Mountbatten's own image, something he refuted, but which seemed to happen remarkably often. The British and American forces' newspapers inevitably tended to give greater emphasis to the role of their own troops in the theatre but, to be fair, Mountbatten explicitly instructed that he wanted even-handed coverage of the US and Chinese roles in both the *SEAC* and *Phoenix* publications. After all, he wanted this to be seen as a unified command.

British and American uses of the media under SEAC

To evaluate British and American use of the media in the Burma campaign of 1944–5 one needs to examine its evolution though certain key events. When Mountbatten first arrived in India in October 1943, relations with Stilwell were good. Shortly after arriving, Mountbatten had met with Stilwell and Chiang Kai-shek at Chungking. Stilwell, at the time, believed that Mountbatten had been partly responsible for Chiang agreeing to his staying in post and this may have contributed to the early warmth in his views on Mountbatten. Stilwell wrote in his diary: 'Louis is a good egg ... full of enthusiasm and also of disgust with inertia and conservatism ... Louis is hot for the "one happy family" idea and is very cordial and friendly.'[9]

The early affability of this relationship did not last long. Stilwell had believed that Mountbatten was a man of action and would quickly galvanize the British into offensive land operations in Burma. He was correct about Mountbatten's drive, but ignored the wartime realities that dictated a Europe-first policy and the consequent lack of military equipment for the amphibious landings in Burma that the British priorities required. Mountbatten's scepticism about the viability of Stilwell's priorities of the building of the Ledo Road to connect with the Burma Road to China undoubtedly added to Stilwell's dismay. By the New Year, Stilwell was confiding in his diary: 'The Glamour Boy is just that. He doesn't wear well and I begin to wonder if he knows his stuff. Enormous staff, endless walla-walla, but damned little fighting.'[10] Stilwell regarded Mountbatten as 'publicity crazy'. He criticized his flamboyant and carefully pressed uniforms in comparison with his own very plain, not to say scruffy, look. He was annoyed when Mountbatten flew into his headquarters with an escort of sixteen aeroplanes and found Mountbatten's soapbox talks to his troops rather laughable. Yet the simple, plain-spoken style that Stilwell used, even along with the popularly used epithet 'Vinegar Joe', were also parts of a cultivated image. Although Stilwell did eschew the type of publicity-hunting that generals like Montgomery or MacArthur pursued, he certainly was prepared to use journalists, on occasion, to suit his own ends.[11] For instance, when his troops captured Myitkyina airport he flew in with about a dozen journalists the next day to record the event. They did not stay around to report the subsequent failure to capture the town itself, which took another two and a half months. Early in the advance to Myitkyina, he gave a press conference on 3 March 1944. He had only seen General Slim the day before and had been told that, despite setbacks in British operations in Arakan, some 4,000 Japanese had been killed there. Despite this knowledge, he told reporters provocatively: 'Imagine – there are only foreigners,

American, and Chinese, really fighting to retake a part of the British Empire. That's a hot one.'[12] Stilwell was deeply Anglophobic, as his published diaries attest. It was not just that he disagreed with the British on strategy and believed that they had no real intention to fight in Burma, but he also held deep-seated prejudices. Partly, these were based on his strong patriotism which he linked to America's historic fight for independence from the British Empire.[13] Partly, it seemed to reflect a certain insecurity and a sensitivity to the upper-class nature of the British commanders he encountered.[14] Whatever the reasons, Anglophobia permeates the Stilwell diaries, with the result that he rarely gave the British credit, even for their military successes. His attitudes were inevitably reflected in the work of his public relations team.

Stilwell saw the need to ensure that the American and Chinese advances in the Hukawng valley and towards Myitkyina were well reported as a means of giving weight to the land campaign in North Burma that he favoured and countering the alternative Culverin/Axiom plans of the British that focused on seaborne invasions in Sumatra and Malaya.[15] Without telling Mountbatten, he sent his aides, Generals Ferris and Boatner, to Washington to make his case against Axiom.[16] He wanted to argue for a strengthened land campaign in North Burma as against the SEAC plan based on sea invasions that he knew that Mountbatten's Chief of Staff, US General Wedemeyer, would be taking to London and Washington later in March. Mountbatten was furious when he found out. The fact of differences between the two men had been aired publicly in *Time* magazine of 14 February 1944.[17] This was a serious leak of material from a highly confidential staff meeting and, despite efforts to do so, the perpetrator was never discovered.[18] This was probably because, as in an Agatha Christie murder novel, it would have been difficult to narrow down the large number of potential suspects. John Paton Davies, Anglophobic political attaché to Stilwell, later admitted that he was partly responsible for feeding information to the press, but also said that plenty of correspondents and commentators already knew about the division between the British and Americans over the strategy in South East Asia.[19]

In many ways, Stilwell saw himself acting defensively because of what he regarded as deliberate efforts by the British to accentuate their own role in the Burma campaign and to play down the contribution of the Americans and Chinese.[20] Differences between the two allies could usually be resolved when Stilwell and Mountbatten talked face to face, and there is clear evidence of an improvement in press relations after they met on 6 March 1944 at Stilwell's headquarters at Taihpa Ga in the Hukawng valley. Stilwell had been told by General Marshall to meet with Mountbatten and establish a working accord after the Washington setback.[21] There is no record of any truce between the British and Americans about fair coverage of each ally's role in the campaign, but one can see a marked increase of US reporting of British activities across different fronts in Burma from the 23 March edition of the US forces paper *CBI Roundup* onwards.[22] On the same day, *SEAC* newspaper carried a three-column article by Philip Wynter (Australian Consolidated Press) on the 'Ledo Road – China's Supply Route'. Both Stilwell and Mountbatten had said that they did not want to interfere in the forces' newspapers, but obviously the editors knew what would please their respective generals. It may also be that with Wingate's Operation Thursday starting, British forward action in areas in support of Stilwell's operations were now obvious and needed proper recognition in the American paper.²³ In any case, by the time that the new forces magazine *Phoenix* was brought out in 1945, Mountbatten made it very clear that it was to be a joint Anglo-American enterprise. Stilwell had agreed and provided much-needed journalists to help run it.²⁴ Mountbatten attempted to do the same with the joint film project *Burma Victory*.²⁵

However, a major issue arose over the sending of official communiqués. Stilwell had been used to sending his communiqués through either Delhi or Chungking for approval and forwarding. Mountbatten was keen, however, to move away from separate communiqués being issued by different armed forces or different army commands and wanted one consolidated SEAC communiqué.²⁶ Stilwell agreed in principle, but he was dismayed when he realized that often the SEAC communiqué was not using the full version of his NCAC sector one. The Americans were, therefore, pleased to have held on to the right to send material from their sector direct to China. They argued that this was to ensure an accurate version went out rather than the unreliable Nationalist Chinese one. In addition, they could issue a supplementary press note which could be released from SEAC headquarters and Chungking at the same time. This allowed American correspondents to forward this uncensored material from Chungking to the USA and to Britain. According to Eldridge, in practice the American press note reached Chungking before it was sent to SEAC for release. Added to this, the faster radio connections from Chungking meant that the American version, effectively an expanded version of the communiqué, was the first to reach the outside world.²⁷

It was disappointing that just at the point when British and American forces in Burma were reaching a higher degree of military cooperation in March 1944, serious differences over the roles of their respective public relations organizations should have arisen once more.²⁸ Considering that he had been pressing from some direct aggression by the British against Japanese forces, Stilwell was actually ambivalent about the second Chindit LRP, Operation Thursday. This was despite the fact that Thursday was intended to divert the Japanese from Stilwell's drive through North Burma. Stilwell admired Wingate personally but felt that his military theories were flawed. Commando-style operations were recognized as valuable as a form of getting behind enemy lines, cutting communications and harrying them. However, in Stilwell's view they were a diversion of men and resources from the main thrust of infantry warfare. They could only be useful if they acted in support of the infantry. Stilwell's PROs were full of praise for Colonel Philip Cochran's American Air Commandos who carried out the highly dangerous glider landings in the jungle that started the operation on 5 March. American engineers followed the initial landings.²⁹ The British decision not to name Wingate in the first communiqué on the operation was wrongly seen by the Americans as showing a typical British Army upper-class disdain for Wingate. Much worse though was what they regarded as Philip Joubert's attempt to appropriate to the British the glory for thinking up the campaign and putting it into operation. The first SEAC communiqué told of 'air-borne troops of the <u>Fourteenth Army</u>' [author's emphasis] having made the landing. The American Air Force PROs quickly put out press notes countering that it was USAAF (United States Army Air Forces) commanding General Henry 'Hap' Arnold who thought up the ambitious idea of delivering the Chindits behind enemy lines by plane rather than by land.³⁰

Myitkyina

The problem was that Mountbatten had not approved of Stilwell's ambition to capture Myitkyina before the monsoon broke in May 1944. The aim was a good one because capturing Myitkyina airport would substantially reduce the length of flight over the Himalayas to China. It would also facilitate the drive to complete the connection to the Burma Road. However, Mountbatten had argued that lines of communication were overstretched, and it would not be possible to capture and hold Myitkyina in time before the monsoon set in. However, this was the policy of rapid advance in North Burma which had been approved by both British and American Chiefs of Staff. Stilwell was now acting almost as an independent commander, and he had the necessary Chinese troops which he had trained, and now also his own US LRP group, Merrill's Marauders. Technically, Stilwell reported to General Slim, one of the few British generals he admired,[31] and Slim knew and effectively approved of the rapid advance on Myitkyina. Mountbatten's staff should have known what Stilwell was doing as he posted regular messages on his advance but when Myitkyina airport was captured on 17 May it caught Mountbatten by surprise and, apparently, he was first told of it by a perplexed and angry Churchill. Stilwell, not surprisingly, gloated at this triumph over his 'Limey' critics and made the most of the publicity opportunities by bringing correspondents with him the next day to mark the capture.[32] Unfortunately, taking the airport was only part of the operation, and the Japanese put up fierce and effective resistance that meant it would be several weeks before the town was finally captured.[33]

Philip Joubert briefed correspondents the day after the capture of Myitkyina and played down any expectation that this would lead to any spectacular advance south through Burma. While paying tribute to Stilwell's remarkable success, he also congratulated the Chindits, now under General Lentaigne, for creating 'a situation which has enabled General Stilwell to take full advantage of the position'. He went further and stated that British resistance at Imphal had so tied down Japanese troops that 'except for some detachments from eastern Burma, the original 18th Japanese Division in North Burma has not, as far as we know, received reinforcements'.[34] Matters got worse from the American point of view when on 22 May Mountbatten wrote an Order of the Day aimed at congratulating Stilwell and his troops but balancing this with praise of the Chindit contribution under Lentaigne. It finished: 'Please convey my personal congratulations and thanks to all ranks, including General Lentaigne's forces who are now under your command and who have been severing Japanese communications between Myitkyina and the south'.[35] Even Mountbatten's generous praise did not assuage Stilwell's resentment at the way the British played down the role of his troops and boosted that of their own. Stilwell took the view that the Chindits had failed to provide the required blocks that would stop Japanese reinforcements reaching Myitkyina.[36]

Stilwell continued his complaints against the Chindits over the two and a half months of what General Slim later described as the 'untidy, uninspired, ill-directed siege' of Myitkyina.[37] Stilwell focused his complaints at Chindit withdrawals from their Blackpool 'block' and from Mogaung, south-west of Myitkyina, which they had previously managed to capture at great cost. The truth was that Stilwell was demanding the Chindits perform a conventional combat role against the Japanese which they did not have the armaments or preparations for. The Chindit brigades were operating in the monsoon when it was well past the point in time when they should have been withdrawn and were losing men rapidly to disease and poor diet, let alone combat casualties. Mountbatten, on the other hand, wanted the Chindit role in the battle for Mogaung given publicity in order to show how the Chindits had played an important role in tying down Japanese troops which would otherwise have been used at Myitkyina.[38] Stilwell's callous attitude towards the withdrawal of the four remaining Chindit brigades forced Mountbatten to intervene on their behalf and instruct that the crack 36th Indian Division, which Stilwell, for reasons best known to himself, had refused to use up until then, be sent to Myitkyina to relieve the Chindits.[39]

It was not only the Chindits who had been overtaxed and used beyond their original purpose. Brigadier General Merrill's American troops were also utterly exhausted and severely reduced by injury and disease, certainly no longer marauding by the time they reached Myitkyina, having lost their leader to a heart attack shortly after Myitkyina airport had been captured. Stilwell treated them callously, even recalling some from hospital to serve at Myitkyina. On 6 August 1944, the *New York Times* ran an article on the breakdown in morale among the Marauders. This was based on information released by Stilwell's headquarters following an official inquiry ordered by Stilwell himself. It had been claimed that, at the end of May when the situation in Myitkyina was critical, several hundred of the men had been recalled for duty there when they were physically unfit. The report was careful not to blame medical or combat leaders but rather talked of a misunderstanding of Stilwell's orders that all possible able-bodied men be thrown into action.[40] Troop morale was already badly affected by the initial promises they had been given when they volunteered that this would be for one big operation after which they would be sent home. Merrill himself played down the incident as 'a storm in a teacup'.[41] However, it nearly led to a major fallout between the British and American public relations organizations. According to Eldridge, his counterpart Philip Joubert requested him to prepare an official text acknowledging the fact that the Marauders 'had had their troubles but had won their battles'.[42] This infuriated Eldridge who met with Joubert on 24 August and threatened to brief war correspondents on the secret troubles of the Chindits if the Marauders' press note was published. Eldridge wrote a memorandum of this meeting for Stilwell which recorded Joubert's agreement not 'to re-wash dirty linen'. Joubert went further and said that 'he had always considered that Merrill's forces were the only ones used properly in this campaign and that the Chindits were worthless from a military point of view'. He admitted that the Chindits had been overplayed in publicity terms but that was now ended. He explained the publicity had been the result of orders from the prime minister who was 'strategically sound but tactically always wrong. He has made some frightful blunders.' Joubert blamed many of the differences with the Americans on publicity issues because Mountbatten kept him in the dark.[43] If Eldridge's verbatim record is correct, then these were extraordinary things for Joubert to say and suggested a lack of loyalty to Mountbatten and his prime minister. There is no evidence that Joubert received direct communications from Churchill.

The circumstances around the capture of Myitkyina airport and the subsequent battle for the town marked a low point in the relations between Stilwell and

Mountbatten. It was clear by this time that Mountbatten wanted to completely reform the confused command structure that he had inherited, and that this meant pressing for Stilwell's role to be confined to commanding Chinese forces. It could not have helped that when Stilwell took over temporarily as Supreme Commander at Kandy, while Mountbatten was away in London at the end July 1944 through to 24 August, he seemed to deliberately make a mockery of the role. Refusing the trappings of office that Mountbatten clearly valued – the limousine, spacious office, impeccable dress and long meetings with staff – Stilwell lampooned the Supremo's lavish pretensions.

When Stilwell was finally recalled from Burma in October 1944, he must have believed that Mountbatten played some part in his downfall, and he left only a very sparse farewell message for his chief. However, he would have been wrong. Mountbatten and the British Chiefs of Staff had at various times wanted Stilwell recalled but came to the conclusion that it would be inadvisable for there to be any suspicion of Mountbatten playing any role in this. The American press regarded Stilwell as a national hero and would react strongly.[44] In fact, it was Chiang Kai-shek's demand for Stilwell's recall that was decisive this time, and probably resulted from Stilwell's inability to recognize the grave danger Chiang's regime was in as a result of the Japanese *Ichigo* offensive in 1944, which threatened to drive southwards through Chinese territory to link up with Japanese-controlled Indochina. Stilwell refused to give Chiang the transfer of troops from the Burma front that he wanted. In diplomatic terms, Stilwell was, as he always had been, something of a liability in terms of relations with his allies. With Stilwell gone, the division of the China-Burma-India (CBI) theatre into two separate areas with Major General Wedemeyer appointed Chief of Staff to the Chinese forces made a lot of sense, and Mountbatten had been calling for it for some time. The Burma-India section was now under Lieutenant-General Daniel Sultan. The conquest of central and southern Burma would be considered predominantly a task for the British, thus avoiding American entanglement with colonial reconquest.

The American press was clearly unprepared for Stilwell's recall, especially as he had only very recently been promoted to be a four-star general. As usual, the *New York Times* military correspondent Hanson Baldwin made the most informed comments but admitted that it was guesswork as to why Stilwell had been recalled and that the story could only be told by historians.[45] Within days the story would become much clearer. Before Stilwell left Chungking, he had confided in two journalists, Theodore White and Brooks Atkinson, so that his version would be kept for the historical record. Atkinson was able to smuggle his story out of Chungking and managed to get it to the *New York Times* within days, ahead of Stilwell's own return.[46] The Defence Department wanted to avoid publication of stories, at least while President Roosevelt was in the middle of his re-election campaign. However, Roosevelt approved publication on the grounds that Atkinson's story was substantially true, and it appeared on *The Times* front page on 31 October. It caused a sensation and opened the floodgates to other stories which were highly critical of Chiang and the Kuomintang, which Atkinson described as 'an unenlightened cold-hearted autocratic political regime … unrepresentative of the Chinese people who are good allies'.[47] One of the most devastating indictments came from the normally placid AP correspondent, Thoburn Wiant, who wrote: 'Democracy does not exist in China. There probably is no more effective dictatorship than that of the Kuomintang. There is no freedom of speech, or of press, or of much of anything else ... For years China has been on the verge of falling apart.' He blamed Chinese censorship, but also American hopes that reforms could be achieved for keeping the American public misinformed about China and its heroic struggle against Japan.[48]

Whatever the new willingness of the American press to reveal the truth about the Chinese regime and its role in the war, the fundamental fact remained that America needed to keep China in the war against Japan. However, mainland China was no longer thought of as a key launching pad for the final push to defeat Japan: this was now going to take place in the Pacific through island-hopping and bombing raids on Japanese cities. The land conquest of central and southern Burma was to be primarily a British concern, with crucial American air support.

Conclusion

Anglo-American relations were always going to play a key role in the India-Burma campaigns. The Allies had very different war aims in this theatre, and the balance of power in the Asia area shifted over time in favour of the United States. Britain was trying desperately to restore its territory and prestige in South East Asia and the Far East. America, on the other hand, had very different priorities based on defeating the Japanese in the Pacific, with Burma just a possible stepping stone towards this objective. The differences were highlighted in their respective attitudes to China. The Americans believed that it was vital to keep China in the war with Japan and used Lend-Lease supplies and Stilwell's military role as a pledge of its serious commitment to this end. President Roosevelt envisaged Chiang Kai-shek's China as a key player in the post-war Pacific, ensuring security and prosperity for American interests in the region. The British viewed this with scepticism, partly because they did not believe China could live up to this billing and partly because they feared American hegemony in the larger Pacific area, stretching south to their Commonwealth allies, Australia and New Zealand. In reality, however, Britain could do little to stop the growth of American dominance in the region. Although Churchill was sceptical of China's significance, he recognized how important the country was in American global strategy and that he would have to go along with their North Burma and China priorities if, as a quid pro quo, he was to hold on to the British Mediterranean strategy against American and Soviet pressure for a faster and more direct opening of a second front in France.

These high-level considerations inevitably were reflected in the differences across the Atlantic in reporting of the Burma War. This was exacerbated by General Stilwell's baleful Anglophobia which increased rivalries in reporting the war. Fortunately, the differences only surfaced in potentially damaging ways on a few occasions, notably after *Life*'s revelations in February 1944 and during the long siege of Myitkyina in the summer of the same year. Mountbatten was always aware of how much his position depended upon American support and he did everything to ensure that it was maintained. It would be wrong, however, to exaggerate the importance of these incidents in the overall picture of the war. Neither the British nor the American publics were focused on the war in Burma for any length of time nor were knowledgeable about it. Stilwell's recall improved Anglo-American relations greatly, while American focus shifted away from the Stilwell/Chennault emphasis on a land/air campaign based in China and supplied from India and Burma. When Germany's defeat seemed inevitable after the Normandy invasions, British attention also shifted to trying to ensure that, before Japan was forced to surrender, they regained some of their South East Asian empire and also that they had had some participation in the Pacific naval engagements. This was what they needed if they were to be taken seriously in the peace negotiations. This made it all the more important that they conducted a publicity campaign in the United States to emphasize the key role that they had played in India-Burma in defeating Japan. This is further discussed in Chapter 10.

8

Reporting the War, 1944

In October 1943 Mountbatten appointed General Slim as commander of the new 14th Army and, although every effort was made to play down any large-scale campaign in Burma during the dry season, there was obviously an expectation that steps would be taken to reverse the failings and humiliations of the previous campaigns. It was vital to restore the confidence of the troops in taking on the Japanese in jungle conditions. The amphibious operations planned at the Quebec Conference had to be postponed indefinitely because the landing ships were needed for Italy and northern France. The main Allied emphasis now was on building a road from Ledo in Assam across to the key airfield at Myitkyina in order to improve the supply routes to China. The military part of this task was assigned to General Stilwell and the Chinese troops that he had trained so assiduously in India. They would also have an American long-range penetration (LRP) group attached to them as a land force for the first time, and it was hoped that the Chinese would contribute by attacking northern Burma from Yunnan in south-west China. Wingate's much enlarged second LRP group would be flown deep behind Japanese lines so that they could harry the communications supporting their position at Myitkyina. These operations would be supported by achieving air superiority, allowing the Allies to supply their key troops over long distances. In addition, there was to be a return to the offensive in Arakan. The aims of commanding the mouth of the Naaf river for supply by sea and securing the vital Maungdaw–Buthidaung road were less ambitious than in 1943 but expected to be more attainable.

The problem was that Allied offensive plans came up against even more ambitious Japanese plans to 'March to Delhi' through crossing the Chindwin and reaching the Imphal plain and possibly Dimapur in Assam where the supply routes between Calcutta and Ledo could be cut. This would completely undermine the Allies' North Burma campaign. The irony was that the Japanese assault was probably encouraged by what they had seen of the Chindits' operation in 1943. If British troops could cross this hostile jungle and steeply mountainous terrain, then surely they could. To divert the enemy, the Japanese planned an advance into Arakan aimed at completely encircling the British forces there, and pulling in reinforcements from Assam.

1944 was therefore likely to be a decisive year in the Burma campaign. The fighting in the first half of the year took place at the same time in three completely separate areas: at the Hukawng and Mogaung valleys leading to Myitkyina, at Arakan and at

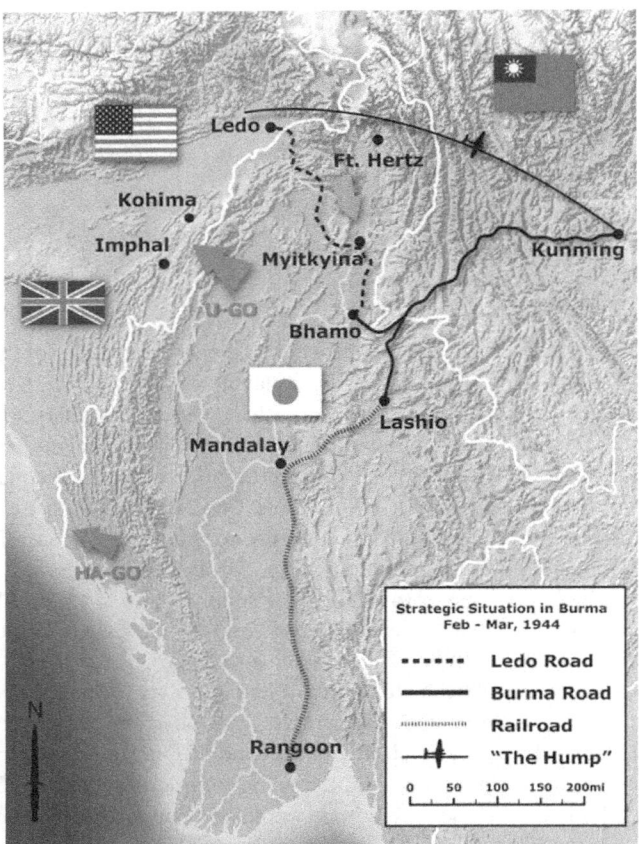

Map 8.1 'The Fall Campaign', in Troy Sacquety, 'A Special Force Model: OSS Detachment 101 in the Myitkyina Campaign, Part 1', *Veritas*, 4, no. 1 (2008), p. 36.

Imphal/Kohima in Manipur state and Assam. This meant there were problems for media coverage. Correspondents had been few on the ground in the second half of 1943 as Burma seemed likely to be a largely static backwater in comparison with the major campaigns taking place in Europe and in the Pacific. Mountbatten was determined that SEAC forces, particularly the 14th Army, should receive much fuller publicity in order to raise troop morale and make the case for more resources. However, it was now established SEAC media policy to play down offensive operations until they had proved to be successful. This was the clear lesson from the successful coverage of the first Wingate expedition, Operation Longcloth. Just as in that operation, there needed to be strict secrecy in the early stages of a second operation, not just for obvious security reasons, but so that expectations were not raised unduly. Then, when success was achieved, it was important to have good material ready for the press. This would include the normal stories of military heroics, but also personalized stories around individual soldiers' accounts, with their names, home town and regiments, too, if possible. It was important to build up the achievements of the 14th Army and its generals. Personal portraits of the generals could be used, alongside other officers and divisions if they could be linked to good stories. The paucity of correspondents covering the Burma War in 1943 needed to be addressed by improving facilities for their movement between fronts and for faster censorship and transmission of their dispatches. Meanwhile, military observers, RAF/AFPU photographers could be used to provide additional material, especially stories that might be attractive to local newspapers in Britain.

1. Arakan – the Admin Box

Because the Arakan campaign of the first half of 1943 had been such a humiliating failure, it was determined that the same mistakes would not be made again there in 1944. Emphasis was placed on improvements in a number of different areas, including training, medical support, troop morale and logistics.[1] Under General Slim, now commanding the 14th Army, there were changes in tactics and in the senior officers who would implement them. Slim was fully supported by Mountbatten as Supreme Commander in the new policy requiring soldiers to stand firm and not retreat when the Japanese tried to encircle them. In order to achieve this, the army needed to coordinate very closely with the RAF and USAAF so that defensive 'boxes' could be supplied by air. In December 1943, Mountbatten persuaded the Americans to place their aircraft under SEAC overall control. This would be crucial during the defence of India in 1944.

Because of the lack of landing craft, no amphibious operation was possible until Germany had been defeated, and this meant that taking the war to the Japanese would mean returning to the very difficult land campaign through North Burma. Plans were drawn up for an offensive in Arakan for the New Year. The aim was to attack the heavy defensive lines protecting the tunnels on the Maungdaw–Buthidaung Road and then move south on either side of the Mayu river to take Indin and Rathedaung. There was certainly an air of déjà vu about these objectives, but this time the troops were better trained, and the objectives were more realistic. Unfortunately, it turned out that the Japanese were planning their own offensive in Arakan, known as *Ha-Go*. This was part of a larger, more ambitious Japanese offensive aimed at crossing the Chindwin and reaching up to the Imphal plain. Thence, the main Allied supply lines could be cut linking Assam to Calcutta. This was a highly ambitious plan which would stretch Japanese lines of communication to the limit. The Japanese had the added incentive that Subhas Chandra Bose's Indian National Army (INA) could be used to support the attack and rouse support from Indian nationalists.

The Japanese plan in Arakan was to drive a wedge between British forces east and west of the Mayu range and to encircle and isolate them. Beginning on 4 February, the Japanese were remarkably successful in their objectives and reached Taung Bazaar, well behind British lines, by the next day. On 6 February, they attacked 7th Division HQ, forcing the commander, Major-General Messervy, to flee in his pyjamas.[2] The 7th Division had to regroup in an administrative area which became known as 'the Admin.

Box', where they were joined by other reinforcements. It was about three-quarters of a mile square and was mostly a flat area of disused paddy fields with two small hills in the centre. This was a large area to defend, especially as the Japanese controlled some of the hills overlooking it. It was not only the army that was caught by surprise, so were the few correspondents covering the Arakan campaign. Only Stanley Wills of the *Daily Herald* seems to have reached the actual fighting at the Ngakyedauk ('Okeydoke') Pass.[3] Stuart Emeny of the *News Chronicle* reported from Army HQ, as did Ian Fitchett of the *Daily Express*. None of them was allowed to write a full report on what had happened in the fortnight of the ruthless fighting that took place at the Box until 28 February when the battle had been won.

Early reports were optimistic, as they had been in the previous year. Maungdaw was captured without resistance. Wills reported the fact that tanks were being used in Arakan for the first time. In fact, they played a major role in the ultimate success in the battle of the Box.[4] He also reported the introduction of West African troops in the Kaladan valley to the east, unfortunately using every racial stereotype available, assuming, quite wrongly, that they were all jungle natives.[5] It was not until the middle of February that reports painted a more worrying picture of setbacks in the campaign, although the papers consistently underestimated the size of the main Japanese thrust as consisting of 2,000 men, whereas, in truth, it was nearer 7,000. Stuart Emeny reported that the Japanese had overrun the divisional HQ and driven into the administrative area, capturing a hospital which was treating the wounded.[6] The Japanese assault on 7 February, which resulted in the killing of doctors, orderlies and patients, marked a peak in stories of enemy atrocities which figured at times throughout the reporting of the campaign.[7]

When the papers were eventually able to reflect on the ultimate victory at the 'Admin Box', they realized that the achievement of air superiority by the British and Americans had played a key role in this the first major victory over the Japanese in Burma.

> This feat is of the greatest military importance and indicates the shape of things to come in jungle warfare. It not only means that we can provide supplies for relatively small penetration groups without ground lines of communication but that we are now in a position to supply whole divisions in roadless jungles, which neutralises the ability the Japanese have so far enjoyed of being able to travel faster and lighter than our troops in jungle country.[8]

Ian Fitchett's report in the *Express* on the same day was given front-page headlines and it also focused on the role of the RAF and USAAF. Pilots were named as were some of the wounded soldiers airlifted from the Box. Participating regiments were named, though Fitchett concluded: 'The battle was a triumph for General Slim's Fourteenth Army, whose name unfamiliar until now, you will soon be hearing often.'[9]

Philip Joubert was delighted to report to Mountbatten that the SEAC PR machine had worked smoothly and come through its first test in battle successfully. Correspondents had been provided with everything they needed and newspapers in Britain and America had given prominence to this major victory.[10] The army's success in Arakan, which included the capture of key Japanese defensive positions, was vitally important and a turning point in the war. However, the Americans saw it, somewhat unfairly, as a defensive success, and this they compared unfavourably with Stilwell's offensive taking place in the Hukawng valley.[11] Perhaps General Wingate's Chindits could provide the offensive success that the British badly needed.

2. Wingate 2, 'Operation Thursday'

The second Wingate LRP operation, named 'Thursday' began on 5 February 1944, almost simultaneously with the height of the Arakan battle. It started conventionally with a very long march of Brigadier Bernard Fergusson's 16th Brigade from Assam into Burma. It would take nearly three weeks for it to cross the Chindwin river. It was at this point that the newly arrived BBC reporter John Nixon flew in with General Wingate to meet the troops. He wrote his dispatch on 2 March, but it was not broadcast until 16 March and, in line with policy, did not mention either Wingate or the Chindits.[12] Nixon was taken with the arduous journey the soldiers had made and their reliance on air support for all their needs:

> During the march, oranges, onions, potatoes, tinned fruit, rum and beer were dropped by air. The men also received magazines by air, and they were able to send mail home. This was put in a container slung between two bamboo poles and was hooked up by an aircraft. One man received a pair of spectacles because earlier on the march he'd broken his original pair … back at base details are kept of all spectacles and false teeth worn by members of the force so that if they lose or break them, a substitute pair or set can be sent with the next aircraft. Spare boots, already broken in, are also kept in readiness for dropping.

This detailed planning typified Operation Thursday. It was a much bigger venture than Wingate's previous one and, crucially, it was very much a joint operation with the USAAF. In fact, the main thrust of the initial advance deep into Japanese-held territory was not to be by land but by air. This involved a series of highly dangerous glider landings in clearings in the jungle deep inside Japanese-held territory which started on 5 March. These were followed by the carving out of an airfield on which Dakota C-47 aircraft could land and bring in Chindit troops. So dangerous was the initial fly-in considered that no journalists would agree to accompany it.[13] Instead Mountbatten arranged for two PR military observers to go in with the first gliders.[14] One, the British Major Dunn, was killed in the fly-in, but the other, US Lieutenant Colonel James W. Bellah, survived and wrote a colourful but realistic seven-page report on the fly-in. He played up the Anglo-American cooperation involved in the venture and pulled no punches about the loss of lives involved as gliders took their chances landing at speed in the dark, trying desperately to avoid trees and other craft which blocked the clearing:

> Two more [gliders] are howling down over the trees, roaring toward the congestion. One of the two sees it in time, zooms over it with the last of its speed and plows in safely just beyond. But the other crashes head on and welds two gliders into a ball

of scrap. Screams tear the night and the wrecker crew claws into the wreckage with bare hands to get at the injured. A British surgeon is already inside doing something under a flashlight, something quite frightful with his kukris after his morphine has stilled the screaming. And there is a quiet North Country voice in there. 'Don't move me – this is where I hit – and this is where I die.' And somebody's damned good sergeant goes out on the tide. You don't have heroes in armies any more. You just have men.[15]

By 10 March, 9,000 men and 1,100 animals had been flown into jungle strongholds. These would be made into a defensive position into which aircraft could land men and materials, and from which columns of Chindits could disperse to harry Japanese lines of communication. It was not intended that the Chindits should fight conventional-style battles with the Japanese as they had no heavy artillery. Other strongholds were soon established: a temporary one named Chowringhee, one named White City at Mawlu, and one named Aberdeen, north of the target town of Indaw.

Graham Stanford of the *Daily Mail* did fly into the Broadway stronghold on 12 March, but correspondents were still not allowed to report that this was another Chindit operation led by General Wingate. Hints were dropped but it was not until 27 March that the full story could be told.[16] GHQ India had released a communiqué on 16 March which just said that operations behind the Japanese lines had been carried out 'by troops of the 14th Army and Air Forces stationed in Assam'. The Americans were not at all pleased that no mention was made of the crucial role played by Cochran's No. 1 Air Commando and US engineers.[17] General Wingate was furious that there was no mention of his name nor that of the Chindits, the 3rd Indian Division as they were called for this operation. He fired off a highly intemperate telegram of complaint to Joubert which led to an unusually robust response from Mountbatten who pointed out that 'you have achieved such amazing success in getting yourself disliked by people who are only too ready to be on your side'.[18] There were good military reasons to keep the nature of the special force assault secret, and this did follow the now established public relations policy of waiting until operations were considered successful until there was a properly orchestrated publicity drive. Wingate did have many critics, especially in Indian Army HQ, and Wingate's paranoid response may not have been entirely without foundation. In any case, Wingate was killed in a plane crash on 24 March, just days before the operation was scheduled to be trumpeted. Along with Wingate, two excellent correspondents were killed in the crash, Stuart Emeny (*News Chronicle*) and Stanley Wills (*Daily Herald*).

With Wingate gone, it seems that Operation Thursday lost some of its thrust and purpose. General Lentaigne who took command did not share all Wingate's convictions about the way that LRP should be used. Military historians disagree about the strategic value of the operation but there is no doubting the heroism and remarkable endurance of the Special Force troops. They did successfully establish 'strongholds' deep in enemy territory, harassed the Japanese when they were focused on their attack on India, and cut railway and other communication lines leading north to Myitkyina. This is where this operation differed from the first Wingate expedition of 1943. It was designed as part of broader operations, particularly in support of Chinese/American advances on

Myitkyina. SEAC publicity concentrated assiduously on making this point. It had to answer Stilwell's criticisms that only his troops were doing the aggressive fighting. This was obviously unfair, and it marked a real division between the British and American public relations teams.[19] This rift became very serious when Chindit forces came under General Stilwell's command on 17 May 1944. Stilwell insisted that the Chindits move out of their strongholds and take up positions where they would come into direct confrontation with Japanese forces trying to maintain their lines of communication to besieged forces at Myitkyina. This was a task for which the Chindits were not suited, and protests from Lentaigne and Calvert led to direct confrontations with Stilwell which Mountbatten had to fly in to try and mediate. The Chindits were being used inappropriately when they were utterly exhausted and reaching the planned limit of ninety days on their operation. It was not just the Chindits who suffered in this way. Stilwell was ruthless also in his use of the US commandos, 'Merill's Marauders', when they, too, were utterly exhausted and carried too many wounded and debilitated men.

3. Imphal and Kohima

The Japanese attack in Arakan in February, was actually a feint to a much larger attack, codenamed *U-Go*, across the Chindwin, aimed at the Imphal plain in Manipur state, north-east India. The aim was to capture the key positions of Imphal, an important Allied base, and Kohima, which was a much smaller hospital and supply base at a high point on the road to the most important base at Dimapur. Dimapur was the railhead of the Bengal–Assam railway which supplied the fighting fronts. This was the real Japanese 'March to Delhi', which, if successful, could break all Allied lines of communication for their campaign in North Burma.

On 17 March, Japanese columns crossed the Chindwin and made rapid progress northwards. Within five days they had crossed the border of India and were threatening Imphal and Kohima. On 18 March, Graham Stanford of the *Daily Mail* filed a report, having been a distance away in a Chindit stronghold: 'I have just reached the Burma border to find that a big battle has broken out behind our backs – a large force of Japanese has crossed the River Chindwin and has launched a major offensive in the Chin Hills sector towards India.' His report did not get published until four days later, indicating the potential delays in reporting this war.[20]

At this stage, Stanford hardly knew which front he should be reporting from: Arakan, Wingate 2 or Imphal/Kohima. He had to constantly move between them. On 3 April 1944, the *Daily Herald* gave front-page news to a report that the Japanese had cut the road running north from Imphal to Dimapur at the hill station of Kohima. The anxiety that this report indicated did not seem to be shared in London or New Delhi. General Auchinleck as Commander-in-Chief of the Indian Army told the Indian Assembly that he was 'convinced that the security of Assam had never been in danger, let alone the security of India'. On 8 April, the Indian government made the rather baffling statement that 'other than attacking the key towns and gaining full possession of the roads, the Japanese effort can now be of little else than nuisance value'.[21] The Indian press, however, reflected deep concerns that the truth was not being told. It was not just the Indian public who were kept in the dark, even the British Cabinet was given misleadingly optimistic information.[22] 'As for the British public,' Fergal Keane argues, 'the extreme peril of the Kohima garrison and the scale of the Japanese threat were unknown.' However, he says, 'This was not in any way exceptional or suspicious. It simply reflected the nature of wartime communications and censorship, and the peripheral nature of Burma to the overall scheme of the war.'[23] Although there is some truth in Keane's argument, it lets the army's media censorship off the hook rather too easily. Failure to allow reporting of the gravity of the situation at Kohima risked repeating the mistakes in the reporting of the losses of Singapore and Rangoon. Over-optimistic information about a military situation could only lead to public mistrust of the media if it turned out to be misleading or plain wrong. On 13 April, the censorship of a report on the threatened defence of Kohima filed by five correspondents had led to an unprecedented strike by them which forced Mountbatten to intervene and promise a liberalization of censorship and improvement in reporting facilities for correspondents in SEAC.[24]

Kohima was an extremely difficult location for newspaper correspondents to report from as it was so isolated, 5,000 feet up in the Naga hills, and surrounded by Japanese troops. Military observers had the advantage of attachment to army units and were able to send reports and interview casualties and soldiers who had been relieved and had been brought to Dimapur. Fergal Keane tells how the observers 'were directed not to any of the Indian regiments but to the West Kents' for the publicity opportunity about heroic individuals and regiments. However, it was not permitted to name the regiments for security reasons, which caused resentment among the soldiers. It was not until 13 June that *SEAC* newspaper named the West Kents, a regiment which played a key role in the defence of Kohima. Other regiments had to wait longer.'[25]

Richard Sharp sent dispatches from Kohima for the BBC, and Fergal Keane tells of how the troops were able to have the broadcasts relayed to them. In one, which was not broadcast until 17 May, Sharp told of walking across the Deputy Commissioner's devastated and body-strewn tennis court, shortly after it had been secured.[26] Graham Stanford was able to interview Charles Pawsey, the heroic Deputy Commissioner, on 28 April outside of Kohima after the garrison had been relieved.[27] Later, on 2 June 1944, he wrote up a full story on Pawsey and the Nagas. Both articles revelled in colonial-era stereotypes, both of the Sanders of the River-style colonial administrator, and of his childlike, potentially savage but loyal wards, the Naga headhunters.[28] The article did at least explain the geography of the area to readers and also the strategic importance of the Kohima ridges that had been so viciously fought over.

Mountbatten also asked for the defensive heroics at Kohima to be mentioned in *SEAC* newspaper.[29] The problem for gaining wider publicity was that it coincided with the build-up to D-Day in Europe and therefore struggled to get the attention in Britain that it deserved. There was still a lot of fighting to do as the Japanese continued fighting hard during their abandonment of their positions at Kohima on 22 June. Lieutenant-General Carton de Wiart warned Mountbatten, shortly after Kohima was relieved, that over-optimistic press communiqués were misleading in giving the impression that the fighting around Imphal-Kohima was more or less over: 'If there is a setback now, it will seem far worse than if the situation had been represented more accurately.'[30] Fortunately the optimism proved well founded, although very high casualties were suffered in the process, and on 5 July the Imphal operation was declared ended.

The important thing now was to have the fullest publicity for the achievements of British and Indian troops in Burma. There was a determination to make the 14th Army's name and successes as well known as the 8th Army's deeds in North Africa and Italy. One way was to have profiles of its commander General Slim placed in the British press. Mountbatten regretted that he had not done enough to publicize Slim, but the War Office public relations section insisted that they had already been working on this and feature articles, such as that by Victor Thompson in the *Daily Herald* of 14 August 1944, showed that their work was showing fruits already.[31] Reports in August showed army morale was high and there was appreciation of the recognition given by the British press and by Churchill to the 14th Army.[32] Philip Joubert and Frank Owen went to London in November 1944 and worked on giving more publicity to the 14th Army. One result was a four-page article, 'The Hell of Burma', in *Picture Post* on 25 November which paid a moving tribute to British and Indian troops in Burma. It listed its achievements:

> Together with Indians, there are 750,000 troops on the biggest single front facing the Japanese in the whole Pacific war (250,000 are British) ... They have knocked out more Japanese than any other force. And they are tired of being 'The Forgotten Army' ... The Burma Army has killed 100,000 Japanese and kept India free ... They are away for years. They can, in the nature of things, get little or no leave. They are badly off for entertainment, books and magazines to read, and mail from home. All this they accept ... But they don't see why, on top of everything else, their exploits should be so little recognised.

The problem, said the magazine, was that people in Britain, while they could visualize war in Europe, had no real concept of Burma and jungle warfare. A series of photographs was included to help readers understand the appalling conditions that the soldiers fought in.[33]

4. Indian war correspondents report the 1944 campaigns

Indian war correspondents came late to being accredited to report the Burma War but played an important and distinctive role in the 1944 campaigns. Their geographical proximity to the SEAC area meant that they could stay longer in Burma as they were less likely to be moved when editors believed that other theatres were more active or required more attention. In addition, they could pay more attention to the role of Indian troops in combat. Two reporters, D. F. Karaka and D. R. Mankekar, left memoirs which give a good picture of their roles in Burma.

Dosabhai Framji Karaka, a Parsi, had been president of the Oxford Union before returning to Bombay in 1938 and taking up work as a journalist with the *Bombay Chronicle*. He had already published a number of books based on his experiences as an Indian in Britain.[34] He was posted as a war correspondent to China to cover the war with Japan, and in 1944 was moved to report on the war in Burma. In his book *With the Fourteenth Army*, Karaka presents himself as a very green war correspondent who struggles with all the acronyms of the various army organizations he had to deal with.³⁵ However, he soon established himself as a very effective journalist who was prepared to challenge the official army line and the censorship system that backed it up. He was pleasantly surprised after his experience in Chungking that SEAC gave him more information than he expected and that its censorship was limited to security issues. In his view, it was Indian Army censorship that held up material on 'policy' grounds, though this may well have been SEAC censors passing the buck.³⁶ It is not surprising that Karaka had problems with censorship as he had developed his own views on military strategy and liked to second-guess future military objectives. As an example, he was not at all impressed with the Wingate/Cochran fly-in in March 1944, believing that it had to be a deliberate diversion of attention from a forthcoming major Japanese offensive. He turned out to be correct about the Japanese offensive but wrong in believing that no serious British offensive action could be undertaken during the monsoon.³⁷ When he was reporting from 14th Army HQ on the defence of Imphal and learnt that the Japanese had actually crossed the Indian border, he was advised to 'play it down' because it would not pass Indian censorship. Karaka was furious that he was not allowed to report what he regarded as a scoop. Worst of all, rival reporters – in this case D. R. Mankekar (Reuters/API) and Richard Sharp (BBC), sitting comfortably in Calcutta – would be able to beat him to the story.³⁸ In fact, Mankekar had also had the same experience of being stopped from reporting this story but had gone to Calcutta to persuade the censor to let a modified version through. He was successful and was widely congratulated for his scoop. The poor censor was demoted, however.³⁹

Nothing annoyed war correspondents more than feeling that unfair advantage had been given to rivals. In order to at least show that he had his own version of the story from the front, Karaka was forced to resort to a form of complex subterfuge that would keep the censor happy but indicate to the intelligent reader that the Japanese had crossed the Indian border. The key was to inch forward in your dispatch from what had been previously approved information and to match any account of a Japanese threat with soothing words that implied the threat was well under control.⁴⁰ In the end, though, he found so many of his messages being stopped that he decided to leave the Imphal/Kohima area for Calcutta, hoping for another assignment.⁴¹

Mankekar stayed on and took a more phlegmatic view of SEAC censorship and PR support. He saw the initial phase of censorship at Imphal/Kohima as being comparable to the earlier jittery phases of the war in South East Asia. As at Singapore, the use of the world 'siege' was initially forbidden. Once Mountbatten had made his peace with the striking correspondents, the censorship settled down and Mankekar admitted that he found the censors sometimes useful in correcting errors in his despatches.⁴² However, he continued to find reporting on Kohima difficult because, as far as he was concerned, Kohima had actually been lost to the Japanese as they held three-quarters of the area, including the town. British and Indian troops were confined to the ridge overlooking the road. Correspondents, in his view, were forced later to tell of the recapture of a town which they were supposed never to have lost.⁴³

For correspondents, Burma was a difficult theatre to report on. There was no front as such, but three or four areas where campaigns were taking place. Even in these areas there were rarely set-piece battles but rather constant skirmishing. Mankekar described it thus:

> A modern war is more heard than seen ... Modern war and particularly the war against the Japanese in Burma was essentially a war of manoeuvre, and long-range artillery and aircraft played a major part in it. The infantry came into the picture only at the final stage of an operation, to clinch the issue. And then it often turned out to be a fierce hand-to-hand battle, in which a reporter rubber-necking would be getting in everybody's way and would be wise to keep out. He should be content to remain, if he must, at the battalion headquarters at the nearest – situated not more than a few hundred yards from enemy positions but well sheltered – collecting his 'dope' as latest reports of the progress of the operation flashed in. Now and then he snatches glimpses of the fighting from various points of sheltered vantage-point like a foxhole, bunker and trench and absorbs 'local colour' for his story.[44]

These were difficult conflicts for correspondents to keep up with. Furthermore, it was difficult to transmit dispatches quickly. Mankekar complained that Stilwell's HQ provided journalists in the field with a mobile wireless radio transmitter.[45] In the British areas, no such facility existed so correspondents had to fly dispatches to 14th Army HQ at Comilla, or to Calcutta where Allied Land Forces HQ was based. In these cases, journalists had to trust to luck that their dispatches were transmitted quickly and not delayed by censorship, or that rival dispatches had not been given priority. It was very difficult to fly to and from where the fighting was taking place. Mankekar said that he often waited days for a suitable plane, and in Arakan it very often was a very small one, the L-5 Sentinel, which was designed to pick up individual wounded soldiers only. Space was at a premium even in the large planes.[46] As a result of these difficulties, correspondents often preferred to stay at base and rely on army communiqués for information, which could be transmitted with some additional colourful material relatively quickly. Mankekar, as a Reuters/API reporter, felt obliged to continue in forward areas, even when colleagues left the theatre in the monsoon period when fighting was expected to be much lighter. He had his reward with what he regarded as a scoop when he was able to report the relief of the siege of Imphal in June 1944.[47]

Although they were rivals as reporters, Mankekar shared with Karaka a pride in the role of the Indian soldiers who formed the largest part of the Allied forces fighting in Burma. They wanted to ensure that they received fair coverage in the newspapers. Mankekar was the first correspondent to reach and report on the 7th Indian Division under Major-General Messervy as they moved in the Naga hills to cut off the Japanese retreat from Imphal/Kohima to the Chindwin. He says that he was very much welcomed by the Division which felt its important role had been neglected:

> Hitherto, apart from an occasional brief mention in the daily communiqué, the Division had received little publicity in the Press, even though it was engaged on a

vital assignment of delivering a left-hook at the jaw of the enemy as he retreated down the Manipur Road under the pressure of the British 2nd Division. The latter operated on a fine tarmac road, easily accessible to the correspondents, and got all the publicity and credit for the Allied progress on the front, while few had heard of the gallant and pivotal contribution made by the 7th Indian Division.[48]

Mankekar also made great efforts to report on the 51st Indian Infantry Brigade, the only all-Indian brigade at Kangaw in Arakan. It was so-called because for the first time all three battalions in the brigade were Indian and were also commanded by Indians.[49] Mankekar said that he found the soldiers 'keen as mustard, and their personal devotion to their commanding officers was inspiring, belying the British officers' claims that Indian officers could never command the loyalty of the sepoys the Britishers did!'[50] This pride in the role of the Indian troops was also reflected in the work of an Indian Army Observer, P. R. S. Mani, whose dispatches and radio scripts have recently come to light.[51] Indian newspapers often had to rely on officer observer reports to fill in war news about Indian forces' contributions when Indian newspaper correspondents were thin on the ground.

5. Stilwell advances to Myitkyina

The introduction of American troops trained in long-range penetration (LRP) techniques, 'Merrill's Marauders' as they were known in the media, into the Burma War marked the first use of American forces in a land campaign on the Asian continent. There was therefore a growing interest in reporting their involvement at first hand. The 5307 Composite Unit (Provisional), to give the Marauders their official title, would fight alongside Stilwell's Chinese troops in a drive to reach the key town and airfield at Myitkyina in northern Burma. This would shorten the flying time for US transport to China considerably and begin the process of reopening the Burma Road, with an oil line to China also. Stilwell aimed to reach Myitkyina before the monsoon broke by advancing down the Hukawng valley. Mountbatten doubted that this was possible in the time available, but General Slim supported Stilwell's ambitious plan. The Marauders started down the valley in the last week of February 1944. There were only three battalions of Marauders, but they would be the ones assigned to actually reach Myitkyina airport first, having marched 100 miles in twenty-five days, over an extremely arduous mountain route.[52]

A large number of correspondents accompanied General Stilwell through the Mogaung valley and/or at Myitkyina airport.[53] Some of the best reports came from *Life* magazine which had photographers William Vandivert and Bernard Hoffman covering the Stilwell advance.[54] Stilwell had a very effective public relations set-up headed by Fred Eldridge. Eldridge claimed in his memoir *Wrath in Burma* that Stilwell spoke to journalists on 24 February but initially kept the involvement of the Marauders secret.[55] The secrecy was broken on 6 March when it was announced that while Chinese troops had taken Maingkwan, the American troops had captured Walawbum, 10 miles to the south-east.[56]

1. T/Sgt. Dave Richardson (Yank Magazine), 2. Capt. Clancy Topp, 3. T/Sgt. Warren Bechlen, 4. Sgt. David Quaid, 5. Cpl. William Safran, 6. Pvt. Joseph Razkowski, 7. Pvt. Daniel Novak, 8. Tillman Durdin (N.Y. Times). Myitkyina Airstrip, May 19, 1944. Photo by B. Hoffman

Figure 8.1 'Seven Men, one a correspondent, hug the ground after a sniper's bullet pings by', adapted from *Life* magazine, Myitkyina airfield, 26 June 1944, p. 90. Note the typewriter, essential equipment wherever. Private collection.

One of the American correspondents who had been in Burma longest was Thoburn Wiant of the AP. He had arrived in India in December 1942 and had reported from Arakan in the first months of 1943. Wiant had gained a reputation as 'Good Luck Wiant' for his remarkably incident-free reporting record while on countless bombing sorties with the USAAF operating from India and China.[57] In January 1944 he returned to reporting land battles when he joined Stilwell's drive in the Hukawng valley. He was impressed with the Chinese troops but even more so with General Stilwell, whom he praised for his accessibility to journalists.[58] However, it proved slow in these inaccessible areas to get his stories back to New York. They had to go back by whatever means of transport was available to rear HQ at Ledo, then get sent to Delhi by army radio, then take twelve hours to go through censorship, and another twelve hours to reach New York. 'It would take from 24 to 36 hours for our stories to get through, while the PRO report and official communiqué would invariably beat us by 12 to 14 hours.'[59] Wiant spent three months in the jungle, culminating in reporting the Marauders' capture of Myitkyina airport on 17 May. This would not be an exclusive, however, as he counted as many as fourteen other British and American reporters brought in by air from Stilwell's HQ to report the triumph.[60]

It was much quicker to send reports from SEAC HQ in Kandy, where advanced communication equipment allowed reports to reach the States between one and a half to four hours maximum. The irony was, therefore, that the AP staffer in Kandy probably got the Myitkyina airport capture story to New York several hours in advance of the reporters on the spot.⁶¹ At least Wiant was able to persuade Stilwell to drop a word limit on reports sent via army radio from Myitkyina.⁶²

Stilwell's reputation had reached a high point but declined rapidly with his troops as well as with correspondents as the siege of Myitkyina town dragged on for weeks. Stilwell's conduct of the campaign and treatment of the Marauders and the Chindits under his command came under criticism. Myitkyina did not fall until 3 August. One week later the Marauders were disbanded. The force had been reduced to only 130 combat-effective men, out of the original 2,997. On 19 October Stilwell was recalled from his command. This triggered an outpouring of US press criticism of the Chiang Kai-shek regime which was thought to be responsible for Stilwell's demise. Wiant, who had always wanted journalists to be allowed to tell the truth in their reporting, wrote one of the most excoriating critiques of the Chinese regime, datelined 31 October 1944, from London. He had been perhaps the most moderate and restrained of reporters on the China-Burma-India (CBI) War but now, angered by Stilwell's treatment, it all came out. Chiang's regime, he said, was corrupt and dictatorial, and was conserving its resources to fight the Communists. Wiant told how reporters had been stopped by Chinese censorship and US wishful thinking from writing the truth about China.⁶³

Conclusion

1944 had been the pivotal year in the Second World War. On all fronts, the Axis powers were now inexorably in retreat. In Burma, the battle of the 'Admin Box' in Arakan had shown that better training and tactics of 'no retreat' backed by air supply was the way forward. Stilwell had stolen the limelight in May by an audacious move to capture Myitkyina airport. His public relations team taunted the British that all the offensive activity in Burma was being carried out by Stilwell's command. The British countered with publicity of the remarkable fly-in of the second Chindit operation and argued that the Chindits played an important role in supporting Stilwell's drive to capture Myitkyina town. It took time for the brilliant and heroic British defences at Imphal and Kohima to turn into – still quite long drawn-out – offensives to drive the Japanese back across the Chindwin. In the process, the 14th Army had proved itself to be a more effective fighting force than the Japanese, and that it was capable of fighting through the monsoon and through appalling terrain. Churchill and the Chiefs of Staff, however, still remained dubious about the efficacy of continuing a land campaign through Burma. It would be up to Slim, supported by Mountbatten, to take the initiative in 1945 and prove them wrong.

9

Broadcasting: BBC, All India Radio and Radio SEAC

The Government of India (GoI) had shown itself remarkably reluctant before the war to engage with using newer forms of media such as cinema and radio for propaganda purposes.[1] Cinema was seen as an expensive medium which was best left to private enterprise. However, radio had the advantage of the successful model of the BBC to show how government could establish a financially viable system while keeping at arm's length from operational concerns. Radio seemed to offer great opportunities to reach India's large, highly dispersed, predominantly illiterate and diverse population in a way that traditional print media could not. There had been plans put forward in the past for the use of radio in rural development and education.[2] However, there were severe practical, political and financial difficulties that stood in the way. During the interwar years, financial retrenchment had been the order of the day and the costs of setting up radio transmitters and staffing just seemed too expensive and risky. Licence fee payers would inevitably be concentrated among the European and Indian urban elites, and it would be very difficult to reach the millions of rural Indians, who were seen as the key audience for army recruitment, political propaganda or agricultural improvement, for instance. There were long debates about the best system for organizing the broadcasting system in India. Enthusiasts, such as Sir John Reith and John Coatman, argued the case for the model of a centralized system based on the public corporation which the BBC had moved to in 1927. The GoI decided, however, to rely on private enterprise to establish the initial radio provision, a decision that backfired when the company chosen failed financially. In 1935 a centralized All India Radio (AIR) was finally established with a BBC protégé, Lionel Fielden, serving as Controller of Broadcasting.

In addition to the practical problems, there were, as Partha Sarathi Gupta argues, doctrinaire prejudices among the Indian civil servants against the idea of investing public money in pioneering industries.[3] The result was that the system was run on a very tight budget and staff were not even placed on permanent contracts until 1940. There was also a fear that radio could come under the control of Indian ministers within the reformed Indian political system. Worse than that was the possibility that nationalist politicians could use the airwaves to project their own political messages. There was, therefore, a negative, defensive attitude towards the development of broadcasting. Politics were to be kept out of broadcasting and this was even applied to

Figure 9.1 Lionel Fielden (front row, second from right) surrounded by AIR station managers. Ahmed Bokhari is on Fielden's right; Zulfaqar Bokhari is on his left. GoI, *Report on the Progress of Broadcasting in India (up to the 31st March 1939)* (Simla, 1939), IOR/V/27/970/2.

the 1937 Indian provincial assembly elections. All of this was greatly frustrating for Fielden, who, as Joselyn Zivin has shown, was temperamentally totally unsuited to dealing with the bureaucrats of the Home and Industries Departments. He did not respect the official and social hierarchies, and socialized with Indian nationalist leaders like Jawaharlal Nehru. While the officials had a defensive and restrictive view of broadcasting, Fielden's vision was creative, expansive, and convinced of the unifying and educative powers of radio.[4]

Fielden left India in 1939 due to illness, and in 1940 his contract was not renewed. He took with him Zulfiqar Ali Bokhari, who took up a role as Programme Organizer in the BBC's Indian Service. When Fielden came to write of his time in India he expressed disillusionment with his lack of achievement, calling AIR 'the biggest flop of all time'.[5] Zivin reckons that Fielden was unfair to himself and his achievements: 'Though broadcasting audiences remained limited through the 1940s, post-colonial Indian radio would not have taken off without Fielden's groundwork. Under his leadership, AIR successfully established more than a dozen new stations and substantially overcame numerous technical, bureaucratic and social obstacles.'[6] Even so, at the beginning of the Second World War, radio provided very limited opportunities to reach beyond the Indian urban educated classes. These were the very people likely to be most critical of any British propaganda. Indeed, it became pretty clear that they were more likely to listen to German and Japanese broadcasts in the early stages of the war. From 1942 onwards the broadcasts on Azad Hind Radio by Subhas Chandra Bose and Ras Behari Bose on behalf of the Indian National Army (INA) were very popular with their message that India was soon to be liberated from colonial rule by the defeat of the British. As Yasmin Khan argues: 'Ultimately, the INA lost their military battles but they won the propaganda war.'[7]

The early stages of the war with Japan, in which the British suffered major setbacks with the loss of Malaya and Burma by May 1942, presented real problems for radio propaganda in India and Burma. It is indicative of the government's limited ambitions that in September 1941, when the India Office asked the GoI whether it would be beneficial for AIR to rebroadcast BBC Hindustani news bulletins, the reply was in the negative. The regular audience for these bulletins was estimated at 20–30,000 out of a maximum possible audience of 60–70,000, and this was thought to be satisfactory. It was argued that AIR rebroadcasts would not add much to this number and, in any case, AIR would find it difficult to fit an extra half-hour into its programme, which would end up too much weighted towards war content.[8]

Could the BBC improve its provision? Laurence Brander, Eastern Intelligence Officer at the BBC, was sent out to India in March 1942 to report on listener feedback in India. He was appointed to set up a skeleton audience intelligence operation. He stayed until October and was in India at just about the worst time militarily and politically for the British in India and Burma. After the crushing army defeat in Burma and the loss of airbases there, the Japanese now threatened Indian cities such as Madras and Calcutta which housed broadcasting stations.

In this situation, Brander focused on improving BBC programmes for the troops. In this he was responding to the request of Brigadier Jehu, head of PR at Army HQ: 'Light music, music-hall, variety, sentimentality and vulgarity suggested. Mingle entertainment with brief and never patronising references to their good work and fighting spirit. In fact, be with them.'[9] Jehu's advice was in line with criticisms in Britain that the BBC needed to lighten its Reithian seriousness if it were to reach wider wartime audiences. From 17 May, the BBC added a daily evening hour of light entertainment with forces' requests included. Brander next pushed for the BBC to provide a messaging service for both troops and civilians, which he said would 'put the BBC on the map'.[10] Brander's feedback raised the much broader issue of what the BBC should concentrate on in its limited broadcasting opportunities in India. The pressure from troops and civilians was for more entertainment, but this could not be allowed to take away from the news remit. Brander reported the views of the Governor of Madras, Arthur Hope, which made an implied criticism of current BBC news provision. These were the points Hope emphasized:

> First, stop attempting to balance grave news with trivial successes
>
> Second, stop padding out the news
>
> Third, tell the truth as much and as quickly as possible. No use softening the blows. Indians in Madras at any rate can take it. Suspense of suspecting bad news coming worse than hearing bad news. Indians very intelligent and never taken in. We must get back to our reputation for telling truth
>
> Fourth. Do not be sarcastic about our enemies. Makes us look stupid as if we did not realise the hidings we have taken.[11]

These points actually also amounted to very pertinent criticisms of general British media reporting of the retreat from Burma in the first half of 1942.[12]

Brander wrote his report on 3 November 1942 on his return from India.[13] The report was fuller on Brander's view of the Indian political situation than of the broadcasting situation in India. He had been in India during the worst months for Britain in the war, and in India there was the failure of the Cripps Mission and the resulting Quit India movement and arrest of Congress leaders. He reported that, as a consequence, British prestige which was already low was now lower still: '[T]he bitterness against us had intensified ... That Congress now has the sympathy of the people, there can be no doubt.' Leo Amery, the Secretary State for India, was none too impressed with Brander's views on Indian politics but admitted: '[I]t may be that so far as the "listening" public (which I assume is the urban intelligentsia) is concerned, it has some foundation in fact.'[14] He saw more value in Brander's views on broadcasting, although they were somewhat contradictory. He reported the widespread availability of enemy broadcasts, and the use they made of open (beam radio) transmission of American correspondents' critical dispatches home. He recommended jamming these broadcasts if possible. On the other hand, he praised the BBC and AIR provision of news and said that the 9.30 p.m. BBC news bulletin was listened to 'with great respect' throughout British India and the Indian States. He argued that AIR needed a great deal of financial help to allow it to put on the best programmes. Brander repeated to George Orwell 'that the Indians listen to the BBC news, because they regard it as more truthful than that given out by Tokyo or Berlin. He considers that we should broadcast news and music and nothing else.'[15] Orwell then revealed that he was actually responsible for writing the news broadcasts.[16]

In fact, Orwell and his colleagues in the BBC in London had been doing much more than just providing news commentaries and broadcasts to India and Burma. Much of what they did could be described as cultural propaganda aimed at the educated elites. They formed the Eastern Services section of the BBC's Empire Service, which in turn was answerable to the Ministry of Information (MoI). The director was

L. F. Rushbrook Williams, a distinguished civil servant and scholar of India who had been brought over from the ministry. There was, therefore, a strong connection with MoI propaganda aims, although an image of BBC independence was to be projected to the public. It was during the Second World War that the BBC really established itself as a public service broadcaster with a global reputation for impartiality and integrity in its news broadcasting. As Edward Stourton and others have pointed out, this was not inevitable at the start of the war, when even its own domestic audience was critical of its output and suspected it was a mouthpiece for government news bulletins and exhortations.[17] Certainly, before the war the BBC had tended to follow establishment views on issues such as empire and appeasement of the dictators.[18] The BBC took time during the war to establish its reputation of independence of government control and to hold to a policy of telling the truth in its news reporting. Obviously, in a patriotic war with the fascist dictatorships the national broadcaster was not going to be a truly impartial news provider, but even so, most of the public at the time did not realize how close the BBC was to the government. Chandrika Kaul says that '[d]uring the war, officials instructed the BBC on the imperial interpretations of political and military developments', but she concludes that 'the BBC often successfully resisted official demands' and retained its 'independence of spirit' and 'relative freedom of maneuver'.[19] The line between truthful and accurate reporting of news and outright propaganda could be a very thin one, easily crossed. The general public may not have realized either that BBC broadcasts were subject to censorship. W. J. West has described this censorship as 'more thorough than that imposed on any other media ... Not a single talk could be broadcast that had not been censored twice, once for security and once for policy.'[20]

BBC broadcasts from London to Burma/India were mostly in English but also in local languages on a more limited basis. The English broadcasts were aimed at both home and colonial audiences, but also, over time, at the large number of troops serving in India and Burma. West has described an aim of the broadcasts to establish a 'university of the air' for Indian students, 'coupled with weekly news broadcasts that enabled educated Indians generally to follow the progress of the war around the world'.[21] Certainly, the speakers employed were of a very high quality and included key literary and cultural figures from both India and the United Kingdom, such as Mulk Raj Anand, Prem Chand, Herbert Read, T. S. Eliot, Stephen Spender, Nevill Coghill, Edwin Muir and E. M. Forster. The talks could be quite critical of British imperial policies. Perhaps the most recognized contributor was Orwell himself. He was employed in the Eastern Services from late 1941 until September 1943 when he resigned to take up editorial and literary work.[22] Orwell, who had served in the Burmese police during the 1920s, was one of a number of left-wing contributors to the BBC who saw their work as their means of contributing to the defeat of fascism. He was only too aware that, although he insisted on only broadcasting the truth, he was, in effect, doing the work of a propagandist.[23] Clearly, the BBC worked closely with government departments. Fleay and Saunders point out that Orwell attended meetings of the Eastern Services Committee which met fortnightly and included representatives from the India Office and Foreign Office (FO), alongside the BBC and MoI. One function of the committee was stated as enabling the coordination of the BBC resources with policy guidance from the government.[24]

Orwell's Burmese expertise sometimes came in useful, most notably when it was clear in May 1942 that the Japanese had driven the British and Chinese forces out of Burma. This was a humiliating defeat which army propagandists and the governor of Burma in India tried to explain away. The BBC's analysis of Burmese opinion was not very profound, if Rushbrook Williams's memo, 'Notes on why some Burmese are helping Japs to Fight us', is anything to go by. It is full of stereotypes of the Burmese character, noting that the Burmese were 'not very industrious' and were prone to violence. 'Thus,' it concluded, 'many Burmese find the Japanese a refreshing break in the monotony of ordered government, and readily join up with the invaders.'[25] Orwell, however, knew the questions which really needed answering. Under his real name, Eric Blair, he forwarded eleven very apposite questions for the Government of Burma, then in exile in India. He wanted to find out what the response of people in Burma was to the Japanese invasion, and how they might be reached by the BBC. Had ministers and civil servants remained loyal? Were there divisions between the Burmese ethnic majority and the tribal minorities in their loyalties? What was the strength of the nationalist Thakin party and support for their army, and what links did the party have with outside organizations? How many people in Burma possessed short-wave receivers? This information was needed for any form of propaganda exercise to be targeted effectively, but it was difficult to obtain clear answers in the post-retreat situation.[26] Orwell's questions were forwarded, along with those of Bokhari, who had been seconded from All India Radio (AIR) as an adviser to the BBC and who was particularly interested in the fate of Indians who had been residing in Burma. The BBC asked what line the Government of Burma would like the broadcaster to take.[27] Dorman-Smith, the governor of Burma, replied that he would like the BBC:

> 1. To express sympathy with those loyal to Burma who temporarily have to suffer from the occupation of a barbarous people and assure them that we will not forget them. If some comfort could be given to Govt. servants left behind about their salaries, pensions, Provident Funds etc. it would be all to the good.
>
> 2. Dispel any idea that we will come back to 'Reconquer' the Burmese people ... We will come back as friends to assist Burma to refashion her life and once more to take her place in the comity of nations.[28]

The BBC indicated it was ready to comply with the governor's requests. However, as Dorman-Smith had pointed out, there were not likely to be many radio receiver sets working in Burma at this stage. Anyway, in December 1942 the Japanese announced severe penalties for anyone in Burma listening to any other than Rangoon Radio. In terms of broadcasts to Burma, the BBC were completely outgunned by the stronger and more effective efforts of their Japanese and German rivals.

The BBC sends war correspondents to Burma

Although the BBC set up a small office in Delhi in the summer of 1942, this was mostly to conduct listener research. It was impossible to provide their own correspondents on the spot and it had to rely on news agencies for the first two years of the war. It was more successful during 1944 and 1945 as it was able to send correspondents and engineers to north-east India and Burma, and to broadcast, often directly, from the battles taking place there. The BBC had been slow to establish a cohort of war correspondents working independently even in Europe, let alone further east. At the beginning of the war, it possessed only two roving reporting units. The reasons were partly historical, partly political, and partly practical. Before the war, the BBC had been limited in how much news it could broadcast, and at what time of day, because of fear of competition felt by the newspaper proprietors. Even at the highest level of government there was scepticism about the role that the BBC could and should play in the war. During the war, the BBC came under the auspices of the MoI, which initially prioritized print media over radio broadcasting in terms of independent news reporting. In any case, the ministry was still reliant on the armed forces' departments which determined what could and could not be reported on security grounds. Live radio reporting was seen as more immediate and therefore more difficult to control. In practical terms, the problems were that radio recording equipment was very cumbersome and difficult to use in live combat situations. The BBC reporter needed to be accompanied by a recording engineer and a transmission engineer, and a vehicle was needed to move the staff and equipment. Live recording proved successful in the Blitz of 1940–1, but until 1943 there were only limited opportunities for BBC reporters, like Wynford Vaughan-Thomas or Richard Dimbleby, to report live from combat situations. When Dimbleby did report live from the North Africa campaign in 1942, he was faced with numerous restrictions and was withdrawn after getting caught up in the conflict over tactics between the commander General Auchinleck and Prime Minister Winston Churchill.[29] By 1943, however, the BBC had proved itself in live reporting from bomber raids over Berlin and from successfully covering a major military exercise – a six-day 'raid' on Oxford, Operation Spartan. It built up a cohort of well-trained, professional reporters and engineers – War Reporting Units, as they were called. The BBC had also acquired a reputation for accurate reporting and a worldwide reach thanks to improvements in its broadcasting equipment and training. Even so, broadcasting from India and Burma was still highly problematic.

The movement of equipment was extremely difficult and there were doubts whether it would stand up to the monsoon conditions that prevailed for several months of the year. The arrival of BBC correspondents coincided with Mountbatten's drive to achieve better recognition in Britain of the Burma campaign. On appointment as Supreme Commander, Mountbatten had asked the BBC for more coverage of the SEAC theatre.[30] Throughout, he remained very supportive of the BBC's reporting and was careful not to alienate the Corporation. In London, A. P. Ryan, the BBC's Controller of News, who was appointed by the MoI to oversee the BBC's Overseas programmes, was kept informed through regular meetings of up-to-date war news and the spin that the government would like to put on this. These background, off-the-record briefings show the close connections between the MoI, FO and the BBC.[31] Ryan was well informed about the India-Burma campaign because he had spent the cold-weather months of 1943 to 1944 liaising with officials in India, Burma and Ceylon and visiting the troops. He reported that General Auchinleck had told him that his visits had had a good effect, '[b]ecause the troops feel forgotten and appreciate a BBC man sent out from home to describe what they are doing'.[32] One of Ryan's recommendations had been that the BBC should appoint a director in New Delhi and, accordingly, Donald Stephenson was appointed in February 1944. Stephenson built better relations with AIR, which resulted in more BBC programmes being relayed in India.[33]

When Mountbatten came to London in August 1944, he had a private meeting with Ryan in which he said that he had seen the BBC correspondents working in SEAC first-hand and praised their work. He gave important guidance on future strategy and Ryan recorded that he let slip his negative view of Stilwell's northern Burma strategy of reaching China with land forces:

> As regards the Stillwell [sic] end, Mountbatten said, in answer to my question as to whether he thought there was any chance of going through to Canton, 'Oh Stillwell thinks there is, and we let him go bumbling along.' In fact, more supplies will be got to China, but Mountbatten does not expect to be able to carry on any substantial military operations against the Japs from that side.[34]

The first BBC correspondent to arrive was Richard Sharp, who reported from Arakan front at the end of January into March 1944.[35] His dispatches were recorded on discs – the machine was called a 'telediphone' – which were then transmitted to London and were read by a BBC announcer. Sharp was present with the 7th Indian Division at the famous battle of the 'Admin Box', which is sometimes seen as a turning point in the Burma campaign as the Japanese were successfully repelled by troops who stood their ground and were supplied by air.[36] The Japanese attack in the Arakan was part of a two-pronged campaign. The other assault was directed at advancing into Manipur and Assam in north-west India and cutting Allied communication lines for reconnecting to the Burma Road to China. Sharp reported from the heroic defence of Kohima in a memorable dispatch from the district commissioner's famous tennis court, which had been the centre of vicious fighting.[37]

Another BBC reporter, John Nixon, was one of the few correspondents to join the 2nd Wingate 'Chindit' long-range penetration (LRP) operation in February 1944 and was with Bernard Fergusson's 16th Brigade at the crossing of the Chindwin in late February/early March. It seems likely that Nixon flew in with General Wingate in a light aircraft. He later reported on the setting up of 'strongholds' towards Lake Indaw in late March/April. Sharp was joined at Kohima by the sound recordist, Eugene 'Jerry' Girot, who had arrived in India in April 1944.[38] Girot, a Glaswegian, wrote home regularly to his mother and to his fiancée Sheila who was a Wren at Kandy, SEAC HQ in Ceylon. Fortunately, his family donated these letters to the BBC Archive at Caversham, and they give a wonderful impression of Girot's work and leisure activities during 1944 and 1945. At Kohima in May 1944, he had his first taste of war. He told his mother on 13 June about his recording of Kohima battles, and also a rather gruesome recording he made of a Japanese soldier committing suicide: 'We actually saw him doing it. We thought he was aiming a hand-grenade at us, but he suddenly held it to his chest ... it went off, and he dropped dead about 50 yards in front of the [recording] truck ... I took a picture of him, and I hope it comes out all right.'[39] In June, Girot

Figure 9.2 Richard Sharp reporting for the BBC from Burma, crossing the river Irrawaddy, February 1945, courtesy of Timothy Sharp.

reached SEAC HQ Kandy where he was eventually assigned to set up a recording studio. This gave him the opportunity to meet and record Mountbatten, the Supreme Allied Commander. 'He was very nice indeed to us, and seems to take a good view of the BBC's efforts.'[40] In August he and Nixon took part in a naval raid on Sabang, Sumatra. Shortly afterwards, Nixon was recalled to Cairo.

The main action for the BBC correspondents in SEAC was the 14th Army's advance on Mandalay. Sharp and Girot were joined by Douglas Cleverdon, who had been sent out at the request of SEAC PR in London, to make a full-length feature programme on the Burma campaign.[41] Richard Sharp sent a dispatch entitled 'Outside Mandalay' on 12 March. By chance, the BBC were among the first into Fort Dufferin when it fell on 20 March. Girot wrote excitedly of the BBC's truck entering Mandalay:

> ... and who was waiting behind us, to raise the Union Jack on the flagstaff, but the General [Rees] himself! Three jeeps had got in before us ... And he shouted out; 'Who the hell is holding up the show?' He just grinned when he was told it was the BBC truck! Eventually we got in ... the first truck to get into the Fort! We drove on, and recorded the General raising his flag ... and the Union Jack. Then we interviewed some Anglo-Burmese who had been in Mandalay all during the occupation. They were pleased to see the British back again ... and they told us so ...[42]

Figure 9.3 Major-General T. W. ('Pete') Rees, GOC 19 Indian Division, directing the battle for Mandalay, 9 March 1945, IWM (SE 3257).

The BBC was also first to report the capture of Mandalay and to broadcast a pre-recorded message announcing this by Mountbatten. They had apparently jumped the gun by broadcasting one hour earlier (21.30 IST) than the official communiqué which they should have waited for. This annoyed the Indian newspapers and the agencies they relied on. Joubert said it was not the first time the BBC had done this, which suggests a sense of lively, competitive journalism by the national broadcaster. It has been suggested that Mountbatten was unhappy that he had not been present for the 'triumphal entry' into Mandalay and had requested that there be an official ceremony with himself and representatives of the forces.[43] However, this was turned down by his new Commander-in-Chief Oliver Leese and by General Slim on the grounds that '[t]he decisive battle is in its opening stages. Heavy fighting is in progress and the thoughts and eyes of all troops must be forward to battle and not resting on a historic success which however is incidental in the main battle.'[44] Mountbatten did visit Mandalay two days later. Girot's letters suggest something rather less than awe for the aristocratic Supreme Commander. 'We've just been told that the Lord and Master has torn himself away from his Island Fortress ... the Green Hell of Kandy ... and is coming to tell the boys how good they are this afternoon. The BBC is just not interested ... anyway we're not allowed to use his stuff.'[45] Girot commented wryly on Mountbatten's soapbox talks to the troops, but seemed to be won over when Mountbatten decided to take tea with the press corps in their hut rather than in the officers' mess.[46]

Girot tells of the problems for the sound recordist in Burma: the delays in equipment arriving, the dust getting into equipment, the blackout at night stopping the writing up of transcripts, the sound of aircraft overhead droning out recordings, etc. However, it was rewarding when recordings had gone well, as in Mandalay, and when they were told by London that most of the recordings had been used. Sometimes, they could actually listen to their recordings being broadcast from London, too, and as Girot said, '[I]t makes you realise you're not wasting your time.'[47]

The BBC missed out on the actual recapture of Rangoon: Girot was stuck with the army in Meiktila, unable to move his recording equipment in monsoon conditions. At the end of May, Richard Sharp returned to England for some well-deserved home leave but returned in time for the Japanese surrender ceremony in Singapore on 12 September. The day after Japan surrendered, he sent a dispatch to the BBC which reflected on how the troops felt about the victory. He looked back on the events that most stuck in his mind over the twenty months he had been reporting from the BBC. They covered the incredible difficulty of attacking Japanese bunkers in the Arakan; the noise the jackals made at night and everyone wondering whether they were really Japanese imitating the animals; the West African troops advancing down the Kaladan valley; the fierce fighting at Imphal and Kohima and the stench at the tennis court at Kohima when it was relieved; and the exhausted Chindits at Mogaung.[48]

Radio SEAC

Along with a forces' newspaper, Mountbatten had also asked on his appointment that a SEAC radio station be set up to broadcast to British and American troops. This was more difficult to implement than the newspaper and Mountbatten had to rely on American broadcasts and, as a temporary measure, a joint forces programme set up by SEAC and India Command in Delhi.[49] Charles Eade, who had been brought out from London, where he was Editor of the *Sunday Dispatch*, was charged with setting up the new radio as Public Relations Adviser to Mountbatten. Eade chaired an Inter-Services Radio Committee with representatives including the MoI and its American equivalent, the Office of War Information. The development of SEAC Radio met a number of requirements. The first was welfare of the troops, who clearly needed more entertainment and news, which according to Eade were just as likely to be provided at the time by Japanese broadcasts.[50] Secondly, there was a need to establish better two-way contact between the forces and home audiences so that the 'Forgotten Army' syndrome was countered and troop morale boosted. Thirdly, effective radio provision could counteract German and Japanese radio propaganda and could potentially be used in political warfare to relay propaganda to the enemy. In February 1944, Radio SEAC began broadcasting to the 14th Army. It was only for an hour in the evening but

Mountbatten, who had a chance to sample the station in March 1944 while recuperating from an eye injury, wrote that it was 'really excellent and tremendously popular and a much-needed innovation'. Significantly, Mountbatten described it as the 'Anglo-American All Forces' broadcast. He was emphasizing that it was a joint Allied enterprise and so was distinct from the BBC and American forces transmissions.[51]

Serious criticisms in Britain of amenities for troops in the Far East led Churchill to have Lord Munster, Under-Secretary of State for India and Burma, go out and investigate in October 1944. One of the complaints was about the lack of radio receivers and suitable transmitters. A recommendation resulting from Munster's visit was that a powerful 100kW short-wave transmitter should be made available for SEAC along with a smaller 7.5kW transmitter. The intention was 'to ensure reception by "British and Colonial" troops in South-East Asia of news and entertainment programmes where it has been found the BBC is not generally receivable. It will largely act as relay station for Home and General Forces BBC programme.'[52] The War Office agreed to fund what was to be a very expensive operation but there were still questions to be settled, particularly between SEAC and India Command.[53] These were about the target audience, the location of the transmitters – whether in Delhi or Ceylon – and the name of the radio station. On all these issues, India had effectively to concede to Mountbatten's will. Ceylon inevitably won out over Delhi for good broadcasting reasons, despite the fact that this would mean moving many of the Delhi staff to help make up the establishment at Colombo.[54] Ronald Adam, the Adjutant General, wrote: 'SACSEA has stated his personal wish to provide a broadcasting service for the forces under the command SEAC over which he can exercise direct control through his HQ and make personal broadcasts.'[55] It seems that Mountbatten saw an opportunity to use Radio SEAC to enlarge on his policy of talking to the troops, and perhaps to bypass Churchill's ban on his broadcasting through the BBC. Both he and Auchinleck were briefed to broadcast messages on the opening of the new station. Auchinleck was worried that broadcasts directed specifically at Indian troops would lose out as Mountbatten insisted that the new service was for British troops whether they served under SEAC or in India Command. Whatever the name of the station, it would largely be relaying BBC broadcasts with some local additions.[56]

Unlike the forces' newspaper and magazine, the radio initiative was not as successful as hoped. The larger transmitter was sunk by Japanese torpedoes off Ceylon and did not go on air until May 1946. Although the smaller transmitter seemed to be successfully received in Burma and northern India, there was still a severe shortage of receiver sets. Even so, although the American use of atomic bombs brought the war in the Far East to an earlier conclusion than expected, there was a continued and expanded role for SEAC troops to play in post-war South East Asia. Radio SEAC helped relieve some of the frustrations of troops who found their tours of duty extended and it became a valuable asset for the independent government of Ceylon.

Conclusion

Radio proved a difficult medium to use to reach large numbers of citizens of both India and Burma. As P. S. Gupta has argued, All India Radio (AIR) suffered from a lack of funding and departmental caution. There were only a limited number of radio receivers in private hands. In India there were only 92,782 at the end of 1939.[57] This may have increased up to twofold during the war but still remained a fraction of the 380-million population.[58] In Burma, the number of radios surviving the Japanese occupation must have been very limited and, in any case, their use to receive Allied broadcasts was strictly forbidden. Those who owned radios in India, mostly the urban middle classes, were the least likely target for army recruitment and the most likely to be sympathetic to the nationalist cause. There is evidence that, at least for a time, they were more likely to listen to Axis broadcasts, including those of Subhas Chandra Bose, which were considered more attractive in message and presentation. The lack of high-powered transmitters and the inability to jam enemy broadcasts also hampered the propaganda effort. Unfortunately, we do not know enough about audience responses to judge what were likely to be complex responses to radio broadcasts. As the war progressed and the Japanese were clearly being defeated, it is likely that the standing of BBC and AIR transmissions improved as the BBC gained a stronger reputation for truthful and accurate reporting. In the last year and a half of the war, radio transmissions from SEAC and by the BBC did play a role in counteracting the 'Forgotten Army' syndrome. Mountbatten's powers of persuasion in setting up Radio SEAC and encouraging direct reporting by the BBC from the front paid off in this respect.

10

The 'Forgotten Army'? Stepping up Publicity for the 14th Army

From August 1944, SEAC stepped up its campaign to bring the Burma campaign to the attention of the British and American publics. This took a number of forms. First, Squadron Leader Charles Gardner, in civilian life a BBC man, was sent from Kandy PRO to London to head a SEAC News Division in the Ministry of Information (MoI). His role was an intermediary one in that he publicized SEAC through the British media, but he also acted as a conduit for British media requests for more information and stories from SEAC.[1] Within two months of setting up office at Senate House in London, it was reported that the number of feature articles on SEAC published in the British press had doubled.[2] A typical example was the *Sunday Pictorial*'s request for background material for a planned feature on General Lentaigne who had taken over from Wingate in command of the Chindit operation.[3] It was difficult to replicate Wingate's charisma, but the second prong of the media campaign was to bring leading figures to London to talk to the press. Mountbatten gave an important press conference while he was in London on 21 August. He was followed in November by Philip Joubert and Frank Owen who gave a number of press conferences. These seem to have been very effective in publicizing the 14th Army, particularly the role of the 17th Indian Division and the Chindits.[4] Joubert's speech was interesting for setting a context for the British and Commonwealth contribution as against the Americans, who, it was often complained, gained greater publicity:

> We have the biggest single front against the Japanese in the whole Pacific war. During last summer our men engaged a bigger number of Japanese than any other force, and up to date have inflicted a larger number of casualties on them than any other force in the Pacific ... At Myitkyina there were more British killed, wounded and missing than were Americans. Although the Americans did their duty gallantly.[5]

Tribune magazine pointed out in November that there were at least a dozen officers in Britain providing information about SEAC: 'These include two Air Marshals, two of Gen. Slim's best field commanders, his Chief of Staff and other officers who have had first-hand experience of the fighting.'[6]

One of the key initiatives to enlighten the British public about the exploits of the 14th Army was the use of officers returning home from SEAC for publicity purposes

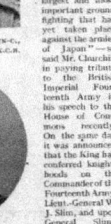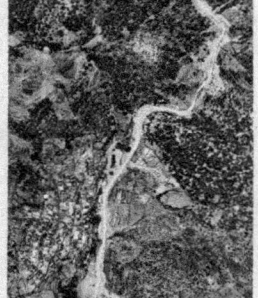

Figure 10.1 The achievements of the 14th Army publicized. *Illustrated London News*, 7 October 1944, courtesy of Mary Evans Picture Library.

at a local community level. This scheme was launched by Philip Joubert in August 1944 and operated under MoI auspices.⁷ The talks in local cinemas, theatres and clubs proved highly popular as they were usually linked to particular local regiments. In addition to these lecture tours, there was an interesting venture undertaken by film enthusiast Lieutenant Colonel Frank Hodgkinson of the 2nd Burma Rifles. He seems to have been employed by Mountbatten to make 16 mm colour film during 1944 which he then took to Britain to show under the title 'Burma Battle Ground', with his own spoken commentary. He claimed audiences from 50 to 3,500 people.⁸ The MoI invited him to show his film all over Britain in November and December 1944. He gave private viewings in the House of Commons to MPs and at Buckingham Palace to the royal family on 1 March 1945.⁹

The use of officer observers

Another form of publicity which was aimed particularly at the local press in Britain was the use of 'officer observers', as they were known. These servicemen, who usually had journalistic experience, had been used for reporting in Burma since 1943 during the Chindit and Arakan campaigns. Brigadier Jehu, Indian Army Public Relations (IAPR), had been keen on using them as a supplement to the war correspondents working for the commercial sector, partly because they added a dimension to the reporting of the campaigns, particularly providing information to the Indian press about the role of Indian soldiers which could not readily be covered by the few Indian war correspondents in Burma.¹⁰ It was also the case that they could be more readily controlled. They could be trusted to maintain confidentiality, especially in campaigns such as Wingate's first expedition which, because of its long march-in, required a substantial period of strict secrecy. Captain M. L. Katju, who followed the first Chindit expedition and was actually killed during it, was one of the first such officer observers. He might easily have been the only reporter on the expedition were it not for the last-minute inclusion of three professional war correspondents.

Officer observers operated without the need of conducting officers and could therefore be used in situations where there were greater dangers to reporters. They were armed, unlike the war correspondents. They could also provide a different type of reporting. First, they could observe and report campaigns for the military and historical record. This was important for future training and for learning about the strengths and weaknesses of particular weaponry. In contrast, war correspondents were under pressure to provide immediate stories, preferably with a strong and exciting narrative. Secondly, the officer observers could provide stories of the activities of individual soldiers and broadly named regiments, which would appeal to local newspapers in the United Kingdom and India. An example is that of Captain J. A. Borthwick, an officer observer who followed the Highland Division and, perhaps unusually, wrote under his own name in the Scottish papers. This helped to establish a rapport with his readers.¹¹

During 1944, under SEAC's determination to improve the coverage of the exploits of the 14th Army and the Burma campaign, there was a need to substantially increase the number of officer observers. Ideally, observers would be recruited from men with previous journalistic experience. One such man was Captain Roy McKelvie who had been a reporter with the *Star* newspaper, but who had nearly four years of regimental soldiering before being called upon to join public relations in GHQ India. McKelvie described the role very well:

> The Officer Observer ... is not meant to be a vicarious war correspondent or even an aspirant journalist. He should be a professional but one who aims to cover that side of army life left uncovered by the war correspondent ... Essentially an observer of men and events, the observer, by virtue of being a soldier, has no authority to criticize or speculate.[12]

A rare example of an Indian Army observer whose dispatches survive in the archives has been explored by Heather Goodall and Mark Frost.[13] Captain P. R. S. Mani, a Tamil journalist, acted as an observer from the Imphal campaign right through to the SEAC advance to Indonesia. Like many other Indians who took up roles in the fight against fascism, Mani was strongly sympathetic to the Indian nationalist cause. Goodall and Frost argue that he tried to report on Indian soldiers from all regions of the subcontinent, in effect subverting the traditional British emphasis on the so-called 'martial races' of northern India. In addition, Mani collected information about the Indian National Army (INA) and about Indian civilian populations in Burma, which he is reported to have shared with his friend, the *Hindu* journalist T. G. Narayanan and even with Jawaharlal Nehru. It must have been very difficult for Mani as a nationalist to work for army public relations as a propagandist. His role would have been very restricted, and certainly he could not have written anything about Subhas Chandra Bose and the INA during the campaign. His reporting on the variety of Indian troops would have been precisely what the army wanted, as by this time the army had to recruit from all regions. The strain in reporting in Indonesia after the war was too much for Mani and he left the army and returned to journalism.

Another appointment was Captain Douglas Atkinson, previously of the *Daily Express*. He divided the work with McKelvie: Atkinson taking the Arakan front and McKelvie the Imphal front.[14] The advantage of using observers was particularly obvious during the short correspondents' strike in April 1944 but was also apparent when correspondents were thin on the ground or found it difficult to report from the fighting front as in the Arakan, Chindit 2 and the Imphal/Kohima fighting. They filled in where newspaper correspondents were not available. In the Wingate fly-in it was difficult to persuade correspondents to join what was a highly hazardous operation. Officer observers were therefore relied on: Colonel James Bellah for the US Air Force, and Major Jerry Dunn for the British. Major Dunn was killed in the first wave of gliders. Another observer was also killed, Captain John Webb.[15]

It was important that the officer observers did not undermine or challenge the position of the commercial war correspondents. As McKelvie pointed out, 'In the field, the observer has no transmission privileges over the correspondents. Only if no correspondents are operating can he use Army signals and then only for a "hot" story which correspondents at base can pick up.' Indeed, he believed that often observers risked their neck for a story which correspondents located at base could rewrite but, in fairness, they mostly gave credit to the observer. There was never a question of scooping correspondents.[16] The use of officer observers proved a very effective and economical form of publicity.[17]

British public attitudes to the war in Burma

There is evidence from Home Intelligence weekly reports (HIWR) that the publicity campaign was working. Generally speaking, from the end of the retreat in 1942 until the second half of 1944, these reports showed a lack of interest and knowledge among the general public about the war in Burma and the Far East. In fact, there seemed to be more interest and enthusiasm for the American campaign in the south-west Pacific than there was for the war in Burma. This was partly because of the lack of progress that the army seemed to be making there, and partly a lack of news reaching the papers because of censorship or paucity of correspondents on the ground. When news did get through, the public often proclaimed that they found it confusing to follow and they wanted better maps to explain it. Of course, Burma seemed a long way away, except to those who had travelled east of Suez or who had relatives serving there. A detailed survey of public attitudes to the Far Eastern War and Japan was conducted in the last week of May 1944 by the British Institute of Public Opinion for the MoI.[18] It confirmed that general knowledge of the Far Eastern campaign was slight, although nearly 90 per cent of respondents believed that Britain should continue the war against Japan until it was defeated. Perhaps the most surprising statistics were in response to the question, 'Which country has done the most fighting against Japan?' The great majority said China (72 per cent), while the USA came second (15 per cent) and Britain and the Dominions lagged well behind (8 per cent). It was not that this was an inaccurate evaluation of Allied contributions but rather that the answers seemed to reflect the way in which the effective contributions of the different countries had been reported up to that point. However, when asked, 'Do you know the names of any places where the Allies are fighting the Japanese?', 46 per cent of respondents named Burma, while New Guinea was next at only 10 per cent. Only 41 per cent correctly named the Allied Chief with his headquarters in Ceylon, so Mountbatten obviously had more work to do on his own publicity. It should be remembered that this survey was conducted at a time when the war in Europe was reaching a climax with preparations nearly complete for the invasion of Normandy, so that war in the Far East was seen by the public as something that could be really focused on only once Germany had been defeated.

During August and September 1944, there was, at last, recognition in the reports of the good work that soldiers were doing in Burma under very tough conditions. There were complaints that not enough information about the campaign was given though, and that news was often relegated to the back pages. In September and October this criticism led to calls from the public for more praise for the 'Forgotten Army'.[19] It is in the last quarter of 1944 that a marked increase in interest in the Burma fighting is noted, and there was recognition of the BBC's role in this.[20] The publicity campaign, which had emphasized the appalling conditions in Burma, led to a public concern for the health and welfare of the soldiers.[21] The improvement in provision of news from

Burma continued up until the end of the year when the intelligence reports were ended. The final report showed that, despite this, 'letters from men themselves show, despite denials, that they do in fact consider themselves forgotten'.[22]

The propaganda campaign in the USA

Simultaneously with the push to publicize in Britain the importance of the Burma campaign, there was a determination to step up propaganda in the United States. This reflected the concern during the 1944 campaigns in India/Burma that General Stilwell's public relations staff had deliberately downplayed the British contribution in Burma. It was felt that they had portrayed the British role in Arakan, Imphal and Kohima as essentially defensive, whereas Stilwell's forces had taken offensive action to successfully capture Myitkyina airport. Stilwell's recall in October 1944 opened up the possibility of a more cooperative working relationship with the USA, something which Mountbatten was very keen to promote. Another very important consideration was that, as hopes grew of an early end to the war with Germany, it was expected that the focus would shift to South East Asia and the Pacific. Harold Butler, head of British Information Services (BIS) in Washington, put this consideration most clearly:

> From a political point of view it is of the greatest importance that the British share in the war against Japan should receive the fullest possible publicity. The extent of British participation, or rather the American opinion of its extent, will considerably affect both the American attitude towards the Far East settlement and Anglo-American relations in general. If the American public believes that Britain has taken a considerable and effective part in the Japanese war, they are likely to be much more sympathetic to our claims when the peace is made, more particularly as they are suspicious that we intend to leave as much of the work as possible to them.[23]

Butler was aware, however, how difficult it would be to get these arguments across when the American press and public continued to see the Japanese war as essentially an American war. The American public took very little interest in Burma or the contribution of British Commonwealth forces there. Butler suggested that it was important to give every facility to American correspondents and photographers, particularly those working for very influential magazines such as *Time* and *Life*. It was also crucial to ensure that these correspondents in the British zones had the best facilities for transmitting stories home as fast as possible, otherwise they will want to be transferred to the American theatre where they could get better facilities.[24] Butler knew that, despite the need to show that US and British strategies in Burma were not at odds, once Germany was defeated and attention turned to defeating Japan, there would be inevitable divergences as each country planned for demobilization and post-war economic recovery.[25]

One of the most effective forms of propaganda to the USA was to give figures showing the relative size and composition of British forces fighting in Burma. The Minister of Information Brendan Bracken had called for this type of information to 'counter US misunderstandings'.[26] British propagandists successfully fed information to American newspapers through their own military correspondents. The best example was the relationship with the respected *New York Times* correspondent Hanson W. Baldwin. Baldwin's article of 23 October 1944, which emphasized the complete British success in repelling the Japanese invasion of India, was based on information given to him by the SEAC section of the MoI.[27] It was remarkable in that it tried to put American illusions about their relative contribution to the land war in Burma in its proper place, and to acknowledge the contributions and sacrifices the British had made and how these were now paying off. While recognizing that American airmen were the largest number in the Burma theatre, he said:

> ...few Americans realize that the ground forces in Burma and on its borders, which are far more exposed to disease, hardship and privation than are the fliers, are preponderantly British and Empire troops ... In northern Burma the forces under the command of General Joseph Stilwell – usually thought of in this country as chiefly American and Chinese – are actually largely British, British Empire and Chinese troops.

He went on to point out that Stilwell's Chinese troops

> were trained, armed and organised in India under American leadership, but were fed, paid and housed with British help ... The American ground troops form a very small percentage of the total ... There has not been and is not a single American combat division in Burma. There is no reason why they should be, for this is primarily a British sphere ... and available in nearby India is the considerable reservoir of the Indian Army.

Baldwin concluded: 'Thus Admiral Mountbatten's command cannot properly be accused of a "do-nothing" policy – as it sometimes is in this country – or of failure to employ a sizable land force on the borders of and inside Burma.'[28] It may well be that Baldwin's article was written by a British propagandist but went out under Baldwin's name. It was recognized in British circles that this was the only way to get material into American newspapers and magazines.[29]

For all the improvements made in British propaganda about the Burma campaign directed at the United States, it proved impossible in 1945 to take American minds off their focus on the Pacific war and their own role in defeating Japan. Despite the victories at Mandalay and Rangoon, British propaganda lacked the vital political ingredient of a firm time-limited promise of Burmese independence, which could have assuaged American opinion.

The propaganda campaign suffers setbacks

The media campaign did not all go smoothly. It might have been expected that the prime minister would help to publicize the heroic deeds of the 14th Army. Churchill returned from America and gave a speech in the House of Commons on 28 September 1944 that was intended to counter the strong impression across the Atlantic that American and Chinese troops were doing all the offensive fighting in Burma and that the British forces were holding back. His speech started in the right direction but soon veered off into praising the American contribution at Myitkyina and in flying aid to China over the Hump. The section of the speech dealing with SEAC focused on the high number of casualties it had incurred through malaria. Although the speech helped bring the Burma campaign to public attention, this was not the morale-boosting speech that Mountbatten would have wanted. It showed up Churchill's biases against the Indian Army and the whole land-based Burma campaign. Although Churchill acknowledged the role of Indian and African troops in Burma, he returned to his old imperial prejudice of describing the fighting force as the '14th British Imperial Army'.[30]

While the press generally responded reasonably well to encouragement from Joubert and Owen to do more to publicize the Burma campaign, some editors took any criticism to heart. The *Daily Mirror* wrote angrily that any failure to report the campaign more fully was not the responsibility of the press but of the governments of Britain and India who had 'done nothing to secure adequate "publicity" for a campaign of equal importance to any other in this great struggle'. The paper said that it had previously withdrawn its correspondent in Burma but would send another if there were assurances that their dispatches would not be subject delays and 'vexatious interference'.[31] The *Mirror* never did send another correspondent to Burma but focused its coverage on stories relating to the welfare of the soldiers in Burma. In December, the paper was highly critical of the deficiencies in provision of food, drink and entertainment which were revealed in Lord Munster's report on troop morale.[32] A front-page article on 15 December reported that the government was so shocked by the report that Churchill wanted it kept secret but indicated that he wanted to take personal control of the issue. On 21 December, the day after the prime minister had answered questions in the House of Commons on the report, the *Mirror* was still not satisfied that conditions for the troops in India-Burma would improve before Germany was defeated. There was particular annoyance at the fact that when Lord Munster held a press conference at the MoI, Secretary of State Amery insisted that the Q&A session should be kept 'off the record'.[33]

A row over the respective responsibility of press and government flared up around Noel Coward's BBC radio broadcast on 19 November in which he confusingly complained of the 'cruel and bitter press invention' and use of the term 'Forgotten Army' but blamed newspaper editors for prioritizing trivial domestic stories over the exploits of 'our soldiers in the Far East'.[34] This triggered a defensive response from the press. The *Herald* argued that Coward ignored the major difficulty editors had in reporting news from Burma which was 'a censorship so rigid that the correspondents themselves have constantly complained of it'.[35] It pointed out that it was not the press that invented the term 'Forgotten Army' but the soldiers themselves some eighteen months previously.[36] Coward's broadcast probably went down badly with the troops who had recently stayed up late at night to hear a promised BBC broadcast on repatriation of troops from the Far East which was cancelled at the last moment.[37]

When Frank Owen returned to London in November 1944, he began a very fruitful collaboration with *Pathe Gazette* on three newsreels, which were shown between January and March 1945. These newsreels show the remarkable closeness of relations between the newsreel companies and official propaganda, which will be brought out in more detail in the next chapter. There is no doubt that these propaganda efforts paid dividends and marked a much more dynamic approach to publicizing the final year of the Burma campaign. However, this was swimming against the tide to a large extent because, as the war in Europe reached a climax in the first months of 1945, it was difficult to keep public attention, in either Britain or the USA, focused on what was a very distant campaign.

11

Film and Photography in SEAC

Visual media were very much valued by propagandists in the Second World War. This could encompass a wide range of media including feature films, non-fiction (documentary) films, newsreels, commercial photography for magazines, and armed forces film and photography. Some of the most successful forms were those, such as fictional films shown commercially in cinemas, which audiences believed were not made by government bodies, and were not therefore seen as propaganda. However, one way or another, the government had a direct influence on these as well as all other visual media. In Britain, government, through the Ministry of Information (MoI), provided the guidance about required subject matter, the necessary film stock, exemptions for key personnel from military service, censorship approval, and even military weaponry and facilities, if necessary. The attraction of visual media to government was that it reached potentially large audiences, not just in Britain, but across the globe. In the days before television, newsreels and pictorial magazines were the main means by which people could envisage the nature, scale and scope of this global war. The problem was that each country, including the Axis powers, had their own powerful systems of visual propaganda. It was necessary for the British not only to counter enemy propaganda but, more importantly, to develop their own distinctive way of successfully communicating their war aims, strategies and post-war ideals for home, Allied and empire audiences.

Despite the fact that Britain had built up a very strong reputation in documentary film in the interwar years, it took the MoI some time to find the right messages and tone for their visual propaganda for home audiences, let alone those in the empire. There were very special problems for the use of film and photographs in the India-Burma theatre. There were material problems – shortages of equipment and of skilled personnel – but also difficulties of finding the appropriate ways of communicating with diverse audiences, some of these being Indian nationalists who were opposed to the war effort altogether. For example, the plummy, upper-class, overly patriotic commentaries on British newsreels did not go down well in India, and it was eventually recognized that India needed its own newsreel. Even the image of the rotund Prime Minister Winston Churchill smoking a cigar and giving a V for Victory salute, which went down well with most Britons, did not resonate with Indians who preferred their heroes to be more ascetic in appearance and behaviour.[1] In this chapter, there is coverage of newsreels, both British and Indian, and the work of the Army Film and Photographic Units (AFPUs). These fed into the main focus which will be on the making of the full-length documentary film *Burma Victory* as this epitomized Mountbatten's drive for recognition of the 14th Army but also for a cooperative Anglo-American approach to covering the combined Allied war effort in 1944 through 1945.[2] It used film from the AFPU, its American equivalent the US Army Signals Corps, and the newsreels.

Mountbatten and the movies

Louis Mountbatten was a keen supporter of modern means of communication and propaganda. He was very enamoured of cinema, Hollywood and American glamour. As Supreme Commander he was completely committed to Anglo-American cooperation across the board, and in the case of film he would definitely need American help. Partly this was because of a serious lack of British personnel and equipment in this theatre, priority being given to Europe, the Middle East and North Africa. The Americans had the best equipment, cine cameras, stills cameras, sound equipment and also colour film at times. They provided equipment to the British under Lend-Lease terms when requested, but it took a time to arrive. As for personnel, the Americans had a head start in that the Hollywood studios provided large numbers of skilled cameramen, directors and technicians who could join the various photographic units. Facilities for producing the films were much better in American studios and, of course, America controlled much the largest exhibition circuit, which was crucial if the films were to reach large audiences. This American dominance in filmmaking was one of the reasons that the British looked to cooperate with them on larger-scale documentaries such as *Tunisian Victory*, though wartime cooperation in filmmaking between the Allies could be almost as difficult as in agreeing overall military objectives and strategies. This would certainly prove to be the case with the Burma war version, *Burma Victory*. Films that involved allies with very different priorities in their war aims and strategies would inevitably involve a good deal of diplomatic discussions and delays. This would be exacerbated when the various armed services fought to protect their own special interests in the filmmaking. The film *Burma Victory*, the focus in this chapter, is a case in point. It was first conceived by Mountbatten in July 1944 as a joint Anglo-American production to show the public how the war in Burma was being fought and to raise troop morale. It was not finally released until 5 November 1945, nearly two months after the war in the Far East was suddenly ended by the two atomic bombs dropped on Japan in August 1945. It became more of an historical record than a morale-booster, though it did help the public realize the conditions under which the Burma campaign was fought. In the process of making it, serious differences arose between the Americans and the British about the objectives of the film and its length.

Mountbatten had for a long time been interested in film and photography as an important means of communication and propaganda. He had shot and edited HMS *Revenge*'s weekly newsreel in 1923 and made links with industry moguls such as Jack Warner in his quest to ensure that the Navy had access to popular feature films in the 1930s. In 1939 he set up the Royal Naval Film Corporation and became its president. The high point of this fascination for film came in 1942 when he took a very close interest in the making of Noel Coward's *In Which We Serve*, which was patently based on the story of the sinking of his own ship, the *Kelly*.³ Despite being in command of Combined Operations, Mountbatten took time to closely vet the whole process of scriptwriting through to production. The film was one of the most popular of the Second World War, but it did earn some criticisms that the hero was a thinly disguised Mountbatten and that it was a form of self-promotion. Adrian Smith has summarized the attraction of filmmaking to Mountbatten: 'Movies offered modernity, mystique, meritocracy and a medium in which the mechanics of production and distribution, as well as the film-making itself, appealed to Mountbatten the technocrat, the logistician, and perhaps above all, the networker and wheeler-dealer.'⁴

In SEAC, Mountbatten wanted to use film in the same way that he had promoted it in the Navy, to provide entertainment for the ranks, but more importantly to establish a record of the campaign, support the propaganda effort, and boost the morale of troops in this theatre. A Mr Kimberley came out to SEAC in early 1944 to report on what was required to provide film production and film entertainment for the forces. He produced his report in March and one outcome was the establishment of a Director of Kinematography for India, who would deal with the film requirements of India Command and SEAC, except for operational cine photography.⁵ Colonel Grove was appointed and continued in this role until the end of the Far East war. He had in this time greatly increased the number of mobile cinema units from 24 to 350, and in addition 130 static cinemas had been set up to meet the needs of the troops. Grove reported that the quality of films shown had greatly improved and there were now *Gaumont British News* and *Indian News Parade* newsreels to counter complaints that most newsreels shown were pro-American.⁶ In addition, *Calling Blighty* short films, which recorded messages from the troops to those at home, were apparently having a good effect on morale and it was aimed to produce one each month.⁷ However, there was a shortage of British soldiers trained as projectionists which lessened the effectiveness of the mobile cinemas.⁸

Forming a SEAC film unit

There were existing film and photographic units established or in training within Indian Army Public Relations (IAPR), and within the RAF, in particular. Also, there was a very effective American Signals Corps film and photographic unit.⁹ However, Mountbatten wanted a British SEAC unit and believed that he had received an undertaking when taking on the role of Supreme Commander that there should be a British film and photographic unit in SEAC to balance the American one.¹⁰ He was clear that the two units should work together <u>within</u> SEAC. This was a difficult ambition to achieve for a number of reasons. First, the approval of the US War Department and of the British War Office would be needed as they would have to provide the personnel and equipment for the SEAC unit. Secondly, there were various interests on the ground who would have to be prepared to cooperate. This was especially true of military commands, some of which already had their own public relations film and photographic units and who might well resent SEAC attempts to take them over.

The most important of these were the Indian Army and the RAF. The former had already set up its own unit based in Calcutta under Brigadier Jehu, and it guarded its interests jealously. The RAF was also using its own film unit as it felt it had not been given due recognition in comparison with the USAAF. In fact, it had a very well-developed set-up, the RAF Film Production Unit, which even produced its own newsreel, *The Gen*. The Admiralty wanted to keep control of public relations within its own sphere, while the 14th Army under General Slim wanted to ensure that their activities were not overlooked by a focus on the glamorous activities of General Wingate's Chindits. Finally, there was General Stilwell's China-Burma-India (CBI) command which had trained Chinese troops in India in preparation for an attempted land assault in North Burma to reopen the Burma Road to China. Stilwell was contemptuous of the British military leadership and was determined that the USA should not be seen to be supporting the return of British imperial rule in South East Asia. He made it clear that any American film and photographic units sent to his command should be under his control. Indeed, according to Mountbatten, Stilwell went further and insisted that all cameramen of whatever national allegiance in his area of operations should be under his direction.

A joint Anglo-American production

Mountbatten overcame the first obstacle of obtaining American support with his usual charm. The American Chief of Staff General George Marshall readily agreed to help SEAC set up its film unit, and to provide personnel and equipment. The Indian Army was more difficult to persuade as it felt that its troops had not been sufficiently covered in the previous US–UK collaborations, *Desert Victory* and *Tunisian Victory*. It had previously persuaded the War Office to provide the British film director Alex Bryce to coordinate their film and photographic unit and was reluctant now to meet SEAC requests to hand over key personnel. The American 'cavalry' fortunately came to the rescue of Mountbatten in the form of Major Irving Asher, a Warner Brothers producer, who had worked in Britain since 1938, where he had been involved in making Alexander Korda's pro-empire film *The Four Feathers* (1939). Asher, who headed up the American SEAC unit, went to America in September and October of 1943 to try to build up a film unit for SEAC. He met with Colonel Kirk Lawton, Head of Army Pictorial Service in the War Department, and obtained authorization for US personnel and equipment to be sent to India and for the use of laboratory facilities in Calcutta. Unfortunately, part of the film personnel offered, the 164th Signal Photo Company, was assigned in the first place to General Stilwell, and his staff insisted that the Company stay under CBI command rather than be transferred to SEAC. This presaged future conflicts between SEAC and CBI over this issue. It is significant that Asher planned to train and use this company to film the forthcoming second Wingate long-range penetration (LRP) expedition which was being planned and would be based on Anglo-American cooperation. On his way back to India, Asher had stopped in London for talks with the MoI and the RAF which was setting up on its own film unit in India. He found them supportive but, ominously, it became clear that the IAPR Directorate was not so cooperative and wanted to hold on to the key film personnel, Major Keen and Lieutenant Colonel Alex Bryce.[11]

The project for a fuller-length American documentary film was first put forward by General 'Hap' Arnold, Commander of the USAAF, who sent a photographic unit under Major William Whitley (10th Air Force Combat Unit) to make a film of the Cochran fly-in of Wingate's Chindits as part of Operation Thursday.[12] This was bound to be a very exciting operation which would show the importance of air support in aid of land forces, but also because it would involve the highly dangerous landing of gliders at prearranged clearances in the jungle behind Japanese lines.[13] Mountbatten, who at that time still lacked a British SEAC film unit, borrowed an Indian Army film unit under Bryce (from a very reluctant India Command) to take pictures of the land-based element of the Wingate operation, which it was planned to have produced at the US Air Force Picture unit in Culver City, California. Mountbatten told General Marshall that he was anxious for the Cochran-Wingate film to be a joint Anglo-American production along the lines of the film *Tunisian Victory*, and therefore needed archive film and studio assistance in editing the film. He had sent Bryce and Major Whitley to America to oversee this process.[14] It seems likely that Mountbatten was aware of the limitations of the film stock and equipment that he had available and needed American help to make the film. In any case, Marshall agreed to offer all facilities needed.[15]

Mountbatten was enthusiastic for the film project as it would showcase the Anglo-American air cooperation which he had brought about. However, when he toured the various fronts and talked to General Slim, he realized that a film focusing on the Wingate expedition would not reflect the wider aspects of the campaign and would probably be resented by other forces, most notably Slim's 14th Army, which regarded itself as badly neglected at home. Mountbatten, therefore, pressed for a larger US-British film which would show the whole campaign from the retreat of 1942 to operations in 1944.[16] However, Asher had pointed out to Mountbatten the difficulties of a SEAC unit making a more ambitious 'Battle for Burma' film, namely that they did not have access to the large amount of film taken by 'military and naval organizations, such as OSS [Office of Strategic Services], CBI Signal Units, India Command, numerous RAF and USAAF film organizations and PR Film Units.'[17] In view of this lack of film, Asher recommended that they try to work with the famous Hollywood director, now US Signal Corps officer, Frank Capra, and his studio facilities. He thought that Capra might well be thinking of making a Burma film himself, and that working with Capra's studio would ensure a more balanced film between army and air force contributions than the Culver City studios.[18] The SEAC commanders approved the new film. General Wedemeyer emphasized the importance of completing it quickly so that people in the Allied nations would realize the conditions of fighting in Burma and this would help bring material support for the SEAC campaign at a time when the European campaign was ending, which was optimistically expected to be during 1944.[19]

In persuading United States allies, the SEAC Chiefs of Staff, Chiefs of Staff at home, the War Office and the MoI in London, Mountbatten used a series of different arguments in support of developing film and photography in SEAC. He varied the priority given to the various arguments according to his audience, but it does seem that the overwhelming concern was to maintain and improve troop morale which had been at such a low point in 1943 when he arrived. It was vital to overcome the 'Forgotten Army' syndrome and film was the best way to convey the appalling conditions that the troops faced in monsoon conditions in the jungle. This in turn would encourage families of the troops to contact them and encourage them that they were doing well. Good film could be provided by the various service film units which were arriving in greater numbers, and they would also be added to by the commercial newsreel cameramen. Newsreels were an important source of visual news during the war, as they were shown to large audiences in most cinemas twice a week. However, newsreel cameramen were thin on the ground in the Burma campaign during 1943 and 1944, partly owing to the difficult conditions for filming and transmitting material from the various fronts, but, more importantly, because of the much more pressing need for film from Europe and North Africa. The newsreel companies relied predominantly on official film to make up their Burma segments until 1945. Still photographs were also important as they would be provided to the MoI for transmission to the newspapers and magazines. Another objective that might have appealed to the service chiefs was that the film was valuable as a record of what had taken place and could be used in the histories but also in practical training and military analysis situations.[20]

Mountbatten was successful in securing the cooperation of General Marshall for the joint Anglo-American film project and also in having his preferred choice, Frank Capra, produce the film in Hollywood with British participation.[21] By the middle of September, the facilities were all set up with the Americans and the British fully cooperating on making the Burma campaign film under Capra in Hollywood, with Bryce as co-director.[22] There were still two potential obstacles to the making of the film, one of which was more serious than Mountbatten realized. The first was that General Stilwell appeared to be lukewarm about the film and required to see and approve a rough cut of the film before it was given public release.[23] This mattered because Stilwell's CBI command came to include the latter stages of the Chindit operations and the role of the British 36th Division at Myitkyina and after. Stilwell had taken a view that he was in charge of any cameramen in his area of command. It seemed that Stilwell's staff were concerned that 'insufficient credit would be given to Stilwell for all that he had achieved in spite of British apathy and inertia in order to spare British feelings'.[24] This attitude went absolutely against Mountbatten's view that he ran an integrated command in which each section relied upon the actions of others. In any case, this obstacle was removed when Stilwell was himself dismissed from his command in October 1944 and replaced by General Sultan who was far more cooperative.[25]

The second obstacle mattered much more in the long run because it went to the heart of the problems with these joint Anglo-American films, namely that the two parties often had very different views of their aims in the military campaigns. This could result in serious differences about the overall objectives of the films and also the balance of coverage of the nations' armed forces. This had already proved the case with the film *Tunisian Victory*, which was jointly produced by Frank Capra (USA) and Colonel Hugh Stewart (UK). *Tunisian Victory* had been fraught with difficulties relating to rival aims in the North African campaign, but also in different approaches to documentary filmmaking. Capra, who was making the 'Why We Fight' propaganda series, was much more prepared to use reconstructed material than was the British preference.[26] In any case, the film was not completed until 1944 when the North African campaign was over. The MoI eventually approved the making of the Burma film in August 1944 but the minister, Brendan Bracken, warned Mountbatten about the dangers of making films with the Americans:

> You do not know what trouble you have launched on in projecting a film on the whole Burma campaign with British and American ends. We have had some experience of this with Tunisian campaign and now the Normandy operations and there is no doubt that an overall campaign film which is to suit British and American tastes is slow to produce and that the effectiveness of the film suffers in the process.[27]

Capra saw the objectives of the campaign as three basic simple ones: '1. The importance of stopping the Jap, so that he could not join with the Nazies [sic]. 2. To re-establish communications with China, in order to keep China in the war. 3. To capture bases and airfields for the final offensive against Japan.' These were, in essence, the American priorities, not necessarily the British ones, which were less enamoured with the idea of using China as the basis for a land/air campaign against Japan. This should have alerted Mountbatten to potential problems for the making of the film. Perhaps he was too taken with the aura of Capra and Hollywood glamour, symbolized by Capra's description of events in the Burma campaign as 'truly "Dick Tracy"'.[28]

It became clear towards the end of November that the film was taking longer to complete than expected and would not be finished before the spring of 1945. Ian Jarvie has shown that there were important players on the American side, notably John Paton Davies and Cordell Hull, who opposed any film that might be seen to be in any way supporting British imperial aims in the region.[29] Capra's film, which he promised would stay clear of politics and stick only to military events, would probably only cover the campaign up until November 1944.[30] The film still needed to satisfy the various parties involved – for instance, the Indian Army and the RAF both felt that their roles had not been properly recognized in previous films and kept a watch on the production to ensure this would not be repeated. Colonel K. S. Himatsinjhi had been deputed by the Indian Army to go to Hollywood in order to look out for India's interests in the Burma campaign film. He reported on 6 November 1944: 'I feel that although half or more of the picture will be made up of our material, the narrative will be full of General Stillwell [sic], the Merrill Marauders, General Chennault's Flying Tigers, etc., and the references of the Indian Army will be few and brief.'[31] Though it is clear that General Auchinleck conveyed some of Himatsinjhi's concerns about the lack of India Command's activities in the film's narrative to Mountbatten, he did not pass on his full report which would surely have rung alarm bells in the Supreme Commander's mind about the way that the film was likely to focus on American interests.[32]

Joubert had already realized that if Capra's film only covered the campaign up until November 1944, there would need to be a sequel covering the liberation of North Burma.[33] Mountbatten used his contacts with Commander Arthur Jarratt,[34] with a view to making a film on the planned offensive to retake Mandalay and Rangoon. Jarratt had recommended that the War Office be approached for permission to use Lieutenant Colonel David MacDonald, who produced *Desert Victory*, to produce the film. Fortunately, the War Office agreed to release MacDonald, whom they described as 'the best man either side of the Atlantic for this type of film' [emphasis in original]. He was to go to SEAC for three months, and then return to Pinewood studios, and MacDonald expected the film to be completed within six weeks. MacDonald arrived at SEAC HQ at the very end of 1944, only to be surprised to find that Mountbatten had laid down new terms for his employment.[35] These put him under SEAC (not War Office) control with no time limit on his stay.[36] Mountbatten also still maintained that this second film should also be a joint Anglo-American production.[37]

The Americans and British decide to make their own films

Early in 1945, Mountbatten became worried by the delays in producing the Capra film. However, he must have been shocked to receive General Marshall's letter of 21 February 1945 which, although it promised that a rough cut of some 10,000 feet of film was almost completed, indicated that the War Department was only prepared to release a short two-reel film (2,000 feet or 22 minutes long) on the North Burma campaign from this footage. The reason given was that US exhibitors did not want lengthy official war films. Marshall admitted: 'This will limit the story somewhat, but since all these activities affected General Stilwell's original plan to reopen the Burma Road, there is a common theme uniting the numerous campaigns which contributed to ultimate success.'[38] Although Marshall offered the film material if the British wanted to make a longer film, it should have been very clear by now that the Americans had very different objectives for their film from the one that Mountbatten had set down. Ian Jarvie indicates that Marshall's reasons for reducing the length of the film may have reflected a genuine decision based on the nature of the American film market, but it may also have reflected a recognition of the fundamentally different type of film he wanted Capra to make.[39] In any case, he seemed to leave the matter open for discussion and this was in many ways unfortunate because the next few months were taken up with endless British attempts to reconstruct Capra's film on lines that reflected the British service chiefs' views of how the campaign should be presented.

Although Mountbatten had taken steps to prepare for a separate British film, it was not until 25 May that he finally concluded that it was best to make a separate up-to-date British film using the raw material that Marshall had offered. While still open to the possibility of a suitable reconstruction of the Capra film, he warned: 'I do not think, however, that we should overlook the fact that AMERICAN object in BURMA IS NOT repeat NOT the same as ours ... Any film likely to pass critics eyes in the War Department and State Department is bound to reflect US outlook.'[40] He, therefore, favoured letting Macdonald go to America as soon as possible to obtain approval to use the 140,000 feet of film available, which he did successfully. Mountbatten had finally realized that the Americans did not want to be involved in a film about the recapture of a British imperial possession. In May, Mountbatten received the official War Office and MoI approval to go ahead with the separate British film.[41] Mountbatten congratulated MacDonald on cutting the Gordian knot with what he described as the 'rival Burma film'.[42] He clearly felt that shackles had been removed from him and that he could now give MacDonald a more detailed set of ideas of how he envisaged the film, which was tentatively called 'Jungle Victory'. In view of his later criticisms of the sections of *Burma Victory* showing staged film of the various service chiefs and himself, it is interesting how this was precisely what he requested MacDonald to include at this stage. It is typical of his ambivalent approach to self-publicity that he asked for the insertion of additional film of himself speaking to the company of a French Navy ship so that other allies could be included. 'Although, as you know, I am not anxious to appear too often in the film,' he reminded MacDonald.[43]

The two films are finally released

It was ironic, considering the amount of fuss it had generated in its making, that the American film *The Stilwell Road* never received a theatrical release in the United States. According to the International Movie Database (IMDB), it was given its initial telecast on 26 November 1945 on New York City's pioneer television station WNBT (Channel 1).[44] The film was longer than the two-reeler that Marshall had predicted and ran for fifty-one minutes. It had a clear focus on the combined British-American-Chinese plan to help the Chinese continue their war effort against Japan by reopening the all-important Burma Road. It was very well made and used animated maps to make a complicated campaign seem clear. Colonel Bryce had obviously done a good job in improving on the original rough cut that the British service chiefs had savaged in March. Mountbatten saw the film and, recognizing that each of the two rival Burma campaign films would naturally include more about their own nation's contributions, said that it 'gave a very fair picture', which it did.[45]

The fact that *The Stilwell Road* did not get a theatrical release in America must have suited those marketing *Burma Victory*, especially as they managed to have Warner Brothers exhibit theirs in their cinemas. It was ten minutes longer than the American film. The film was released in British cinemas on 5 November 1945, directed by Roy Boulting, who also wrote the script with Frank Harvey. It probably also gained an additional audience due to the furore in September 1945 when Warner Brothers had been forced to withdraw its feature film, *Objective Burma*, starring Errol Flynn, after the British press gave it a very critical reception for its pro-American inaccuracies.[46] *Burma Victory* was a very effective documentary which gave a vivid picture of the appalling monsoon and jungle conditions in which troops had to fight.[47] The main difference with the American film was that, while the former focused on the Allied drive in North Burma to reopen the Burma Road to China, the British film emphasized the 14th Army drive south to recapture Mandalay and Rangoon. Mountbatten's beloved combined sea assault on Rangoon, like a previous assault on Akyab, gave disappointing filmic results as the Japanese had already abandoned the Burma capital when the seaborne invasion arrived, and monsoon conditions made filming difficult. Even so, *Burma Victory* is a fitting culmination to the work of the AFPU in recording the different campaigns of the war.

Forces' film and photographic units

An informal SEAC publicity committee was set up at the beginning of February 1944 in London chaired by Francis Williams of the MoI. The intention was to coordinate photographic requirements of the various services and liaise with India and the Dominions. At the second meeting on 14 February, Williams stated:

> ...the principle had been established that only official photographers would be sent out from Britain. The presence of accredited photographers gave rise to conducting difficulties and the Ministry of Information did not consider that press photographers would improve the quality of photographs. He said that the Committee which represented the British Press were satisfied with the present arrangements.[48]

This decision, which was strongly backed by the War Office and the RAF representatives, presumably suited the press in that it saved them the cost of sending out their own

Figure 11.1 Sergeant Basil Wishart of No.9 Army Film and Photo Section films Indian troops crossing a river near Meiktila, Burma in 1945. IWM, SE5423.

cameramen. However, it put the British at odds with the Americans who insisted on sending both official and commercial (accredited) photographers.

Clearly, the success of *Burma Victory* depended on a whole number of cameramen contributors, men of the different services' film and photographic units who risked their lives to capture images of the Burma campaign. Enormous risks were taken by those who filmed RAF reconnaissance, supply and bombing raids. In terms of number, though, it is the Army Film and Photographic Unit (AFPU) which deserves closest attention. It took quite a long time for it to be assembled and to receive suitable equipment, but during 1944 personnel grew in number under the direction of a Burma Rifles officer, Colonel Frank Outram Hodgkinson. Captain Philip Daniels, who was assigned to the SEAC film unit in April 1944, lists four other officers joining the unit, one sergeant clerk, eighteen sergeant cameramen, 'and three stills cameramen, all inexperienced in the field'.[49] The unit had to work between headquarters in Calcutta, Kandy in Ceylon, and at advanced headquarters, wherever that might be. In August 1944 Philip Joubert set out plans for the aims and organization of the SEAC film unit which indicated that, in addition to a headquarters unit, there would be six combat camera teams. These would supply film to GHQ India PR facilities at Tollygunge, Calcutta, and an American production unit at Kandy, with an animation unit and laboratories for developing and forwarding still and cine film. Combat camera teams would be located as the campaign required, but pools of three cameramen would be kept with the 14th Army Advanced HQ and SACSEA HQ for special assignments. One presumes that the latter included filming Mountbatten's special talks to troops on the various fronts.[50] The SEAC unit was increased in size at the end of October 1944 when a new contingent arrived under Lieutenant Colonel Derek Knight, who took over from Hodgkinson in charge of the SEAC film unit. However, the British unit was still considered deficient by Mountbatten who told Brendan Bracken, Minister for Information, that the 'US Photo unit has magnificent up-to-date equipment for 50 cameramen in the field, half for stills and half for motion pictures, as well as all processing requirements. British Unit is understaffed and equipment is hopelessly inadequate both in the field and at HQ'.[51] Mountbatten became increasingly concerned that the Americans might withdraw some or all of their SEAC photo unit in order to cover other theatres.[52] In March 1945, the Americans did just that, disbanding their SEAC photo unit but generously allowing Asher to remain, and for fixed laboratory equipment to be given to SEAC.[53]

At this stage in March 1945 the comparative figures for the British film units clearly indicate the significance of the loss of the American personnel (see Table 11.1).

SEAC film unit production reached a peak at this time: 39,783 feet of film had been shot in one week together with 1,562 stills.[54] In June 1945, the SEAC unit was transferred over to No. 9 AFPU, by which time much of the heaviest fighting in Burma had finished and the unit would soon turn to focus on the liberation scenes and Japanese surrender ceremonies in SEAC's enlarged command.

Table 11.1

1. Present Position Personnel	Cameramen – Motion & Still	Laboratories – Motion & Still	Admin.	Total
SEAC Photo Unit (US)	62	16	10	38	126
SEAC Film Unit (Br)	25		6	8	39
Royal Navy	1	-	-	-	1
RAF Film Unit	13		3	15	31
TOTAL		39	9	23	71
2. Personnel required to reach Photo Unit (US) strength if RAF participates	23	16	1	15	55

Source: Present Position SEAC Photo Unit; Joubert to Mountbatten, 19 March 1945, WO203/5161.

Newsreels

During 1943 and 1944 there were a very small number of British newsreel cameramen covering the war in Burma. In March 1944 there was only one cameraman: F. Oscar Bovill (Pathé) was based at Chittagong with the 14th Army for the campaigns in Arakan and in the Chin Hills.[55] This meant that the newsreels had to rely to a great extent on using film from the IAPR, the AFPU and the RAF film units.

The News Reel Association (NRA) expressed its concern in September 1943 at the poor film coverage of the South East Asian theatre and said that their cameramen blamed this on the inefficiency of the PROs. It is not quite clear whether this meant the PROs on location in India and SEAC or those organizing their accreditation and transport from Britain. In fact, London was taking an inordinately long time to accredit and provide transportation for cameramen.[56] Whatever or whoever caused the improvement in newsreel coverage of the Burma War at the end of 1944, it elicited the following highly unusual commentary for a newsreel titled 'The 14th Army in the Arakan': 'At long last someone is putting a foot down on the SEAC Publicity accelerator. Chances are brighter of our getting bigger and better film and press reports from South East Asia.'[57]

Perhaps the most effective newsreel publicity for SEAC and the Burma campaign were three Pathé newsreels which resulted from Frank Owen's return to London in November. The first, 'The Road to Mandalay', in January 1945, included his commentary to Oscar Bovill's film of the 5th Indian Division crossing the Chindwin river.[58] This was short, but the second newsreel, 'Front Line Newspaper', was over three minutes long and was a brilliant plug for the *SEAC* newspaper, for which its publisher Owen again provided the spoken commentary. This showed the editorial office, with photostat copies of the overseas editions of British newspapers being used. The climax was the daily air delivery of the paper to soldiers with a close-up of them admiring the 'Jane' cartoon strip in the paper.[59] The final newsreel, shown in March, was about the Ledo Road connecting India and China.[60] The closeness of this collaboration between the commercial newsreels and SEAC public relations seems remarkable. Clearly, the newsreels depended on armed forces photographic units for much of their film, but to have Owen not only write the commentaries but also speak to them was very effective propaganda.

At the end of 1944 and into 1945, as the war in Europe looked as if it would soon be coming to an end, more newsreel cameramen were assigned to SEAC.[61] As the 14th Army advanced on Mandalay and then Rangoon in the first months of 1945, there were six British newsreel cameramen covering the fighting:

Alec Tozer	Movietone (Mandalay and Rangoon)
James Wright	Paramount (coordinated cameramen)
Oscar Bovill	Pathé (Mandalay, Rangoon)
G. B. Oswald	Universal (Mandalay)
Ronnie Noble	Universal (covering RAF missions and later Singapore capture)
John Turner	Gaumont British[62] (naval operations)

This marked an ambitious approach by the newsreels to implement the lessons learnt in other campaigns to ensure a more 'scientific' approach to filming the Burma front. Jimmy Wright was appointed liaison between SEAC HQ and the cameramen at the front. He promised:

> Every battle will be planned in advance. We shall use maps, drawings, charts, and even cartoons to support the actual shots and make a sort of newsreel documentary. When a place is taken we shall screen explanatory diagrams showing what the strategy was and how the situation has altered. Nowadays people want a planned pictorial illustration of what war means. We are going to give it to them.[63]

This was going to be much more difficult to deliver than Wright realized. For one thing, the studio facilities at Kandy were not yet completed. Also, the Burma front posed difficulties for cameramen that were exceptional. Captain Alan Lawson, a SEAC cameramen, pointed to the technical difficulties of filming in such strong sunlight, deep jungle and monsoon dampness. Even more difficult was finding the front in what was a highly mobile war with several different dagger thrusts at the enemy. The line of communication back to the railhead was over 600 miles.[64] The key for cameramen was mobility and that meant reliance on that mobile workhorse, the jeep. For the SEAC cameramen this involved two cine cameramen and a still photographer sharing a jeep, searching for the action. For the commercial newsreel cameramen, the logistics were even more difficult as they needed to travel with a conducting officer and, most importantly, to be able to return their film by whatever transport was available as quickly as possible. Finding the right sort of subject matter was difficult because, in the nature of the fighting, it was rarely possible to see the enemy and, if you did manage to see Japanese troops in action, you were in danger for your life. The end result was that both sets of cameramen often had to settle for shots of air force bombing targets or dropping supplies, or of engineers building roads and bridges across rivers. Lawson admitted that 'such pictures as these do not give you a complete and true picture of the

Burma front'.[65] Because of these difficulties the SEAC cameramen resented the superior claims of the professional newsreel men. Lawson went so far as to accuse them of faking some of their material, saying: 'Because of these strange conditions some of the newsreel lads occasionally lay on their own private wars to whet the appetite of the dear old B.P. [British Public]' It is very difficult to pin down staged footage, but 'faking' certainly did take place in the Burma campaigns, despite instructions from the newsreel managers forbidding it.[66]

The newsreel cameramen were still outnumbered by the AFPU and RAF cameramen. Although the film from all the various units, whether commercial or service-based, was pooled and available to all, it is possible to distinguish the different approaches and outputs of the professional and service cameramen. The newsreel cameramen were more professional, in the sense of having much longer training and an in-built sense of the need to create an attractive newsreel story. They also had the advantage of having better cameras with telephoto lenses, enabling them to film from a safer distance.[67] The RAF film unit could be said to also have some of these skills as they made their own newsreel, *The Gen*, eighteen issues of which were produced between April 1943 and September 1945. This was a highly skilled operation which was aimed primarily at RAF audiences at home and overseas. It deliberately mixed informative topical items with entertainment, such as the story of the young Gurkha boy 'Jimmy Nathu', who served as an RAF mascot. The RAF film was of very good quality and was often used by the newsreel companies.[68] The AFPU, IAPR and SEAC units could create stories, but they were also concerned with creating a photographic record of the campaign, which meant photographing weaponry and tactics in operation, subjects which might have limited attraction to newsreel editors and in any case would be liable to be stopped by the censors. From the point of view of the service PROs, the newsreel cameramen were more difficult to direct and could move location if they wished. The official cameramen could be assigned to particular tasks and locations, which might include making film messages of the forces for *Calling Blighty* or recording Mountbatten's regular visits to the troops.[69] Their dope sheets indicate their function as recorders of events because they include a good deal of naming of regiments and places, which they must have known would not pass the censor for immediate use in newsreels.

Cameramen obviously found it easier working when armies were advancing than when they had filmed the retreat in 1942 and the more static fighting in the Arakan and Assam. Even so, their editors did not always use the film they shot. This was a normal but frustrating experience for them. Ronnie Noble flew on eight RAF bombing missions over a two-week period and was proud of the film he sent home. Three weeks later his boss cabled to tell him that the photography was outstanding but that he could not use the film because events in Europe were 'so important and outstanding' that they took priority.[70] John Turner was supposed to film the navy but found very little activity and so he somehow persuaded Gaumont British that he should seek navy-related stories in the areas where the army was fighting. He had not realized quite how far from the sea this would be and, although he followed the army into Rangoon, he found that he had missed the amphibious operation which was part of the actual recapture of the city in the first days of May.[71] Turner was able to compensate by filming the Japanese surrender of Singapore which took place on board HMS Sussex on 4 September. As the official naval cameraman, he had exclusive access, something which did not please the other correspondents.⁷² The official Japanese surrender was taken by Mountbatten on 12 September. As in Rangoon, the newsreel coverage was coordinated by James Wright. There were three newsreel cameramen and in addition there was film taken by the Army and Navy film units, so there was plenty of material for editors to choose from. The resulting Paramount and Pathé newsreels were released on 24 September and given full coverage.⁷³

From a situation in 1943 and the first months of 1944 when there had been a dearth of cameramen and film coverage of the Burma campaign, the situation had been transformed during 1945. The quality of film that went into *Burma Victory* and *The Stilwell Road* is testament to the value of the work of the various film and photographic units, which ensured that those who participated in the Burma campaign would never be forgotten.

12

Race to Rangoon and Victory, 1945

The British and the Americans continued with their different priorities in Burma during 1945. They both had major successes which could be used to boost publicity about the theatre. The Americans started the year with a fanfare about the opening of the completed Ledo–Burma Road, which Chiang Kai-shek renamed the Stilwell Road after his old adversary. This was a magnificent achievement by a combination of local labourers, American engineers (60 per cent African Americans), Chinese soldiers, and American soldiers and airmen.[1] It was accomplished in the face of appallingly dangerous geographical, climatic, disease and technical conditions. The first part began construction in Assam in December 1942 and did not reach a junction near Wanting with the Burma Road until the end of January 1945. It covered 1,079 miles from Ledo to Kunming in China, at a cost in lives calculated at approximately at least one person a mile. On 12 January 1945, the first convoy left Ledo and reached Kunming in China on 4 February. Newspapers in both Britain and America provided good coverage, especially using the photographic opportunities provided by the series of hairpin bends and US-Chinese celebrations across the border. However, reporting in American papers was greatly outshone by MacArthur's exploits in retaking the Philippines.

In truth, American media interest in Burma had decreased greatly since Stilwell's departure in October. There was a realization that the Burma land campaign really was a sideshow in the defeat of Japan and that Pacific island-hopping, though costly in manpower, was the only way forward. Even the Stilwell Road, the culmination of American efforts in Burma, proved to be something of a disappointment in terms of the amount of supplies it could carry to China compared with the air route. The capacity of the air route increased greatly once Myitkyina airport could be used with new larger transport planes. The planes could then fly a more southerly route which was shorter and safer. By the end of the war, ten times as many tons were being transported by plane as through the Stilwell Road. However, it has to be factored in that, alongside the road, oil pipelines were built, which by July provided valuable fuel to China, and that the Myitkyina air route would not have been safely in Allied hands without the road providing support to Stilwell's forces. The road would provide further publicity when the American documentary film on the Burma War was shown on American television in November 1945 with the title *The Stilwell Road*. By March, Chinese and American forces (Mars Task Force) were leaving Burma and the only US ground force left to harry the Japanese was Detachment 101 of the Office of Strategic Services (OSS).[2] This had started out in 1942 as a small group of agents carrying out

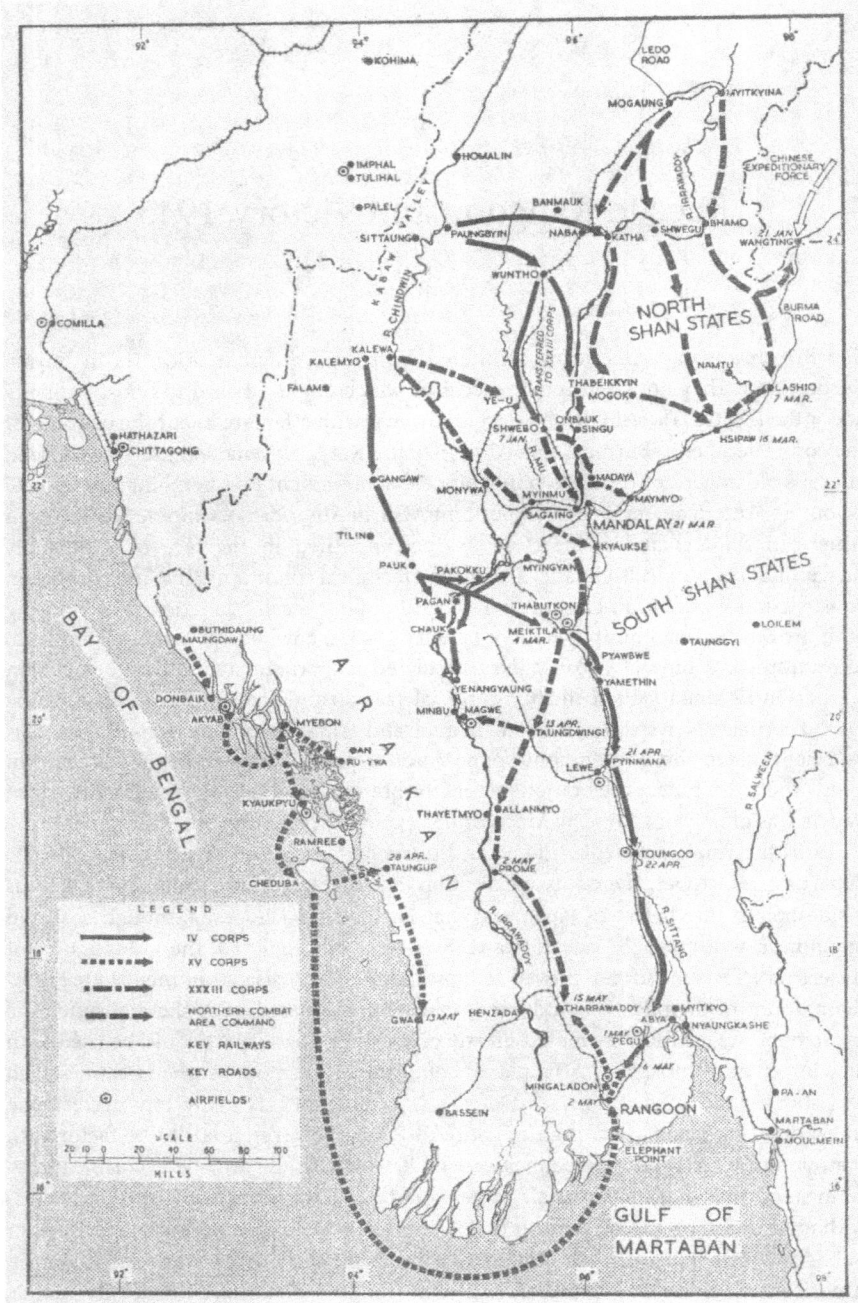

Map 12.1 The Reconquest of Burma, November 1944–May 1945, Hilary St George Saunders, *The Royal Air Force 1939 to 1945*, Vol. III: 'The Fight Is Won', HMSO Official History of WWII, London: HMSO, 1953, p. 356.

intelligence and guerrilla operations in conjunction with local peoples in Burma. As with the British equivalent, SOE, with whom they often had a competitive relationship in North Burma, Detachment 101 worked with Burmese groups, especially Kachins and later Karens.[3] By 1945, Detachment 101 had developed from guerrilla operations into conventional warfare in support of harrying the Japanese in eastern Burma. It is estimated that they killed over 1,200 Japanese in the final months of the war.[4] Because of the need for secrecy and the safety of native families, the work of Detachment 101 was not covered by the media at the time.

British advance by land and sea

When Mountbatten was chosen as Supreme Commander, one of his strengths, in the view of both the British and the Americans, was his experience of organizing combined operations which were aimed at landing troops on the coasts of enemy-held territory. At that time, the British expectation was that the best way to reconquer Burma and Singapore was not by land but by sea. Unfortunately, the landing craft for this amphibious operation were needed elsewhere in North Africa and Europe, and so Admiral Mountbatten was a naval commander having to coordinate what were essentially land/air operations in Burma during 1944–5. SEAC would have to wait for the Normandy invasion to be successful and for Germany to be defeated before the resources would be available for a major amphibious operation to retake Malaya and Burma. Slim's orders still prioritized American plans to secure territory in North Burma which would protect the full reopening of the Burma Road to China. However, Slim was planning to go further than the original Operation Capital which aimed to capture Mandalay. He planned an audacious advance which was designed to retake Rangoon before the monsoon broke in May. The most innovative part of this Operation Extended Capital was a flanking manoeuvre towards Meiktila, south of Mandalay, which, if successful, would cut Japanese forces in two. This was a major gamble against strong Japanese forces holding internal lines of communication, without the availability of Chinese and American troops to protect his north-east flank. It would also be a race against time as the monsoon which was due in May would put an end to the advance by land. Graham Dunlop has described the 14th Army's advance on Rangoon as 'the last and greatest victory of the British Indian army'. There was nothing inevitable about its success, and it rested on air power supporting troop movements at the limits of their capability, especially when the Americans threatened to move their aircraft from Burma to China. Air support required the capture of coastal airfields which would bring the planes in reach of Rangoon. This meant continuing with the long-standing attempts to capture Akyab on the north-east coast and then to take Ramree Island further down the coast. It turned out that the Japanese would abandon Akyab without resistance but defend Ramree much more strongly. These were the sort of combined operations that Mountbatten had always wanted, and he tried to ensure that they were given good press coverage.[5]

The first coastal assault took place on 3 January 1945. The aim was to capture the island port of Akyab, at the southern end of the Mayu peninsula in Arakan. This had been the objective of Allied offensives since the end of 1942. It had been bombed by aircraft endlessly. This was an opportunity for good press coverage of the first amphibious operation in the retaking of Burma. The air force was readied to begin the assault in preparation for the naval/commando assault. Commanders from the services were prepared to watch the assault: Lieutenant General Christison, Air Marshal Coryton and Air Commodore the Earl of Bandon. General Christison's 15th Corps had advanced down the Mayu peninsula much faster than was expected and it was planned to bring the Akyab operation forward. However, Christison believed that Mountbatten had tried unsuccessfully to delay the operation to ensure the publicity operation was fully in place.[6] On the day before the intended operation, it was realized that there were no Japanese left in Akyab and the aerial bombardment was called off. What was left was more like a rather embarassing training exercise.

What is interesting from the media management point of view is the very different ways in which the media reported this event. The 'official' message was that the Japanese had only very recently left Akyab, maybe even the day before, and that Allied forces had been helped by locals who welcomed them, and had even taken up weapons against the Japanese. A two-day embargo was placed on the release of press stories. Fortunately, there are copies of the 'press collect' dispatches of one of the newspapers correspondents, the Australian Ronald McKie.[7] A series of telegrams to his editor of the Sydney *Daily Telegraph* between 3 and 7 January show changes in these dispatches over time, from initially accepting the official line to strong, even sarcastic, criticism of the operation and a demand for an inquiry into the failure of intelligence involved. McKie's initial telegrams on the first two days of the 'invasion' reflect this 'misinformation' about a last-moment Japanese withdrawal from Akyab.[8] The emphasis on the welcome given to the 'liberators' was encapsulated in the story of a Burmese headman from a nearby village organizing locals to resist Japanese pressure for them to leave Akyab, and taking up arms which had been buried during the retreat in 1942 to emphasize their point. This gentleman was decribed as a graduate of Rangoon University who spoke perfect English and wore a green college blazer. Villagers had assisted the first British artillery officer to land his plane and gave him their their last chicken to eat. McKie's next telegram on 5 January gave a slightly more differentiated account by pointing out that while local Muslims, who formed the majority of the local population, had welcomed them, Buddhists were still holding back. He said this was a legacy of the Japanese deliberately stirring up communal suspicion.[9] McKie, along with other correspondents who had crossed the island to reach the port of Akyab were struck by the almost total desolation they found:

> Port of Akyab has neither been used nor occupied by Japanese since British pulled out more than two years ago. This is glaringly obvious from state of town which is completely overgrown and bombed burnt out in part by our own air attack. Docks have neither been used nor destroyed by Japanese and practically all defence positions on island are old and lined with water marks from the last monsoon ... Personally – and I am only amateur – I doubt whether there has ever been more than a small token force on island at any time. Maybe one battalion with good bloodhound could have captured place any time in past year. Before we went in we heard lot about island being littered with mines, booby traps, but no traps. Town is wilderness of tropical growth etc.[10]

Figure 12.1 Akyab, Burma. *c.* 3 January 1945. Lieutenant General Sir Philip Christison, Commander of the 15th Indian Corps, Group Captain W. D. David, Air Liaison Officer to the Corps, and Air Commodore the Earl of Bandon, Air Officer Commanding No. 224 Group RAF in the Arakan, landed on a village green which the local people had prepared for them. The white flag on the right of the Earl of Bandon was used by the natives to guide the aircraft down. Courtesy of Australian War Memorial Collections, SUK13681.

By this time, McKie had come to the same conclusion as other correspondents that the Japanese had performed an enormous bluff in exaggerating their strength at Akyab. He shared the opinion of the troops that it was a SABU – a self-adjusting balls-up.[11] Two days later, McKie went on to the offensive and called for '[a]n immediate investigation and explanation should be made of facts behind occupation Akyab. This is urgently needed in interests of military and general public confidence.'[12] McKie was angry for a number of reasons. One was that he had withdrawn from reporting the advance on Mandalay in order to report on what was supposed to be the first and largest combined operation involving Australians. This had meant an arduous 1,000-mile journey. Secondly, the two-day delay in releasing their stories meant that correspondents reporting from Kandy or Calcutta would have the same chance of getting their stories through first.

The British public received contrasting reports on Akyab when they read their papers on 6 January. The *News Chronicle*'s reporter Stuart Gelder, a close friend of McKie's, took a similar line, treating it as a farce. 'By denying us the Arakan port for two years the enemy has put up the largest and most successful bluff of this war. Two men could have taken this town.'[13] The *Times* report of the same day would have been written by Ian Morrison who was in Burma but not participating in the operation. It was a much more sober assessment. In typical *Times* fashion it gave prominence to the early arrival of the commanders of the land and air forces. Unlike the other correspondents who had built up the importance of the capture of Akyab, Morrison admitted the prestige factor in capturing the fifth town of Burma but played down its strategic importance. He described it as 'a poor port' whose land communications towards Rangoon were not ideal.[14]

Many more members of the British public would have seen the news from Akyab in cinema newsreels. They would have to wait some three weeks to view this. Oscar Bovill of Pathé was in Akyab filming on behalf of all the newsreels. Additional film would be provided by the RAF film unit. The troop landings provided some footage for Bovill as there was a nine-mile trudge from the coast to the centre of town. Despite some shots of cheering locals, it was depressing film as most of Akyab had been destroyed long before. *British Paramount News* made the most of the film, tidying up what was actually quite a messy landing with marines wading knee-deep through mud. The commentary said that the operation was made possible because of supplies and armaments provided by British factories, not least the square mesh which had allowed tanks to cross the beach.[15] Typically, the newsreel reporting was anodyne and non-controversial.

McKie's allegation of failed intelligence echoes complaints which General Slim had made earlier in 1944 when he called for an overhaul of the intelligence system.[16] Could the intelligence in the Arakan really have been as badly informed as McKie argued? It seems more likely that the Japanese had based three battalions in Akyab but moved out two of the battalions in response to the unexpectedly rapid advance of XV Corps down the Mayu peninsula. British intelligence had only picked up on the movement of one battalion. It is likely that the Japanese had kept away from the town, port and airfields which were heavily bombed. Once XV Corps had reached the tip of the Mayu peninsula, there was no possibility of the Japanese holding Akyab. Further pressure was put on them by the rapid advance of the 81st West African Division down the Kaladan valley.[17] The Japanese had to respond to this two-pronged attack. This seemed to be an example where correspondents following fighting in person could add valuable correctives and colour to official communiqués, but could be too close to have an overall picture. SEAC PR wanted the positive reactions to the Akyab capture played up in *SEAC* newspaper. Joubert was obviously concerned at the negative reactions of the troops to the critical press reports which seemed to indicate that the Japanese had left willingly and that the Allied advances were too cautious. He instructed the newspaper to make it plain that the Japanese only withdrew because of the pressure brought by Allied advances.[18]

There was a final twist in the tale of Akyab's recapture because, less than a fortnight later, Philip Joubert was recommending that Stuart Gelder should be moved to another theatre. This was to be a censure for a clear attempt to avoid censorship regulations by sending a press story by air from Akyab which was intended to reach Ian Stephens, editor of the *Statesman* newspaper in Calcutta. Gelder could be a difficult man, but this was a very unusual step for Joubert to take against one of the most respected correspondents, and the threat does not seem to have been carried out. Gelder continued to report right through to the fall of Mandalay when he finally took a deserved rest and gave in to the amoebic dysentery that had dogged him for a long time.[19]

Correspondents, including McKie, continued to cover the combined operations which took place further south at the Myebon peninsula, Ramree and Cheduba, which were more important strategically for the advance on Rangoon than Akyab. There were no commercial cameramen covering them. However, Paramount used SEAC and Indian Army Public Relations (IAPR) photographers' material.[20] The aim of these operations was to establish air bases in time to protect the assault on Rangoon, which needed to take place before the monsoon set in in May. They were successful in their objective and provided valuable training for the amphibious assault to capture Rangoon.

Advance from the Irrwawaddy to Mandalay and Meiktila

A good deal of attention was played by correspondents to the capture of Mandalay. This proved to be a long, time-consuming operation and correspondents must have been quite frustrated by the time it took to capture the heart of the city, the famous Fort Dufferin. *The Times* was sceptical about the focus given to capturing places like Mandalay:

> It would be a pity if the influence of Kipling were to confuse the operational picture; and it might be noted that the road which he undoubtedly had in mind, where the flying-fishes play, &c., was a sea road – a gentle reminder, perhaps, that amphibious operations, if undertaken, might still provide the quickest route to Mandalay, and certainly to the reconquest of Burma as a whole. Not Mandalay, but control of the road, rail, and river communications system of central Burma is the objective. Thebaw's capital is still 356 miles from Rangoon.[21]

The army was also concerned that unrealistic expectations of speedy landward advances were being promulgated by the press and called for PR to rein them in.[22] Whatever pressures may have been brought, the lure of the road to Mandalay stories was just too big an attraction for the correspondents. Clive Graham of the *Daily Express* homed in on the role of the romantically named Dagger Division, the 19th Indian Division, commanded by the diminutive Welsh general Thomas Wynford 'Pete' Rees. 'The stocky general was tireless and inspired all by his brisk confidence,' wrote Graham. 'There was nothing incongruous in seeing him wielding a pick and shovel with his men. His staff call him "Nap" from a resemblance to Napoleon.'[23]

The press emphasis on the capture of Mandalay may, however, have served to distract Japanese attention from the very bold manoeuvre by which Slim planned to send mobile troops much further south to capture the key Japanese position at Meiktila. This required a long period of secrecy from the correspondents as the Japanese needed to remain convinced that Mandalay was the main British objective and that moves to the south were feints.[24] Clive Graham triumphantly told of the capture of Meiktila at the beginning of March, revelling in the fact that he rode into the town on a tank. He predicted rather optimistically: '[I]f Meiktila stands firm we have virtually won the Burma war.'[25] Graham was able to rush back to Mandalay to report its capture on

21 March. He described its captor, General Rees, as 'another Monty'.[26] By this time, SEAC PR were very well established to help correspondents get stories and transmit them quickly. Brian Reynolds, *Daily Sketch* correspondent, reported:

> Five signallers from the 33rd Corps of the 14th Army worked in eight-hour shifts in a portable wireless transmitter van flashing to the world war correspondents' stories of General Rees' battle for Mandalay. News from the front was flown by light casualty planes and dispatch riders waited for it at the airport. The time that elapsed from the moment the story was written till it reached London office was often less than three hours.[27]

Advance to Rangoon

Rangoon was still a long way from Mandalay and the monsoon was imminent. When it came, the roads would become quagmires and advance would be slow. The lines of communication were becoming very stretched and there was the danger that American air support might be withdrawn to China.

This time the newsreel cameramen were in place, well most of them. John Turner, *Gaumont British News* cameraman, who was assigned to the navy, was actually stuck inland at Meiktila and missed the operation. It was left to Ronnie Noble and Oscar Bovill to film for the newsreels but the RAF and army film units were well placed to cover Operation Dracula. This was a combined operation which was necessary in case the 14th Army was not able to reach Rangoon in time for the breaking monsoon. It involved a parachute assault by Gurkhas on Elephant Point, south of the city and at the mouth of the Rangoon river leading into Rangoon. This took place on 1 May and, unfortunately, some of the troops were injured by misplaced aerial bombing. These troops became bogged down in deep mud as the monsoon had begun early and there was a spring tide. However, minesweepers were now able to clear a passage up the river and landing craft were able to come ashore on 2 May. It was becoming clear that the Japanese had actually evacuated the city some days earlier and either withdrew south to Moulmein or helped to hold up the 14th Army's advance at Pegu, north of the city. Oscar Bovill filmed the landings on the beaches and at jetties in Rangoon itself. He reported: 'A great reception was given to the troops by the Burmese, Indians and Chinese still left in Rangoon. There was not a shot fired by either side.' Filming was very difficult due to the rain and poor light.[28]

Rangoon was found to be in an appalling state, in part caused by Allied bombing but also by deliberate scorched earth tactics by the Japanese as they left. Noble described it as 'a scene of desolation. No water system in operation, no sewerage, no electricity, or gas. Small oil lamps provide the town's illumination, wells in the main street provide water, and the filth provides the breeding ground for the disease carrying flies.'[29] If the British evacuation from Rangoon in March 1942 had involved much deliberate destruction of resources, the Japanese withdrawal at the end of April 1945 left the city in a far worse state.[30] The capture of Rangoon was not the end of the Burma War by any means. The Japanese put up continued resistance for some time. However, it was an opportunity for the press to reflect on the achievement of the British, Indian, Gurkha, African, American and other troops involved in the long land campaign to regain Burma. Recognition was also given to the role played by the Burma and Indian navies, and above all the crucial role of the air force. Without air supremacy and the close support of the armed forces by air power, the Burma victory would have been unlikely. The RAF had always been very good at publicizing its role and this was brought to the forefront in the final stages of the campaign. *The War Illustrated* published an article extolling the role of the air force, with a picture and caption that indicated the role of Commonwealth airmen in the campaign. *The War Illustrated* was a British publication so perhaps its focus on the RAF might be excused; however, US transport, bomber and fighter planes had played a crucial role throughout the campaign.[31]

Victory raised new problems

The nearer the Allies came to defeating Japan in Burma the more difficult it was to keep the war correspondents 'on message'. The issue of political censorship had not gone away, but now resurfaced as journalists felt freer to vent the frustrations they had felt over a long campaign. American correspondents felt particularly aggrieved when Joubert cancelled a press conference that was planned to be given in April by the US General Stratemeyer.[32] The correspondents were particularly annoyed because this would have been their first chance to interview the commander of the Eastern Air Command in SEAC, who had been in charge of what they rightly regarded as the key American contribution to the reconquest of Burma, air supply to the ground forces. Apparently Joubert, as an Air Chief Marshal, was sensitive to the idea that the RAF's role would not be properly represented in the press conference. The correspondents' complaints reached Mountbatten who was clearly angry at the way this had been handled. Mountbatten always prioritized good relations with the Americans so that the complaints that Joubert had, over a period of time, played down American contributions to the war hit home hard. This became one of a number of issues in deteriorating relations between Mountbatten and Joubert in the last months of the war. Both men were strong, determined characters and, in some respects, it is remarkable that they worked together so well for so long.[33] However, Joubert's multiple roles in charge of PR, information, political warfare and civil affairs must have taken their toll on his health and temperament. In the previous month, he had been taken to task for his peremptory treatment of the BBC in negotiations over planned victory programmes and, worst of all, Mountbatten came to see him as disloyal for obstructing his conciliatory policy to Aung San and the Burma National Army (BNA).[34] Joubert returned to England for hospital treatment and did not return. He strongly denied charges of disloyalty but had differed with Mountbatten for some time over civil affairs issues.[35]

As any campaign came towards a close, particularly a victorious one, journalists felt freer to reflect on some of the wider issues involved. With large numbers of correspondents coming to Rangoon and later to Singapore to cover the final victory over Japan, it was more difficult to control them and keep them focused on army communiqués. There were newly released prisoners of war to interview, and the whole question of Burma's future, its economic recovery and future independence to raise. Independence brought to the forefront the future of the minority ethnic communities such as the Karens, Chins, Kachins, Nagas and Muslims who had helped the British and Americans during the war. Journalists were well aware from early on of the ethnic rivalries in Burma that meant that the Burman majority tended to support the Japanese occupation while minority ethnic groups, especially the hill tribes, were more likely to be hostile to their occupiers and could be recruited to act as guerrilla resistance to their new rulers.[36] The tribal levies, as they were known, were mobile guerrillas who were used to gather intelligence, support Special Operations Executive (SOE) operatives who were dropped behind Japanese lines, cut communications and generally harass enemy forces as much as possible. Correspondents inevitably came into contact with the levies and reported their activities when it was safe to do so. It is not clear whether they were encouraged to do so by army public relations. As Richard Duckett has pointed out, it took time for the Indian Army command to be convinced of the value of SOE activities: 'The military generally tended to worry that SOE was expensive in money and people and had a poor track record of successful operations.'[37] The ethnic groups worked in conjunction with the SOE and the OSS for the Americans. By their nature, these operations were secret and not reported on in any detail until nearer the end of the war. Publicity could lead to Japanese retribution against local villagers. It is now recognized that the SOE made an important contribution to the war, particularly in its early and later stages.[38] First, in 1942 by establishing Kachin levies the Japanese advance northwards was delayed, thus allowing British and Chinese forces to escape over the borders into India and China. They also managed to maintain a zone free from the Japanese in North Burma around Sumprabum that contained the airfield of Fort Hertz. This was important for protecting the 'Hump' air route over the Himalayas and for rescuing Allied pilots forced to land in that area. It was also the launching point for Stilwell's advance toward Myitkyina. In the latter stages of the war, SOE operated in conjunction with Karens to harry the retreating Japanese and facilitate the 14th Army's remarkably rapid advance southwards to recapture Rangoon.

Journalists also picked up on the question of where British military commitments in South East Asia would end, and when soldiers would be able to return home. This last issue related to the morale of the 14th Army, which had been involved in an incredibly long and arduous campaign. Arthur Helliwell wrote an impassioned front-page column in the *Daily Herald* which was headlined 'Send the 14th Army Home'. He depicted an army of 'veterans', some of whom had served abroad for five years in the most demanding conditions. These men had talked to him of longing to reach Rangoon and then going home. He argued that now they had reached Rangoon they 'should not embark on another campaign or fight another battle'.[39] Clive Graham of the *Daily Express* took up soldiers' complaints about the lack of cigarettes and beer and commented that the entertainment unit ENSA seemed 'to have forsaken Burma for the time being'.[40]

One correspondent, in particular, picked up the issue of what was happening to the Burmese peoples whose lands had been devastated during the war and who were in the process of being liberated from the Japanese. This was Ian Morrison of *The Times*.

Morrison was probably the most well-versed correspondent in the politics of South East Asia and the Far East. He had lived in Japan and China before the war and was proficient in their languages. He went to Singapore in 1941 and worked as Deputy Director of the Far Eastern Bureau of the MoI. When war with Japan broke out, he became a full-time war correspondent with *The Times* and provided realistic assessments for the paper during the losses of Malaya and Singapore. Like other journalists in Singapore, he clashed with the strict censorship organization there. He wrote critically of British colonialism in Malaya and published two books analysing the reasons for the debacle.[41] He escaped to Java and reported on the war in the south-west Pacific where he was injured more than once. In 1945 he was reporting in Burma as the 14th Army advanced into central Burma. Morrison was very aware of the desperate situation which the Burmese people faced with spiralling prices and shortages of basic commodities. Many people had been badly treated by the Japanese and lived in fear of the Japanese military police, the Kempeitai. It was very important for the Government of Burma and the Civil Affairs Service (CAS(B)), which was mostly manned by old Burma civil service hands, to try to quickly establish some form of civil administration and policing in liberated areas, while bringing in urgent supplies for the local population. Morrison wrote an article on 22 February 1945 which was highly critical of the failure to get supplies into these areas. In fact, it was the Government of Burma which he blamed more than civil affairs officers on the ground. According to Morrison, it seemed to be running the whole operation on 'traditional secretariat lines'.[42] This article and an accompanying editorial really annoyed Philip Joubert, who asked why the censors had let it through, and that Morrison should be put in touch with the CAS(B) to understand the true picture.[43] Wing Commander Maurice Thackrah, the 14th Army Chief Censor, defended the censor's decision, saying that Morrison was 'one of the more responsible journalists in this theatre who has availed himself of ample opportunity to see Civil Affairs officers at work and to discuss its problems with Civil Affairs officers'.[44] Thackrah said that Morrison's criticism of the Government of Burma reflected the views of other journalists. He also pointed out that censoring the article might cause embarrassment as Joubert was known to be in charge of both civil affairs and censorship.[45] This, he said, did not promise well for dealing with the complicated political problems which were now arising as Burmese national feeling had been much strengthened by the war.

Morrison was aware that some Burmese nationalists had already turned against the Japanese and formed an anti-fascist organization with armed forces ready to rise up. In fact, the British resisted any premature uprising of the BNA and waited until March 1945 when Mountbatten gave instructions that arms should be supplied to those BNA soldiers who would assist in the defeat of the Japanese. Mountbatten and General Slim could see the advantages of the intelligence and harassing measures which the BNA could use to speed up the 14th Army advance on Rangoon before the monsoon broke. However, Mountbatten looked beyond the immediate military benefits and could see wider political advantages, too. As Vernon Donnison put it, '[H]e would be able to leave the civil government a useful, if not valuable, legacy of having helped the Burmese to liberate themselves.' It would be better to have the BNA assistance seen as helping the British rather than opposing them.[46] Another factor was that now that 'political' censorship had been circumscribed, it would be very difficult to avoid news of a British refusal to allow the offer of help from Burmese nationalists becoming public and this would not go down well with world opinion.[47]

Mountbatten sympathized with Burmese nationalist aspirations, believing that the Anti-Fascist People's Freedom League (AFPFL), as the umbrella nationalist organization was known, was the only organization that had substantial popular support in the country. This view was not shared by Dorman-Smith, the governor, who was concerned that some of the more traditional political leaders and ethnic groups who had been loyal to the British throughout the campaign were being displaced by those who, for most of the war, had supported the Japanese and who had only switched sides when they realized what the outcome would be.[48] This difference of opinion was to have long-term repercussions for Burma as it reflected different views about how quickly Burma could be granted self-government. Mountbatten believed that recognizing the inevitability of a rapid transition to independence would result in Burma staying in the Commonwealth. Dorman-Smith, on the other hand, believed that the British should, while promising early independence, stay on long enough to help rebuild the country, to ensure the security of their long-term political and ethnic allies, and ensure a stable transition. In retrospect, Mountbatten was proved correct, but Dorman-Smith was actually implementing the agreed policy of the British government at that time.

Mountbatten was keen, as soon as Rangoon was retaken on 2 May, to advertise the role of the BNA in helping to defeat the Japanese, which he dated back to 26 March and praised its 'notable contribution to the liberation of Burma'.[49] He even had Joubert write to Brendan Bracken, Minister of Information, asking for his personal intervention in securing publicity for this in Britain.[50] A further story detailing the exploits of the BNA in fighting the Japanese in central Burma and in support of the capture of Rangoon was put out with the request from Joubert that it be given the widest possible publicity. The story was significantly entitled 'The Burmese Partisans', which linked these guerrilla forces with those in Europe which were helping the Allies.[51] This was significant because it aligned Mountbatten with a pragmatic view that, just as in places like Italy, Greece and Yugoslavia, it was necessary to work with the most powerful partisan groups even if they were politically aligned to the Communists.[52] In March, the War Cabinet Committee had warned Mountbatten against giving publicity to the AFPFL, which some saw as a Communist organization like the EAM-ELAS resistance movement in Greece, which was causing the British a good deal of trouble at the time.[53] Mountbatten was treading a very thin line.[54] Events would work in his favour. First, because the BNA proved its military value in the final stages of defeating the Japanese. Secondly, it was becoming clear that expanding SEAC military obligations in South East Asia and the need to repatriate British and Commonwealth troops after a very long campaign would mean it would be very difficult to suppress a nationalist uprising in Burma. There were also obvious political difficulties of using Indian troops to put down any Burmese nationalist insurgency. The election of a Labour government at the end of July 1945, which was looking to find a quick way out of India, and the obvious popular support for Aung San and the AFPFL, all pointed in the direction of a much more rapid transfer of power in Burma than Dorman-Smith and the coalition government could have expected.

However, not all journalists conformed to Mountbatten's line. Alan Humphreys of API caused annoyance in SEAC with an article in the *Hindustan Times* of 9 May which warned: 'Greatest potential threat to civil order exists in elements of the Burma Defence Army. As measure towards firm control of Rangoon this body is being disarmed but by no means all weapons are coming in and many firearms going underground.'[55] Rangoon was pretty lawless in the period after its recapture and Humphreys reflected the views of senior army personnel about the 'bad apples' within the patriot forces. Mountbatten was clearly annoyed at such reports coming at a time when he wanted to win Aung San and the BNA over, although he opposed censoring such views, preferring to give wider circulation to 'approved' articles.[56]

Mountbatten realized that in the delicate process of separating the nationalist sheep from the goats, of integrating the better elements into the army and trying those guilty of serious crimes, there was a danger of negative press comments leading to a dangerous breakdown in negotiations with Burmese nationalists. It was important to keep in mind the position of Dorman-Smith who would soon start discussions with various interests in Burma and would eventually return in charge of civil government at some point. It was also important to remember that Burma policy would ultimately be made by the British government. Articles about the BNA would need to go through the chief censor, but it would have to be made clear this was not political censorship but was imposed on security grounds.[57] It seems that Ian Morrison and Clive Graham wrote to Mountbatten protesting about the censorship restrictions. Morrison was able to write two very full articles in *The Times* which very much took the Mountbatten line, although they had a sting in the tail. He explained to readers the history of the BNA and the broad-based AFPFL, of which it was the armed part.[58] He recognized: 'There is a lawless and self-seeking element among them, but for the foreseeable future these Burmese will be easily the most potent political force in the country. Their nationalism is intense. Their aim is simple – full independence for Burma ... Dominion status, it may be frankly said, holds little appeal.'[59] Mountbatten's entire strategy was based on the belief that by offering Burmese nationalists early independence they would agree to keeping Burma within the Commonwealth as a Dominion.[60] Mountbatten used the same strategy later when Viceroy of India. It worked in India but not in Burma where Morrison's reading of the situation was the more accurate one, and Burma stayed outside the Commonwealth on independence in 1948.[61]

General Slim, who met with Aung San on 16 May, was impressed with the Burmese nationalist leader on a personal level but argued in a meeting with Mountbatten that great care should be taken not to build him up as a national hero: 'in fact the less said about Aung San the better. It should also be remembered that the BNA was originally a Japanese-inspired organisation and that a part of them were still under Ba Maw.'[62] Mountbatten agreed, but argued that what was needed was a clear distinction in guidance to the press between the Burmese nationalists who were fighting for the British, whom he now preferred to be called the Local Burmese Forces (LBF) and those BNA who were attached to Ba Maw who were fighting for the Japanese.[63] However, Aung San had his own ideas about what his followers should be called and said they were to be called Patriot Burmese Forces (PBF). Mountbatten agreed and instructed that the press be told of the new name, but it be given no special publicity until its forces would be formally integrated into the Burma Army.[64]

There was still the need to convince Burmese nationalists that the British were the power to work with and, as Richard Duckett has argued, 'one way of doing that was through the spectacle of a victory parade in Rangoon on 15 June 1945'.[65] Mountbatten was keen to ensure that seventeen American correspondents who were attending the victory parade were given a grandstand view.[66] Special arrangements were made to fly correspondents from Rangoon and Mountbatten placed his own Mercury aircraft at the disposal of the press for the speediest transmission to Kandy.[67] The *Daily Express* reported on the parade that 5,000 troops of nine nations took part in it. Graham wrote rather ominously: 'When the local Burma forces contingent reached the saluting base, they broke into the Japanese ceremonial goose-step'. However, as if to reassure readers, he added that 'they were clad in British jungle green, the first step to absorbing them into armed service under the Crown'.[68]

If the victory parade was supposed to show Aung San that rebellion against such strong forces would be suicidal, Mountbatten was also prepared to proffer the political carrot of a formal meeting with Dorman-Smith, the governor of Burma in exile since 1942. This would be an indication of moves towards the restoration of civil government. Unfortunately, the good intentions rather backfired. The meeting had to take place offshore on board a navy ship because military government remained in place on the mainland.[69] It took place on 20 June and Mountbatten intended that it should be given good publicity.[70] The meeting was filmed by Ronnie Noble for the British newsreels and was linked with the Rangoon victory parade in the newsreels.[71] Correspondents reported favourably, if rather uncritically, on the meeting, seeing it as the beginning of a swift move to independence for Burma, a way of reconciling the different ethnic and political interests in Burma. Clive Graham had already written: 'Our handling of the Burmese situation is wise, liberal and stamped with sincerity'.[72] After the meeting he quoted Dorman-Smith's promise: 'We do not mean to wait until 1948 to give Burma her independence ... As soon as electoral rolls are ready Burma will be free to elect her own government'.[73]

In fact, this meeting was very important in defining the attitude of Aung San and the AFPFL towards the British Government. Although Dorman-Smith seemed to please Burmese leaders by promising moves to reconstruct Burma and recognizing the need to move towards independence, Aung San realized that, by including in the meeting ethnic groups like the Karens and more conservative figures like Sir Paw Tun, Dorman-Smith was continuing to try to work with the old discredited politicians.[74] 'Above all,' Bayly and Harper argue, 'the Governor's reappearance brought to the surface the underlying conflicts between the British and the nationalists in Burma.'[75] The British were not setting any date for independence and Burma was still intended to be within the Commonwealth, something that the nationalists would not accept.

Conclusion

1945 had been a very good year for SEAC, and the media were in place to tell that story. The Japanese had been driven back across the Irrawaddy and the Allies had recaptured Mandalay and Rangoon. The facilities for correspondents to cover the fighting and transmit their dispatches home rapidly had been achieved. The story the reporters told necessarily became more complicated as it broadened from discussing details of military activities to much broader and more complex issues such as those of troop and POW welfare and repatriation. New political issues arose relating to the post-war future of Burma, restoring its ruined economy and stabilizing its long-standing ethnic rivalries. However, it was just at this time that it became harder for Burma stories to grab the headlines. The American media had lost interest in the Burma campaign and had moved their attention to the dramatic stories of island advances in the Pacific. The British media was focused on the final stages of the war in Europe and the victory celebrations that took place at its end. People needed to be reminded that the war was not yet over in the Far East, and this is the point in time when the soldiers felt increasingly forgotten by those at home. Resentments built up around fears that many combatants would not be going home for some time but would be kept on for unpopular operations to restore colonial rule in Malaya, Indonesia and Indochina. There was a strong feeling that the 14th Army and its brilliant commander Bill Slim had not been give due recognition in London. It was this revived notion of being a 'Forgotten Army' which would feed into long-lasting images of the Burma War.

13

Conclusion

What lessons for army media management were learnt during the India-Burma War?

The first and most obvious lesson learnt in media management during the India-Burma War was that generals and PROs should avoid any 'overselling' of campaigns or military operations in advance of knowing whether they were likely to be successful. This was the lesson learnt from the advance into Burma to try and recapture Akyab in late 1942 and spring 1943. In fact, the army had tried to play down the advance into Arakan but because of public expectations that there would be a rapid attempt to erase the defeats of 1942, the message did not get through clearly enough. The disastrous failure of this campaign coincided with the first Chindit expedition. While historians may disagree about the effectiveness of Wingate's operation, it was seen at the time, and since, as a morale-booster and media management triumph. The irony is that there was in fact very little media coverage planned for the early stages of Wingate's advance and the presence of correspondents was almost accidental. The fact that correspondents maintained a promise of silence about the operation for three months was also remarkable. The eventual media fanfare was a triumph of organization, however. It did not last long but it set a pattern for all future media planning of operations. Media coverage would be set up in advance, but publication would be kept low-key until it was known that operations would be safe and likely to be successful.

Following on from this, it was important to have good stories prepared in advance for the media with a timed blanket news coverage. This meant keeping government publicity organizations informed of forthcoming operations so that they could prepare material in advance – for instance, background stories on the generals or regiments involved. This was only really achieved by the second half of 1944 when SEAC established a presence at Ministry of Information (MoI) headquarters in London, and British Information Services (BIS) in Washington was geared up to provide material to the American media. This publicity could be sustained if extended with the release of photographs and stories that were suited to the pictorial magazines, which were not quite so concerned with only using 'hot news'.

The fullest coverage depended on having representatives of the main media available to cover the operations. Key media would always include correspondents from the main international news agencies, such as AP, UP and Reuters, whose reports would receive the widest global coverage. Newsreel cameramen were also in demand because they were one of the main visual sources of war news in Britain and America. The presence of cameramen in particular theatres could be encouraged and organized in Britain by the Newsreel Association, which also conveniently arranged facilities for footage to be pooled so that it was widely available, even globally. It was not so easy to arrange for the presence of correspondents from particular representatives of the print media. Owners and editors largely followed their own priorities of which areas to cover and when.[1] Pictorial magazines, especially *Life* and *Illustrated*, were recognized as especially important to attract for the depth of the stories they told and for their undoubted audience impact, and international readerships.

It was crucial to ensure that correspondents had good facilities to ensure fast censorship and transmission of their stories. Burma news was difficult enough to get into the newspapers: old Burma news virtually impossible. Burma presented particular problems not only of transmitting dispatches from the jungle fighting fronts but also over large distances to Britain and America. Fast transmission was achieved first from SEAC headquarters at Kandy in 1944 and then was available to correspondents as the 14th Army advanced into upper and central Burma in 1945.

Censorship was necessary but it was important to limit it as far as possible to reasons of military security. This was the lesson painfully learnt through the correspondents' strike of 1944. Correspondents accepted the need for security censorship, indeed many welcomed it as a form of protection from making costly errors, but they disliked what they called 'policy' or political censorship. The problem was that the political situation in India, and the reliance on Indian troops and support of all types, inevitably meant that political considerations impinged on censorship in this theatre. What correspondents really wanted was fairness in the way they were treated by censors. Correspondents who troubled to reach distant fighting fronts were really annoyed if they felt that their reports were delayed and were then scooped by rival correspondents based at headquarters, with faster transmission facilities. They particularly resented any form of multiple censorship, i.e. where dispatches approved in one military theatre were subject to a second censorship elsewhere.

Lastly, extended periods of news blackout proved counterproductive. These had been imposed at times when campaigns were going badly, such as at Arakan in 1943 and Kohima in 1944. The problem was that the absence of news led to the spread of unfounded rumours, which could spread very fast in the febrile atmosphere of cities like Calcutta. This could have a deleterious impact in the form of mass civilian evacuation and the loss of key workers. It also caused disquiet among newspaper editors and led to questions in Parliament. These censorship controversies led to real improvements in censorship policies, and some determination to bring Indian censorship policies into line with overall empire ones.

Did the media act as propagandists for the armed forces?

There has been much criticism from historians of the way in which the media in both Britain and the United States failed to report truthfully what they experienced in the Second World War. Most correspondents, it is argued, succumbed too readily to government and military pressures to withhold stories or to tell misleadingly optimistic ones during the Second World War. As far as Phillip Knightley was concerned, there was far too cosy a relationship between the war correspondents and the military during the war. In his highly influential book, *The First Casualty*, he castigated those journalists who knew the truth in wartime but failed to report it. He attributed this to a misplaced sense of patriotism, a belief that the truth would damage the nation's war effort or morale. War correspondents, he argued, 'went along with the official scheme for reporting the war because they were convinced that it was in the national interest to do so. They saw no sharp line of demarcation between the role of the press in war-time and that of the government.'[2] Other historians have supported Knightley's view, and some have expressed it even more strongly, such as Connelly and Welch:

> During much of the twentieth century, governments and military leadership could generally rely on the journalists and news agencies to cooperate in supporting nationalistic and patriotic causes. The media willingly collaborated in disseminating propaganda justifying war aims, sustaining the morale of the home and fighting fronts and demonising the enemy. Such collaboration inevitably resulted in a form of war reporting that was less concerned with accuracy than with propaganda.[3]

A word like 'collaborated' has a very particular resonance in a Second World War context and seems inappropriate when discussing the contribution of journalists, most of whom put their lives at risk over long periods of service, and some of whom were killed in pursuit of their profession. Much more nuanced studies have come out of detailed research into the reporting of the war. Richard Fine, examining reporting in North Africa and Europe, has argued convincingly that the military and the media were 'far more adversarial during the Second World War than most accounts would have it'.[4] Steven Casey's meticulously researched and detailed studies of the American media in the European and Pacific theatres spell out a similar message.[5] Of the reporters in the European theatre, he concludes that their most striking characteristic was 'their lack of docility. They were not compliant cheerleaders who abandoned all thought of impartiality to trumpet the official line. Nor did they always give the home front an anodyne version of war that conveniently airbrushed out all the gruesome bits.'[6]

My previous study of war correspondents during the Burma retreat of 1942 tends to support the views of Fine and Casey that it is too simple to see the journalists as mouthpieces for the military.[7] In the retreat, the army tended to rely on censorship to maintain morale at a very difficult time. However, reporters constantly tried to find ways round that censorship and challenged it wherever they could, sometimes successfully. Some correspondents behaved well and others badly, incurring the wrath of the civilian government and the army censor alike. However, they tried their best to keep the public informed while not in any way undermining the war effort. It is far too simple to see them as propagandists for the government or the military.

This book did not set out to test the veracity of the correspondents' reporting but rather to look at how the media responded to military attempts to manage their coverage of the India-Burma War. Following Casey's argument of changes in correspondents' attitudes according to how the war was progressing, one can see such changes taking place over the course of the war in Burma. In 1942, many of the journalists were more experienced in warfare than the PROs they dealt with. Some had come from the debacle in Singapore with its strict censorship, and they were not prepared to meekly accept limitations on their reporting freedom, especially when criticizing non-military matters such as civilian evacuation, arrangements to move Lend-Lease equipment from the docks in Rangoon, and civil defence arrangements. They had little choice but to submit to censorship on military matters as they relied on the army to provide them with transport and transmission arrangements. There were challenges to censorship, but they were rarely successful. As the war progressed, the main complaint related to political censorship which they regarded as being imposed by India Command out of sensitivity over the impact on Indian public opinion. This reached a climax with the correspondents' strike in April 1944, after which it became clearer that censorship was primarily a SEAC responsibility and would be limited to security issues only. Correspondents generally accepted the reasons for this censorship. As the Burma campaign headed to a successful outcome in 1945, many more correspondents came into Burma, and there was a general feeling that censorship would inevitably be wound down as Japanese forces were defeated. Correspondents pursued stories that previously would have been considered off limits. Topics that were reported derived broadly from questions about Burma's political future after Japan was defeated. These included the role of Civil Affairs officers as areas of Burma were liberated, the role of ethnic minorities in Burma's political future, and, most important, how Burmese nationalists and their armed forces could be integrated safely into a phased transition to Burmese independence. These were sensitive issues, potentially involving military security, but they were also political. It was a tribute to Mountbatten's political skill that he realized this and maintained the principle of press freedom.

Was this a 'Forgotten War'? What part did the media play in improving soldier morale in Burma?

Captain Cyril Falls, the eminent military correspondent of the *Illustrated London News*, wrote a very perceptive article towards the end of the war commenting on media coverage of the different campaigns.[8] He was writing at a time when there were many complaints, not least from the soldiers themselves, that the army in Burma was not given enough attention in the media, especially considering the hardships and long, still-continuing service that many endured. Falls argued it was only in twentieth-century warfare, which coincided with technological improvements in the speed of media coverage, that the ordinary soldier could be said 'to have taken a deep and continuous interest in what was said about him and his campaigns'. Soldiers in all theatres could receive up-to-date news of the campaigns they were involved in through the radio and military newspapers which included quotes from the home press. Public relations organizations had developed which ensured that news was transmitted more speedily from the front, and the use of military observers meant that news of individual units and personnel could reach local newspapers. He concluded:

The British fighting man has thus become what is called 'publicity conscious.' If a feat of arms should in error be attributed to the wrong formation or unit, there is heartburning and a prompt protest, whereas formerly such a thing would have passed unnoticed. At the same time, he has begun to demand up-to-date comment. If the unit to which he belongs has accomplished something of note within the last week or two, he wants to hear about that.

Falls played down the idea that the army in Burma was unfairly forgotten by the media. At certain times, such as the Chindit expeditions or the capture of Mandalay and Rangoon, it had received very full attention. At other times, the media had given priority to more active, or what they regarded as more important, theatres. These were inevitably based on professional judgments about the interests of their audiences and readerships, which changed according to the progress of the war. He concluded:

To put the whole matter as shortly as possible, every campaign or theatre of war must make its own news all over the world. On the other hand, an intelligent democracy should not require to be reminded at length every day that men are fighting and dying for it in distant and obscure theatres of war. If we do forget, then the reproach cannot be confined to the news services; it must extend to the whole country.

At a time when the last Burma campaign veterans are rightly receiving the attention that is their due, Falls's arguments may seem harsh, but the evidence suggests that he was broadly correct. Media coverage of the Burma campaign waxed and waned at different times and for a variety of reasons. In 1942 there were many correspondents who arrived in Burma having covered the war from Singapore, Thailand or China. As a result, there was plenty of media coverage of the loss of Rangoon and the long retreat in 1942, whatever the quality of that reporting might be considered to have been. In 1943, the advance in the Arakan was deliberately played down and there were few reporters present to cover it. From the government's point of view, this may have been just as well, considering how badly it went. Wingate's first experiment in long-range penetration (LRP) warfare, Operation Longcloth, turned out, almost accidentally, to have been a masterstroke of publicity. Even so, it was short-lived and may have backfired in terms of the longer-term military implications. The real turning point in publicizing the Burma campaign came after October 1943 when Mountbatten was appointed Supreme Commander South East Asia. Before accepting his appointment, Mountbatten had insisted that he needed to be provided with material support for a much-enlarged media campaign. His personal contacts in the newspaper, radio and film industries ensured that he would get the best people to come out to India-Burma to put his ideas into practice. Mountbatten realized, along with his army commanders, notably General Slim, that it was vital to restore the morale of the fighting forces in Burma, and that regular news coverage of their activities should be given much greater attention. Mountbatten's interest in media coverage was detailed and persistent. It ranged from his own roving soapbox talks to the troops, to the limitation of press censorship to security issues only, to the provision of forces' newspapers and magazines, and to a Hollywood collaboration on a Burma campaign film. He did not always get his way. He was prohibited from broadcasting directly to the troops for some time, and he could not overcome the commercial priorities of the media that Falls pointed out.

During the 1942 retreat, the army public relations organization had been set up too slowly and had limited resources. In the circumstances, it was probably inevitable that censorship was the main tool to be used, and that this led to negative feedback from many correspondents. Media management was largely confined to helping the correspondents with transport and communication issues. In 1943, censorship, particularly Indian Army censorship, was still an important factor. The news blackout when the Arakan campaign went badly wrong was an example of how over-rigorous censorship could lead to newspapers being unwilling to send correspondents to what was, in any case, a very difficult war to cover. The technique of using off-the-record press conferences also had its limitations. There needed to be greater openness. It might be thought that the media handling of the return of Wingate's first Chindit operation was masterful in comparison with what had gone on before. The army had not originally planned for correspondents to cover the expedition, but the fact that three correspondents were attached to its early stage meant that at least some newspapers had very good material ready to hand when publicity was released to coincide with Wingate's large press conference at Delhi on 21 May 1943. The stories of ordinary soldiers getting behind enemy lines and carrying out sabotage operations would have been enthralling enough, but they were also backed by personal stories of valour and eccentricity which guaranteed front-page coverage. No one was more eccentric and charismatic than Wingate, and journalists linked him with Lawrence of Arabia and called him 'Clive of Burma'. The propaganda coup was short-lived and papered over the very heavy casualties incurred by the Chindits. It propelled Wingate to fame and even to the Allied conference at Quebec where Wingate won American approval for a second, much larger operation.

Although the coverage of Operation Longcloth was a success and a boost to morale after so many setbacks, it did not offer the long-term boost to morale that was needed by the Indian soldiers who had not been used by Wingate, but who comprised the majority of the forces in the larger campaign. The improvement of army morale was something which derived from much improved training and tactics. It paid off in 1944 when the Japanese assaults in Arakan and into Assam were turned back and proof was given that the Japanese were not the sole masters of jungle conditions. In recent years, historians have given more attention to the question of troop morale in the Second World War. This has particular importance in the India-Burma context because British troops fighting in appalling conditions generally disliked their distant posting, especially when it seemed to mean a postponed demobilization. The morale of Indian troops was potentially much more problematic as the Indian Army had been expanded so quickly and by so many men that unquestioned loyalty to the British Raj could no longer be taken for granted. The loss of thousands of soldiers to Bose's Indian National Army (INA), and the fact that this could never be mentioned by the media, was indicative of this. Yet, despite the evidence that most Indians serving in the army wanted India's independence, there was overwhelming adherence to seeing the war through successfully. The ingredients of good morale are many, but it is strange that the recent studies give little attention to the role of the media in boosting morale. This is surprising because it was the first topic raised in each of the two reports on troop morale and welfare instigated by Churchill from September 1944 through to the end of the war. Lord Munster in his report headed this section 'Publicity at Home', while General King used the peculiar heading 'Indoctrination'.⁹ In fact, this was not a matter of conveying propaganda, which seemed to have little purchase with soldiers, but rather of maintaining a contact with home and family, and of their seeing recognition of the value of what they were doing in Burma. The daily airdrop of *SEAC* newspapers along with mail to even distant frontline troops was recognized as important to boosting morale. It had been arranged that British national newspapers would provide *SEAC* with up-to-date stories. Soldiers could let off steam about the lack of entertainment or the quality of food in the letters columns of the paper. On a smaller scale, officer observers could relay stories about local regiments and personnel to local newspapers, and even return home to give talks, too. The opportunity for soldiers to record filmed messages, *Calling Blighty*, to their loved ones at home was also much appreciated. The BBC had sometimes been seen as out of touch with reality in the earlier stages of the war, but in the last two years the presence of BBC correspondents relaying stories direct from the frontline was a boost to soldiers as they could listen to the broadcasts on camp radios. Broadcasts were also increased on Burma and Far East topics at home.

The correspondents' strike resulting from censorship in the early stages of the defence of Kohima marked the end of the old censorship regime and the beginning of a personal determination on Mountbatten's part to reduce censorship strictly to security issues only. Trusting the correspondents, as seen elsewhere in the war, proved to be the best policy. Technological improvements in cameras, transportable broadcasting equipment and fast radio transmission of photographs meant that in the later stages of the war the quality and speed of media coverage was much improved. The visual results could be seen in the remarkable quality of the film *Burma Victory*. Good coverage was given to the last stages of the war in Burma when newsreel cameramen were organized in numbers, and events such as the capture of Akyab and Ramree could be, in effect, 'staged' for cameramen and journalists.

Improved media communications meant that, just after weary Allied soldiers were struggling through the monsoon mud to recapture Rangoon and to face a long struggle with surviving Japanese forces, they would have learnt on 8 May of the celebrations of victory in Europe. Inevitably, coverage of this jubilation relegated news from Burma to minor coverage in the home media. Servicemen in Burma wanted people at home to know that this was not the end of the war and that the end might well be a long way off.¹⁰ This is where the 'Forgotten Army' image seems to have become more firmly entrenched as issues of demobilization and the return of prisoners of war came to the forefront.

The year 2020 saw an unprecedented amount of attention to the India-Burma War as part of the celebrations of the 75th anniversary of victory over Japan. Ironically, it has tended to lead to a repetition of the clichéd term, 'Forgotten War', even in the act of remembering the bitter and prolonged campaign. We have seen how the efforts of Mountbatten, SEAC publicists and the media contributed to the image through the very process of trying to counteract it. Yet its longevity derived from the way that it became embedded in the first major history of the Second World War written by Winston Churchill. His six-volume history was immensely popular when published between 1948 and 1953. It set a broad pattern for popular understanding of the war, but it was written from the very personal viewpoint of a wartime leader who was looking to return to power and to operating in a new Cold War situation. It was written by a team of eminent military figures but reflected Churchill's views and prejudices.[11] Churchill gave relatively little space to the war in Burma and failed to even mention the 14th Army in the relevant volume.[12] This was in part because it reflected his long-standing prejudices against the Indian Army, but also because Burma had been a military embarrassment in 1942–3 and a cause of Anglo-American strategic differences throughout the war. However, as Cat Wilson points out, it was not Churchill alone to blame for the failure to give the Indian Army its proper due, but it was true that the official history, which was published in 1958 and might have rectified the situation, was eclipsed in the popular mind by Churchill's epic volumes.

In the last few decades, there have been many books, films and television programmes on the India-Burma War and it can no longer be considered a forgotten war in that respect.[13] Should the clichéd terms 'Forgotten Army' and 'Forgotten War' now be avoided? For historians, they can still be useful if confined to the particular limited time and issues they referred to. From the soldiers' point of view, this began in 1943 when reporters were thin on the ground and, apart from the first Chindit expedition, there was relatively little media coverage of the Burma War compared with other theatres. However, complaints of being forgotten were particularly strong in the last quarter of 1944 at the time of the Munster Report, and also as the fighting was coming to an end in May–August 1945. The first date marked the point at which the government looked forward to the end of the war with Germany and the need to focus on defeating Japan. This triggered questions of how existing troops could be encouraged to see this long campaign through, and indeed extended into recovering territories in South East Asia about which they probably cared little. There was also the need to persuade navy recruits of the justification for sending them to fight in the Pacific when it was still expected that it might take a long time to defeat Japan. Service personnel were cynical of politicians' motives and promises in focusing on issues of troop morale at this stage when so little had been done before.[14] The closer it came to the defeat of Germany in 1945, the more soldiers were sensitive to the increased attention their comrades in Europe were receiving in comparison with their own apparent neglect by the press. The British public's joyous reaction to victory in Europe and the attempt to return to normal life, while obviously welcomed by those serving in the Far East, also seemed to alienate those who wanted to assert their war was far from over. There were serious issues to be addressed about deficiencies of pay, provisions and amenities, and, most of all, questions of when and how soldiers who served in the longest British campaign of the war would return home.

However, even when issues of soldier morale were receiving their greatest attention, the term 'Forgotten Army' was widely challenged as inappropriate by politicians from the prime minister down. The general public also responded by increasing support for those serving in the Far East in both words and practical deeds. Those in public relations roles such as at the MoI or the editors of *SEAC* newspaper vehemently argued that the Burma campaign was not forgotten by the media, although, of course, they would not have wanted to admit what would have been a failure of publicity on their part.[15]

Journalists resorted to clichés as shorthand all the time, and 'Forgotten Army' came into this category. At the time it may have served a purpose in helping people to identify with a multinational army in a complicated war in a very distant part of the world, but such hackneyed terms should not be allowed to become unchallenged myths. Just as historians have recognized how myths like those attached to Dunkirk, the Blitz spirit, 'Britain alone' in 1940, and 'The People's War' can have a misleading, and perhaps damaging, historical legacy, the idea of the Burma campaign as a 'Forgotten War' needs to be critically reassessed.[16] This should be done, however, while continuing to give deserved recognition and admiration to those who fought in that most difficult campaign.

Notes

1 Introduction

1. https://www.britishlegion.org.uk/get-involved/remembrance/remembrance-events/vj-day/remembering-the-forgotten/why-is-the-fourteenth-army-known-as-the-forgotten-army, accessed 5 November 2021.
2. Graham Stanford conducted a mini-campaign when he was on home leave during the summer of 1943 to rouse interest in what he described as the 'forgotten front': *Daily Mail*, 29 June 1943, p. 2; 26 August, p. 1; 16 September, p. 2.
3. Mountbatten addressing 136 Field Regiment Royal Artillery on 15 December 1943 in Arakan.
4. China and Chinese troops were also very much involved in Burma but there were very few Chinese correspondents accredited to SEAC, so that no attempt has been made to look at Chinese media management in the war. I could only find one accredited Chinese correspondent, Eddie Tseng of the China Central News Agency, who was with Stilwell in the Hukawng valley in 1944.
5. Philip Woods, *Reporting the Retreat: War Correspondents in Burma, 1942*, London: Hurst & Co., 2016.
6. 'Heroes: Glimpse of an Epic', *Time*, 10 August 1942.
7. Nicholas Reeves, *The Power of Film Propaganda: Myth or Reality?*, London: Cassell, 1999, pp. 140–6.
8. Brigadier Desmond Young, who was appointed Director of Public Relations, Army HQ, India, in December 1944, claimed in his memoir that when he visited Washington, he learnt that Churchill had ordered a ban on publicizing the Indian Army. Naturally, he overturned this order for which he could see 'no military reason': *Try Anything Twice*, London: Hamish Hamilton, 1963, p. 320.
9. Somerset Struben de Chair (Norfolk South West), House of Commons Debates, 12 December 1944.
10. See Woods, *Reporting the Retreat*. Appendix 1 lists the twenty-six correspondents in Burma during 1942 with details of the dates of their arrivals and departures. Two women correspondents, Claire Booth Luce and Eve Curie, were not formally accredited.
11. D. R. Mankekar, *Leaves from a War Reporter's Diary*, New Delhi: Vikas, 1977, p. 99.
12. Some examples of excellent military histories of the Burma campaign are: Louis Allen, *Burma: The Longest War 1941–1945*. London: Phoenix Press, 2000; Jon Latimer, *Burma: The Forgotten War,* London: John Murray, 2004; Robert Lyman, *Slim, Master of War: Burma and the Birth of Modern Warfare*, London: Constable & Robinson, 2004; Raymond Callahan, *Churchill and His Generals*, Lawrence, KS: University of Kansas Press, 2007; Robert Lyman, *Kohima: The Battle That Saved India*, Oxford: Osprey, 2010; Frank McLynn, *The Burma Campaign: Disaster into Triumph, 1942–45*, New Haven: Yale University Press, 2011; James Holland, *Burma '44: The Battle That Turned Britain's War in the East*, London: Corgi, 2016; Robert Lyman, *A War of Empires: Japan, India, Burma & Britain 1941–45*, Oxford: Osprey, 2021.

13 An exception were two pioneering studies which focused on the crucial inter-Allied relationship in the Far East theatre: Raymond Callahan, *Burma, 1942–1945*, London: Davis-Poynter, 1978; Christopher Thorne, *Allies of a Kind: The United States, Britain and the War against Japan, 1941–1945*, London: Hamish Hamilton, 1978.
14 Christopher Bayly and Tim Harper, *Forgotten Armies: Britain's Asian Empire & The War with Japan*, London: Penguin Books, 2005.
15 For the SOE and its connections to ethnic groups, see Richard Duckett, *The Special Operations Executive (SOE) in Burma: Jungle Warfare and Intelligence Gathering in World War II*, London: I.B. Tauris, 2017; Robert A. Farnan, 'Indigenous resistance as irregular warfare. The role of Kachin forces in SOE and OSS covert operations during the Burma campaign' in Chris Murray (ed.), *Unknown Conflicts of the Second World War: Forgotten Fronts*, London: Routledge, 2019, pp. 120–38.
16 See Woods, *Reporting the Retreat*, pp. 109–11.
17 The mass exodus has been very well covered in two books by Michael Leigh: *The Evacuation of Civilians from Burma: Analysing the 1942 Colonial Disaster*, London: Bloomsbury Academic, 2014; *The Collapse of British Rule in Burma: The Civilian Evacuation and Independence*, London: Bloomsbury Academic, 2018.
18 In the case of Burma, this was most clear in his organization of the Rangoon victory parade (15 June 1945) and the shipboard meeting of the governor of Burma with Burmese politicians (20 June 1945). See Chapter 12 for more details. The parallel examples for India would be his stage-managed swearing-in ceremony as viceroy on 24 March 1947, and the press conference on 4 June to announce the plan for independence and the partition of India. For a vivid description of the swearing-in, see Alex von Tunzelman, *Indian Summer: The Secret History of the End of an Empire*, London: Simon & Schuster, 2007, pp. 164–6. For the 4 June press conference, see Philip Ziegler, *Mountbatten: The Official Biography*, London: Collins, 1985, pp. 387–9.
19 This is an important theme in Lyman, *A War of Empires*.
20 Srinath Raghavan, *India's War: The Making of Modern South Asia 1939–1945*, London: Allen Lane, 2016; Yasmin Khan, *The Raj at War: A People's History of India's Second World War*, London: Bodley Head, 2015.
21 Ashley Jackson, *The British Empire and the Second World War*, London: Hambledon Continuum, 2006. The standard work on African troops, who also played an important part in the Burma campaign, is still David Killingray and Martin Plaut, *Fighting for Britain: African Soldiers in the Second World War*, Woodbridge: James Currey, 2010. Barnaby Phillips, *Another Man's War: The Story of a Burma Boy in Britain's Forgotten African Army*, London: OneWorld Publications, 2014, has added a human element to that story.
22 Tarak Barkawi, *Soldiers of Empire: Indian and British Armies in World War II*, Cambridge: Cambridge University Press, 2017.
23 Alan Allport, *Browned off and Bloody-Minded: The British Soldier Goes to War 1939–1945*, New Haven: Yale University Press, 2015, esp. ch. 9, 'Fighting Bloody Nature'; Jonathan Fennell, *Fighting the People's War: The British and Commonwealth Armies and the Second World War*, Cambridge: Cambridge University Press, 2019.
24 For examples of this radicalization in the 1942 cohort of correspondents, see Woods, *Reporting the Retreat*, pp. 141–5.
25 Phillip Knightley, *The First Casualty: The War Correspondent as Hero, Propagandist and Myth Maker from Crimea to Iraq*, 3rd edn, Baltimore: Johns Hopkins University Press, 2004.

26 Mark Connelly and David Welch, *War and the Media: Reportage and Propaganda, 1900–2003*, London: I.B. Tauris, 2005, p. x.
27 *Picture Post* had a circulation in Britain of 1,950,000 copies a week in December 1943.
28 Anthony Aldgate and Jeffrey Richards, *Britain Can Take It: British Cinema in the Second World War*, London: I.B. Tauris, 2007, p. 3.
29 An outline of such views relating to distortions of the truth through censorship and propaganda in Britain during the Second World War can be found in Ian Garden, *Battling with the Truth: The Contrast in the Media Reporting of World War II*, London: History Press, 2016.
30 Welch gives the example that when in the war the British government tried to inform the public about Nazi extermination camps, it was not immediately believed: David Welch, *Propaganda: Power and Persuasion*, London: British Library, 2013, p. 93.
31 The PWE reported to the FO and included BBC staff. It is interesting, however, that the BBC took care to distance itself from PWE activities which involved radio transmissions.
32 Welch defines propaganda as 'the dissemination of ideas intended to convince people to think and act in a particular way and for a particular persuasive purpose. Although propaganda can be unconscious, it is most often the conscious, deliberate attempt to use the techniques of persuasion for specific goals.' Welch, *Propaganda: Power and Persuasion*, p. 2 (see pp. 201–5 for alternative definitions from previous decades).
33 This is clear from his resignation letter to L. F. Rushbrook Williams, 24 September 1943, quoted in W. J. West (ed.), *George Orwell: The War Broadcasts*, London: BBC Books, 1985, pp. 57–8.
34 I am grateful for Iain Farquharson, who is researching British Army attitudes to the reform of staff training in the interwar period, for this information.
35 A good example of a general who recognized the importance of the media is Montgomery. See Miles Hudson and John Stanier, *War and the Media: A Random Searchlight*, Stroud: Sutton Publishing, 1997, pp. 81–2.
36 General Eisenhower epitomized this policy of trusting correspondents, no more so than in the highly secret D-Day operations. See Steven Casey, *The War Beat, Europe: The American Media at War Against Nazi Germany*, New York: Oxford University Press, 2017, pp. 6–7, 218–23.
37 Ian Stewart and Susan L. Carruthers (eds), *War, Culture and the Media: Representations of the Military in 20th Century Britain*, Trowbridge: Flicks Books, 1996.
38 A good overview is Susan L. Carruthers, *The Media at War: Communication and Conflict in the Twentieth Century*, London: Macmillan, 2000.
39 For a critical view of the policies of pooling and embedding correspondents in the two Iraq wars, see Douglas Kellner, 'War Correspondents: Propaganda, Witnessing, and Truth-Telling', *International Journal of Communication*, 2 (2008), pp. 298–330.
40 For the First World War, see Tim Luckhurst, 'War Correspondents', in Ute Daniel et al. (eds), *1914-1918-online. International Encyclopedia of the First World War*, issued by Freie Universität Berlin, 15 March 2016. DOI: 10.15463/ie1418.10862, accessed 5 November 2021.
41 The most powerful criticism of Mountbatten is Andrew Roberts, *Eminent Churchillians*, London: Weidenfeld & Nicholson, 1994, pp. 55–136. Roberts recognizes Mountbatten's 'genius' for PR and personal relations but these do not seem to weigh much against his other failings, indeed they add to them by his ability to present his failures as successes. For a powerful argument in favour of Mountbatten's use of self-publicity, see Lyman, *A War of Empires*, p. 492.

2 Media Covering the War in India-Burma

1. See Milton Israel, *Communications and Power: Propaganda and the Press in the Indian Nationalist Struggle, 1920–1947*, Cambridge: Cambridge University Press, 1994, ch. 2.
2. The Free Press of India (FPI) was established in 1925. The finances of FPI were always rocky because it could not attract enough newspapers, especially English-language ones, to its service. In addition, it also suffered increased hostility from the Home Department for its nationalist stance. Pressure was put on it and its subscribers, and increased securities were demanded during the early 1930s. In 1935 it was forced to close.
3. See Michael Mann, *Wiring the Nation: Telecommunication, Newspaper-Reportage, and Nation Building in British India, 1850–1930*, Oxford: Oxford University Press, 2017.
4. Israel, *Communications and Power*, p. 309.
5. Gordon Waterfield, *Morning Will Come*, London: John Murray, 1944, p. 118.
6. There was nothing like the scale of ill-feeling between agency reporters and newspapermen in Burma as there was in the European theatre where the very large number of correspondents involved meant that Army PR had to set limits to the number who could witness important events such as D-Day or coverage of the German surrender. See A. J. Liebling, 'The A.P. Surrender', *The New Yorker*, 19 May 1945, in Samuel L. Hynes et al. (eds), *Reporting World War II: American Journalism, 1938–1946*, New York: Library of America, 2001, pp. 646–55.
7. D. R. Mankekar, *Leaves from a War Reporter's Diary*, New Delhi: Vikas, 1977, pp. 129–30.
8. Ibid., p. 58.
9. James Curran and Jean Seaton, *Power Without Responsibility: The Press and Broadcasting in Britain*, 5th edn, London/New York: Routledge, 1997, p. 67.
10. The reduction in size might mean papers were only a quarter of their pre-war size. There were government-imposed cuts on American newspapers in 1943 but they still remained much larger than their transatlantic equivalents.
11. Ibid., pp. 68–9.
12. In fact, the leftward political trend could be seen in a number of newspapers including Beaverbrook's *Evening Standard*. Stephen Koss, *The Rise of the Political Press in Britain, vol. 2: The Twentieth Century*, London: Hamish Hamilton, 1984, pp. 607–8.
13. Kevin Williams, *Read All About It! A History of the British Newspaper*, London: Routledge, 2009, p. 154.
14. Ibid., p. 165.
15. See Ziegler, *Mountbatten*, pp. 172–3, for what Mountbatten thought was the origin of Beaverbrook's hostility. In fact, Beaverbrook's anger at Mountbatten's responsibility as Commander of Combined Operations for the large loss of Canadian soldiers in the Dieppe Raid of August 1942 was surely more important than any supposed slur on the *Daily Express* arising from the film *In Which We Serve*.
16. Hanako Ishikawa, *Winston Churchill in the British Media*, London: Palgrave Macmillan, 2019, pp. 195–6.
17. See Chapter 10 for more details on officer observers.
18. Copies can be found on the excellent CBI website: https://www.cbi-theater.com/menu/cbi_home.html, accessed 5 November 2021.
19. Harold Butler memorandum, 'The Publicity Problem in the United States during Stage II', 3 August 1944, WO 203/5080, TNA. AP and UP were well represented throughout

the India-Burma campaign. I can only find one INS correspondent, James Brown, who was with Stilwell's forces in 1944.
20 Michael S. Sweeney, *The Military and the Press: An Uneasy Truce*, Evanston, IL: Northwestern University Press, 2006, p. 115.
21 For details of US media reporting of the Indian political situation in the early stages of the war, see Auriol Weigold, *Churchill, Roosevelt and India: Propaganda during World War II*, New Delhi: Routledge, 2008. Journalists Preston Grover (AP), Edgar Snow (*Saturday Evening Post*) and Louis Fischer (*The Nation*) provided reporting from India that was sympathetic to the Indian nationalist position. Some of their reports went directly to President Roosevelt.
22 Srinath Raghavan, *India's War: The Making of Modern South Asia 1939–1945*, London: Allen Lane, 2016, p. 240.
23 Sweeney, *The Military and the Press*, pp.53–60.
24 Ibid., p. 3. For the broader context of US censorship policies in the war, see Jeffrey A. Smith, *War and Press Freedom : The Problem of Prerogative Power*, New York: Oxford University Press, 1999, esp. ch. 6, 'The Bureaucratization of Wartime Censorship'.
25 For media management of the news of Pearl Harbor and Hiroshima/Nagasaki, see Steven Casey, *The War Beat, Pacific: The American Media at War Against Japan*, New York: Oxford University Press, 2021, pp. 11–21, 280–8.
26 Sweeney, *The Military and the Press*, pp. 117–19.
27 See Casey, *The War Beat, Pacific*, pp. 150–1.
28 'Journalists accredited to the GoI and SEAC', File 462/87, IOR/L/I/1/107. 7. See Chapter 7 for more information on Indian war correspondents.
29 Fay Anderson and Richard Trembath (eds), *Witnesses to War: The History of Australian War Reporting*, Melbourne: Melbourne University Publishing, 2011, p. 137.
30 The Trove website, National Library of Australia, provides excellent digitized copies of the whole range of Australian newspapers: https://trove.nla.gov.au/newspaper.
31 Briggs, 'Watch the Burma Front', *Collier's*, 5 June 1943; De Luce, 'Oil for the Planes of China', 13 October 1943.
32 See Mark Gayn, 'The Cause of China's Tragedy', *Collier's*, 13 January 1945, pp. 18, 19, 66, 68, 69; 'Can China Unite?', 3 February 1945, pp. 14, 15, 30.
33 James L. Baughman, 'Who Read *Life*? The Circulation of America's Favorite Magazine', in Erika Doss (ed.), *Looking at Life Magazine*, Washington, D.C.: Smithsonian Institution Press, 2001, pp. 41–51.
34 Harold Butler directive, 'Publicity Requirements for the War in Asia', n.d., WO203/5080, TNA.
35 I owe much of the information in this paragraph to the work of Susan Moeller, *Shooting War: Photography and the American Experience of Combat*, New York: Basic Books, 1990, ch. 8.
36 In a set of essays published in 2006 under the title 'Media and the British Empire', thirteen out of fifteen essays focused on print media, especially the press: Chandrika Kaul (ed.), *Media and the British Empire*, Basingstoke: Palgrave Macmillan, 2006. Important studies of print media include: Gerald N. Barrier, *Banned: Controversial Literature and Political Control in British India 1907–1947*, Columbia, MO: University of Missouri Press, 1974; Israel, *Communications and Power*; Chandrika Kaul, *Reporting the Raj: The British Press and India, c.1880–1922*, Manchester: Manchester University Press, 2003.
37 For an explanation and an informative history, see Linda Kaye, 'If You Build It, Will They Come? Researching British Newsreels', in Ciara Chambers et al. (eds),

Researching Newsreels: Local, National and Transnationals Case Studies, London: Palgrave Macmillan, 2018, pp. 285–300. There are many examples of individual researchers publishing work on newsreels, but a lack of a coherent body of research and teaching on the use of newsreels in historical research. Pioneering work on film in colonial Africa was done by Rosaleen Smyth, also by Jude Cowan for India and Burma. See also Ian Kikuchi, 'From "Oriental Quarrel" to "Bloody Vengeance!": British Newsreels and War in the Far East, 1937–1942', Lisbon: Instituto de História Contemporânea da Faculdade de Ciências Sociais e Humanas da Universidade Nova de Lisboa, 2013, pp. 304–10.

38 Lee Grieveson and Colin MacCabe (eds), *Empire and Film*, London: Palgrave Macmillan/BFI, 2011; *Film and the End of Empire*, London: Palgrave Macmillan/BFI, 2011. One outcome of this research is the recent book by Tom Rice, *Films for the Colonies: Cinema and the Preservation of the British Empire*, Berkeley: University of California Press, 2019.

39 In the US, newsreel series included *The March of Time* (1935–51), *Pathe News* (1910–56), *Paramount News* (1927–57), *Fox Movietone News* (1928–63), *Hearst Metrotone News & News of the Day* (1914–67) and *Universal Newsreel* (1929–67). *Pathe News* was distributed by RKO Radio Pictures from 1931 to 1947, and then by Warner Brothers from 1947 to 1956. These newsreel companies have made their archives available through university libraries and through digitalization. This has contributed to a growing academic interest in historic newsreels as can be seen in Mark Garrett Cooper et al., *Rediscovering U.S. Newsfilm: Cinema, Television, and the Archive*, New York: Routledge, 2018.

40 Nicholas Pronay, 'British Newsreels in the 1930s: 1. Audience and Producers', *History*, 56, 188 (October 1971), p. 416.

41 Nicholas Pronay, 'British Newsreels in the 1930s: 2. Their Policies and Impact', *History*, 57, 189 (February 1972), p. 70.

42 This compares with weekly daily newspaper readership of 10.48 million, Sunday papers of 13.59 million, and nearly 9 million radio licence holders: Pronay, 'British Newsreels in the 1930s: 1', p. 415. These figures are likely to be underestimates because newspapers were read by more than one person and radio was often listened to in family groups or in communal places like factories or canteens.

43 Nicholas Pronay, 'The News Media at War', in Nicholas Pronay and D. W. Spring, *Propaganda, Politics and Film, 1918–45*, London: Macmillan, 1982, pp. 202–3.

44 The following paragraph is based on Philip Woods, '"Chapattis by Parachute": The Use of Newsreels in British Propaganda in India in the Second World War', *South Asia*, XXIII, no. 2 (2000), pp. 89–109.

45 The United Newsreel was a compilation newsreel made for the Office of War Information for overseas consumption. It operated from mid-1942. See Phillip W. Stewart, 'A Reel Story of World War II The United News Collection of Newsreels Documents the Battlefield and the Home Front', *US National Archives Prologue Magazine*, 47, no. 3 (Fall 2015).

46 Leach to Chisnell, 24 February 1943; Chisnell to Leach, 26 February 1943, Leach to Thapar, 3 March 1943, L/I/1/569, BLOIOC.

47 'Film for Propaganda Purposes. Army Films Units – coordination of cameramen. Minutes of Newsreel Meetings', L/I/1/699, File no. 462/14F, BLOIOC.

48 See the minutes of the Newsreel Association, Book 2, Minutes, 21.4.1941–15.12.1943, British Film Institute (BFI), London. For details of the Association's work as seen through its minute books, see Jeff Hulbert, 'The Newsreel Association of Great Britain

and Ireland', http://bufvc.ac.uk/wp-content/media/2009/06/newsreel_association.pdf, accessed 5 November 2021.
49 Philip Woods, 'Filming the Retreat from Burma, 1942: British Newsreel Coverage of the Longest Retreat in British Army History', *Historical Journal of Film, Radio and Television*, 35, no. 3 (2015), pp. 438–53.
50 For further information, see Philip Woods, 'The British Use of Film Propaganda in India in the Second World War', *Indian Horizons*, 48, no. 4 (March–April 2001), pp. 11–24; 'From Shaw to Shantaram: the Film Advisory Board and the Making of British Propaganda Films in India 1940 to 1943', *Historical Journal of Film, Radio and Television,* 21, no. 3 (August 2001), pp. 293–308.

3 Managing the Media in the Burma Retreat, 1942

1   Leland Stowe, *They Shall Not Sleep*, New York: Alfred A. Knopf, 1944, p. xvi.
2   T. E. Healy, *Tourist Under Fire: The Journal of a War-Time Traveller*, New York: H. Holt & Co., 1945, p. 91.
3   Fred Eldridge, *Wrath in Burma; The Uncensored Story of General Stilwell and International Maneuvers in the Far East*, New York: Doubleday, 1946.
4   Chiang was against allowing his troops to come under British command, so Stilwell acted as intermediary.
5   This is very well dealt with in Chen Li, 'The Chinese Army in the First Burma Campaign', *Journal of Chinese Military History* 2, no. 1 (2013), pp. 43–73; Hans Van de Ven, *China at War: Triumph and Tragedy in the Emergence of the New China*, Cambridge, MA: Harvard University Press, 2018.
6   Diary entry for 1 April 1942, Theodore White (ed.), *The Stilwell Papers*. New York: Schocken Books, 1972 [1949], p. 80. He expressed similar views in the diary entry for 7 April, p. 83.
7   *Time*, 24 April 1942, pp. 16–17. The fuller illustrated articles did not appear until after the retreat was over, *Life*, 'Burma Mission', 15 and 22 June 1942.
8   Casey, *War Beat, Pacific*, ch. 9, 'The CBI'.
9   Barbara Tuchman, *Sand Against the Wind: Stilwell and the American Experience in China 1941–45*, London: Futura, 1981, p. 454.
10 *Dunkirk Evening Observer*, 11 May 1942, p. 1, https://newspaperarchive.com/dunkirk-evening-observer-may-11-1942-p-1/, accessed 5 November 2021.
11 Although the memoirs were more outspoken in their criticisms of the way the retreat had been handled by civil and military authorities alike, one should not assume that with greater freedom their accounts were necessarily more reliable. Indeed, the governor of Burma and his officials devoted much effort to refuting some of the claims made by the journalists in their memoirs. Journalists undoubtedly wanted the opportunity to publish for a wider audience what they saw as the 'true story' which they were unable to put into print during the retreat. However, there was always the temptation to make their story more saleable with colourful 'I was there' accounts. See Woods, *Reporting the Retreat*, ch. 9, 'Making the Government of Burma's Case'.
12 This was probably Maurice Ford, Paramount's cine cameraman, who had his accreditation withdrawn by General Alexander for reasons that are not entirely clear but may have resulted from a misdemeanour in a previous theatre. He was reaccredited by Jehu. War News Film Committee, Minute 13 April 1942; Jehu to Gennings, 4 March 1943, L/I/1/699, OIOC.

13 This was in line with policies in other theatres where women reporters were initially not allowed at the fighting front. See Woods, *Reporting the Retreat*, pp. 60–2.
14 One clever but unusual way for reporters to cover two fighting fronts at once was to come to an agreement with a rival reporter on a different front to share their material when they met up again. They would then reword the rival's dispatches and send them to their respective editors. This is what Thomas Healy (*Daily Mirror*) and William Munday (*News Chronicle*) did. See Woods, *Reporting the Retreat*, pp. 100–1.
15 Ian Stephens, *Monsoon Morning*, London: Ernest Benn, 1966, p. 220.
16 Ibid., p. 57 n. 13.
17 Burma Censorship Regulations, 1938, chapter vi, 'Press Censorship', p. 88, WO33/1567, TNA.
18 Paul L. Moorcraft and Philip M. Taylor, *Shooting the Messenger: The Political Impact of War Reporting*, London: Biteback Publishing, 2011, ch. 2, esp. p. 68, which describes reporters as 'patriots with pens and cameras ... cheerleaders, not objective reporters'.
19 An example might be the reporter O'Dowd Gallagher who decided to volunteer for the Royal Armoured Corps when he returned to Britain later in 1942: HS 9/555/2 (SOE Personnel Files), TNA.
20 Pictures of dead American soldiers were banned by US censorship until the policy changed in October 1943 when there was a concern that the public were becoming too complacent about winning the war quickly: Sweeney, *The Military and the Press*, pp. 117–19.
21 Bill Munday report, *News Chronicle*, 12 March 1942, p. 2.
22 For more details, see Woods, *Reporting the Retreat*, pp. 97–100.
23 Ibid., pp. 109–11.
24 Ibid., pp. 69–73.
25 E. C. V. Foucar, *I Lived in Burma*, London: Denis Dobson, 1956, pp. 133–4.
26 Hodson's report, *Sunday Times*, 1 March 1942, p. 1; Jordan, *News Chronicle*, 8 March 1942, p. 2. Leland Stowe picked up the story about the same time but must have felt it was too late to form any sort of scoop. Stowe notebook iv, entries for 26 February, 2 March, 8 March, Stowe MSS, Wisconsin Historical Society.
27 See, for instance, Allen, *Burma*, appendix 2, 'The debate on the Sittang Bridge'.
28 Wavell to War Office et al., 10 May 1942, BBC WAC, E1/475/1.
29 Ibid., 6 May 1942.
30 Idem.
31 F. S. V. Donnison MSS, Eur B357, f. 374, OIOC.
32 See Woods, *Reporting the Retreat*, pp. 132–4 for details.
33 John T. Correll, 'Chennault and Stilwell', *Air Force Magazine*, December 2015, p. 65.
34 *Life*, 'Flight from Burma', 10 August 1942, pp. 26–7.
35 J. Belden, Retreat *with Stilwell*, New York: Alfred A. Knopf, 1943.
36 'Heroes: Glimpse of an Epic', *Time*, 10 August 1942.
37 Eldridge, *Wrath in Burma*, pp. 125–6.

4 Managing Media Coverage of the First Arakan Campaign, 1943

1 Field Marshal Viscount Slim, *Defeat into Victory*, London: Pan Macmillan, 2009 edn, p. 151. Slim says that when he arrived in Burma, he was glad that there was no press

fanfare before he had time to become known to his own troops. 'All that can be most helpful *afterwards*', ibid., p. 37. Slim is largely sceptical of the value of publicity but he is pragmatic in believing it useful if the timing is correct. See his views on publicizing Wingate's second operation, ibid., pp. 265–6.
2. Ibid., p. 163.
3. MoI Home Intelligence Division weekly report no. 116, 24 December 1942, INF 1/292, http://www.moidigital.ac.uk/reports/home-intelligence-reports/home-intelligence-weekly-reports-inf-1-292-1-2/idm140465674143520/, MoI Digital and TNA, accessed 5 November 2021. Interestingly, the report cited public expectations being based partly on the fact of General Wavell being in overall command. Wavell enjoyed a strong reputation as a military leader both in Britain and India. See Linlithgow to Amery, 21 April 1943, IOR/L/WS/1/939, ff. 695–9. However, by the start of the Burma campaign he had lost the confidence of Churchill, and military historians tend to share Churchill's view that in 1942 and 1943 he was something of a 'spent force'. Amery to Churchill, 31 May 1943, ibid.
4. Fennell, *Fighting the People's War*, p. 330.
5. *Courier-Mail* (Brisbane) 21 December 1942, Trove, National Library of Australia website, http://trove.nla.gov.au/newspaper/article/50125742, accessed 5 November 2021.
6. Callahan, *Burma*, pp. 48–9.
7. See Raghavan, *India's War*, pp. 308–11.
8. See Peter Murray's private paper, 'North Arakan in 1942', written 26 October 1980 and kindly provided to me by Derek Tonkin. Murray was involved in the military administration of North Arakan in 1943.
9. *News Chronicle*, 23 July 1942, pp. 2, 3–5.
10. He surmised that this was to avoid inflaming communal feelings in India: Waterfield, *Morning Will Come*, p. 104. This area is known as Rakhine State today and the Arakanese Muslims are also known as Rohingyas.
11. 'Jap Terror War in Burma', 7 December 1942, p. 4.
12. *Daily Mail*, 13 January 1943, pp. 3, 4.
13. Bayly and Harper, *Forgotten Armies*, p. 276; General Irwin letter to Sir Alan Hartley, 14 May 1943, enclosing Zainuddin, Assistant Liaison Officer, Kyautaw area, 'Confidential account of my experiences prior to and during the re-occupation of the Kyautaw area by the British', Irwin Papers, Box 2/1, IWM.
14. Robert Lyman, *The Generals: From Defeat to Victory, Leadership in Asia, 1941–45*, London: Constable, 2008, p. 148.
15. Raghavan, *India's War*, p. 311.
16. Wavell to Brooke, 19 December 1942, WO106/3760, TNA.
17. Brooke to Wavell, 22 December 1942, ibid.
18. Thoburn Wiant, the AP correspondent in Burma, reported that agency sources were saying that the Chinese were hailing the advance into Arakan as the first step in the promised offensive to reopen the Burma Road. See Susan E. Wiant, *Between the Bylines: A Father's Legacy*, New York: Fordham University Press, 2010, pp. 62–3.
19. An interesting exception was the *New York Times* which, although it recognized that the capture of Akyab would not be the springboard for the invasion of Burma, argued that, in addition to other airfield advantages, it 'would cut 500 miles off the aerial supply line to China', 20 December 1942, p. 1, cont. p. 38. This indicated the American priorities in Burma, but the paper immediately took up the British message that played down the significance of the Arakan advance.

20 Jehu to Bromhead, 27 January 1943; Minute 515, 8 February 1943; F. Burton Leach (MOI) to J. F. Gennings (IO), 27 February 1943, L/I/1/699, File 462/14F, 'Film for Propaganda Purposes: Army Film Units – Coordination of cameramen: Minutes of newsreel meetings', OIOC.
21 Minutes of War News Film Committee, 2 November 1942; Burton Leach (MOI) to Gennings, India Office, London [IO], 27 February 1943; Jehu to Gennings, 4 March 1943, L/I/1/699, OIOC.
22 'Burma-Arakan Front', *Pathe Gazette*, issue no. 43/28, 8 April 1943, http://bufvc.ac.uk/newsonscreen/search/index.php/story/99919, accessed 5 November 2021; 'Movietone's Wartime News – Reported by Leslie Mitchell: Bombs over Burma', *British Movietone News*, issue no. 724A, 22 April 1943. http://bufvc.ac.uk/newsonscreen/search/index.php/story/12676, accessed 5 November 2021.
23 Burton Leach (MOI) to Gennings (IO), 27 February 1943; Jehu to Gennings, 4 March 1943, L/I/1/699, File 462/14F, 'Film for Propaganda Purposes: Army Film Units – Coordination of cameramen: Minutes of newsreel meetings', OIOC.
24 Stephens, *Monsoon Morning*, p. 111.
25 Burchett was able to use his time in hospital to write up his Burma experiences in a book, *Bombs Over Burma*, Melbourne: F. W. Cheshire, 1944. Chapter XXII tells the story of his first Arakan campaign experiences. Waterfield gave details of his experience to *The Newspaper World*, 9 January 1943. He told of being shot at by Japanese planes firing at least 1,400 rounds of 'mushroom' bullets, which he described as being as deadly as the dum-dum bullets of the last war. This must surely count as journalistic exaggeration.
26 *Daily Mail*, 11 January 1943, p. 4.
27 Waterfield, *Morning Will Come*, pp. 105–6.
28 Though this was disputed by Unni Nayar who said that two Calcutta *Statesman* reporters, M. J. Pritchard (1st Burma campaign) and Norman Devine (Assam/Burma frontier), should have been acknowledged, too. Captain M. K. Unni Nayar, Indian Army PR unit, GHQ MEF, to Ian Stephens, 3 June 1943, Box 33, Stephens Papers, Centre of South Asian Studies [CSAS], Cambridge University.
29 For a summary of the achievements of Indian troops in Arakan, see Moraes, 'Praiseworthy Role of Indian Troops in Arakan Campaign', *Times of India*, 6 May 1943, p. 1. Some of his dispatches were inexplicably delayed in the Calcutta telegraph office for a ten-day period. *Times of India*, 2 April 1943, p. 4; Stephens to Unni Nayar, 21 June 1943, Stephens Papers, Box 33, CSAS.
30 Frank Moraes, *Witness to an Era: India 1920 to the Present Day*, London: Weidenfeld & Nicolson, 1973, p. 113.
31 Ibid., p. 115.
32 *Indianapolis News*, 4 February 1943, 'Slippery Burma Japs Fire And Disappear in Covered Foxholes' by Thoburn Wiant 'with British front-line troops on the Mayu Peninsula', Burma, 30 January 1943 (Delayed) (AP), cited in Wiant, *Between the Bylines*, pp. 75–6.
33 *The Advertiser* (Adelaide), 6 January 1943, p. 4, Trove, http://trove.nla.gov.au/newspaper/article/48896881, accessed 15 November 2021.
34 Jehu to Joyce, 9 January 1943, L/I/1/731, f. 308, OIOC.
35 Cutting in L/I/1/731, f. 294, OIOC.
36 A North American Newspaper Alliance correspondent, who must have been Wilkie, is reported in the *Sydney Morning Herald* of 28 December 1942 as saying that the advance of British and Indian troops in Burma was made through soaking tropical

rains which made the newly built roads and jungle tracks almost impassable, even for mules. He went on to say that military observers did not expect the rapid British advance to continue because of difficult communications. Wilkie's longer articles appeared in *Cairns Post*, 10 December 1942, 'Recapture of Burma'; *The Advertiser* (Adelaide), 6 January 1943, p. 4, Trove, http://trove.nla.gov.au/newspaper/article/48896881, accessed 5 November 2021.
37 *News Chronicle*, 22 March 1943, pp. 4, 5.
38 *Sydney Morning Herald*, 29 March 1943, p. 6, Trove, http://trove.nla.gov.au/newspaper/article/17842187, accessed 5 November 2021.
39 Waterfield, *Morning Will Come*, p. 113.
40 *Courier-Mail* (Brisbane) 13 March 1943, p. 2, Trove, http://trove.nla.gov.au/newspaper/article/42033867, accessed 5 November 2021.
41 Cavendish was killed by his own forces' artillery fire in what was an act of brave defiance of his captors. https://www.bbc.co.uk/history/ww2peopleswar/stories/27/a4894527.shtml, accessed 5 November 2021.
42 The story is told in Stephens, *Monsoon Morning*, ch. 9.
43 Statement on the Arakan campaign, attached to Stephens to Sir Gilbert Laithwaite, 7 June 1943, Stephens Papers, CSAS.
44 *Statesman*, 6 April 1943, p. 2, cols 2–3, copy in Stephens Papers, Box 36, CSAS.
45 Stephens to Vyvyan Edwards, 16 April 1943, Box 33, Stephens Papers, CSAS.
46 Stephens to Irwin, 9 April 1943; Irwin to Stephens, 17 April 1943, Stephens Papers, Box 36, CSAS.
47 Jehu to Stephens, 21 April 1943, Stephens Papers, Box 36, CSAS.
48 *Times*, 9 April 1943, p. 4c. But this was not what Stephens had intended to say.
49 For the power of the rumour mill in Calcutta, see Stephens, *Monsoon Morning*, pp. 115–16.
50 Stephens' predecessor as editor, Arthur Moore, clashed with the GoI over a number of issues. He was later employed in SEAC PR writing communiqués.
51 Ibid., ch. 6, 'Bombs'.
52 Ibid., p. 114.
53 Irwin to Stephens, 17 April 1943, Stephens Papers, Box 36, CSAS.
54 Stephens to Sir Gilbert Laithwaite and Reginald Maxwell, 26 April 1943, Stephens Papers, Box 36, CSAS.
55 Jehu conducted a press conference in Delhi on the previous day.
56 'Gen. Irwin's Conference 9.4. 1943' by W. N. P. Devine, Stephens Papers, Box 1, CSAS, [hereafter 'Devine transcript'].
57 Rough Shorthand Note of Army Commander's Press Conference dated 9 May 1943, Irwin Papers, File 2/1, Correspondence with HE the Commander in Chief, India, IWM.
58 Idem.
59 General Irwin's Conference, Devine transcript, CSAS.
60 Idem.
61 Walter Briggs (UP) wrote an article for *Collier's* magazine in the United States that followed the British line on the positive outcomes of the campaign and future objectives almost entirely: 'Watch the Burma Front', 5 June 1943, pp. 13, 46–7.
62 General Irwin's Conference, Devine transcript, CSAS.
63 See Irwin's weekly report to Wavell, no. 9, 9 March 1943, Irwin Papers, File 2/1, IWM.
64 Bayly and Harper, *Forgotten Armies*, p. 275; 'Note on our capacity to operate offensively against Burma, May 1943', Irwin Papers, File 2/1, IWM. Historians have

since focused more on problems of training and troop morale for the failure in Arakan. See Tim Moreman, *The Jungle, Japanese and the British Commonwealth Armies at War, 1941–45: Fighting Methods, Doctrine and Training for Jungle Warfare*, London: Routledge, 2014; Fennell, *Fighting the People's War*.
65 Message from Martin Moore to *Daily Telegraph*, 11 May 1943, Irwin Papers, File 2/1, IWM.
66 Irwin to General Sir Alan Hartley, Deputy C-in-C India, 8 May 1943, Irwin Papers, File 2/1, IWM.
67 *Daily Mail*, 10 April 1943, p. 4; 12 May 1943, p. 4.
68 *Daily Mail*, 17 May 1943, p. 4.
69 Wilfred Burchett, *Democracy with a Tommygun*, Melbourne: F. W. Cheshire, 1946, p. 123.
70 Waterfield, *Morning Will Come*, pp. 117–18.
71 Ibid., pp. 206–7.
72 'Reconquest of Burma, July 1942–June 1943', CAB121/681, TNA.

5   Media Coverage of Operation Longcloth: Wingate's First Expedition into Burma, 1943

1 A good summary of different views of the two Wingate Chindit operations in 1943 and 1944 is provided by Raymond Callahan, *Triumph at Imphal-Kohima: How the Indian Army Finally Stopped the Japanese Juggernaut*, Lawrence, KS: University Press of Kansas, 2017, Appendix C, 'Note on Chindit Historiography,' pp. 145–9.
2 Slim, *Defeat into Victory*, pp. 162–3; S. N. Prasad et al. (eds) *The Reconquest of Burma*, Vol. 1, June 1942–June 1944, *The Official History of the Indian Armed Forces in the Second World War*, Calcutta: Combined Inter-Services Historical Section (India & Pakistan), 1958, p. 135; McLynn, *The Burma Campaign*, pp. 156–8. The most up-to-date and convincing analysis of the strengths and weaknesses of Wingate and Longcloth is Lyman, *A War of Empires*, ch. 18.
3 Allen, *Burma*, pp. 147–9. A balanced view of the historiography is provided by Tony Redding, *War in the Wilderness: The Chindits in Burma 1943–1944*, Stroud: History Press, 2011, pp.73–5. He concludes with the widespread but seemingly strange defence of the operation that it inspired the Japanese to take major offensive actions in Burma in 1944, which was ultimately disastrous for them.
4 Frank McLynn argues powerfully that the publicity was misleading, unnecessary and counterproductive in the long run. However, his argument that ultimate victory in the war was obvious in 1943 is not a convincing argument that the Wingate publicity was unnecessary at that time: *The Burma Campaign*, pp. 157–8.
5 Allen, *Burma*, p. 118.
6 Richard Rhodes James, *Chindit*, London: John Murray, 1980, cited in Redding, *War in the Wilderness*, p. 75.
7 Phillip Knightley, *Burchett Reporting the Other Side of the World 1939–1983*, London: Quartet Books, 1986, pp. 7–8.
8 Alaric Jacob, *A Traveller's War: A Journey to the Wars in Africa, India and Russia*, London: Collins, 1944, p. 321.
9 Antony Beauchamp, *Focus on Fame*, London: Odhams, 1958, p.39.
10 John Deane Potter, *No Time for Breakfast*, London: Andrew Melrose, 1951. Strangely, Potter does not even mention his part in the expedition in his memoirs.

11 Beauchamp, *Focus on Fame*, p. 45.
12 See Steve Fogden's excellent 'Chindit Chasing' website which has a page on the Longcloth journalists: http://www.chinditslongcloth1943.com/war-correspondents-with-the-chindits-including-the-story-of-moti-lal-katju.html, accessed 5 November 2021.
13 Beauchamp told of the hostility of senior general staff at HQ in Delhi to Wingate, which even impacted on the quality of troops he was assigned: *Focus on Fame*, pp. 40, 49.
14 Beauchamp, *Focus on Fame*, pp. 46–7. This can be seen on the Army PR film unit's film 'Into Burma', AYY 444, IWM, sections of which were shown in British newsreels.
15 Note from A. G. Neville (DDIP) to DDPR, 10 April 1943, attached to dope sheet for film 'Into Burma', Army Film Centre, IWM, A444 P2 A35.
16 Idem.
17 The newsreels did use some of the footage: *Gaumont British News*, issue 981, 'Secret Jungle Army in Britain'; *British Movietone News*, issue 730, both released 31 May 1943. This footage was quite a small part of each of the newsreels. Gaumont used 21' out of a total 685'; Movietone used 77'out of 730', while they have more footage to the 2,000 Guineas horse race at 90'. Their commentaries added some colour to the draft commentary 'Into Burma' provided by IAPR, A444, IWM. The newsreels did not show footage of the return of the Chindits which was filmed by the IAPR film unit on 20 April 1943, MWY 83, IWM, which rather confirms the short span of interest in the story in Britain.
18 *News Chronicle*, 13 February 1943, p. 4, col. 1.
19 Jehu memo, 3 April 1943, Irwin Papers, Folder 2/1, IWM, quoted in Allen, *Burma*, p. 146.
20 Trevor Royle, *Orde Wingate: A Man of Genius 1903–1944*, London: Frontline Books, 2010, pp. 257–8.
21 John Connell, *Auchinleck: A Biography of Field-Marshal Sir Claude Auchinleck*, London: Cassell, 1959, p. 739. Connell's brief account of the Chindit expedition and its publicity is more reliable than that of Sykes.
22 Christopher Sykes, *Orde Wingate*, London: Collins, 1959, p. 435.
23 See copy of Reuters message from Delhi, 20 May 1943, which was based on the army communiqué, Wingate Papers, Chindit Box 1, IWM.
24 *The Times* produced a fuller report on the following Monday which added some of the colourful personal stories the other papers had used, 24 May 1943, p. 5, cols 6–7. *The Times* did not give its correspondents bylines, but these reports were from R. W. 'Bob' Cooper who was based with GHQ, Delhi.
25 *Daily Express*, 21 May 1943.
26 It had previously been published in *Life* magazine, vol. 14, no. 26, 28 June 1943.
27 For further details, see the excellent article in https://www.chinditslongcloth1943.com/the-piccadilly-incident.html, accessed 5 November 2021.
28 *Daily Mail*, p. 2, cols 3–5. Sykes, *Orde Wingate*, incorrectly dates Stanford's article as 22 May.
29 Churchill referred to the 'Clive of Burma' expression in his message to the Chiefs of Staff Committee, 24 July 1945. Connell, *Auchinleck*, p. 740.
30 Harold Butler memo, 'The Publicity Problem in the United States during Stage ll', pp. 4–5, 3 August 1944, WO203/5080, TNA.
31 Borrow Papers and *Milwaukee Journal*, 13 October 1943: http://mymilitaryhistory.blogspot.co.uk/2015/03/wingates-raiders-by-charles-j-rolo.html, Viking Press, New

York, 1944, and London: Harrap, 1945. A part-comic strip version was serialized in the *Milwaukee Sentinel* in May–June 1944, http://mymilitaryhistory.blogspot.co.uk/2015/03/wingates-raiders-by-charles-j-rolo.html, accessed 5 November 2021.
32 W. G. Burchett, *Wingate's Phantom Army*, Thacker & Co., Bombay April 1944. A British edition of this book was published in 1946, London: Frederick Muller, 1946, and this is the edition used here. It was also published in Australia as W. G. Burchett, *Wingate Adventure*, Melbourne: F. W. Cheshire, 1944.
33 Wilfred Burchett, *At the Barricades*, London: Quartet Books, 1980, p. 87.
34 Burchett, *Wingate's Phantom Army*, 1946, p. 43.
35 Sykes uses Wingate's failure to be interviewed by the press when he first reached India at Imphal, and this initial reluctance to be interviewed, as evidence of his indifference to publicity, *Orde Wingate*, pp. 435–6. The evidence does not support this view. Wingate was ordered not to speak to the press at Imphal but to go straight to Delhi. When Burchett met him, he was still recovering from a serious illness. In fact, he had every need for further publicity, and resented when it was withheld.
36 Idem, p. 5.
37 For the full flavour of Burchett's critical views on the Delhi 'Blimps', see his *Democracy with a Tommygun*.
38 Burchett, *At the Barricades*, p. 91.
39 Burchett, *Wingate's Phantom Army*, p. 178.
40 Phillip Knightley, 'Cracking the Jap: Burchett on World War Two', in Kiernan (ed.), *Burchett Reporting the Other Side of the World 1939–1983*, p.7.
41 Ibid., p. 8. Frank McLynn has gone further than Knightley and described the publicity for the expedition as 'lying propaganda' which was unnecessary at a time when it was obvious that the Allies would win in the long run. McLynn drew the parallel with Dunkirk – the deliberate turning of a defeat into a victory by propaganda, *The Burma Campaign*, pp. 155–8.
42 *The Times*, 24 May 1943, p. 5, cols 6–7.
43 *Daily Telegraph*, 24 May 1943, p. 3, col 4.
44 A copy can be found with other newspaper cuttings in the Borrow Papers at the IWM.
45 The Chindit coverage had to compete with a strong story nearer to home, the so-called Dam Busters Raids on the Ruhr dams. Home Intelligence reports report public 'admiration' for what are described as 'commando operations' in Burma, whereas the exploits of Guy Gibson VC and his pilots elicit great praise for the raid – 'the audacity of its conception and execution'. MoI Home Intelligence Division weekly reports, nos. 138 & 139, 27 May 1943, http://www.moidigital.ac.uk/reports/home-intelligence-reports/home-intelligence-special-reports-inf-1-292-2-a/idm140465682860304/; 3 June 1943, http://www.moidigital.ac.uk/reports/home-intelligence-reports/home-intelligence-special-reports-inf-1-292-2-a/idm140465683155632, INF 1/292, MoI Digital and TNA, accessed 5 November 2021.
46 Latimer, *Burma*, p. 168.

6 Mountbatten Takes Charge: Publicity and Censorship

1 Churchill to Ismay, 2 October 1943, Broadlands Archive, A C147, quoted in Ziegler, *Mountbatten*, p. 252. Churchill's wish seems to have been fulfilled. Thorburn Wiant, the AP correspondent, wrote to his parents on 17 October 1943: 'You may be wondering why we haven't sent more news about Mountbatten. The fact is, we've sent all we could.

A hold-down has been imposed, for reasons that seem sound. Don't expect much out of us war correspondents here for three or four months.' Wiant, *Between the Bylines*, p. 142.
2 'Report by Charles Eade of *Sunday Dispatch* 1946', WO 203/4869, TNA.
3 Stephens, *Monsoon Morning*, p. 205 n. 18.
4 In his autobiography, Joubert devoted a chapter to his SEAC career and, perhaps acknowledging his ultimate fallout with his boss, admitted that it 'only just failed to be a resounding success'. *The Fated Sky*, London: Hutchinson, 1952, pp. 243–4.
5 Although not a newspaper, there was a monthly publication, the *Army Digest*, aimed at the army in India, which was first produced in December 1943. It took the form of a compendium of articles from a wide range of British and American publications. It was published by the Directorate of Welfare and Education in India, and was edited and produced by the *Times of India* in Bombay. For details of this, see Chandrika Kaul, 'Service Newspapers and the British Empire', *Service Newspapers of World War Two: Material from the Imperial War Museum 1938–1946*, Adam Matthew Digital, 2019, accessed 22 December 2020.
6 The history of the negotiations for setting up *SEAC* newspaper is very well explained in Stephens, *Monsoon Morning*, ch. 15, 'Enter Mountbatten', and Appendix XIII, 'Stephens memorandum', 11 December 1943.
7 The papers were *Contact* for India Command, *CBI Roundup* for the US forces, and *Il Corriere del Campo* for Italian POWs.
8 The rupee was divided into 16 annas. One rupee was worth 1s 6d or 7.5p in modern decimal currency. Basic pay for a sepoy (private) in the Indian Army in 1944 was 37 rupees 8 annas a month: Khan, *The Raj at War*, p. 220.
9 Stephens, *Monsoon Morning*, p. 213.
10 Pownall to Mountbatten, 2 January 1944, WO 203/5073, TNA.
11 Draft of message from Supreme Commander to readers of *SEAC* sent for comment, 31 December 1943, for the first number of *SEAC* to H. R. Pownall and others, WO 203/5073.
12 Joubert to War Office, 26 January 1944, WO 203/5073; Mountbatten to War Office, 20 June 1944, WO 203/5085; Report to Combined Chiefs of Staff by Supreme Commander SEAC, 1947, vol. II, Annexure 8, p. 344, FO 371/63551, TNA.
13 'Air Delivery' – Arakan Front, 26 February 1944, L/I/1/1050, OIOC.
14 Peter Burchett, 'Immortal Rearguard', *SEAC*, 11 January 1944, p. 2.
15 *SEAC*, 11 February 1944. Beaton, essentially a society fashion photographer, had been recruited by the MoI to make a photographic record in various theatres of war. He toured India and Burma in 1944. For his Burma experiences, see Cecil Beaton, *Indian Diary & Album,* Oxford: Oxford University Press, 1991, ch. 4. Fuller coverage of his photos can be found in Cecil Beaton, *Theatre of War*, London: IWM/Jonathan Cape, 2012.
16 Joubert to Mountbatten, 14 June 1944, WO 203/5073, TNA.
17 'Extract from Minutes of Meeting at HQ 15th Corps on 9 September 1944', WO 203/5073.
18 Mountbatten to Joubert, 16 August 1944, referring to *SEAC*, 19 July 1944. Grigg did not let the matter rest: in a Cabinet discussion of General King's report on the morale and welfare of troops he made criticisms of Owen's role in publicizing soldiers' unsubstantiated grievances. War Cabinet minutes, 11 April 1945, CO 968/98/1, TNA.
19 'Morale Report for British troops of SEAC, quarter ended 31 Aug 1944', WO 203/4536, f.18a, TNA; 'Morale in Manipur', 4 August 1944, no. 144, IOR/L/WS/1/1433, 'India – Weekly Intelligence Summaries'.

20 Mountbatten Diary entry, 20 January 1945, in Philip Ziegler (ed.), *Personal Diary of Admiral the Lord Louis Mountbatten, Supreme Allied Commander, South-East Asia, 1943–1946*, London: Collins, 1988, p. 176.
21 Mountbatten to Wheeler, 'Phoenix magazine: reports', 31 December 1944, WO 203/5085, TNA.
22 Idem.
23 IWM holds copies of *Phoenix*.
24 Ralph Arnold, *A Very Quiet War*, London: Rupert Hart-Davis, 1962, p. 153.
25 The Australian journalist Geoffrey Tebbutt, who had plenty of opportunity to see the Supreme Commander in action, also believed that Mountbatten eschewed personal publicity: 'New Era for Mountbatten', *Melbourne Herald*, 13 October 1944, p. 4.
26 Arnold, *A Very Quiet War*, p. 153.
27 Douglas Gardner, 'Censorship in India – War Correspondents' Difficulties', *Sydney Morning Herald*, 5 October 1944, L/I/1/731, f. 57, OIOC.
28 Devika Sethi, *War over Words: Censorship in India, 1930–1960*, Cambridge: Cambridge University Press, 2019, pp. 129–30.
29 Ibid., pp. 147, 152, 159–61.
30 *New York Times*, 'Confusion Over Burma Warfare', 12 April 1944, p. 10. The story spread quickly in America and Britain and was taken up by the Japanese propaganda machine. Stories circulated also about a supposed antagonism between General Auchinleck and Mountbatten, which the GoI thought potentially damaging to the Indian war effort. The issue is very fully dealt with in File 462/18(k) 'Censorship: Stilwell-Mountbatten dispute, SEAC', IOR/L/I/1/735.
31 SACSEA DPR to WO DPR, 21 April 1944, WO203/5076, TNA.
32 Fergal Keane, *Road of Bones: The Siege of Kohima 1944: The Epic Story of the Last Great Stand of Empire*, London: Harper Press, 2010, pp. 283–4. Questions were asked in Parliament on the censorship issue on 20 April and 3 May 1944.
33 File 462/18(k) 'Censorship: Stilwell-Mountbatten dispute, SEAC', IOR/L/I/1/735, ff. 118–20, 22 April 1944.
34 Message from Martin Moore to A. E. Watson in SACSEA to MoI, 29 April 1944, WO 203/5076, TNA.
35 Idem.
36 The INA included many Indian civilians in Malaya in addition to army POWs, and at its height it was thought to comprise some 40,000 soldiers. The Japanese only allowed the INA to have a very restricted support role, but they fought in the battles for Imphal and Kohima in 1944 and played a part in supporting the retreating Japanese army in Burma in 1945. The existence of the INA was a very sensitive issue for the Indian Army which prided itself on its traditions of having an army of loyal volunteers. However, the rise of nationalism, the pressure of the army's setbacks in the first two years of the war, and the much wider net of recruitment for the war undermined the hold of traditional army values for some soldiers. For the INA under Bose, see Srinath Raghavan, *India's War: The Making of Modern South Asia 1939–1945*, London: Allen Lane, 2016, pp. 282–95, 424–5; Bayly and Harper, *Forgotten Armies*, pp. 322–7, 371–4, 401–2. For a sympathetic study of the motivations of those joining the INA, see Gajendra Singh, *The Testimonies of Indian Soldiers and the Two World Wars: Between Self and Sepoy*, London: Bloomsbury, 2015, ch. 6.
37 Most correspondents considered that the fly-in was too dangerous and the operations would mean that they would be out of communication with their newspapers for too a long time. See Chapter 8, 'Reporting the War, 1944', for details.

38 Idem.
39 5 May minute, WO 203/5076.
40 See Chapter 7, 'Allies of a Kind'.
41 The circumstances are most clearly laid out in a letter and enclosures from General Auchinleck to Mountbatten, 13 May 1944, https://archives.soton.ac.uk/records/MS62/MB/1/C/138/16, Mountbatten papers, Southampton University, online, accessed 5 November 2021. This letter reveals just how angry Auchinleck was with Philip Joubert's handling of this issue at a press conference in London on 21 April. In his view Joubert, who came under strong questioning from the press, implied that the censorship was the responsibility of India Command and was based on internal Indian considerations.
42 MoI Home Intelligence Division weekly report no. 186. 27th April 1944, INF 1/292, http://www.moidigital.ac.uk/reports/home-intelligence-reports/home-intelligence-special-reports-inf-1-292-2-c/idm140465677631552/, MoI Digital and TNA, accessed 5 November 2021.
43 The text is reproduced in WO203/5078b, TNA.
44 Mountbatten to Joubert, 30 May and 1 June 1944, WO203/5078b.
45 Chief Press Censor memo for Joubert, re. SAC's minute on Martin Moore's article for DICA, n.d., WO203/5078b.
46 GoI External Affairs Dept to SSI, 6 May 1944, IOR/L /PS/12/919.
47 SSI to GoI, 6 May 1944, ibid.
48 GoI External Affairs to SSI, 6 May 1944, ibid.
49 Viceroy to SSI, 8 May 1944, ibid.
50 SSI to Viceroy, 11 May 1944, ibid. In fact, the paper's editorial alongside Gelder's original article was much more circumspect about criticizing 'a great Allied Power'. Whereas Gelder had written of tendencies to fascism in the Kuomintang regime, the editorial talked of Chiang Kai-shek as the only one who could unify the country and argued that, in the sort of crisis that China was in, some sort of temporary limitations on freedom of expression were likely.
51 SSI to Viceroy, 17 May 1944, ibid.
52 Jehu to Joyce, 11 June 1944, ibid.
53 Joyce to Jehu, 15 June 1944, ibid.
54 SSI to Viceroy, 23 June 1944; 8 July 1944, ibid.
55 V to SSI, 10 July 1944, ibid.
56 V to SSI, 22 Sept 1944; AF Morley (IO) to W. Ridsdale (FO), 22 September 1944; SSI to Viceroy, 1 October 1944, ibid. It was not Gelder's last clash with SEAC censorship. In January 1945 he nearly lost his accreditation for trying to bypass censorship by sending a message from Akyab to the editor of the *Statesman* in Calcutta. Joubert to Robertson, 22 January 1945, CAB105/175, TNA.
57 *Adelaide News*, 'Arakan Front Folds up for Monsoon', 30 June 1944, p. 2.
58 Melbourne *Herald*, 10 July 44, p. 2, Trove, accessed 5 November 2021.
59 Burma Front publicity, w/e Friday 21 April Part II, M/3/1389, 'Propaganda: guidance reports on situation in Burma 22 April 1944–29 August 1945', TNA.
60 The issue of what motivated Indians to volunteer to serve in such large numbers for this war is persuasively argued by Lyman, *A War of Empires*, pp. 500–2. Tebbutt's pessimism about the ability of this polyglot army to cohere effectively proved to be unfounded in the campaigns of 1944 and 1945.
61 C. R. Lamplough (DoI) to Joubert (DICA) 5 July 1944; Joubert's detailed comments on Tebbutt's article, 15 July 1944, WO203/5078b, TNA.

62 Tebbutt to Brigadier G. P. Oldfield (DPR SEAC), 15 July 1944, ibid.
63 Mountbatten to Joubert, 16 July 1944, ibid.
64 Carbon copy of a typescript letter from Lord Louis Mountbatten to General Sir C. J. E. Auchinleck concerning problems with Tebbutt, an Australian war correspondent, 19 July 1944, https://archives.soton.ac.uk/records/MS62/MB/1/C/139/11, Mountbatten Papers, Southampton University, online, accessed 5 November 2021.
65 Melbourne *Herald*, 19 July 1944, p. 4, Trove, accessed 5 November 2021.
66 Mountbatten to Joubert, 16 July 1944, WO203/5078b, TNA.
67 The GoI cited the cases of two American correspondents, Alex Small (*Chicago Tribune*) and John R. Morris (UP). The former had apparently been accredited under pressure from the MoI but had 'never been near the scene of operations'. E. Conran-Smith (HD GoI) to A. F. Morley (Inf Dept IO), 12 July 1944, L/I/1/1078, OIOC.
68 A. H. Joyce, memo, 12 August 1944, L/I/1/1078, OIOC.

7 Allies of a Kind: Public Relations Officers at War

1 See Barbara Tuchman's very influential book, *Sand Against the Wind: Stilwell and the American Experience in China 1941–45*, London: Futura, 1981. Contrast this with later histories which have taken a more sympathetic approach to Chinese strategies: Hans Van de Ven, *War and Nationalism in China: 1925–1945*, London: Routledge, 2003; Rana Mitter, *China's War with Japan, 1937–1945: The Struggle for Survival*, London: Penguin Books, 2013; Chen Li, 'The Chinese Army in the First Burma Campaign', *Journal of Chinese Military History*, 2, no. 1 (2013), pp. 43–73; Hans Van de Ven, *China at War*.
2 See the sympathetic account of the influence of Protestant missionary children on more liberal American attitudes to other cultures, David A. Hollinger, 'The Missionary Children Who Taught Empathy to Americans', *What it Means to be American*, 29 January 2018, http://www.whatitmeanstobeamerican.org/encounters/the-missionary-children-who-taught-empathy-to-americans/, accessed 5 November 2021.
3 There are two pioneering studies focused on Anglo-American rival policies in the war against Japan. The first, from which I took the title for this chapter, is Christopher Thorne, *Allies of a Kind: The United States, Britain and the War against Japan, 1941–1945*, London: Hamish Hamilton, 1978. Also, Callahan, *Burma*.
4 For MacArthur's use of the media, see Casey, *War Beat, Pacific*.
5 Eldridge, *Wrath in Burma*, p. 200.
6 See, for example, Geoffrey Tebbutt, 'Jungle Fighter Joe Stilwell', *Perth Daily News*, 20 May 1944, p. 5, Trove, accessed 5 November 2021.
7 Tuchman, *Sand Against the Wind*, p. 360.
8 Churchill to Charles Eade, n.d., Churchill Archives, Eade2/2, cited in Andrew Roberts, *Churchill: Walking with Destiny*, London: Allen Lane, 2018, p. 799 n. 74.
9 Theodore H. White (ed.), *The Stilwell Papers*, New York: Schocken Books, 1972, p. 230, cited in Jonathan Templin Ritter, *Stilwell and Mountbatten in Burma: Allies at War, 1943–1944*, Denton, TX: University of North Texas Press, 2017, p. 66.
10 Stilwell Papers, 12 January 1944, cited in Ziegler, *Mountbatten*, p. 247.
11 For an example of the idolatry that some American journalists could show Stilwell, see Tillman Durdin, '"Uncle Joe" Footslogs with His Soldiers', *New York Times*, 30 April 1944, pp. 122, 142. Durdin praised the general's openness with reporters which he describes as 'in accordance with his liberal concepts of the role of the press'.

12 Eldridge, *Wrath in Burma*, pp. 220-1.
13 See, for example, the letter to his wife, 2 July 1944, which incorporates all his prejudices about the British, in White, *The Stilwell Papers*, p. 306.
14 This may be one of the reasons that Bill Slim, a man of modest social origins, was one of the few British commanders that he really respected.
15 Eldridge, *Wrath in Burma*, p. 238.
16 This whole issue is very well explained in Ritter, *Stilwell and Mountbatten*, ch. 9.
17 *Time*, 'Battle of Asia: Difference of Opinion'. The article also claimed: 'The Allied chain of command, furthermore, is badly divided. Lord Louis Mountbatten, in nominal command of the entire fighting front, can get no troops from General Auchinleck, in charge of India, except through orders from London.' The article caused much consternation in British government circles. British political intelligence on Stilwell's behaviour was well informed. See Eden to Churchill, 2 March 1944, enclosing a note on the history of Stilwell's relations with Mountbatten from M. E. Dening, political adviser to Mountbatten, PREM 3/53/12, TNA.
18 The leak spread into the British press and then to China and inevitably to the Japanese. Mountbatten's Chief of Staff, Henry Pownall, commented that a censor stop was put on the story in India. Brian Bond (ed.), *Chief of Staff: The Diaries of Lieutenant-General Sir Henry Pownall, Vol. 2, 1940-1944*, London: Leo Cooper, 1974, entry for 5 March 1944, p. 147.
19 John Paton Davies, *Dragon by the Tail: American British Japanese and Russian Encounters with China and One Another*, New York: W.W. Norton & Co., 1972, p. 302. Theodore White (*New York Times*) was in America at the time of the leak and was a confidante of Stilwell. Mountbatten clearly thought Davies was the likely source of this security breach: see Ziegler (ed.), *Personal Diary of Admiral the Lord Louis Mountbatten*, pp. 104-5.
20 Eldridge, *Wrath in Burma*, pp. 235-6.
21 Dill to British COS, 2 March 1944, PREM 3/53/12, TNA. Marshall asked specifically that Mountbatten should not be shown his letter to Stilwell.
22 This edition contained coverage of the Wingate expedition as well as British successes in the Arakan and, most importantly, Mountbatten's Order of the Day praising Stilwell and his American and Chinese troops. *CBI Roundup* vol. II, no. 28, 23 March 1944.
23 *CBI Roundup*'s interest up in British and Indian troop involvement tailed off pretty steeply after Stilwell was dismissed and American troops were not involved in the operation to retake central and southern Burma.
24 Eldridge, *Wrath in Burma*, p. 236.
25 See Chapter 11 for more details.
26 It was not just Stilwell who resisted SEAC's control of publicity and communiqués. US General George Stratemeyer, who commanded the unified Eastern Air Command, also resisted Mountbatten's centralizing demands. See Robert Gardner, *Battle of Britain Broadcaster: Charles Gardner, Radio Pioneer & WWII Pilot*. Barnsley: Air World, 2019, p. 189.
27 Ibid., pp. 236-9.
28 For military cooperation, see the meetings of 3 March and 3 April between Slim and Stilwell, in which the former gave his tacit support for the rapid advance on Myitkyina – Slim, *Defeat into Victory*, pp. 254-5, 271-3.
29 Cochran attracted much publicity, partly as the model for the All-American daring pilot Flip Corkin in the comic strip *Terry and the Pirates*. Cochran's role in rescuing wounded soldiers by flying low to latch on to gliders on the ground won him admiration from British and American combatants alike.

30 Joubert said in an AIR broadcast that Mountbatten had thought up the idea of the airborne attack and that General Arnold had agreed to implement it, *The Times*, 21 March 1944, p. 4. Mountbatten confirmed this when he wrote to President Roosevelt: Mountbatten to Roosevelt, 28 March 1944, FDR MSS, http://docs.fdrlibrary.marist.edu/psf/box36/a331f01.html, accessed 5 November 2021. Whoever was the true initiator, Arnold had offered at the Quebec Conference to give air support for the Wingate operation, but this was only conceived originally as supply and evacuation support to troops who would march into Burma. He later determined that it made better sense that Wingate's troops should be flown in, and he appointed two US Army fighter pilots, Colonels Philip Cochran and John Alison, to lead the First Air Commando Group to carry this out. It was Cochran and Alison who suggested the use of gliders to Wingate. See Bob Bergin, 'The Development of a British-American Concept of Special Operations in WWII Burma', *Studies in Intelligence*, 61, no. 4 (December 2017), pp. 19–25, https://www.cia.gov/resources/csi/studies-in-intelligence/volume-61-no-4/the-development-of-a-british-american-concept-of-special-operations-in-wwii-burma/, accessed 5 November 2021.
31 Another was General Festing who commanded the 36th Indian Division which joined NCAC for the advance south from Myitkyina.
32 White, *Stilwell Papers*, p. 296, diary entry for 17 May 1944.
33 Hans van de Ven is highly critical of Stilwell's Myitkyina operation, describing it as 'a gamble that did not work out and that did little to contribute to the defeat of Japanese forces in Burma, let alone to that of Japan itself', *War and Nationalism in China*, p. 51. This does not make enough allowance for the importance of the advance in showing American support for China's continuing war effort.
34 Quoted in Eldridge, *Wrath in Burma*, pp. 265–6. This claim infuriated Eldridge who believed that the Japanese at Myitkyina had been able to receive reinforcements from up the Irrawaddy river, despite the fact that the Chindits were supposed to be blocking them south of the town.
35 Idem.
36 Idem.
37 Slim, *Defeat into Victory*, p. 275.
38 Mountbatten for DICA/DCOS, 17 June 44, WO203/5083, TNA.
39 Mountbatten to Stilwell, 15 July 1944, Stilwell Papers, Hoover Institution, cited in Ritter, *Stilwell and Mountbatten*, p. 136.
40 *New York Times*, 6 August 1944, pp. 1, 17, 'Merrill Marauders Break in Morale'. Steven Casey tells of Stilwell's efforts to 'spin' what was a potentially very damaging story to his advantage, *War Beat, Pacific*, pp. 206–11.
41 *New York Times*, 26 August 1944, p. 7, 'Merrill Says Mistake on Order Sent ill Marauders to War Front'.
42 Eldridge, *Wrath in Burma*, p. 271.
43 Ibid., pp. 271–2.
44 Keswick [Deputy to Dening, Political Adviser to SEAC], SAC to FO, 1 May 1944, PREM 3/53/12, TNA.
45 *New York Times*, 30 October 1944, p. 7.
46 See Tuchman, *Sand Against the Wind,* pp. 646–7.
47 *New York Times*, 31 October 1944, pp. 1, 4.
48 Ibid., p. 4.

8 Reporting the War, 1944

1. This is very well brought out in Holland, *Burma '44*, ch. 2, 'The Four Challenges'.
2. 'Pyjama General Beats Off Attack', *Daily Express*, 28 February 1944, p. 1. This story has all the marks of a colourful story prepared by Army PR: 'Dressed only in pyjamas, he organised the defence. He led his men to the top of a hill, a grenade in each hand, wading through one river up to his neck.'
3. *Daily Herald*, 26 February 1944, p. 4. Perhaps unexpectedly, Cecil Beaton, the MoI photographer, found himself in the thick of the Arakan fighting: Holland, *Burma '44*, pp. 181–2, 200–1.
4. *Daily Herald*, 3 February 1944, 'I Watch Our Tanks Fight in Burma'.
5. *Daily Herald*, 14 January, GHQ SEAC, 'They're Jungle Experts. Thousands of tall coal-black West African troops, experts to a man in jungle craft, are ready to play their part in throwing the Japs out of South-east Asia. . . . Most of these men were born in the jungle.'
6. *News Chronicle*, 14 February 1944, p. 4.
7. *Daily Herald*, 28 February 1944, p. 1, 'Massacred by Japanese'. An editorial warned that the Japanese would have to answer for this atrocity after the war: 'Japs Bayonet British Wounded', *Daily Express*, 28 February 1944, p. 1.
8. *News Chronicle*, 29 February 1944, p. 4, 'Trapped Division Saved by Air. Planes Drop 15,000 Tons'.
9. *Daily Express*, 29 February 1944, p. 4. Initially, there had been a stop on mentioning the name 14th Army.
10. Joubert memo for Mountbatten, 2 March 1944, WO/203/5160, TNA.
11. See, for instance, Tillman Durdin's comments, *New York Times*, 16 March 1944, p. 9. See the more balanced assessment of the campaign in Lyman, *A War of Empires*, pp. 309–11.
12. 'Fighting on Japanese Ground in Burma', 16 March 1944, Talks Scripts, John Nixon, BBC WAC.
13. Only one British correspondent, Alan Humphreys of Reuters/API, initially volunteered to join the larger operation, but he was later joined by Ian Fitchett of the *Daily Express* and John Nixon of the BBC. Reporting on Operation Thursday was later augmented by three officer observers and two army photographers.
14. P. Joubert, 'Notes for the Supreme Commander on News Coverage of 3rd. Indian Div. (Chindits)', SEAC Publicity 1, 14 March 1944, WO203/5159, TNA.
15. Bellah was an author of westerns who was serving as a SEAC PRO. There is an original, uncensored version of Bellah's seven-page report in President Roosevelt's papers: http://docs.fdrlibrary.marist.edu/psf/box36/a331f04.html, accessed 5 November 2021. A censored version is in WO203/5162, TNA. The US War Department asked for the report to be published and the British agreed that the censored version could be published later on 22 April, WO to DPR SACSEA 18 April 1944, Idem. Apart from one small security cut, it was only the names of British regiments involved that were excised.
16. Stanford gave a pretty strong hint when he repeated his 'Clive of Burma' sobriquet for the expedition commander in his report filed on 15 March and published in the *Daily Mail* on 20 March. Martin Moore's report in the *Daily Telegraph* on 15 March told in general terms of Fergusson's land advance and its purpose in supporting allied attacks on Myitkyina but he knew nothing of the aerial invasion which had taken place. He

later complained that correspondents had not been forewarned, but, of course, he should have known better because of his fortuitous, last-minute participation in the high-level secrecy of the first Wingate expedition. SACSEA to Miniform 30 April 1944, L/I/1/1376, OIOC.

17 The London edition of the US forces' newspaper, *Stars & Stripes*, published an article which praised the role of US Major William H. Taylor in the fly-in, who, it said, 'planned, organized and personally led the recent glider thrust behind Jap lines in Burma'.
18 Mountbatten to Wingate, 19 March 1944, Broadlands Archives, C288, cited in Ziegler, *Mountbatten*, pp. 275–6.
19 See Chapter 7, 'Allies of a Kind', for more detail.
20 *Daily Mail*, 22 March 1944, p. 4.
21 Cited in Keane, *Road of Bones*, p. 283.
22 Ibid., p. 282.
23 Ibid., p. 283.
24 For details of changing censorship policies, see Chapter 6, 'Mountbatten Takes Charge'.
25 Keane, *Road of Bones*, pp. 361–2.
26 Ibid., pp. 283–4. Sharp's scripts at the BBC archives have the following listed: 'Attack on Kohima', 11 April 1944; 'Fighting across the District Commissioner's Tennis Court in Burma', 15 May 1944; 'The Tennis Court at Kohima', 17 May 1944; undated script, 'Battle for Kohima', WRV 231, Talks Scripts, Richard Sharp, BBC WAC. It suggests that Sharp reached the Kohima tennis court shortly after the Kohima Ridge was cleared on 13 May.
27 *Daily Mail*, 1 May 1944, p. 3, 'Undaunted by the Japs the White Chief stays at Kohima'.
28 *Daily Mail*, 2 June 1944, p. 2.
29 Copy of a signal from [C.] Eade to [Lieutenant F.] Owen 25 April 1944, https://archives.soton.ac.uk/records/MS62/MB/1/C/62/10, Mountbatten Papers online, accessed 5 November 2021. *SEAC* newspaper did respond with articles on Kohima and the crucial role the Nagas played in its defence and recapture. The best pictorial coverage of the Nagas was that marking Lord Wavell's visit to Kohima in August, *SEAC*, 30 August 1944, p. 4. Wavell also called for more media coverage of the loyal contribution of the Nagas, Wavell to Amery, 1 August 1944, IOR/L/WS/1/93, f. 316.
30 Letter from Lieutenant-General Carton de Wiart, Personal Representative of the Prime Minister to China, to Lord Louis Mountbatten, n.d. ante 21 May 1944, https://archives.soton.ac.uk/records/MS62/MB/1/C/42/28/2, Mountbatten Papers online, accessed 5 November 2021.
31 Mountbatten to Giffard, CinC, 11 Army Group, 19 September 1944; Major L. Hope, for DPR, to DICA, 14 September 1944, WO 2013/5088, TNA; *Daily Herald*, 14 August 1944, p. 2.
32 'Report on the Morale of British Army Personnel under the Command of 11 Army Group for the month of August 1944', WO 203/4536, f. 19c, TNA. At the same time, anger was expressed about the disproportionate publicity given to US forces and other allied troops in all theatres. 'Individual units and formations are excessively touchy about press and wireless comments, and frequently a unit will object because it has not been cited by name for its part in a particular operation, whereas other units have received specific mention.'
33 *Picture Post*, 25 November 1944, vol. 25, no. 9, pp. 7–10.
34 http://www.open.ac.uk/researchprojects/makingbritain/content/dosabhai-framji-karaka, accessed 5 November 2021.

35 D. F. Karaka, *With the Fourteenth Army*, Bombay: Thacker & Co., 1944.
36 Ibid., pp. 7–8.
37 Ibid., pp. 52–7.
38 Ibid., pp. 63–4.
39 D. R. Mankekar, *Leaves from a War Reporter's Diary*, New Delhi: Vikas, 1977, pp. 46–7.
40 Ibid., pp. 64–6.
41 Karaka, *With the Fourteenth Army*, p. 114.
42 Ibid., pp. 53–6.
43 Mankekar, *Leaves from a War Reporter's Diary*, pp. 52–4; 85–7.
44 Ibid., p. 126.
45 Ibid., p. 60. It is not clear that Mankekar was correct about this. See Thoburn Wiart's views on the delays in reporting from Stilwell's advance to Myitkyina in Wiant, *Between the Bylines*, letter to his parents, 23 May 1943, pp. 206–7.
46 Ibid., p. 40.
47 Ibid., pp. 92–3.
48 Ibid., p. 97.
49 Ibid., p. 120.
50 Ibid., p. 122.
51 https://opus.lib.uts.edu.au/handle/10453/28087, accessed 5 November 2021. See Chapter 10 for more details.
52 See the excellent Library of Congress website which brings together Marauder recollections in audio and visual recordings. This is constructed around the film taken at the time by official photographer Sergeant David L. Quaid, https://www.loc.gov/vets/stories/cbi-marauders.html, accessed 5 November 2021.
53 These included, according to Thoburn Wiant, in Wiant, *Between the Bylines*, p. 171: Darrell Berrigan (UP), Jim Brown (INS), A. T. Steele (*Chicago Daily News*), Tillman Durdin (*New York Times*), Ed Cunningham (*Yank* magazine), Bob Bryant (International Newsphotos), Eddie Tseng (China Central News Agency), Charlie Grumitt (AP), Frank Hewlett (UP) and Jim Shepley (*Time*). In addition, George Johnston (*Melbourne Argus*), Jack Bell (*Miami Herald*), John Graham Dowling (*Chicago Sun*) were there.
54 *LIFE*, 17 April 1944, 'Joe Stilwell's War', http://www.cbi-theater.com/stilwellswar/stilwell.html; 24 April 1944, 'Trouble in Burma', http://www.cbi-theater.com/life042444/life042444.html; 26 June 1944, 'Foot Soldiers in Burma', http://www.cbi-theater.com/life062644/life062644.html, accessed 5 November 2021.
55 Fred Eldridge, *Wrath in Burma*, p. 219.
56 *New York Times*, 7 March 1944, pp. 1–2.
57 See Wiant, *Between the Bylines*, letter to his parents, 31 July 1943, pp. 122–3.
58 Letter to his parents, 23 May 1944, ibid., p. 206.
59 Ibid., pp. 206–7.
60 They did not stay for long though, and on 23 May Bernard Hoffman, the *Life* photographer, reckoned that he was the only correspondent remaining with the Marauders at Myitkyina: *Life*, 26 June 1944, 'U.S. Foot Soldiers in Burma', http://www.cbi-theater.com/life062644/life062644.html, accessed 5 November 2021.
61 Wiant letter to parents, 23 May 1944; Wiant, *Between the Bylines*, p. 193.
62 Ibid., pp. 206–7.
63 *San Francisco Chronicle*, 1 November 1944, quoted in ibid., pp. 224–8.

9 Broadcasting: BBC, All India Radio and Radio SEAC

1. For interwar radio, see Chandrika Kaul, who concludes that 'the Raj had neither the inclination nor the imagination to pursue the broadcasting dream'. '"Invisible Empire Tie": Broadcasting and the British Raj in the Interwar Years', in Kaul, *Communications, Media and the Imperial Experience: Britain and India in the Twentieth Century*, London: Palgrave Macmillan, 2014, p. 170.
2. For a discussion of the difficulties for government using radio for rural propaganda in pre-war India, see Clive Dewey, *Anglo-Indian Attitudes: Mind of the Indian Civil Service*, London: Hambledon Press, 1993, pp. 51–2, 92–3, 237–8.
3. P. S. Gupta, *Radio and the Raj 1921–47*, Calcutta: K. P. Bagchi Centre for Studies in Social Sciences, 1995, pp. 6–8. More recent studies of the establishment of radio broadcasting in India have largely endorsed Gupta's pioneering study. See Alasdair Pinkerton, 'Radio and the Raj: Broadcasting in British India (1920–1940)' *Journal of Royal Asiatic Society*, Series 3, 18, no. 2 (2008), pp. 167–91; Colin R. Alexander, *Administering Colonialism and War: The Political Life of Sir Andrew Clow of the Indian Civil Service*, Oxford: Oxford University Press, 2019, ch. 3.
4. Joselyn Zivin, 'Bent: A Colonial Subversive and Indian Broadcasting', *Past & Present*, 162 (February 1999), pp. 195–220. Chandrika Kaul agrees with this assessment: see '"The Meek Ass between Two Burdens"? The BBC and India during the Second World War', in Simon Eliot and Marc Wiggam (eds), *Allied Communication to the Public during the Second World War: National and Transnational Networks*, London: Bloomsbury, 2019, pp. 163–4.
5. Ibid., pp. 219–20.
6. Idem.
7. German radio content proved to be very popular with Indian audiences and had a wider geographical coverage than AIR could manage. Gupta, *Radio and the Raj*, pp. 33–5; Khan, *The Raj at War*, pp. 40–1, 218–19.
8. SSI to GoI, 9 September 1941: GoI, HD to SSI, 22 September 1941, L/I/1/962, OIOC.
9. Brander to Macmillan (BBC), 12 May 1942, L/I/1/962, OIOC.
10. Brander to Davenport, 1 June 1942, ibid.
11. Brander to Rushbrook Williams, 6 July 1942, ibid.
12. Sadly, Arthur Hope was less open to Indian papers' reporting the truth, as he had a reputation for strict censorship of the Indian press at the time of the Quit India movement.
13. An anonymous copy was sent by Cripps to Amery, 3 November 1942, L/PO/3c, ff. 660–3, 'Files on broadcasting and propaganda, 1926–46', OIOC.
14. Amery to Linlithgow, 3 November 1942, ibid.
15. W. J. West (ed.), *George Orwell: The War Broadcasts*, London: BBC Books, 1985, p. 42; Orwell diary, 5 October 1942, CE II, p. 507; https://orwelldiaries.wordpress.com/, accessed 5 November 2021.
16. West (ed.), *George Orwell*, p. 42.
17. Edward Stourton, *Auntie's War: The BBC During the Second World War*, London: Penguin Books, 2018, pp. 70–1.
18. For BBC support for monarchy and empire, see Thomas Hajkowski, *The BBC and National Identity in Britain, 1922–53*, Manchester: Manchester University Press, 2010. Examples of the care the BBC took in the interwar years not to come into conflict with the government are in James Curran and Jean Seaton, *Power Without*

Responsibility: The Press and Broadcasting in Britain, 5th edn, London/New York: Routledge, 1997, pp. 120–3.
19 Kaul, '"The Meek Ass between Two Burdens"', pp. 210, 218. There was more opportunity to put pressure on the BBC over sensitive Indian political issues such as the failure of the Cripps Mission of 1942 or the Bengal Famine of 1943 than over reporting of military matters. In most cases, conflicts were resolved by discreet dialogue rather than by overt demands.
20 West (ed.), *Orwell*, p. 21.
21 Ibid., p. 12. See listing in 'Masterpieces of English Literature' Series of Talks on English Literature for Indian students', L/I/1/962, 'BBC Empire Intelligence Service', OIOC.
22 Orwell was perhaps influenced in his decision by a memorandum from Brander which told of poor Indian audience figures, and that Orwell's own ratings were low, too. West (ed.), *Orwell*, pp. 57–8.
23 Jutta Paczulla brings out the tensions between Orwell's anti-imperialism and his wartime propaganda work for the BBC. She concludes that his determination to defeat fascism took precedence: '"Talking to India": George Orwell's Work at the BBC, 1941–1943', *Canadian Journal of History*, 42, no. 1 (Spring/Summer 2007), pp. 53–70.
24 C. Fleay and M. L. Sanders, 'Looking into the Abyss: George Orwell at the BBC', *Journal of Contemporary History*, 24, no. 3 (July 1989), p. 506.
25 2 April 1942, E1/475/1, Countries: Burma: Burmese Service File 1, 1940–1946, BBC WAC.
26 Eric Blair was Orwell's real name. He was not allowed to use the name Orwell for broadcasting until the end of 1942. Memo to E. Rowan-Davies, 'Information re. Burma Campaign', 16 May 1942, E1/475/1, Countries: Burma: Burmese Service File 1 1940–1946, BBC WAC, reprinted in West (ed.), *Orwell*, pp. 34–5. Orwell's questions were so good that historians have still not been able to answer them with any accuracy. This is partly due, perhaps, to the fact that so many of the Burma government records were destroyed in the retreat, but also because of the chaotic conditions that prevailed.
27 E. Rowan Davies to Rushbrook Williams and governor of Burma, 18 May 1942, E1/475/1, Countries: Burma: Burmese Service File 1 1940–1946, BBC WAC.
28 Joyce tel. to Puckle and Cook, 22 May 1942, Countries: Burma: Burmese Service File 1 1940–1946, BBC WAC. This seems to represent Dorman-Smith's views.
29 Morale reports found the troops in the Middle East theatre very critical of the BBC, partly for following over-optimistic army communiqués. It was even said that Dimbleby 'was a far more unpopular man than Rommel during the period of the Eighth Army's withdrawal': 'War Office Quarterly Morale Reports for February–May 1942; May–July 1942', item 15, WO 32/15772, TNA.
30 Carbon copy of a typescript letter from Lord Louis Mountbatten to Air Chief Marshal Sir P. B. Joubert de la Ferté, 17 March 1945, https://archives.soton.ac.uk/records/MS62/MB/1/C/148/46, Mountbatten Papers, Southampton University, online, accessed 5 November 2021.
31 Explanatory Notes vol. 2, 1 October 1947, R28/19/2 News. Background Notes (A. P. Ryan's Papers), File 2 October 1943–January 1945, BBC WAC.
32 Memo from A. P. Ryan to Director General W. J. Haley, 17 February 1944, L/2/178/1, 'Ryan, Alfred Patrick CBE 1936 to 1947' [left staff file] BBC WAC.
33 A. H. Joyce memo for Mr Patrick, 20 September 1944, L/I/1/950, 'Liaison Arrangements Between India and Burma Office and the BBC', OIOC.
34 'Note on meeting with Admiral Mountbatten at Norfolk House, St James's Square, on Monday 21st August 1944 at 6.30 pm': R28/19/2 News. Background Notes (A. P. Ryan's Papers) File 2 Oct. 1943–January 1945, BBC WAC.

35 There is good material on Sharp and his BBC colleagues in India/Burma on the website 'Old Radio Broadcasting Equipment and Memories': http://www.orbem.co.uk/repwar/wr_people.htm, accessed 5 November 2021.
36 Excerpt from dispatch written by R. Sharp, With 7th Indian Division in the 'Box', 24 February 1944, broadcast Home Service, 29 February 1944, Talk Scripts, Richard Sharp, BBC WAC.
37 'The Tennis Court at Kohima', 17 May 1944, Talk Scripts, Richard Sharp, BBC WAC.
38 'Fighting on Japanese Ground in Burma', 16 March 1944; 'Despatch from Burma – What Life is Like Behind the Enemy Lines', 23 March 1944; West Country Men Serving with the Chindits, 8 May 1944. Talk Scripts, John Nixon, 8 May 1944, BBC WAC.
39 S491/1/1/1 'Girot – Eugene James – Letters to his mother, Mrs C. Girot, Glasgow', 13 June 1944, BBC WAC.
40 S491/1/1/1 'Girot – Eugene James – Letters to his mother, Mrs C. Girot, Glasgow', 25 June 1944, BBC WAC.
41 Cleverdon had been a co-producer on the very successful radio programme *The Brain's Trust*.
42 S491/2/1, Girot – Eugene James: Letters to Sheila Macleod (later Sheila Girot), 22 March 1945, BBC WAC.
43 Ziegler, *Mountbatten*, p. 290.
44 Leese to Mountbatten, 21 March 1945, WO203/5088, TNA.
45 S491/2/1, Girot – Eugene James: Letters to Sheila Macleod (later Sheila Girot), 22 March 1945, BBC WAC. There was a ban on Mountbatten and other generals broadcasting imposed by the Chiefs of Staff, but this is more likely to be Mountbatten's sense that publishing his speeches would undermine the troops' confidence in these being personal addresses to them.
46 S491/2/1, Girot – Eugene James: Letters to Sheila Macleod (later Sheila Girot), 24 March 1945, BBC WAC.
47 S491/2/1, Girot – Eugene James: Letters to Sheila Macleod (later Sheila Girot), 1 April 1945, S491/2/1, BBC WAC. Cleverdon's programme on the capture of Mandalay was given full-page publicity in the *Radio Times* of 8 June 1945, 'Five Hundred Miles on our Flat Feet', and was given star billing when broadcast in the Home Service on 11 June at 21.35 for fifty-five minutes.
48 'The Formal Ending of the War', 16 August 1945, Talks Scripts, Richard Sharp, BBC WAC.
49 Carbon copy of a typescript letter from Lord Louis Mountbatten to General Sir C. J. E. Auchinleck concerning broadcasts to British and American forces, 7 February 1945, Mountbatten Papers, MB1/C142/4.
50 'Report by Charles Eade of *Sunday Dispatch* 1946', WO203/4869, TNA.
51 Ziegler (ed.), *Personal Diary of Admiral the Lord Louis Mountbatten*, entry for 7–14 March 1944.
52 SACSEA to CinC India; Thomas to DPR, 19 February 1945, WO 203/5207, TNA.
53 Eric Hitchcock reckons that the original estimated cost of £100,000 was multiplied threefold by completion, equivalent to £10 million today. *Making Waves: Admiral Mountbatten's Radio SEAC 1945–49*, Solihull: Helion, 2014, p. 87.
54 The broadcasts went out under the name Radio SEAC Kandy, despite the fact that they were actually located at Colombo. This was presumably for security reasons. See http://www.ontheshortwaves.com/Wavescan/wavescan120603.html, accessed 5 November 2021.

55 War Office (Adjutant General) to CinC India, 14 December 1944, WO203/5207, 'Radio S.E.A.C.: co-ordination of broadcasting stations'.
56 Idem.
57 Gupta, *Radio and the Raj 1921–47*, p. 3.
58 Diya Gupta, 'The Raj in Radio Wars, Media History', *Media History*, July 2019, p. 6. Brander calculated radio ownership in India at 121,000 (0.4% of the population) and that very few students had access to wireless sets: Paczulla, 'Talking to India', p. 64. Sanjoy Bhattacharya, *Propaganda and Information in Eastern India 1939-45: A Necessary Weapon of War*, Richmond: Curzon Press, 2001, pp. 65–71 provides a detailed study of the limitations of radio broadcasting during the war.

10 The 'Forgotten Army'? Stepping up Publicity for the 14th Army

1 For more information on Charles Gardner's role, see Gardner, *Battle of Britain Broadcaster*.
2 *The Newspaper World*, 30 December 1944, p. 13.
3 Gardner, SEAC News Division Miniform, to Joubert, 27 August 1944, WO203/5087, TNA. Chief of Staff to General Slim, Brigadier S. F. Irwin, gave a remarkable nationwide tour, giving lectures using the title of 'Forgotten War'.
4 Clipping from *SEAC*, 9 November 1944, ibid.
5 *Birmingham Daily Gazette*, 8 November 1944, p. 3.
6 24 November 1944, ibid.
7 Joubert to Sir Ronald Adam (Adjutant-General), 7 August 1944, WO203/5087, TNA.
8 *Chelmsford Chronicle*, 22 December 1944.
9 IWM catalogue of Hodgkinson material, diaries etc.; Dorman-Smith to Mountbatten, 17 February 1945; Joubert to DDPR, Adv. ALFSEA, 2 March 1945, WO203/5087, TNA.
10 General Auchinleck to Mountbatten, 13 May 1944, https://archives.soton.ac.uk/records/MS62/MB/1/C/138/16, Mountbatten papers, Southampton University, online, accessed 5 November 2021.
11 Roy McKelvie, *The Newspaper World*, 9 December 1944, p. 2.
12 Idem.
13 'The Transnational Mission of an Indian War Correspondent: P. R. S. Mani in Southeast Asia, 1944–1946', *Modern Asian Studies*, 51, no. 6 (November 2017), pp. 1936–68. The scripts of Mani's dispatches and radio broadcasts have been digitized: https://opus.lib.uts.edu.au/handle/10453/28087, accessed 5 November 2021.
14 List of other correspondents from *The Newspaper World*, 3 June 1944, p. 2.
15 Some of the other newspapermen who were brought in for public relations duties were Major Hope (*Daily Mail*, Manchester), Major Russell (*Glasgow Herald*), Major Martin (Reuters), Captain Pankhurst (Associated Scottish Newspapers, Glasgow), Captain Eliot (*Daily Sketch*), Captain Bodkin (Allied Newspapers) and Captain Smallwood (*Daily Mail*, Manchester), *The Newspaper World*, 3 June 1944, p. 2.
16 McKelvie, *The Newspaper World*, 9 December 1944, p. 2.
17 Geoffrey Tebbutt, an Australian journalist, criticized officer observers for being too close to the units they were allocated to and therefore incentivized to overplay their role in combat. *Melbourne Herald*, 19 July 1944, p. 4. On the other hand, they could

also gain recognition for units that were previously neglected as Mani did for Indian divisions.
18 MoI Home Intelligence Special Report, 'Public attitudes to the Far Eastern War and Japan', INF 293, 11 July 1944, MoI Digital and TNA, http://www.moidigital.ac.uk/reports/home-intelligence-reports/home-intelligence-special-report-inf-1-293/idm140465704367760/, accessed 5 November 2021.
19 HIWR, nos. 208 and 208, 28 September 1944; 5 October 1944, INF 1/292, MoI Digital and TNA, http://www.moidigital.ac.uk/reports/home-intelligence-reports/home-intelligence-special-reports-inf-1-292-2-c/, accessed 5 November 2021.
20 HIWR, no. 212, 26 October 1944, ibid. An editorial in *SEAC*, the forces' newspaper, pointed out that in one recent month the BBC had made thirty-two broadcasts referring to the 14th Army and other fighting forces in Burma, SEAC, no. 384, 27 January 1945.
21 HIWR, no. 216, 23 November 1944, ibid.
22 HIWR, no. 221, 29 December 1944, ibid.
23 Butler directive, n.d. [October 1944?], 'Publicity Requirements for the War in Asia', WO203/5080, TNA.
24 Idem.
25 Butler memo, 'The Publicity Problem in the United States during Stage ll', 3 August 1944, ibid.
26 Bracken to Mountbatten, 21 September 1944, WO203/5080.
27 Gardner to Joubert, 24 October 1944, WO203/5078a, TNA.
28 *New York Times*, 23 October 1944, p. 9. Another article by Baldwin on 24 November, 'The Outlook in Burma', which was very positive about Indian Army progress, contained data provided apparently by Colonel Himatsinjhi who was attached to the Agency General for India in Washington as military liaison officer.
29 Butler, 'Suggestions for the improvement of Publicity in America of the British effort of the war in Asia', p. 3, WO203/5080, TNA. Brigadier Desmond Young stated in his autobiography that he had been the person to enlighten American military correspondents like Hanson, Walter Lippmann and Fielding Elliot about the realities of British military contributions in Burma. Desmond Young, *Try Anything Twice*, London: Hamish Hamilton, 1963, pp. 320–1. He said that he had visited Washington and was surprised to find that there was a stop on publicizing the Indian Army on the orders of Winston Churchill. He put this down to the prime minister's prejudices against the Indian Army and effectively countermanded it. This is difficult to verify as Young did not take up his post as Director of Public Relations for the Indian Army until December 1944, sometime after Baldwin's articles.
30 *The Times*, 29 September 1944, p. 6, WO203/5087. Churchill's prejudices relating to the Indian Army went back even to his days as a subaltern in India in the 1890s and he seemed to refuse to adjust to the fact that this was no longer an army that was predominantly British or solely British-officered. This is very well brought out in Cat Wilson, *Churchill on the Far East in the Second World War: Hiding the History of the 'Special Relationship'*, London: Palgrave Macmillan, 2014, esp. ch. 6, 'Churchill's Indian Army and the Reconquest of Burma'.
31 *Daily Mirror*, 16 November 1944, p. 2. See also Raymond Callahan, 'Did Winston Matter? Churchill and the Indian Army, 1940–1945', in Alan Jeffreys and Patrick Rose (eds), *The Indian Army, 1939–47: Experience and Development*, Abingdon: Routledge, 2017, pp. 73–84.

32 Churchill sent Lord Munster, Under-Secretary of State for India, to report on troop morale in the India Command and SEAC in September 1944. His report largely focused on British troops and was submitted in November 1944.
33 *Daily Mirror*, 21 December 1944, p. 4. For a fuller discussion of the importance of the morale issue, see Andrew Muldoon, '"India is a fine country after all!" The cultivation of military morale in colonial India', in Ashley Jackson, Yasmin Khan and Gajendra Singh (eds), *An Imperial World at War: Aspects of the British Empire's War Experience, 1939–1945*, London: Routledge, 2017, pp. 176–92; Kaushik Roy, 'Discipline and Morale of the African, British and Indian Army Units in Burma and India during World War II: July 1943 to August 1945', *Modern Asian Studies*, 44, no. 6 (2010), pp. 1255–82.
34 *Daily Herald*, 20 November 1944, p. 4. Coward had visited Burma to entertain the troops so perhaps felt that he could speak on their behalf.
35 Ibid., p. 2.
36 *Tribune*, 24 November 1944, WO 203/5087, TNA.
37 *Sunday Post*, 19 November 1944, p. 4, ibid.

11 Film and Photography in SEAC

1 Monthly Intelligence Summary, no. 7, 6 July 1942, p. 7, IOLR/ L/WS/i/3475.
2 There were no feature films made by British studios in this period covering the Burma campaign. The Americans did release a film, *A Yank on the Burma Road* (MGM: 1942), which was made just before America entered the war, and a very timely film called *Flying Tigers* (Republic Films: 1942) starring John Wayne, on the American Volunteer Group of pilots. In 1945 they released *Objective Burma* (Warner Bros), a film starring Errol Flynn, which had to be withdrawn from cinemas in Britain after protests that it gave the impression that it was only the Americans who fought in Burma.
3 Ziegler, *Mountbatten*, pp. 170–2.
4 Adrian Smith, 'Mountbatten Goes to the Movies: Promoting the Heroic Myth through Cinema', *Historical Journal of Film, Radio and Television*, 26, no. 3 (August 2006), p. 397.
5 Operational film was used to record the use of weaponry, tactics etc. in battle situations. Auchinleck to Mountbatten, 31 March 1944, https://archives.soton.ac.uk/records/MS62/MB/1/C/136/70, Mountbatten Papers, Southampton University, online, accessed 12 October 2019.
6 For more information on wartime newsreels in India, see Woods, '"Chapattis by Parachute"', pp. 89–109; Paul Sargent, '*Indian News Parade*: The First Indian Newsreel', *Imperial War Museum Review*, no. 12 (1999), pp. 29–35.
7 For more information on the *Calling Blighty* films, see the North West Film archive website: https://www.nwfa.mmu.ac.uk/blighty/index.php, accessed 5 November 2021.
8 Brigadier I. R. Grove to Mountbatten, 10 August 1945, enclosure to Ducker to Brockman, 22 August 1945, Mountbatten Papers, MB1/C108/71.
9 For example, see the remarkable film by Sgt David Quaid of Merrill's Marauders advance to Myitkyina: https://www.youtube.com/watch?v=8zLp08KhVqo, accessed 5 November 2021.
10 Extract from 'Minutes of Meeting held 30 May 1944, Alternative record proposed by DDPR India', WO 203/5161, f. 70, TNA.

11. 'Report to the Supreme Commander SEAC on Photo Film Unit for South East Asia Command' by Major Irving Asher (with enclosures) 20 November 1943, WO 203/5161, TNA.
12. Mountbatten to Field Marshall Sir John Dill, JSM Washington, 25 July 1944, WO 203/5165, ff. 145–6, TNA.
13. Idem.
14. Mountbatten to General George Marshall, Chief of Staff US Army, 3 June 1944, ibid., f. 176.
15. Joubert later noted: 'The film shot of the Wingate operation is not of a very high order of excellence although this difficulty may be overcome if more and better film is available in America', Joubert to Bracken, 31 July 1944, ibid., f. 139.
16. Mountbatten to Marshall, 14 July 1944, WO 203/5161, f. 66.
17. Asher to Mountbatten, 7 July 1944, ibid., f. 167.
18. Idem.
19. 'Extract from SAC's 1231st Meeting of 14.7.44', ibid., f. 67.
20. Joubert listed some nine different uses for the film and photographic units, 'Standard Operating Procedure, SEAC Film Unit (British)', 9 August 1944, ibid., f. 624.
21. Marshall to Mountbatten, 28 June 1944, WO 203/5165, f. 174.
22. Marshall to Mountbatten, 16 September 1944, ibid.
23. 'Extract from SAC's 135th meeting of 21 July 1944', W203/5165; Mountbatten to Field Marshal Dill, JSM Washington, 25 July 1944, ibid., ff. 150–1.
24. Idem.
25. One can almost sense Mountbatten's relief: W0203/5161, Mountbatten to Marshall, 1 November 1944, WO 203/5161, f.68. He wrote: 'I intend to tell Sultan that I demand absolute operational priority for the Anglo-American Film Units which I shall send about under Asher's direction.'
26. Clive Coultass, *Images for Battle: British Film and the Second World War, 1939–1945*, Cranbury, NJ: Associated University Presses, 1989, pp. 140–2.
27. Bracken to Joubert, 27 July 1944, 'Burma Campaign Film No. 1', WO 203/5165, f. 140.
28. Marshall to Mountbatten, 16 September 1944, WO 203/5165.
29. Ian Jarvie, 'The Burma Campaign on Film: "Objective Burma" (1945), "The Stilwell Road" (1945) and "Burma Victory" (1945)', *Historical Journal of Film, Radio and Television*, 8, no. 1 (1988), pp. 60–1.
30. Colonel Frank Capra to Mountbatten, 27 November 1944, WO 203/5165, f. 77.
31. Himatsinji to DPR, GHQ India, 6 November 1944, enclosure to Brigadier Cornwall Jones, 24 March 1945, CAB 122/1163, f. 61, TNA.
32. Auchinleck to Mountbatten, 11 November 1944, WO 203/5165, f. 74.
33. Joubert to Burnham, 19 December 1944, WO 203/5166.
34. Jarratt was Film Industry Liaison Officer of the Royal Naval Film Corporation.
35. Major General Lord Burnham (DPR-WO) to Joubert, 7 December 1944, WO 203/5166.
36. Jarvie, 'Burma Campaign on Film', pp. 61–2.
37. Mountbatten to Joubert, 4 January 1945, WO 203/5166; this coincided with his preoccupation with the joint Anglo-American forces magazine and a pamphlet and book on the Burma campaign. See Chapter 6.
38. Marshall to Mountbatten, 21 February 1945, ibid.
39. Jarvie, 'Burma Campaign on Film', p. 62.
40. Mountbatten to Grigg et al., 25 April 1945, CAB 122/1163, f. 98.
41. Field Marshal Wilson and Mr Butler, JSM Washington to Minister of Information and Secretary of State for War, repeated to Mountbatten, 3 May 1945, WO 203/5166.

42 Mountbatten to Macdonald 16 May19 45, ibid., f. 38.
43 Idem.
44 https://www.imdb.com/title/tt0246953/trivia?ref_=tt_trv_trv, accessed 5 November 2021.
45 Mountbatten to Marshall, 22 September 1945, WO203/5166, f. 74.
46 See I. C. Jarvie, 'Fanning the Flames: Anti-American Opposition to Operation Burma (1945)', *Historical Journal of Film, Radio and Television*, 1, no. 2 (1981), pp. 117–37.
47 There are good analyses of the strengths and weaknesses of the film in Coultass, *Images for Battle*, pp. 193–6; Richard Osborne's entry in the Colonial Film Database: http://www.colonialfilm.org.uk/node/2509.
48 'SEAC Publicity – Policy re. Accreditation of Correspondents. Minutes of meetings of SEAC Public Relations (London) Committee', File 462/87 (A) IOLR/L/I/1/1078.
49 Philip Daniels, unpublished MSS, cited in Fred McGlade, *The History of the British Army Film & Photographic Unit in the Second World War*, Solihull: Helion & Co., 2010, pp. 158–9.
50 SEAC Film Unit (British) by Joubert, 9 August 1944, WO203/5161, ff. 62–4.
51 Mountbatten to Bracken, 29 November 1944, ibid., f. 56.
52 Mountbatten to Asher, 29 January 1945, ibid.
53 Marshall to Wheeler, SEAC, 17 March 1945, ibid.
54 Extract from 6th I & CA Meeting, 27 March 1945, ibid.
55 Chart of location of cameramen coordinated by the War News Film Committee, 23 March 1944, L/I/1/699, OIOC. This compared with six RAF cameramen assigned to SEAC and seven IAPR cameramen and one from the MoI.
56 Minutes of Newsreel Committee Meeting, 4 September 1944. Looking at the example of newsreel cameraman Oswald of Universal, one can see where the problem lay. He was nominated to join SEAC by the NRA on 3 April 1944 and was still in process of RAF accreditation on 22 May, he eventually left England on 10 July and finally arrived at SEAC on 21 August. The process had taken over four months. Minutes of War News Film Committee, 3 April, 24 April, 22 May, 12 June, 19 June, 10 July, 21 August 1944, L/I/1/699, OIOC.
57 *Pathe Gazette*, issue no. 44/95, 27 November 1944.
58 'The Road to Mandalay', *Pathe Gazette*, issue no. 45/5, 15 January 1945, http://bufvc.ac.uk/newsonscreen/search/index.php/story/100606, accessed 5 November 2021.
59 'Front Line Newspaper', *Pathe Gazette*, issue no. 45/10, 1 February 1945, http://bufvc.ac.uk/newsonscreen/search/index.php/story/100621, accessed 5 November 2021.
60 'The Road to China – Story of the Ledo–Burma Road Told by Major Frank Owen', *Pathe Gazette*, issue no. 45/20, 8 March 1945, http://bufvc.ac.uk/newsonscreen/search/index.php/story/100654, accessed 5 November 2021.
61 Minutes of Newsreel Committee Meeting, 4 December 1944, L/I/1/699, OIOC.
62 Colombo with the navy initially but then to Meiktila with the army, searching for 'some navy angle', John Turner, *Filming History: The Memoirs of John Turner Newsreel Cameraman*, London: BUFVC, 2001, p. 93.
63 Interview dated 1 February 1945, *The Cine-Technician*, May–June 1945, https://archive.org/stream/cinetech911asso/cinetech911asso_djvu.txt, accessed 5 November 2021.
64 Alan Lawson, *The Cine-Technician*, May–June 1945.
65 Idem.
66 Idem. One likely example of 'faking' seems to be Oscar Bovill's film for Pathe entitled 'Action in Burma'. This film was proclaimed in the commentary to be 'the first combat pictures from regions of the Arakan front'. Shown on 17 January 1944, it was also an early

use of the naming of the 14th Army. However, the footage looks very much like training material, showing soldiers falling and quickly being taken away by stretcher bearers. 'Action in Burma', *Pathe Gazette*, issue no. 44/5, 17 January 1944, http://bufvc.ac.uk/newsonscreen/search/index.php/story/100249, accessed 5 November 2021. For a fuller discussion of an earlier example of faking, see Woods, *Reporting the Retreat*, pp. 70–3.

67 Philip Daniels, quoted in McGlade, *History of the British Army Film & Photographic Unit*, p. 163.
68 Tom Rice, analysis of The GEN, no. 14, Colonial Film database, http://www.colonialfilm.org.uk/node/5890, accessed 5 November 2021.
69 See, for instance, Mountbatten's visit to General Wingate, 4, filmed by US M/Sgt Widmayer HQ SEAC Film Unit, Dope Sheet, 'Tribute to Hero', *British Paramount News*, issue no. 1372, 24 April 1944, http://bufvc.ac.uk/newsonscreen/search/index.php/document/39139_dope, accessed 5 November 2021.
70 Ronnie Noble, *Shoot First! Assignments of a Newsreel Camera-Man*, London: Pan Books, 1957, pp. 79–83.
71 Turner, *Filming History*, pp. 92–3.
72 Ibid., pp 95–6; Stopford, 12 Army, to HQ SACSEA, 22 Aug 1945, WO 203/5088, TNA.
73 'Lord Louis Humbles the Japs', *British Paramount News*, issue no. 1520, 24 September 1945, http://bufvc.ac.uk/newsonscreen/search/index.php/story/39710. On the same day, Pathe gave two minutes to the HMS Sussex surrender and four minutes to Mountbatten's speech at the final surrender, https://www.britishpathe.com/video/singapore-surrender/query/45+77; https://www.britishpathe.com/video/order-of-the-day-mountbattens-words-to-his-men, accessed 5 November 2021.

12 Race to Rangoon and Victory, 1945

1 I have relied on two excellent websites for the Ledo/Stilwell Road: https://www.cbi-theater.com/ledoroad/; https://eucmh.com/2020/10/28/the-ledo-stilwell-road/, both accessed 5 November 2021.
2 After Stilwell left the theatre in October 1944, American forces were integrated under SEAC Command. It is a remarkable fact that nearly 280,000 Americans served in SEAC in 1945 (out of a total of 1.3 million men and women) and that many more Americans served in SEAC than did Britons. This included the large numbers of Americans in logistical support, on the railways, airfield construction and the Hump: Lyman, *War of Empires*, p. 488.
3 Duckett, *The Special Operations Executive (SOE) in Burma*, pp. 87–92, 96–7.
4 George L. MacGarrigle, *Central Burma*, Washington, D.C.: U.S. Army Center of Military History, 1996, p. 17. MacGarrigle's conclusions, pp. 19–22, form a very hard-headed assessment of the relative contributions of LRP operations, as against OSS/hill-tribe guerrilla harassment and the main land armies. He also sets the Burma War in context saying that it was of 'little strategic importance for completing the triumph over Japan'.
5 For the military planning, see Graham Dunlop, 'The Re-capture of Rangoon, 1945: The Last and Greatest Victory of the British Indian Army', in Jeffreys and Rose (eds), *The Indian Army, 1939–47*, pp. 161–80.
6 The full story is very well told by Latimer, *Burma*, pp. 364–5. The most detailed contemporary report was by the API correspondent D. R. Mankekar, *Times of India*, 6 January 1945, p. 7.

7 These are in the papers of his close friend Stuart Gelder of the *News Chronicle*, MSS Eur F332, OIOC.
8 Ibid., 3 January 1945.
9 Ibid., 4 January 1945.
10 Ibid., 5 January 1945. The telegrammese has been tidied up by the author to make the message more easily intelligible.
11 Ronald McKie, *Echoes from Forgotten Wars*, Sydney: Collins, 1980, pp. 163-4.
12 Press collect telegram, 7 January 1945; published *Sydney Daily Telegraph*, 9 January 1945, p. 6.
13 *News Chronicle*, 6 January 1945, p. 4.
14 *The Times*, 6 April 1945, p. 4. Of course, it was the airbase potential which was much more important.
15 'British Land at Akyab', *British Paramount News*, issue no. 1452, 29 Jan 1945, http://bufvc.ac.uk/newsonscreen/search/index.php/story/39466, accessed 5 November 2021. This includes dope sheets.
16 Duckett, *The Special Operations Executive (SOE) in Burma*, p. 156.
17 Slim, *Defeat into Victory*, pp. 459-60. Slim acknowledged that it was the advance of the 81st African Division down the Kaladan which forced the Japanese to move their troops and was key to the fall of Akyab. Robert Lyman agrees and says that this avoided a 'battle that would have consumed considerable time, scarce material and lives'. *A War of Empires*, p. 462.
18 Joubert to ADICA for *SEAC* newspaper, 9 January 1945, WO203/5067, TNA.
19 Joubert to Robertson, 22 January 1945, CAB105/175, TNA.
20 'Burma Landing Outwits Japs', *British Paramount News*, issue no. 1459, 22 February 1945; 'British Storm Island off Burma', *British Paramount News*, issue no. 1468, 26 March 1945.
21 *The Times*, 'The Road to Mandalay', 14 December 1944, p. 3.
22 Walsh, Adv. HQ ALFSEA to Joubert, SACSEA, Cawthorn (India), 14 January 1945, WO203/5087, TNA.
23 *Daily Express*, 13 February 1945, p. 4.
24 Brigadier Michael Roberts claimed that in making this bold manoeuvre Slim 'mystified and misled ALFSEA, the British Press and the Japanese': Roberts Papers, Churchill Archives Centre, cited in Callahan, *Churchill and His Generals*, p. 228 n. 33. It seems more likely that the press were forbidden to report on this diversionary attack. Clive Graham of the *Daily Express* seemed to break that embargo when he told on 10 February 1945 of a surprise advance by the British south of Mandalay to Chauk area/Seikpyu, which was actually the point on the Irrawaddy due west of Meiktila, *Daily Express*, 10 February 1945, p. 4.
25 *Daily Express*, 6 March 1945, p. 4.
26 *Daily Express*, 23 March 1945, p. 4.
27 *Newspaper World*, 24 March 45, p. 11. In fact, Reuters and British United Press agencies reported the fall of Mandalay first, see *Daily Express*, 21 March 1945, p. 4, 'Mandalay Flies the Dagger'. Some Indian newspaper editors were furious that the news of the capture of Mandalay reached London through the BBC and the press in the evening, faster than it reached India, where it was too late for the morning editions: *Times of India*, 23 March 1945, p. 4.
28 Bovill dope sheet, dated 3 May 1945, 'Rangoon Captured (First Pictures)', *British Paramount News*, issue no. 1487, 31 May 1945, http://bufvc.ac.uk/newsonscreen/search/index.php/document/39586_dope, accessed 5 November 2021.

29 Idem.
30 See Bayly and Harper, *Forgotten Armies*, pp. 437–40.
31 *The War Illustrated*, 16 March 1945, vol. 8, no. 202, pp. 686–7.
32 Carbon copy of a typescript letter from Lord Louis Mountbatten to Air Chief Marshal Sir P. B. Joubert enclosing papers concerning the cancellation of Stratemeyer's conference and political censorship, 24 April 1945, MB1/C148/50, Mountbatten Papers, Southampton University, online. The enclosures included two messages from John Grover (AP) dated 12 and 14 April 1945, which represented the views of correspondents of different nationalities. Grover said: 'It has not only been American journalists who have complained about the over emphasise [sic] of the British role in the reconquest of Burma. Accusations of Joubert's "eighteenth century empire building" have come from British correspondents.'
33 For some insights into Joubert's character, see *The Times* obituary, 22 January 1965. Joubert's papers held at RAF Hendon and his autobiography, *The Fated Sky*, concentrate on his career in the RAF and are not revealing on his time in SEAC.
34 Carbon copy of a typescript letter from [Lord Louis Mountbatten] to Air Chief Marshal Sir P. B. Joubert de la Ferté concerning a dispute with the BBC over the victory broadcast, 17 March 1945, MB1/C148/46, Mountbatten Papers, Southampton University, online. For the accusation of disloyalty, see Mountbatten diary entry for 15 July 1945, Ziegler (ed.), *Personal Diary of Admiral the Lord Louis Mountbatten*, pp. 226–7.
35 Joubert to Lieutenant General F. A. M. Browning, 15 July 1945, MB1 /C148/59, Mountbatten Papers, Southampton University, online.
36 Richard Duckett has shown in recent research that these broad generalizations about hill tribe versus Burman support for British secret operations against the Japanese during the war may need to be revised. He demonstrates that, in one group in a very significant SOE operation, Burmans substantially outnumbered other ethnic groups. https://soeinburma.wordpress.com/2020/10/29/a-force-136-special-group-ferret/, accessed 5 November 2021.
37 Duckett, *The Special Operations Executive (SOE) in Burma*, p. 77.
38 This is very well argued by Duckett, *The Special Operations Executive (SOE) in Burma*, Conclusion.
39 *Daily Herald*, 14 May 1945, p. 1.
40 *Daily Express*, 23 May 1945, p. 3.
41 *Malayan Postscript*, London: Faber & Faber, 1942; *This War Against Japan*, London: Faber & Faber, 1943.
42 'Responsibility in Burma', *The Times*, 22 February 1945, p. 5.
43 Joubert to DDPR Adv. ALFSEA, 2 March 1945, WO203/5087, TNA.
44 Thackrah, 14th Army, to Joubert, 5 March 1945, ibid.
45 The work of CAS(B) during the reoccupation of Burma was given a good deal of attention by official cameramen. The following titles from the IWM film catalogue indicate the types of subject that were filmed: JFU 30 (Medical Attention And Food Distribution To Burmese); JFU 98 (Civil Affairs Service [Burma] – Medical Treatment Of Burmese In Mandalay); JFU 176 (Civil Affairs Service Activities In Mandalay); JFU 275 (The Work of The Civil Affairs Service [Burma] At Meiktila, Shwebo And Maymyo). These films emphasized the restoration of civil order and government on a benevolent basis.
46 F. S. V. Donnison, *British Military Administration in the Far East, 1943–46*, London: HMSO, 1956, p. 353.

47 Mountbatten was very aware of the publicity benefits of working with the BNA. See Mountbatten to British Chiefs of Staff, 27 March 1945, PREM 3/149/5, ff. 394–7, TNA. For an earlier, prescient view of the propaganda benefits of working with the BNA, see Alec Peterson, Force 136, SACSEAC, to Dorman-Smith, 7 November 1944, MSS Eur E215/16, OIOC. Peterson went so far as to say: 'In fact one might almost say that if this Burmese resistance movement did not exist it would be justifiable to invent it.'
48 Dorman-Smith was supported in mistrusting Aung San by Frederick Pearce, Chief Civil Affairs officer, and some army officers. Significantly, Joubert also was against backing Aung San and the BNA.
49 SACSEA to ADV ALFSEA, 2 May 1945, WO 203/5088, TNA.
50 Joubert to Bracken, 3 May 1945, ibid. The story was published verbatim in the *Ceylon Evening Times*, 12 May 1945.
51 SACSEA to ADV ALFSEA, 7 May 1945, WO 203/5088.
52 The *New York Times* picked up on this issue, Tillman Durdin article, 19 May 1945, p. 3.
53 War Cabinet Committee to Mountbatten, 30 March 1945, cited by Donnison, *British Military Administration*, pp. 353–4.
54 Mountbatten admitted that he did actually cross the line by trying to promote AFPFL and BNA participation within the political discussions that were taking place in Burma in June 1945. The British government and Chiefs of Staff were trying all the time to keep Mountbatten limited to the military negotiations and to avoid any political commitments. See Mountbatten to Chiefs of Staff, 16 May 1945, PREM 3/149/5, ff. 365–6, TNA.
55 Rear SACSEA to SACSEA, 10 May 1945, WO 203/5088. Later, on 16 June, in discussions with four representatives of the AFPFL and BNA, Mountbatten interpreted the government's White Paper as offering Dominion status within three and a half years. This was much more definite than the governor or British government were committing themselves to. It had the effect, however, of receiving a positive response from nationalist leaders. See Minutes of SAC's 12th Misc. Meeting, 16 June 1945; Extract from 13th Misc. Meeting of 23 June 1945, WO203/5238, TNA.
56 Mountbatten memo, 15 May 1945, ibid. It is interesting to speculate whether Joubert was actually feeding journalists like Humphreys with a line that was hostile to Aung San and the BNA, despite Mountbatten's instructions to the contrary. Mountbatten seems to have suspected this and was relieved when Joubert came to the end of his term of office, Ziegler (ed.), *Personal Diary of Admiral the Lord Louis Mountbatten*, 15 July 1945, p. 226.
57 Mountbatten draft tel. to Rear Link, no date, ibid.
58 *The Times*, 31 May and 1 June 1945.
59 *The Times*, 31 May 1945, p. 5.
60 See Ziegler (ed.), *Personal Diary of Admiral the Lord Louis Mountbatten*, 16 June 1945, p. 215.
61 The practical problem for Burma was that, before India set a precedent in 1950, no republic, that is states which rejected the monarch as head of state, had ever been allowed to join the Commonwealth.
62 Ba Maw was regarded as a Japanese Quisling. He had been head of state and prime minister under the Japanese between 1943 and 1945.
63 Extract from SAC's 8th Misc. Meeting, 30 May 1945, W0 203/5088.
64 Extract from 12th I & CA Meeting of 25 June 1945, WO 203/5160, TNA. This was formalized in 'Burma Front publicity', w/e 7 July 1945, M/3/1389, OIOC.
65 Duckett, *The Special Operations Executive (SOE) in Burma*, p. 175.

66 Extract from 10th I & CA meeting, 6 June 1945, WO 203/5160.
67 Extract from 11th I & CA meeting, 11 June 1945, ibid.
68 Clive Graham, *Daily Express*, 16 June 1945, p. 3. Mountbatten, who seemed sanguine about this, said in his diary that the BNA wore Japanese uniforms with a large red armlet to distinguish them from the Japanese at the march-past, Ziegler (ed.), *Personal Diary of Admiral the Lord Louis Mountbatten*, p. 213.
69 Civil government was not restored until 16 October. Mountbatten reluctantly agreed to this under strong pressure from Dorman-Smith. He later described it as the one mistake of his career, Ziegler, *Mountbatten*, p. 322. Historians might wish to add to the list.
70 Extract from 11th I & CA meeting, 11 June 1945, WO 203/5160.
71 *British Paramount News* and Pathe, 19 July 1945. Dope Sheet, 'Through War to Lasting Peace', *British Paramount News*, issue no. 1501, 19 Jul 1945, http://bufvc.ac.uk/newsonscreen/search/index.php/document/39639_dope, accessed 5 November 2021. Although Noble filmed a range of Burmese leaders talking to Dorman-Smith, the edited version missed out film of the most important nationalist leader who was present at this point, Aung San. This may be because Noble's film ran out at one point. He did appear, however, in the Army Film Unit version held at the IWM, JFU 273. This is a reminder that many more official cameramen were filming these events than commercial newsreel cameramen.
72 *Daily Express*, 19 June 1945, p. 3.
73 *Daily Express*, 21 June 1945, p. 4. See also *Daily Herald*, 21 June 1945, p. 3.
74 *The Times*, 21 June 1945, p.4.
75 Bayly and Harper, *Forgotten Wars*, p. 66.

13 Conclusion

1 In Britain, the most popular paper, the *Daily Mirror*, decided not to send any correspondents to Burma from 1944 onwards, citing unreasonable censorship as the cause. Probably more importantly, they preferred to cover stories nearer to home, both geographically and metaphorically.
2 Knightley, *The First Casualty*, p. 300.
3 Mark Connelly and David Welch, *War and the Media: Reportage and Propaganda, 1900–2003*, London: I.B. Tauris, 2005, p. x.
4 Richard Fine, 'Allied War Correspondents' Resistance to Political Censorship in World War II', in Simon Eliot and Marc Wiggam (eds), *Allied Communication to the Public during the Second World War*, London: Bloomsbury Academic, 2019, p. 96.
5 Casey, *The War Beat, Europe* and *The War Beat, Pacific*.
6 Casey, *The War Beat, Europe*, p. 349.
7 Woods, *Reporting the Retreat*.
8 Cyril Falls, 'The Great World War: British Fighting Service and the Public, *Illustrated London News*, 30 June 1945, p. 696.
9 Although publicity was the first item listed, it did not occupy the most attention in the report, which was given to practical issues such as the provision of amenities, entertainment and, of course, beer. The Munster Report (Cmd. 6578) was set up in September and published in December 1944; while General King was sent in December 1944 to look at the implementation of the Munster Report, and his reports on progress were provided to the Cabinet at various points during 1945. Both men

were required to report to the prime minister directly, which is an indication of the importance he attached to British troop welfare as the war shifted to the Far East and the Pacific.

10 *SEAC*'s editorial, 25 July 1945, contrasted the lack of press coverage of the continuing war in Burma with the British newspaper depiction of life being enjoyed at home as if the war had ended and things were returning to normal, as depicted in a photograph of people sunbathing on the deck of a yacht at Henley.

11 For Churchill's views on India and the Indian Army, see Callahan 'Did Winston Matter?', in Jeffreys and Rose (eds), *The Indian Army, 1939-47*, pp. 73-84; Wilson, *Churchill on the Far East in the Second World War*.

12 Wilson, *Churchill on the Far East in the Second World War*, p. 131.

13 Though, Ian Kikuchi has pointed out the tendency in earlier popular films such as *The Bridge over the River Kwai* (1957) and museum exhibitions to focus on the experience of POWs on the Burma-Thailand railway rather than on the Burma War itself: Ian Kikuchi, 'Far-Flung and Forgotten: Britain and the War in Burma', *Despatches* (Summer 2020), pp. 22-6.

14 See 'Report on the Morale of British, Indian and Colonial Troops of Allied Land Forces, South East Asia for the months of August, September, October 1944, items 3 and 4', IOR/L/WS/2/71, 'Morale Reports India & SEAC, Adjutant General in India's Committee on Morale'.

15 The editors of SEAC forces' own newspaper *SEAC* were clearly annoyed at the misuse of the 'Forgotten Army' epithet, e.g. in editorials of 21 March 1944, 26 November 1944, 27 January 1945. The 14th Army in Burma was not the only 'forgotten army' which journalists referred to. It was used to describe the neglected soldiers in Iraq and Persia, New Guinea, and the women in the Land Army at home. Examples include Persian and Iraq Force, *Weekly Dispatch* (London), 15 April 1945, p. 6; New Guinea, *Sunday Mirror*, 13 December 1942, p. 7; Land Army, 15 February 1945, *Liverpool Daily Post*, p. 4.

16 See, for instance, Professor David Edgerton's Emden Lecture 2018 at St Edmund Hall, Oxford, 'The Birth of the British Nation? "Alone", "People's War" and the Mythical Myths of 1948', https://www.youtube.com/watch?v=eg3DI8v1TY0, accessed 5 November 2021; Keith Lowe, *The Fear and the Freedom: How the Second World War Changed Us*, New York: St Martin's Press, 2017, pp. 77-80, 'The Cost of Myth'.

Bibliography

Manuscript sources

BBC Written Archives Centre, Caversham

Douglas Cleverdon Papers, L/1/1, 626/1
E1/475/1, Countries: Burma: Burmese Service, File 1 1940–1946
'Girot – Eugene James – Letters to his mother, Mrs C. Girot, Glasgow'
'Girot – Eugene James: Letters to Sheila Macleod (later Sheila Girot)', 22 March 1945
P/F E15/191, Staff Visits Abroad, Ryan, A. P., 1943
R28/19/2 News. Background Notes (A.P. Ryan's Papers), File 2, October 1943–January 1945
R28/19/3 News. Background Notes (A.P. Ryan's Papers), File 3, January 1945–April 1946
'Ryan, Alfred Patrick CBE 1936 to 1947' [left staff file]
Talks Scripts, John Nixon
Talks Scripts, Richard Sharp

British Film Institute, London

Minute Books of the Newsreel Association of Great Britain

Centre of South Asian Studies, University of Cambridge

Ian Stephens Papers, Boxes 1, 33, 36
William Alfred Barnes Papers – Box 8 – Personal Diary

Imperial War Museum, London

Department of Documents

Captain GH Borrow MC Papers
History of the Royal Air Force Film Production Unit [18 4l0] 868/5, Accession: K37630
Lt Col Frank Outram Hodgkinson: catalogue & background documents
Lt Gen N.M.S. Irwin Papers: Box 2/1, Folders IRW2/2 and IRW/2/3
Lt Gen Orde Wingate Papers: Chindit Box 1

Photographic Department

Cecil Beaton Photographs for Ministry of Information
George Rodger Photos for Ministry of Information.

Film Department

British Paramount News – newsreels and dope sheets
Calling Blighty from Burma films
Films produced by Indian Inter-Service Public Relations Directorate; Indian Public Indian Movietone News
Indian News Parade – newsreels
RAF Film Production Unit, AB56-100, Daily Progress Reports – Shot Sheets
Relations Directorate; Royal Air Force Film Production Unit; SEAC Film Unit

Liddell Hart Centre, King's College London

Major Heard MSS, Box 1

Oriental and India Office Collection, British Library

Arnold Mss, Eur F145
Clague Mss, Eur E252
Collis Mss, Eur D1034
Donnison Mss, Eur B357
Dorman-Smith Mss, Eur E215: including diaries of Lady Dorman-Smith and papers of Major E.T. Cook
Gelder Mss, Eur F332

University of Southampton, Hartley Library

Mountbatten Papers

Official papers

Oriental and India Office Collection, British Library

L/I/1	Information Department Records
L/P&J	India Office: Public and Judicial Department Records
L/P&J/12	Political Intelligence files
L/PO	Secretary of State for India: Private Office Papers
L/WS	India Office: War Staff Papers
M:	Burma Office Records

The National Archives, Kew, London

CAB	Cabinet Office Papers: CAB101, CAB105, CAB122
CO	Colonial Office Papers: CO825, CO875, CO968
FO	Foreign Office Papers: FO371, FO643, FO930, FO954
HS	Records of SOE: HS9, HS47

INF 1   Ministry of Information: Files of Correspondence
PREM   Prime Minister's Correspondence: PRE1, PREM3, PREM4
WO   War Office Papers: WO32, WO106, WO172, WO203, WO208

Newsreels (online)

British Movietone News – online at: http://www.aparchive.com/partner/British%20Movietone
British Universities Film & Video Council database *News on Screen* gives information including documentation, dope sheets and links to Movietone and Pathé newsreels online
Pathé Gazette – online at www.britishpathe.com

Newspapers and magazines (via Newsroom at British Library unless otherwise stated)

Chicago Daily News
Collier's (magazine)
Daily Express
Daily Herald
Daily Mail
Daily Mirror
Daily Sketch
Daily Telegraph
Evening Standard
Illustrated (magazine)
Illustrated London News (magazine)
Illustrated Weekly of India (magazine)
Life (magazine)
Manchester Guardian
News Chronicle
Newsweek (magazine)
New York Herald Tribune
New York Times
Observer
Picture Post (magazine)
Radio Times (magazine)
Sydney Morning Herald (via http://trove.nla.gov.au/, National Library of Australia, for this and other Australian newspapers)
Statesman (Calcutta)
Sunday Express
Sunday Times
The Times
The War Illustrated (magazine)

Forces' newspapers and magazines

CBI Roundup
Phoenix
SEAC
Yank

Bibliography (all Internet references were accessed 5 November 2021, unless otherwise stated)

Aldgate, Anthony, and Jeffrey Richards, *Britain Can Take It: British Cinema in the Second World War*, London: I.B. Tauris, 2007.
Alexander, Colin R., *Administering Colonialism and War: The Political Life of Sir Andrew Clow of the Indian Civil Service*, New Delhi: Oxford University Press, 2019.
Allan, Stuart, and Barbie Zelizer (eds), *Reporting War Journalism in Wartime*, London: Routledge, 2004.
Allen, Louis, *Burma: The Longest War 1941–1945*, London: Phoenix Press, 2000.
Allen, Louis, *War, Conflict and Security in Japan and Asia Pacific, 1941–1952: The Writings of Louis Allen*. Folkestone: Global Oriental, 2011.
Allport, Alan, *Browned off and Bloody-Minded: The British Soldier Goes to War 1939–1945*, New Haven: Yale University Press, 2015.
Anderson, Fay, and Richard Trembath (eds), *Witnesses to War: The History of Australian War Reporting*, Melbourne: Melbourne University Publishing, 2011.
Arnold, Ralph, *A Very Quiet War*, London: Rupert Hart-Davis, 1962.
Anglim, Simon, *Orde Wingate and the British Army, 1922–1944*, London: Pickering & Chatto, 2010.
Barkawi, Tarak, *Soldiers of Empire: Indian and British Armies in World War II*, Cambridge: Cambridge University Press, 2017.
Barnes, John, and David Nicholson (eds), *The Empire at Bay: The Leo Amery Diaries 1929–1945*, vol. 2, London: Hutchinson, 1988.
Barrier, N. Gerald, *Banned: Controversial Literature and Political Control in British India 1907–1947*, Columbia, MO: University of Missouri Press, 1974.
Baughman, James L., *Henry R. Luce and the Rise of the American News Media*, Baltimore: Johns Hopkins University Press, 2001.
Baughman, James L., 'Who Read *Life*? The Circulation of America's Favorite Magazine', in Erika Doss (ed.), *Looking at Life Magazine*, Washington, D.C.: Smithsonian Institution Press, 2001: 41–51.
Bayly, Christopher, and Tim Harper, *Forgotten Armies: Britain's Asian Empire & The War with Japan*, London: Penguin, 2005.
Bayly, Christopher, and Tim Harper, *Forgotten Wars: The End of Britain's Asian Empire*, London: Penguin, 2008.
Beaton, Cecil, *Indian Diary & Album*, Oxford: Oxford University Press, 1991.
Beaton, Cecil, *Theatre of War*, London: Imperial War Museum/Jonathan Cape, 2012.
Beauchamp, Antony, *Focus on Fame*, London: Odhams, 1958.
Belden, J., *Retreat with Stilwell*, New York: Alfred A. Knopf, 1943.
Belden, Jack, *Still Time to Die*, New York: Harper, 1944.
Bergin, Bob, 'The Development of a British-American Concept of Special Operations in WWII Burma', *Studies in Intelligence*, 61, no. 4 (December 2017), pp. 19–25.

Best, Brian, *Reporting the Second World War*, Barnsley: Pen & Sword, 2015.
Bhattacharya, Sanjoy, *Propaganda and Information in Eastern India 1939-45: A Necessary Weapon of War*, Richmond: Curzon Press, 2001.
Bond, Brian (ed.), *Chief of Staff: The Diaries of Lieutenant-General Sir Henry Pownall*, vol. 2, 1940-1944, London: Leo Cooper, 1974.
Briggs, Asa, *The History of Broadcasting in the United Kingdom*, vol. III, *The War of Words*, Oxford: Oxford University Press, 1995.
Brinkley, Alan, *The Publisher: Henry Luce and His American Century*, New York: Alfred A. Knopf, 2010.
Burchett, Wilfred, *Bombs Over Burma*, Melbourne: F. W. Cheshire, 1944.
Burchett, Wilfred, *Wingate Adventure*, Melbourne: F. W. Cheshire, 1944.
Burchett, Wilfred, *Democracy with a Tommygun*, Melbourne: F. W. Cheshire, 1946.
Burchett, Wilfred, *At the Barricades*, London: Quartet Books, 1980.
Burchett, Wilfred, and N. Shimmin, *Memoirs of a Rebel Journalist: The Autobiography of Wilfred Burchett*, Sydney: University of New South Wales Press, 2006.
Burgess, Pat, *Warco: Australian Reporters at War*, Richmond, Vic.: William Heinemann Australia, 1986.
Cady, John F., *A History of Modern Burma*, Ithaca: Cornell University Press, 1958.
Callahan, Raymond, *Burma, 1942-1945*, London: Davis-Poynter, 1978.
Callahan, Raymond, *Churchill and His Generals*, Lawrence, KS: University of Kansas Press, 2007.
Callahan, Raymond, *Triumph at Imphal-Kohima: How the Indian Army Finally Stopped the Japanese Juggernaut*, Lawrence, KS: University Press of Kansas, 2017.
Campion, Garry, *The Good Fight: Battle of Britain Propaganda and the Few*, London: Palgrave Macmillan, 2009.
Campion, Garry, *The Battle of Britain, 1945-1965: The Air Ministry and the Few*, London: Palgrave Macmillan, 2015.
Carruthers, Susan L., *The Media at War: Communication and Conflict in the Twentieth Century*, London: Macmillan, 2000.
Casey, Steven, 'Reporting from the Battlefield: Censorship and Journalism', in Richard Bosworth and Joseph Maiolo (eds), *The Cambridge History of the Second World War*, vol. 2, Cambridge: Cambridge University Press, 2015, pp. 117-38.
Casey, Steven, *The War Beat, Europe: The American Media at War Against Nazi Germany*, New York: Oxford University Press, 2017.
Casey, Steven, *The War Beat, Pacific: The American Media at War Against Japan*, New York: Oxford University Press, 2021.
Charney, Michael W., *A History of Modern Burma*, Cambridge: Cambridge University Press, 2009.
Charney, Michael W., *Imperial Military Transportation in British Asia: Burma 1941-1942*, London: Bloomsbury, 2019.
Chasie, Charles, and Harry Fecitt, *The Road to Kohima: The Naga Experience in the Second World War*, Oxford: Infinite Ideas, 2020.
Chen, Li, 'The Chinese Army in the First Burma Campaign', *Journal of Chinese Military History*, 2, no. 1 (2013), pp. 43-73.
Churchill, Winston S., *The Second World War*, vol. IV, *The Hinge of Fate*, London: Reprint Society, 1953.
Churchill, Winston S., *The Second World War*, vol. V, *Closing the Ring*, London: Reprint Society, 1954.

Collier, Richard, *The Warcos: The War Correspondents of World War Two*, London: Weidenfeld & Nicholson, 1989.
Collis, Maurice, *Last and First in Burma (1941–1948)*, London: Faber & Faber, 1956.
Conboy, Martin, and John Steel (eds), *The Routledge Companion to Media History*, London: Routledge, 2015.
Connell, John, *Auchinleck: A Biography of Field-Marshal Sir Claude Auchinleck*, London: Cassell, 1959.
Connelly, Mark, and David Welch, *War and the Media: Reportage and Propaganda, 1900–2003*, London: I.B. Tauris, 2005.
Connelly, Mark, et al. (eds), *Propaganda and Conflict: War, Media and Shaping the Twentieth Century*, London: Bloomsbury, 2019.
Cooper, Mark Garrett, et al. *Rediscovering U.S. Newsfilm: Cinema, Television, and the Archive*. New York: Routledge, 2018.
Correll, John T., 'Chennault and Stilwell', *Air Force Magazine* (December 2015), pp. 62–7.
Coultass, Clive, *Images for Battle: British Film and the Second World War, 1939–1945*, Cranbury, NJ: Associated University Presses, 1989.
Crosbie, Thomas, 'The Golden Age, Revisited: George C. Marshall's Press Work, 1939–45', *War in History*, 27, no. 2 (April 2020), pp. 249–70.
Curie, Eve, *Journey Among Warriors*, London: Heinemann, 1943.
Curran, James, and Jean Seaton, *Power Without Responsibility: The Press and Broadcasting in Britain*, 5th edn, London/New York: Routledge, 1997.
Davies, John Paton, *Dragon by the Tail: American British Japanese and Russian Encounters with China and One Another*, New York: W.W. Norton & Co., 1972.
Davies, Robert B., *Baldwin of the Times: Hanson W. Baldwin, A Military Journalist's Life, 1903–1991*, Annapolis: Naval Institute, 2011.
Davis, Robert T., *The US Army and the Media in the 20th Century*, Fort Leavenworth, KS: Combat Studies Institute Press, 2009.
Dell'Orto, Giovanna, *AP Foreign Correspondents in Action: World War II to the Present*, New York: Cambridge University Press, 2016.
Desmond, Robert W., *Tides of War: World News Reporting 1940–1945*, Iowa City: University of Iowa Press, 1984.
Dewey, Clive, *Anglo-Indian Attitudes: Mind of the Indian Civil Service*, London: Hambledon Press, 1993.
Donnison, F. S. V., *British Military Administration in the Far East, 1943–46*, London: HMSO, 1956.
Dorman-Smith, Sir Reginald, 'Civil Government under Invasion Conditions', *Journal of the United Service Institution of India*, lxxiii (1943), pp. 240–52.
Dorn, Frank, *Walkout: With Stilwell in Burma*, New York: T. Y. Crowell, 1971.
Doss, Erika (ed.), *Looking at* Life *Magazine*, Washington, D.C: Smithsonian Institution Press, 2001.
Draper, Alfred, *Dawns Like Thunder: Retreat from Burma, 1942*, Barnsley: Pen & Sword, 1987.
Duckett, Richard, *The Special Operations Executive (SOE) in Burma: Jungle Warfare and Intelligence Gathering in World War II*, London: I.B. Tauris, 2017.
Dunlop, Graham, *Military Economics, Culture and Logistics in the Burma Campaign, 1942–1945*, London: Pickering & Chatto, 2009.
Dunlop, Graham, 'The Re-capture of Rangoon, 1945: The Last and Greatest Victory of the British Indian Army', in Alan Jefferys and Patrick Rose (eds.), *The Indian Army, 1939–47: Experience and Development*, Abingdon: Routledge, 2017, pp. 161–80.

Edgerton David, 'The Birth of the British nation? "Alone", "People's War" and the Mythical Myths of 1948', Emden Lecture 2018, St Edmund Hall, Oxford. https://www.youtube.com/watch?v=eg3DI8v1TY0

Eldridge, Fred, *Wrath in Burma: The Uncensored Story of General Stilwell and International Maneuvers in the Far East*, New York: Doubleday, 1946.

Eliot, Simon, and Marc Wiggam (eds), *Allied Communication to the Public during the Second World War: National and Transnational Networks*, London: Bloomsbury, 2019.

Falls, Cyril, 'The Great World War: British Fighting Service and the Public', *Illustrated London News*, 30 June 1945.

Farnan, Robert A., 'Indigenous Resistance as Irregular Warfare The Role of Kachin Forces in SOE and OSS Covert Operations during the Burma Campaign', in Chris Murray (ed.), *Unknown Conflicts of the Second World War: Forgotten Fronts*, Abingdon: Routledge, 2019.

Fennell, Jonathan, *Fighting the People's War: The British and Commonwealth Armies and the Second World War*, Cambridge: Cambridge University Press, 2019.

Fine, Richard A., 'Edward Kennedy's Long Road to Reims: The Media and the Military in World War II', *American Journalism*, 33, no. 3 (Summer 2016), pp. 317–39.

Fleay, C., and M. L. Sanders, 'Looking into the Abyss: George Orwell at the BBC', *Journal of Contemporary History*, 24, no. 3 (July 1989), pp. 503–18.

Foucar, E. C. V., *I Lived in Burma*, London: Dennis Dobson, 1956.

French, Paul, *Through the Looking Glass: China's Foreign Journalists from Opium Wars to Mao*, Hong Kong: Hong Kong University Press, 2009.

Fox, Jo, 'The Propaganda War', in Richard Bosworth and Joseph Maiolo (eds), *The Cambridge History of the Second World War*, vol. 2, Cambridge: Cambridge University Press, 2015, pp. 91–116.

Fraser, George MacDonald, *Quartered Safe Out Here: A Recollection of the War in Burma with a New Epilogue: Fifty Years On*, London: Harper Collins, 2000.

Gallagher, O'Dowd, *Retreat in the East*, London: Harrap, 1942.

Gander, Leonard Marsland, *Long Road to Leros*, London: Macdonald & Co., 1945.

Garden, Ian, *Battling with the Truth: The Contrast in the Media Reporting of World War II*, London: History Press, 2016.

Gardner, Robert, *Battle of Britain Broadcaster: Charles Gardner, Radio Pioneer & WWII Pilot*, Barnsley: Air World, 2019.

Gilbert, Martin, *Winston S. Churchill*, vol. VII, *Road to Victory, 1941–1945*, London: Heinemann, 1986.

Gladstone, Kay, 'The AFPU: The Origins of British Army Combat Filming during the Second World War', *Film History*, 14 (2002), pp. 316–31.

Grant, Ian Lyall, and Kazuo Tamayama, *Burma 1942: The Japanese Invasion; Both Sides Tell the Story of a Savage Jungle War*, Chichester: Zampi Press, 1999.

Grieveson, Lee, and Colin MacCabe (eds), *Film and the End of Empire*, London: Palgrave Macmillan/BFI, 2011.

Grieveson, Lee, and Colin MacCabe (eds), *Empire and Film*, London: Palgrave Macmillan/BFI, 2011.

Gupta, Diya, 'The Raj in Radio Wars: BBC Monitoring Reports on Broadcasts for Indian Audiences During the Second World War', *Media History* (July 2019), pp. 414–29.

Gupta, Partha Sarathi, *Radio and the Raj 1921–47*, Calcutta: K. P. Bagchi Centre for Studies in Social Sciences, 1995.

Hajkowski, Thomas, *The BBC and National Identity in Britain, 1922–53*, Manchester: Manchester University Press, 2010.

Hannon, Brian P. D., 'Creating the Correspondent: How the BBC Reached the Frontline in the Second World War', *Historical Journal of Film, Radio and Television*, 28, no. 2 (2008), pp. 175–94.

Harris, Janet, and Kevin Williams (eds), *Reporting War and Conflict*, London: Routledge, 2018.

Hastings, Max, *All Hell Let Loose: The World at War 1939–1945*, London: Harper Press, 2011.

Healy, Thomas Edward, *Tourist Under Fire: The Journal of a War-Time Traveller*, New York: H. Holt & Co., 1945.

Heenan, Tom, *From Traveller to Traitor: The Life of Wilfred Burchett*, Melbourne: Academic Monographs, 2006.

Herzstein, Robert E., *Henry R. Luce, Time, and the American Crusade in Asia*, Cambridge: Cambridge University Press, 2005.

Hess, Gary R., *America Encounters India, 1941–47*, Baltimore: Johns Hopkins University Press, 1971.

Holland, James, *Burma '44: The Battle That Turned Britain's War in the East*, London: Corgi, 2016.

Hollinger, David A., 'The Missionary Children Who Taught Empathy to Americans', *What it Means to be American*. http://www.whatitmeanstobeamerican.org/encounters/the-missionary-children-who-taught-empathy-to-americans/

Hudson, Miles, and John Stanier, *War and the Media*, Stroud: Sutton Publishing, 1997.

Hughes, T. L., *What Happened in Burma*, London: Brittain Publishing, 1944.

Hulbert, Jeff, 'The Newsreel Association of Great Britain and Ireland'. http://bufvc.ac.uk/wp-content/media/2009/06/newsreel_association.pdf

Hynes, Samuel, et al. (eds), *Reporting World War II: American Journalism, 1938–1946*, New York: Library of America, 2001.

Israel, Milton, *Communications and Power: Propaganda and the Press in the Indian Nationalist Struggle, 1920–1947*, Cambridge: Cambridge University Press, 1994.

Jackson, Ashley, et al. (eds), *An Imperial World at War: Aspects of the British Empire's War Experience, 1939–1945*, Abingdon: Routledge, 2017.

Jackson, Ashley, *The British Empire and the Second World War*, London: Hambledon Continuum, 2006.

Jacob, Alaric, *A Traveller's War: A Journey to the Wars in Africa, India and Russia*, London: Collins, 1944.

James, Lawrence, *Churchill and Empire: Portrait of an Imperialist*, London: Phoenix, 2014.

Jarvie, Ian, 'Fanning the Flames: Anti-American Opposition to "Objective Burma" (1945)', *Historical Journal of Film, Radio and Television*, 1, no. 2 (1981), pp. 117–37.

Jarvie, Ian, 'The Burma Campaign on Film: "Objective Burma" (1945), "The Stilwell Road" (1945) and "Burma Victory" (1945)', *Historical Journal of Film, Radio and Television*, 8, no. 1 (1988), pp. 55–73.

Jeffreys, Alan, and Patrick Rose (eds), *The Indian Army, 1939–47: Experience and Development*, Abingdon: Routledge, 2017.

Jeffreys, Alan, *The British Army in the Far East 1941–45*, Oxford: Osprey, 2005.

Jeffreys, Alan, *Approach to Battle: Training the Indian Army During the Second World War*, Solihull: Helion & Co., 2016.

Joubert de la Ferté, Philip, *The Fated Sky*, London: Hutchinson, 1952.

Karaka, D. F., *With the Fourteenth Army*, Bombay: Thacker & Co., 1944.

Kaul, Chandrika, *Reporting the Raj: The British Press and India, c.1880–1922*, Manchester: Manchester University Press, 2003.

Kaul, Chandrika (ed.), *Media and the British Empire*, Basingstoke: Palgrave Macmillan, 2006.
Kaul, Chandrika, '"The Meek Ass between Two Burdens?": The BBC and India during the Second World War', in S. Eliot and M. Wiggam (eds), *Allied Communication to the Public during the Second World War: National and Transnational Networks*, London, Bloomsbury Academic, 2019, pp. 203–21.
Kaul, Chandrika, 'Service Newspapers and the British Empire', *Service Newspapers of World War Two: Material from the Imperial War Museum 1938–1946*, Adam Matthew Digital, 2019, accessed 22 December 2020.
Kaye, Linda, 'If You Build It, Will They Come? Researching British Newsreels', in Ciara Chambers et al. (eds), *Researching Newsreels: Local, National and Transnationals Case Studies*, London: Palgrave Macmillan, 2018, pp. 285–300.
Keane, Fergal, *Road of Bones: The Siege of Kohima 1944: The Epic Story of the Last Great Stand of Empire*, London: Harper Press, 2010.
Kellner, Douglas, 'War Correspondents: Propaganda, Witnessing, and Truth-Telling', *International Journal of Communication*, 2 (2008), pp. 298–330.
Khan, Yasmin, *The Raj at War: A People's History of India's Second World War*, London: Bodley Head, 2015.
Kiernan, B. (ed.), *Burchett: Reporting the Other Side of the World 1939–1983*, London: Quartet Books, 1986.
Kikuchi, Ian, 'From "Oriental Quarrel" to "Bloody Vengeance!"; British Newsreels and War in the Far East, 1937–1942', Lisbon: Instituto de História Contemporânea da Faculdade de Ciências Sociais e Humanas da Universidade Nova de Lisboa, 2013, pp. 304–10.
Kikuchi, Ian, 'Far-Flung and Forgotten: Britain and the War in Burma', *Despatches* (Summer 2020), pp. 22–6.
Killingray, David, and Martin Plaut, *Fighting for Britain: African Soldiers in the Second World War*, Woodbridge: James Currey, 2010.
Kirby, Major-General S. Woodburn, *The War Against Japan*, vol. II: *India's Most Dangerous Hour*, London: HMSO, 1958.
Knightley, Phillip, *Burchett Reporting the Other Side of the World 1939–1983*, London: Quartet Books, 1986.
Knightley, Phillip, *The First Casualty: The War Correspondent as Hero, Propagandist and Myth-Maker from Crimea to Iraq*, 3rd ed., Baltimore: Johns Hopkins University Press, 2004.
Knightley, Phillip, 'Cracking the Jap: Burchett on World War Two', in B. Kiernan (ed.), *Burchett Reporting the Other Side of the World 1939–1983*, London: Quartet Books, 1986, pp. 3–12.
Koss, Stephen, *The Rise of the Political Press in Britain*, vol. 2: *The Twentieth Century*, London: Hamish Hamilton, 1984.
Latimer, Jon, *Burma: The Forgotten War*, London: John Murray, 2004.
Leigh, Michael D., *The Evacuation of Civilians from Burma: Analysing the 1942 Colonial Disaster*, London: Bloomsbury Academic, 2014.
Leigh, Michael D., *The Collapse of British Rule in Burma: The Civilian Evacuation and Independence*, London: Bloomsbury Academic, 2018.
Liebling, A. J., 'The A.P. Surrender', *The New Yorker*, 19 May 1945, in Samuel L. Hynes et al. (eds), *Reporting World War II: American Journalism, 1938–1946*, New York: Library of America, 2001, pp. 646–55.
Lowe, Keith, *The Fear and the Freedom: How the Second World War Changed Us*, New York: St Martin's Press, 2017.

Lownie, Andrew, *The Mountbattens: Their Lives & Loves*, London: Blink Publishing, 2019.
Luckhurst, Tim, 'War Correspondents', *The International Encyclopaedia of the First World War*, 2016. https://encyclopedia.1914-1918-online.net/home
Lunt, James, '"A Hell of a Licking": Some Reflections on the Retreat from Burma, December 1941–May 1942', *RUSI Journal*, 130, no. 5 (1985), pp. 55–8.
Lyman, Robert, *Slim, Master of War: Burma and the Birth of Modern Warfare*, London: Constable & Robinson, 2004.
Lyman, Robert, *The Generals: From Defeat to Victory, Leadership in Asia, 1941–45*, London: Constable, 2008.
Lyman, Robert, *A War of Empires: Japan, India, Burma & Britain 1941–45*, Oxford: Osprey, 2021.
Macdonald, Roderick, *Dawn Like Thunder*, London: Hodder & Stoughton, 1944.
MacGarrigle, George L., *Central Burma*, Washington, D.C.: U.S. Army Center of Military History, 1996.
Mains, Tony, *The Retreat from Burma: An Intelligence Officer's Personal Story*, London: Foulsham, 1973.
Mankekar, D. R., *Leaves from a War Reporter's Diary*, New Delhi: Vikas, 1977.
Mann, Michael, *Wiring the Nation: Telecommunication, Newspaper-Reportage, and Nation Building in British India, 1850–1930*, Oxford: Oxford University Press, 2017.
Marston, Daniel P., *Phoenix from the Ashes: The Indian Army in the Burma Campaign*, Westport, CT: Praeger, 2003.
Marston, Daniel, and Chandar S. Sundararam, *A Military History of India and South Asia: From the East India Company to the Nuclear Era*, Bloomington: Indiana University Press, 2008.
Marston, Daniel, *The Indian Army and the End of the Raj*, Cambridge: Cambridge University Press, 2014.
McGlade, Fred, *The History of the British Army Film & Photographic Unit in the Second World War*, Solihull: Helion & Co., 2010.
McKernan, Luke, 'Newsreels: Form and Function', in Richard Howells and Robert W. Matson (eds), *Using Visual Evidence*, Maidenhead: Open University Press, 2009, pp. 95–106.
McLaine, Ian, *Ministry of Morale: Home Front Morale and the Ministry of Information in World War II*, London: George Allen & Unwin, 1979.
McKie, Ronald, *Echoes from Forgotten Wars*, Sydney: Collins, 1980.
McLynn, Frank, *The Burma Campaign: Disaster into Triumph, 1942–45*, London: Vintage, 2011.
Mead, Peter, and Shelford Bidwell, 'Orde Wingate—Two Views', *Journal of Contemporary History*, 15, no. 3 (1979), pp. 401–4.
Messinger, Gary S., *The Battle for the Mind: War and Peace in the Era of Mass Communication*, Amherst, MA: University of Massachusetts Press, 2011.
Mitter, Rana, *China's War With Japan, 1937–1945: The Struggle for Survival*, London: Penguin Books, 2013.
Moeller, Susan, *Shooting War: Photography and the American Experience of Combat*, New York: Basic Books, 1990.
Moon, Penderel (ed.), *Wavell: The Viceroy's Journal*, Oxford: Oxford University Press, 1973.
Moorcraft, Paul L., and Philip M. Taylor, *Shooting the Messenger: The Political Impact of War Reporting*, London: Biteback, 2011.
Moraes, Frank, *Witness to an Era: India 1920 to the Present Day*, London: Weidenfeld & Nicolson, 1973.

Moreman, Tim, *The Jungle, Japanese and the British Commonwealth Armies at War, 1941–45: Fighting Methods, Doctrine and Training for Jungle Warfare*, London: Routledge, 2014.
Morenweiser, Konrad, *British Empire Civil Censorship Devices: World War II: British Asia*. Civil Censorship Study Group, 1997. http://c-c-s-g.org/index.php
Morris, Sylvia Jukes, *Rage for Fame: Ascent of Clare Boothe Luce*, New York: Random House, 1997.
Morrison, Ian, *Malayan Postscript*, London: Faber & Faber, 1942.
Morrison, Ian, *This War against Japan; Thoughts on the Present Conflict in the Far East*, London: Faber & Faber, 1944.
Moseley, Ray, *Reporting War: How Foreign Correspondents Risked Capture, Torture, and Death to Cover World War II*, New Haven: Yale University Press, 2017.
Muldoon, Andrew, '"India is a fine country after all!" The cultivation of military morale in colonial India', in Ashley Jackson, Yasmin Khan and Gajendra Singh (eds), *An Imperial World at War: Aspects of the British Empire's War Experience, 1939–1945*, London: Routledge, 2017, pp. 176–92.
Naggar, Carole, *George Rodger: An Adventure in Photography, 1908–1995*, New York: Syracuse University Press, 2003.
Nicholas, Sian, '"The People's Radio": The BBC and its Audience, 1939–1945', in Nick Hayes and Jeff Hill (eds), *Millions Like Us? British Culture in the Second World War*, Liverpool: Liverpool University Press, 1999, pp. 62–92.
Nicholas, Sian, 'War Report (BBC 1944–5) and the Birth of the BBC War Correspondent', in Mark Connelly and David Welch (eds), *War and the Media: Reportage and Propaganda 1900–2003*, London: I.B. Tauris, 2005, pp. 139–61.
Noble, Ronnie, *Shoot First! Assignments of a Newsreel Camera-Man*, London: Pan Books, 1957.
Orwell, George, *Keeping Our Little Corner Clean, 1942–1943* (Collected Works of George Orwell), rev. edn, London: Secker & Warburg, 2001.
Orwell, Sonia, and Ian Angus (eds), *The Collected Essays, Journalism and Letters of George Orwell*, vol. II, *My Country Right or Left 1940–1943*, London: Penguin Books, 1970.
Paczulla, Jutta, '"Talking to India": George Orwell's Work at the BBC, 1941–1943', *Canadian Journal of History*, 42, no. 1 (Spring/Summer 2007), pp. 53–70.
Pe, M. Thein, *What Happened in Burma: The Frank Revelations of a Young Burmese Revolutionary Leader Who Has Recently Escaped from Burma to India*, Allahabad: Kitabistan, 1943.
Phillips, Barnaby, *Another Man's War: The Story of a Burma Boy in Britain's Forgotten African Army*, London: OneWorld, 2014.
Pinkerton, Alasdair, 'Radio and the Raj: Broadcasting in British India (1920–1940)', *Journal of the Royal Asiatic Society*, Series 3, 18, no. 2 (2008), pp. 167–91.
Potter, John Deane, *No Time for Breakfast*, London: Andrew Melrose, 1951.
Prasad, S. N., K. D. Bhargava, and P. N. Khera, *The Reconquest of Burma*, vol. 1, June 1942–June 1944. *Official History of the Indian Armed Forces in the Second World War*, Calcutta: Combined Inter-Services Historical Section (India & Pakistan), 1958.
Prasad, B., *The Retreat from Burma, 1941–42*, Delhi: Combined Inter-Services Historical Section (India & Pakistan), 1959.
Pronay, Nicholas, and D. W. Spring, *Propaganda, Politics and Film, 1918–45*, London: Macmillan, 1982.
Pronay, Nicholas, 'British Newsreels in the 1930s. 1. Audience and Producers', *History*, 56, no. 188 (October 1971), pp. 411–18.

Pronay, Nicholas, 'British Newsreels in the 1930s: 2. Their Policies and Impact', *History*, 57, no. 189 (February 1972), pp. 63–72.

Pronay, Nicholas, 'The News Media at War', in Nicholas Pronay and D. W. Spring, *Propaganda, Politics and Film, 1918–45*, London: Macmillan, 1982, pp. 173–208.

Raghavan, Srinath, *India's War: The Making of Modern South Asia 1939–1945*, London: Allen Lane, 2016.

Read, Donald, *The Power of News: The History of Reuters*, Oxford: Oxford University Press, 1999.

Redding, Tony, *War in the Wilderness: The Chindits in Burma 1943–1944*, Stroud: History Press, 2011.

Reeves, Nicholas, *The Power of Film Propaganda: Myth or Reality?*, London: Cassell, 1999.

Rhodes James, Richard, *Chindit*. London: John Murray, 1980.

Rice, Tom, *Films for the Colonies Cinema and the Preservation of the British Empire*, Berkeley: University of California Press, 2019.

Ritter, Jonathan Templin, *Stilwell and Mountbatten in Burma: Allies at War, 1943–1944*, Denton, TX: University of North Texas Press, 2017.

Roberts, Andrew, *Eminent Churchillians*, London: Weidenfeld & Nicholson, 1994.

Rodger, George, *Red Moon Rising*, London: Cresset Press, 1943.

Rodger, George, *Far on the Ringing Plains: 75,000 Miles with a Photo Reporter*, New York: Macmillan, 1944.

Roeder, George H., *The Censored War: American Visual Experience During World War Two*, New Haven: Yale University Press, 1993.

Rooney, David, *Wingate and the Chindits: Redressing the Balance*, London: Arms and Armour Press, 1994.

Rooney, David, *Stilwell the Patriot: Vinegar Joe, the Brits and Chiang Kai-Shek*, London: Chatham Publishing, 2005.

Rooney, David, *Stilwell*, London: Pan Books, 1971.

Roth, Mitchel P., *Encyclopedia of War Journalism*, Armenia, NY: Grey House, 2015.

Roy, Kaushik, 'Discipline and Morale of the African, British and Indian Army Units in Burma and India during World War II: July 1943 to August 1945', *Modern Asian Studies*, 44, no. 6 (2010), pp. 1255–82.

Royle, Trevor, *Orde Wingate: A Man of Genius 1903–1944*, London: Frontline Books, 2010.

Sacquety, Troy J., *The OSS in Burma: Jungle War against the Japanese*, Lawrence, KS: Kansas University Press, 2013.

Sargent, Paul, 'Indian News Parade: The First Indian Newsreel', *Imperial War Museum Review*, no. 12 (1999), pp. 29–35.

Saunders, Hilary St George, *The Royal Air Force 1939 to 1945*, vol. III, 'The Fight Is Won' (Official History of WWII), London: HMSO, 1953.

Sethi, Devika, *War over Words: Censorship in India, 1930–1960*, Cambridge: Cambridge University Press, 2019.

Singh, Gajendra, *The Testimonies of Indian Soldiers and the Two World Wars: Between Self and Sepoy*, London: Bloomsbury, 2014.

Slim, Field Marshal Sir William, *Defeat into Victory*, London: Pan Macmillan, 2009.

Smith, Adrian, 'Mountbatten Goes to the Movies: Promoting the Heroic Myth through Cinema', *Historical Journal of Film, Radio and Television*, 26, no. 3 (August 2006), pp. 395–416.

Smith, Jeffery A., *War and Press Freedom: The Problem of Prerogative Power*, New York: Oxford University Press, 1999.

Smurthwaite, David (ed.), *The Forgotten War: British Army in the Far East 1941–1945*, London: National Army Museum, 1992.
Stephens, Ian, *Monsoon Morning*: London: Ernest Benn, 1966.
Stewart, Ian, and Susan L. Carruthers (eds), *War, Culture and the Media: Representations of the Military in 20th Century Britain*, Trowbridge: Flicks Books, 1996.
Stewart, Phillip W., 'A Reel Story of World War II The United News Collection of Newsreels Documents the Battlefield and the Home Front', *US National Archives Prologue Magazine*, 47, no. 3 (Fall 2015).
Stourton, Edward, *Auntie's War: The BBC During the Second World War*, London: Penguin Books, 2018.
Stowe, Leland, *They Shall Not Sleep*, New York: Alfred A. Knopf, 1944.
Sutter, Robert G., *U.S.-Chinese Relations: Perilous Past, Pragmatic Present*, 2nd edn, Lanham, MD: Rowman & Littlefield, 2013.
Swanberg, William A., *Luce and His Empire*, New York: Scribner, 1972.
Sweeney, Michael S., *Secrets of Victory: The Office of Censorship and the American Press and Radio in World War II*, Chapel Hill: The University of North Carolina Press, 2001.
Sweeney, Michael S., *The Military and the Press: An Uneasy Truce*, Evanston, IL: Northwestern University Press, 2006.
Sykes, Christopher, *Orde Wingate*, London: Collins, 1959.
Tarling, Nicholas, '"An Empire Gem": British Wartime Planning for Post-War Burma, 1943–44', *Journal of Southeast Asian Studies*, 13, no. 2 (September 1982), pp. 310–48.
Tarling, Nicholas, 'Lord Mountbatten and the Return of Civil Government to Burma', *The Journal of Imperial and Commonwealth History*, 11, no. 2 (1983), pp. 197–226.
Taylor, Jay, *The Generalissimo: Chiang Kai-shek and the Struggle for Modern China*, Cambridge, MA: Harvard University Press, 2011.
Taylor, Philip M., *Munitions of the Mind: A History of Propaganda from the Ancient World to the Present Day*, 3rd edn, Manchester: Manchester University Press, 2003.
Taylor, Robert H., 'Burma in the Anti-Fascist War', in Alfred W. McCoy (ed.), *Southeast Asia under Japanese Occupation*, New Haven: Yale University Press, 1980, pp. 159–89.
Thorne, Christopher, *Allies of a Kind: The United States, Britain and the War against Japan, 1941–1945*, London: Hamish Hamilton, 1978.
Tinker, Hugh, 'A Forgotten Long March: The Indian Exodus from Burma, 1942', *Journal of Southeast Asian Studies*, 6, no. 1 (March 1975), pp. 1–15.
Todman, Daniel, *Britain's War: A New World, 1942–1947*, London: Allen Lane, 2020.
Torney-Parlicki, Prue, *Somewhere in Asia: War, Journalism and Australia's Neighbours, 1941–1975*, Sydney: University of New South Wales Press, 2000.
Toye, Richard, *Winston Churchill: A Life in News*, Oxford: Oxford University Press, 2020.
Tozer, Alec, 'War Filming in the Far East', *Journal of the British Kinematograph Society*, 9, no. 1 (March 1946), pp. 19–21.
Tuchman, Barbara, *Sand Against the Wind: Stilwell and the American Experience in China 1941–45*, London: Futura, 1981.
Tunzelman, Alex von, *Indian Summer: The Secret History of the End of an Empire*, London: Simon & Schuster, 2007.
Turner, John, *Filming History: The Memoirs of John Turner Newsreel Cameraman*, London: BUFVC, 2001.
Van de Ven, Hans, 'Stilwell in the Stocks: The Chinese Nationalists and the Allied Powers in the Second World War', *Asian Affairs*, 34, no. 3 (November 2003), pp. 243–59.
Van de Ven, Hans, *War and Nationalism in China, 1925–45*, London: Routledge, 2003.

Van de Ven, Hans, *China at War: Triumph and Tragedy in the Emergence of the New China*, Cambridge, MA: Harvard University Press, 2018.
Vorley, J. S., and H. M. Vorley, *The Road From Mandalay*, Windsor: Wilton 65, 2002.
Wagg, Alfred, *A Million Died!: A Story of War in the Far East*, London: Nicholson & Watson, 1943.
Waterfield, Gordon, *Morning Will Come*, London: John Murray, 1944.
Webster, Donovan, *The Burma Road: The Epic Story of the China-Burma-India Theater in World War II*, New York: Farrar, Straus and Giroux, 2003.
Welch, David, and Jo Cox (eds), *Justifying War: Propaganda, Politics and the Modern Age*, London: Palgrave Macmillan, 2012.
Welch, David, *Propaganda: Power and Persuasion*, British Library, 2013.
Welch, David, *Persuading the People: British Propaganda in World War II*, London: British Library, 2016.
West, W. J. (ed.), *George Orwell: The War Commentaries*, New York: Schocken Books, 1985.
West, W. J. (ed.), *George Orwell: The War Broadcasts*, London: BBC Books, 1985.
White, Theodore (ed.), *The Stilwell Papers*, New York: Schocken Books, 1972 [1949].
Wiant, Susan E., *Between the Bylines: A Father's Legacy*, New York: Fordham University Press, 2010.
Williams, Kevin, *Read All About It! A History of the British Newspaper*, London: Routledge, 2009.
Williams, Kevin, 'War Correspondents as Sources for History: Problems and Possibilities in Journalism and Historiography', *Media History*, 18, nos. 3–4 (2012), pp. 341–60.
Wilson, Cat, *Churchill on the Far East in the Second World War: Hiding the History of the 'Special Relationship'*, London: Palgrave Macmillan, 2014.
Winkler, Allan M., *The Politics of Propaganda: The Office of War Information 1942–1945*, New Haven: Yale University Press, 1978.
Woods, Philip, '"Chapattis by Parachute": The Use of Newsreels in British Propaganda in India in the Second World War', *South Asia*, xxiii, no. 2 (2000), pp. 89–109.
Woods, Philip, 'The British Use of Film Propaganda in India in the Second World War', *Indian Horizons*, 48, no. 4 (March–April 2001), pp. 11–24.
Woods, Philip, 'From Shaw to Shantaram: the Film Advisory Board and the Making of British Propaganda Films in India 1940 to 1943', *Historical Journal of Film, Radio and Television*, 21, no. 3 (August 2001), pp. 293–308.
Woods, Philip, 'Filming the Retreat from Burma, 1942: British Newsreel Coverage of the Longest Retreat in British Army History', *Historical Journal of Film, Radio and Television*, 35, no. 3 (September 2015), pp. 438–53.
Woods, Philip, *Reporting the Retreat: War Correspondents in Burma, 1942*, London: Hurst & Co, 2016.
Yerkey, Gary G., *Still Time To Live: A Biography of Jack Belden*, Washington, D.C.: GK Press, 2011.
Young, Desmond, *Try Anything Twice*, London: Hamish Hamilton, 1961.
Young, George Gordon, *Outposts of Victory*, London: Hodder & Stoughton, 1943.
Yurkevich, A., 'The Chinese Army in the Burma Campaigns of World War II (1942–1945)', *Far Eastern Affairs*, 38, no. 3 (September 2010), pp. 95–109.
Ziegler, Philip, *Mountbatten: The Official Biography*, London: Collins, 1985.
Ziegler, Philip (ed.), *Personal Diary of Admiral the Lord Louis Mountbatten, Supreme Allied Commander, South-East Asia, 1943–1946*, London: Collins, 1988.
Zivin, Joselyn, '"Bent": A Colonial Subversive and Indian Broadcasting', *Past & Present*, 162 (February 1999), pp. 195–220.

Index

Admin Box, battle of 97–9, 108, 116
air forces
    importance of in Arakan 98
    recognition of crucial role in Burma victory 157
    see also Royal Air Force (RAF); United States Army Air Force (USAAF)
Akyab 37, 38, 41, 42, 44, 45, 47, 48, 165, 171
    recapture of 151–5
Alexander, General Harold 29, 31
All India Radio (AIR) 21, 109, 111, 114, 116, 120–1
    see also radio
Allen, Louis 53
Allport, Alan 7
America, see United States of America
American Volunteer Group (AVG) 32
    see also 'Flying Tigers'
Amery, Leo 59, 112, 130
    and China censorship issue 75–6
    limited role in Burma media management 4
Anti-Fascist People's Freedom League (AFPFL) 160–2
Arakan
    civil conflict in 38–40
Arakan campaign, 1943 45–51, 53, 54, 60, 62, 68
    aims of 37–8
    comparisons with Wingate operation 49
    low level of reporting on 41
    terrain worst for offensive operations 38
Arakan campaign, 1944 77, 97–9, 125, 170
Army Film and Photographic Unit (AFPU) 20, 97, 133–4, 141, 143, 144
    advantages of using armed forces' cameramen 146
Arnold, General 'Hap' 137
Arnold, Ralph 70

Asher, Major Irving 136, 137, 143
Asian nationalisms 6
Atkinson, Brooks 92
Auchinleck, General 57, 60–1, 65, 78, 101, 115–16, 120, 139
    relations with Mountbatten 84
Aung San 157, 160, 161, 162
Azad Hind Radio 111

Baldwin, Hanson 71, 92, 129
Barkawi, Tarak 7
Bayly, C. and Harper, T. 6, 162
Beaton, Cecil 66, 69
Beauchamp, Captain Antony 55–6
Beaverbrook, Lord 13, 14, 68
Belden, Jack 34
Bellah, Colonel James 99–100, 126
Bengal famine 71, 78
Blair, Eric, see Orwell, George
Bokhari, Zulfiqar Ali 110, 111, 114
Boothe, Claire (Luce) 27
Bose, Subhas Chandra 6, 30, 72, 97, 111, 121, 126
Bovill, F. Oscar 144, 145, 154, 156, 205 n.66
Bracken, Brendan 128–9, 139, 143, 160
Brander, Laurence 111–12
British Army (units)
    2nd Division 106
    81st West African Division 154
    Royal West Kent Regiment 102
British Broadcasting Corporation (BBC) 8, 9, 21, 31, 99, 120, 121, 130, 157
    covers Kohima siege 102
    Eastern Services 112, 113
    Indian Service 111
    may have overplayed Arakan operation 37, 40
    public broadcasting model 109
    reports recapture of Mandalay 118
    role in increasing interest in Burma campaign 127, 171

228 Index

sending correspondents overseas 114–19
see also radio
British Information Services (BIS) 59–60, 128, 165
British Universities Film and Video Council (BUFVC) 18
broadcasting, *see* radio
Brooke, General Sir Alan 4, 40
Bryce, Colonel Alex 136–8, 141
Burchett, Wilfred 14, 41, 59, 68
    book on Wingate 60–1
    critique of Indian Army leadership 50
    injured in Arakan 1943 42
Burma
    Allies' plans for in 1944 95
    Japanese plans for in 1944 95
    low on Allied priorities 3
Burma film
    Anglo-American differences in aims 138–9
    see also Burma Victory film
Burma Independence Army, *see* Thakin
Burma National Army (BNA) 157, 159, 161
Burma Road 23, 82, 83, 85, 87, 106, 116, 140, 151
    see also Ledo/Stilwell Road
Burma Victory film 21, 134, 141, 143, 147
    see also Burma film

Calcutta 38, 105, 111, 166
    Tollygunge film studio 21, 143
Calling Blighty short films 135, 146, 171
Calvert, Major Michael 54, 61, 101
Capra, Colonel Frank 137, 138–9, 140
Casey, Steven 167
CBI Roundup newspaper 15, 88
censorship
    in Arakan campaign 1943 43–4
    BBC subject to 113
    of British newspapers in wartime 13
    about Burma National Army 161
    Indian journalists comment on SEAC 104
    issues on which correspondents clashed with censors 31
    at time of Kohima siege 101–2
    overview of 168
    restrictions on reporting retreat 28
    security and political 30
    self-censorship, reasons for 30–1
    of *Statesman* article on Arakan campaign 46–8
    Stowe complains of 25
    substantially changed during 1944 76–7
censorship
    American 15–16
    Chinese 27, 75–6, 93, 108
    Indian 70–9, 104, 166
Chennault, Colonel Claire 25, 34, 85
Chiang Kai-shek 23, 26, 27, 34, 38, 76, 82, 83, 85, 87, 92–3, 149
    regime criticized after Stilwell recall 108
    war aims 81
China
    Communists in north of China 81
    journalists visit Communist HQ at Yenan 82
    war aims 81
    see also Chiang Kai-shek
China-Burma-India theatre 3, 26, 82, 92, 136
Chindits 5, 49, 51, 95, 108, 116, 119, 123, 136, 137, 170
    in Operation Longcloth 57–62
    in Operation Thursday 99–101
    origin of the name 59
    Stilwell's misuse of 90–1
Christison, General Philip 69, 152–3
Churchill, Winston 13, 14, 31, 38, 63, 86, 90, 91, 103, 108, 115, 120
    attitude to Burma campaigns 4
    attitude to China 93
    calls for restraint of SEAC publicity 65
    criticism of Arakan campaign 1943 50–1
    image of did not resonate with Indians 133
    instigated Munster report 171
    invites Wingate to Quebec conference 59
    prejudice against Indian Army 6–7, 172
    speech 28 September 1944 130
    strategy in Far East 83

The Second World War history 172
  wanted regiments named in reports 31
Cleverdon, Douglas (BBC) 117
Cochran, Lt Philip 89, 100
communiqués 9, 29, 31, 32, 40, 43, 58, 74, 78, 102, 105, 154, 157–8
  Chinese 27
  Stilwell keeps control of NCAC 84
  Mountbatten presses for single SEAC 89
conducting officers 10, 25, 29, 125
Connelly, M. and Welch, D. 7, 167
  see also Welch, D.
correspondents, *see* war correspondents
Coward, Noel 130
  In Which We Serve 135

Daily Mirror
  not sending correspondents to Burma 130
  under threat of censorship 13
Davies, John Paton 82, 88, 139
Detachment 101 (OSS) 151
Dimbleby, Richard 115, 199 n.29
Donbaik 43, 45
Donnison, Vernon 159
Dorman-Smith, Sir Reginald 25, 26, 34, 114
  postwar Burma politics 160–2
  refutes fifth-column allegations 32
Duckett, Richard 158, 162, 176 n.15
Dunlop, Graham 151
Dunn, Major Jerry 99, 126

Eade, Charles 68, 73, 119
  appointed publicity adviser 65
Eldridge, Fred 15, 26, 34, 86, 91
  and NCAC communiqués 89
  Wrath in Burma 26
Emeny, Stuart 55, 57–8, 98, 100
evacuation of civilians
  impact of on Burma and India 6

Falls, Captain Cyril 169
Fennell, Jonathan 7
Fergusson, Brigadier Bernard 58, 99, 116
Fielden, Lionel 109–11
fifth columnists 6, 32, 59

films
  documentary/propaganda in India 20–1
Fine, Richard 167
Fitchett, Ian 72, 98
Fleay, C and Saunders, M. L. 113
'Flying Tigers' 25, 26, 139, 203 n.2
  see also American Volunteer Group (AVG)
'Forgotten Army' and 'Forgotten War' epithets 1, 3–5, 103, 119, 121, 127–8, 138, 163
  counteracted by radio broadcasts 121
  how appropriate is its use? 168, 171–3
  Noel Cowards's comments on 130
  not appropriate term for 1942 retreat 34

Gallagher, O'Dowd 24–5, 182 n.19
Gander, Marsland 62
Gardner, Squadron Leader Charles 123
Gardner, Douglas
  complains of censorship system 71
Gelder, Stuart 154
  and China censorship 75–7
  Joubert wants expelled 153
Girot, Eugene, (BBC) 116–17, 118–19
Goodall, H. and Frost, M. 126
Government of India (GoI)
  concerns about correspondent accreditation 78–9
  policies on cinema and newsreels 19–20
  reluctance to develop modern mass media 21, 109
Graham, Clive 155–6, 158, 161, 162
Great Britain
  war aims in Far East 83
Grove, Colonel, Director of Kinematography India 135
Gupta, Partha Sarathi 109

Hartley, General Sir Alan 45, 57
Healy, Thomas 31, 182 n.14
Helliwell, Arthur 158
Himatsinjhi, Colonel K. S. 139
Hodgkinson, Colonel Frank Outram 143
Home Intelligence weekly reports (HIWR) 127–8

Hong Kong 83
Hope, Arthur, Governor of Madras 112
Hukawng valley 88, 95, 99, 106, 107
Hump, the (Himalayan air route) 82, 84, 130, 158
Humphreys, Alan 161, 209 n.56

Imphal 54–5, 57, 60, 72, 77, 90 101, 104, 108, 119, 126
India Command 65
    concerns about planned Burma film 136
    defends its role in Kohima censorship 74–5
India-Burma War 10, 171, 172
    historiography 5–7
    must be seen as involving India in all ways 11
Indian Army (units)
    6th Brigade 46
    7th Indian Division 97, 105–6, 116
    14th Army 1, 3, 5, 74, 95, 98, 100, 108, 134, 141, 143, 144, 151, 158, 163, 195 n.9
    14th Indian Division 40, 42
    16th Brigade 99, 116
    36th Indian Division 91
    47th Indian Infantry Brigade 46
    51st Indian Infantry Brigade 106
    XV Corps 154
    Churchill and the 172
    concern that it be properly represented in Burma film 136–7
    publicizing the 96–7, 103, 123–5, 129–30
Indian Army Public Relations (IAPR) 11, 15, 29, 41, 53, 54, 60, 61, 74, 78
    censorship dispute with Stephens 46–8
    learnt lessons in media management 51
    mistakes in first Arakan campaign 37
    organizes publicity for Operation Longcloth 57–8
    prefer to use officer observers 125
    propaganda line after retreat 33–4
    want to hold on to their own cameramen 135, 136–7
    see also Jehu, Ivor

Indian National Army (INA) 3, 97, 111, 126
    ban on media mention of 30
    in 'March on Delhi' 72
Indian News Parade, newsreel 19–20
Irwin, General Noel 57
    character 40
    criticizes Statesman leader on Arakan 46–7
    press conference to explain Arakan setbacks 48–9
    relieved of his command 49

Jackson, Ashley 7
Jacob, Alaric 55, 59, 60
Japanese offensives
    Ha-Go in Arakan 97
    U-Go towards India 101
Japanese surrender ceremony, Singapore 147
Jarvie, Ian 139, 140
Jehu, Brigadier Ivor 20, 61, 66, 78, 125, 136
    advice for broadcasting 111
    character 42
    control of allocation of cameramen 20
    coverage of Operation Longcloth 55–7
    criticized for lack of film of Arakan campaign 41
    defends news blackout in Arakan campaign 47
    during Arakan campaign 1943 44–50
    organizes publicity for Operation Longcloth 56–7
    see also Indian Army Public Relations (IAPR)
Joubert de la Ferté, Air Marshal Philip 69, 90, 103, 159, 209 n.56
    advertizes role of BNA 160
    and the BBC 118, 157
    appointed DICA 65–6
    differences with Mountbatten 157
    meets with Eldridge 91
    plans for SEAC film unit 143
    reporting Akyab recapture 154
Joyce, Alec 79

Kaladan valley 48, 98, 119, 154
Karaka, Dosabhai Framji 16, 103–4, 105

Katju, Captain Motilal 56, 125
Kaul, Chandrika 113
Khan, Yasmin 111
Kirchner, Bernard 71
Knight, Colonel Derek 143
Knightley, Phillip 7
   criticism of Burchett's book 61
   The First Casualty 167
Kohima 96, 116, 119, 171
   censorship issue at 72–5
   defence of 101–3

Langley, Bryan 21
Latimer, Jon 63
Lawson, Captain Alan 145–6
Ledo/Stilwell Road 15, 16, 82, 83, 87, 88, 144, 149, 206 n.1
   see also Burma Road
Leese, General Oliver 118
Lentaigne, General Walter 90, 100, 101, 123
Life magazine 15, 17, 106
Long-Range Penetration(LRP), *see* Operation Longcloth; Operation Thursday; Merrill's Marauders
Luce, Henry 17
Luce, Claire Boothe, *see* Boothe, Claire (Luce)

MacArthur, General Douglas 84, 86, 149
MacDonald, Colonel David 140
McKelvie, Captain Roy 126–7
McKie, Ronald 152–4, 155
magazines, illustrated 17–18
managing the media
   methods of during the retreat 28–34
Mandalay 5, 32, 139, 141, 144, 145, 151
   BBC covers recapture of 117–19
   bombed by Japanese 28
   railway line from 54, 58
   recapture of 155–6
Mani, P. R. S. 106, 126
   see also officer-observers
Mankekar, D. R. 5, 12, 103, 104–6
Marshall, General George 86, 88, 136, 137, 138
   says only prepared to make short Burma film 140–1

Media
   global nature of 11
   importance of in Second World War 7–8
   overview of coverage of Burma war 170
   see also broadcasting, film, news agencies, newspapers, newsreels
media, visual 133
   American dominance in cinema 134
   valued by propagandists 133
media management 3, 5, 11, 18, 37, 51, 65, 97, 170, 175 n.4
   of Akyab combined operation 152
   in the battle to take Myitkyina 89–91
   government controlled supplies to media 31
   historiography 9–10
   left to the Army in Burma War 4
   lessons from Operation Longcloth 62–3
   lessons learnt in Burma campaign 3–4, 165–6
   preparations for 1944 campaigns 96–7
   and propaganda 8–9
   putting a positive spin on the retreat 32–3
Meiktila 119, 151, 155
Merrill, General Frank 26, 91
Merrill's Marauders (5307th Composite Unit) 15, 84, 90, 91, 101, 106, 203 n.9
   casualties and disbanded 108
Messervy, General Frank 97, 105
Ministry of Information (MoI) 13, 123, 133
   and BBC 112–13, 115
   decide not to send commercial photographers 142
   dissatisfaction with film supplied from India 20
   limited role in media management in Burma 4
Montgomery, General Bernard 3, 86, 87
Moorcraft, P. L. and Taylor, P. M. 30
Moore, Martin 49, 55–6
   and reporters' strike 1944 72–5
Moraes, Frank 42–3

morale, troop 1–2
  issue addressed by historians 7
  role of media in boosting morale 170–1
Morrison, Ian 153–4
  critical of CAS (B) 158–9
  on BNA and AFPFL 161
Mountbatten, Lord Louis 1, 29, 65, 71, 83, 91, 100, 102, 103, 127, 140
  against censorship of *SEAC* 69
  ambivalence about his personal publicity 10, 70, 190 n.25
  arguments for Burma film 138
  attitude to Burma National Army 160
  BBC, encourages it 115, 117
  comparison with Stilwell's use of the media 87–9
  concerned at lack of film resources 143
  differences with Joubert 1945 157
  Dominion status aim for Burma 161
  endorses Radio SEAC 120
  establishes *SEAC* newspaper 67–8
  forced to focus on land campaigns 151
  interest in cinema 135
  lowpoint in relations with Stilwell 91–2
  meets Tebbutt about censorship 77–8
  meets with striking correspondents 73–4
  moves to separate *Burma Victory* film 141
  policies for using media to restore morale 5
  problems of command structure 84
  publicity for victory parade 162
  recapture of Mandalay 118–19
  sets up *Phoenix* magazine 69–70
  surprised at capture of Myitkyina airport 90
  has US aircraft placed under SEAC control 97
Munday, William 31, 38, 182 n.14
Munster, Lord 120, 130, 171, 172
Myitkyina 123, 138, 149
  advance to and capture of 106–8
  aims in capturing 84–5
  air route established 149
  capture and siege of 91, 107–8
  Chindit contribution to capture of 100–1
  Mounbatten's doubts regarding operation 89–90
  railway to 54, 58
  reporting of advance to 87–8
Nagas 102, 158, 196 n.29
news agencies
  compared with newspaper correspondents' 12
newspapers, American 15–16
  which sent reporters to Burma 15
newspapers, Australian 16–17
  which sent reporters to Burma 17
newspapers, British 12–14
  censorship of in wartime 13
  changing character in wartime 13
  coverage of Operation Longcloth 59
  local and regional papers 14
  ownership and political affiliations 13–14
  which sent reporters to Burma 14
newspapers, Indian 16
  show little interest in Operation Longcloth 62
Newsreel Association (NRA) 20
newsreels 138
  and cinema, Britain 18–19
  and cinema, India 19–20
  cameramen, advantages of 146
  characteristics of 18–19
  claims of faking 146
  coverage of Akyab recapture 154
  films of Arakan campaign 1943 41
  ownership 18
  rota system 20
  self-censorship of 31
Nixon, John, (BBC) 99, 116
Noble, Ronnie 145, 146, 156, 162, 210 n.71
Northern Combat Area Command (NCAC) 84

Objective Burma film 141
officer observers 14, 171, 201 n.17
  advantages of using 125–7
  role of 5
  see also P. R. S. Mani
Operation Capital 151
Operation Dracula 156
Operation Extended Capital 151

Operation Longcloth, 1943 49, 51, 53–62, 96, 169, 170
Operation Thursday, 1944 59, 63, 74, 88, 89, 99–101
Orwell, George 9, 112–14
Oswald, G. B. 145, 205 n.56
Owen, Frank 14, 67–9, 103, 123, 130–1, 144–5

Patriot Burmese Forces (PBF), *see* Burma National Army
Pawsey, Charles 102
Phoenix, forces' magazine 69–70, 79, 87, 89
Picture Post 8, 103, 177 n.27
Political Warfare Executive 9
Potter, Captain John Deane 55
Price, Byron 15
Pronay, Nicholas 18–19
propaganda
 black, white and grey 8–9

Quebec Conference 59, 63, 65, 95, 170
Quit India movement 3, 15, 38, 71, 78, 112

radio
 in India 21, 109–14, 121
 see also All India Radio, and British Broadcasting Corporation (BBC)
Radio SEAC 119–20
Ramree Island and Cheduba 151, 155, 171
Rangoon 6, 10, 23, 24, 31, 33, 141
 advance to and recapture 156
 correspondents forced to leave 28
 post-capture press reflections 157
Rees, General Thomas Wynford 117–18, 155–6
refugees, civilian from Burma 23–4
 stories told 28
Reith, Sir John 109
retreat from Burma, 1942 23–6
 journalists response to 28
 managing the media in the 28–35
Reuters/API agency 11–12, 105
Reynolds, Brian 156
Rhodes James, Richard 53
Rodger, George 25
Rolo, Charles J. 59–60
Roosevelt, President Franklin D. 26, 38, 82, 83, 85–6, 92, 93

Royal Air Force (RAF) 25, 32, 59, 97, 98, 139, 143, 157
Royal Air Force (RAF) film unit, 2020 135, 136, 143 54
The Gen newsreel 146
Rushbrook Williams, L. F. 113, 114
Ryan, A. P. 115–16

Scoones, General Geoffrey 55–6
SEAC, *see* South East Asia Command (SEAC)
SEAC cameramen 145–6
SEAC forces' newspaper 66–9, 88, 144
Services Public Relations Organisation (SPRO)
 tasks 24–5
Sethi, Devika 71
Sharp, Richard, (BBC) 102, 104, 117, 119
Sittang river battle 28, 182 n.27
Slim, General William 87, 97, 163, 169
 appointed commander 14th Army 95
 called for improvements in intelligence system 154
 concerns about planned Burma film 136–7
 media coverage of, and 14th Army 4, 5, 98, 103
 plans for 1944 campaign 97
 plans for 1945 campaign 151–5
 vetoes Mountbatten's planned 'triumphal entry' to Mandalay 118
 views on advance to Myitkyina 90, 106
 views on Aung San and Burma National Army 159, 161
 views on publicity 37, 40–1
Smith, Adrian 135
South East Asia Command (SEAC)
 film unit 135–6, 143–4
 HQ, Kandy, facilities 75, 107–8, 117
 overlapping command structures 84
 PR office in London 117
 propaganda in USA 128–9
 quotas for correspondents 107–8
 setting up of 63, 65
Special Operations Executive (SOE) 6, 158

Stanford, Graham 40, 41, 42, 50, 59, 72, 100, 101, 102
   criticism of Arakan campaign 1943 45
   explains Arakan reverses 50
   possible first use of 'Forgotten' war in newspapers, 175 n.2
   on use of sampans in Arakan 42
Statesman newspaper 67, 70
   full coverage of Operation Longcloth 62
   and Arakan censorship 46–8
Stephens, Ian 42, 62
   and forces' newspaper 66–7
   comments on private press briefings 30
   criticizes news blackout in Arakan 46–8
Stilwell Road, *see* Ledo/Stilwell Road
Stilwell, General Joseph 95, 129
   advance to Myitkyina 89–91, 106–8
   appointed 26
   attitude to, and use of the media 15, 26, 27
   atttitude to British 88
   command roles 84
   counters sea invasion plans 88
   critical of Chinese regime 82
   criticism of Chindit role 93–4, 101
   and Mountbatten's use of media 84–7
   protects film interests 136, 138
   recalled, causes and implications 92–3
   on the retreat from Burma 2–3
   rift over strategy with Mountbatten 71, 81
   treatment of Merrill's Marauders 91
   walkout of Burma, 1942 34
Stratemeyer, General George 157
Sykes, Christopher 57

Tebbutt, Geoffrey 77–8
telegraph agencies, role of 11–12
Thackrah, Wing-Commander Maurice 159
Thakin 32, 38, 114
The Stilwell Road film 141
Thompson, Victor 41, 103
Tozer, Alec 41, 145
tribal levies 158
Tuchman, Barbara 27, 81, 86

Tunisian Victory film 134, 136–8
Turner, John 145, 146, 147

United States of America
   war aims in Burma and China 82–3
United States Army Air Force (USAAF) 90, 97, 98, 99, 107, 136, 137

V Force 6, 38, 50
Vandivert, William 59, 106

war correspondents
   accreditation and rules to follow 29
   changing attitudes of military to 9
   claim political censorship operated 3
   concerns about their comments on India 3
   criticise civil government and society 25–6
   embedded with troops 10
   five go on strike 1944 72–5
   forced to leave Burma in retreat 28
   in the 1942 retreat 25
   in the Retreat 2, 24–5
   limited cohort in the retreat 29
   limits on their freedom to roam 29
   maintain silence on Operation Longcloth 57
   memoirs of the retreat 28
   pooling arrangements 10
   radicalized by war 7
   reasons for staying near HQ 31–2
   take up new issues in 1945 157–8
   were they propagandists? 166–8
war correspondents, Americans
   black reporters in India-Burma 16
   criticize Chinese leadership 81
war correspondents, Indian
   complain of slow transmission of reports 105
   cover Indian troops 105–6
   report 1944 campaigns 103–6
Waterfield, Gordon 38–40
   comments on Reuters monopoly 12
   criticism of Arakan campaign 1943 45, 50
   injured in Arakan 1943 42

Wavell, General Archibald 29, 33, 38, 40, 44, 49, 50, 60
   and Chinese censorship issue 75–6
   supports Operation Longcloth 54–5
Wedemeyer, General Al 88, 92, 137
Welch, David 9
   see also Connelly and Welch
West African troops 98, 154
Wiant, Thoburn 92–3
   at Hukawng Valley with Stilwell 107–8
   describes Japanese foxhole system 43
Wiart, General Carton de 102–3
Wilkie, Douglas 43–4
Wills, Stanley 98, 100
Wilson, Cat 172
Wingate, General Orde 74, 89, 95–6, 116, 165, 169, 170
   disliked by Indian Army HQ 56
   killed in plane crash 100
   Operation Thursday 99–101
   Operation Longcloth 53–63
Wright, James 'Jimmy' 145, 147

Yenangyaung oilfields 28
Young, Desmond 71, 175 n.8, 202 n.29

Zivin, Joselyn 111

www.ingramcontent.com/pod-product-compliance
Lightning Source LLC
Chambersburg PA
CBHW062139300426
44115CB00012BA/1980